# Values. Driven. Leadership.

## The History of Accenture

First Edition
ISBN 0-9773882-0-4

Produced by The History Factory
Chantilly, Virginia

Design by Pivot Design, Inc.
Chicago, Illinois

# Contents

# Foreword
# Enduring Values

by William D. Green and Joe W. Forehand



**Accenture is a great success story by any measure. Our history has been more than 50 years in the making—from our earliest days as pioneers in the new world of information technology to our position today as a *FORTUNE* Global 500 industry leader. The men and women of Accenture have anticipated and responded to the changing needs of our clients and in the process built a great company.**

Through this business biography and the accompanying video we capture the events, decisions and commitment to values that define our history and make Accenture such a special place to work and build a career. Although our company looks different today than it did in its early days, many of the hallmarks of the Accenture culture remain: Our commitment to stewardship, our ability to master change to stay relevant to our clients and our passion to be the best. These traits have endured to create the unique and vibrant company we are today.

Our success is based on a core set of beliefs, behaviors and values that transcend generations and geographies. One core value that consistently has guided the decisions and actions of company leadership is stewardship. Stewardship is based on the premise that you leave Accenture a better place than you found it. The concept is simple—and powerful.

Stewardship is also about positioning the company for the future and creating opportunities to develop the next generation of leaders. From the very beginning, our partners invested in our people by sharing knowledge, pioneering world-class training opportunities and upholding our core values through their own behaviors and actions. Today, Accenture continues to invest nearly $400 million annually in developing the best people on the planet in what we do. We equip our people with the knowledge, skills and experience to enable them to serve our clients in a first-class manner.

Throughout the decades, our people became masters of change—embracing technology and transforming our business model to stay relevant to our clients and to respond to dramatic shifts in the marketplace. It has become second nature for our people to stare change in the face. Our ability to embrace change has made us more responsive, relevant—and above all—resilient.

From the earliest days of our existence, our people demonstrated their can-do, entrepreneurial spirit. Born out of a strong work ethic and the desire to uphold the highest professional and ethical standards, our early leaders developed a unique style—known within the company as our "special sauce"—that blends confidence with competence.

Accenture CEO Bill Green (left) and Chairman Joe Forehand.

Our people also have always had a passion to do their very best for our clients and for Accenture. We are known for our commitment to superior execution and delivery. In fact, our clients continually tell us that they choose Accenture because our people are the best in the industry.

All of these traits continue to define Accenture today. We are known in our industry as a high-performance business—as bold, innovative risk takers who do what is right for our people, our clients and our other stakeholders.

The chapters that follow trace the steps that Accenture people have taken as they have pursued their passion to serve our clients and to build one of the world's great enterprises. No matter what crisis or challenge presented itself during the past 50 years—from the early days of pioneering technology in business when we installed the first computer system for commercial use in the United States at General Electric, to difficult leadership transitions, economic downturns and arbitration—our people always have come together in the spirit of "one global firm" to support each other and lead.

Writing this business biography has been an incredible team effort, and we thank everyone who recounted their personal stories and shared their memories with us so that we could educate, energize and inspire our current and future employees. We want to recognize our retired partner Peter Fuchs for leading the business biography project team, which included numerous retired partners, current partners and employees, the writer Scott McMurray and our friends from The History Factory. We congratulate the team on bringing this book to fruition.

Finally, to our past, present and future employees: We created this book for you and hope you enjoy reading it.

Best regards,

| | |
|---|---|
| **William D. Green**<br>**Chief Executive Officer** | **Joe W. Forehand**<br>**Chairman** |

August 2005

# Introduction

**The history of Accenture is, in many ways, the history of global business consulting and information technology services for more than the past half century. Yet in the minds of many of the company's 120,000 employees, and for much of the public, the history of Accenture dates back only to 2001, at best. Why the keen awareness of the most recent years and not the earlier history? The answer lies in the question posed by William Shakespeare nearly four centuries ago: What's in a name?**

Accenture is a top global business brand today, yet the name didn't even exist until October 2000. The company, then known as Andersen Consulting, was required to rename itself by January 1, 2001, as part of a historic international arbitration decision rendered in August 2000. That's when the arbitration ruling severed all ties between Andersen Consulting and the audit and tax firm Arthur Andersen as well as the umbrella organization Andersen Worldwide.

Although Andersen Consulting had operated as a legally separate business unit since 1989, senior management had concluded months before the arbitration decision that the company would need a new name in order to develop its own identity in the marketplace.

This history of Accenture places these seminal events of 2000 and 2001 in the context of more than a half century of pathbreaking global leadership in the fields of information technology and consulting, beginning in the late 1940s. And it traces the core values and principles that have guided Accenture from the beginning in providing industry-leading client service and support for its employees.

Despite the many changes the company has undergone to serve its clients and respond to changing markets, Accenture remains true to its original beliefs. Each generation of Accenture employees has embraced these principles as its own. They have passed on to the next generation a company that remains unmatched in its dedication to helping transform the way the world lives and works.

# The 1950s

## Sparking Innovation

"I've seen something just beyond anything you can comprehend, but it's something that the firm has to get into. It is the coming thing. And if we miss it, we're going to miss the boat."

Joe Glickauf

# The 1950s
# Sparking Innovation



**The world emerged from the 1940s eager to move beyond the limits of postwar economic and political turmoil. Recently invented computers offered corporate America powerful opportunities to boost productivity, but few business leaders recognized their full potential. Visionary Arthur Andersen leaders such as Leonard Spacek, Joe Glickauf and John Higgins were the exception. They helped move computers out of the laboratory and into the commercial mainstream—and developed an important role for consultants in the introduction of computer technology.**

Chapter opening image: Joe Glickauf, technological visionary and gadget guru.

**Leonard Spacek, managing partner of Arthur Andersen & Co., had no way of knowing that the promise he had just made to his largest client in early 1950 would not only dramatically change the future of his firm, but would help create an entirely new industry. What he did know as he walked back to his office at 120 S. LaSalle St. in Chicago's Loop was that Andersen was determined to do what was necessary to stay one step ahead of its client. He also knew he had just the man for the job.**

Leonard Spacek, Arthur Andersen managing partner and lifelong champion of the firm's budding consulting business.

Spacek had met that morning with Willis Gale, the prominent chairman and CEO of Commonwealth Edison Co., the largest utility in the Midwest and one of the largest in the country. Gale was at the helm of a highly regulated utility, but he had the restless spirit and intellectual curiosity of an entrepreneur. He wasn't just interested in Andersen for its ability to audit financial records. He had retained its Administrative Accounting Division, soon to be renamed Administrative Services, for numerous assignments aimed at improving the utility's performance and upgrading systems such as those that tracked its voluminous property records.



Gale kept abreast of the latest technological advances in science and industry, always with an eye toward making Commonwealth Edison more efficient and helping it meet booming postwar demand for electricity. On his mind this particular morning was a device that neither he nor Spacek had ever seen, but one that was being referred to in various journals and at times in the popular press. What, he asked Spacek, did Andersen know about recently invented electronic computers and the impact they might have on business?

Spacek, while running a regulated enterprise, was Gale's match in terms of intellectual curiosity and entrepreneurial spirit. Spacek spent much of his career at Andersen, which began in 1928 and lasted until 1973, involved in administrative accounting activities as opposed to audits. "Most people don't realize that I could count on my fingers the audits I conducted during my career," he recalled in a 1983 interview. "Most of my work involved systems projects for utilities, and that was the genesis of the firm's present Management Information Consulting practice."

Spacek assured Gale that Andersen would look into computers, which to date had been used by only a handful of research universities and the U.S. federal government. When it came to the Andersen employee most suited to the task, Spacek immediately thought of a brilliant engineer (with no accounting training) he had been persuaded to hire right out of the U.S. Navy in 1946: Joe Glickauf.

Glickauf jumped at the offer. A Chicago native and graduate of the Illinois Institute of Technology, Glickauf had a lifelong passion for tinkering with gadgets. He had invented two medical devices, and patented one, by the time he applied for and received a commission in the U.S. Navy in 1942 at age 30. He had hoped to be involved in radar development. Instead, the Navy sent him to develop more efficient payroll and other massive systems at its Bureau of Supplies and Accounts headquarters in Cincinnati. He also saw active duty at sea.

Glickauf met and worked closely with John Higgins in the Navy. Higgins had worked for a few years at both Andersen and IBM before the war. He also met Wally Oliphant, an Andersen employee who eventually would succeed Spacek at the head of the firm. Having designed the highly automated system used to discharge personnel in the Navy, Higgins and Glickauf were nicknamed the "gold dust twins." The workings of the system remained a mystery to most sailors. All they knew was that when the system created by these two chose your name, you felt as lucky as if you had been sprinkled with gold dust.

Higgins' management of mechanization projects for IBM and the Navy, and his previous auditing experience at Andersen, made him an attractive prospect as demobilization approached. When Spacek contacted Higgins about rejoining Andersen, Higgins had one condition: that Spacek also hire his friend Joe Glickauf, who already was weighing

Top: Chicago's mammoth Fisk Street electric-generating station, owned and operated by Commonwealth Edison, Arthur Andersen's largest client in the early 1950s.

Bottom: John Higgins, dynamic leader of the consulting practice and Spacek's right-hand man.

Harris Trust & Savings Bank building, Chicago, home of the firm's first office.

job offers from AT&T, U.S. Steel and his former employer, IBM. After a brief interview in Chicago with Spacek, Glickauf, still in uniform, was offered a job and agreed to start on January 6, 1946. As he was leaving Spacek's office, Glickauf asked Spacek what he expected him to do at Andersen, given that his knowledge of accounting was so limited. "Just keep on doing what you have been doing in the Navy," Spacek replied.

### Consulting's Deep Roots

Higgins and Glickauf helped revitalize the Administrative Accounting Division in the immediate postwar years. They and others kept that side of the business growing even after the 1947 death of founder Arthur Andersen who, with Spacek, had championed such work despite resistance from many audit partners. In fact, the founder had been a proponent of consulting and systems businesses from day one. The December 1, 1913, announcement of the formation of Andersen DeLany & Co. listed lines of business the new firm would pursue, including "investigations for special purposes, such as to determine the advisability of investment in a new enterprise or the extension of an old business," and "the designing and installing of new systems of financial and cost accounting and organization, or the modernizing of existing systems." An industrial engineering department flourished during the 1920s. It analyzed future prospects and management abilities of companies, though it fell dormant during the Great Depression.

A typical work station, circa 1950.

## Punch and Duty.

The increasing use of punch card tabulating and processing machines by major corporations in the years leading up to World War II, combined with the importance the war effort placed on systems mechanization, exposed the emerging generation of postwar corporate leaders to the importance of technological innovation. (Smaller companies would hang on to handwritten ledgers for years.) Well before the advent of electronic computers, Spacek led the effort to pursue what he termed "responsibility accounting," later renamed "responsibility reporting."

Beginning in the late 1930s, Spacek directed pioneering work for Commonwealth Edison and other clients in which the Administrative Accounting professionals used punch cards to sift through reams of data. They sorted out just the relevant expense data, for instance, that had a direct impact on a particular vice president's division. They produced a similar report for the vice president's superior, collecting the expense data from each vice president who reported to that officer. With data collected on punch cards, the reports could be updated frequently. With such reports in hand, utility officials could see what steps they needed to take to control costs or improve performance. Prior to this time, internal accounting in the utility industry tended to reflect the collection of data driven by regulatory requirements, not operating efficiencies.

During the war, Higgins, Glickauf and others saw first hand the enormous productivity gains that mechanization produced for the military. When they started their postwar careers at Andersen, they applied what they had learned to the corporate arena. In 1947, Higgins moved to Los Angeles for a year to lead a responsibility accounting installation at Southern California Edison, the leading utility in the area. At the same time Glickauf moved his family to Texas for a year so he could work out of the firm's Houston office. There he played a leading role in a responsibility accounting engagement with the Tennessee Gas Transmission Co., which was planning to build a natural gas pipeline from Louisiana to New York. That engagement helped establish the Houston office as a leader in systems work. The Administrative Services Division won its first major responsibility accounting engagement for an industrial company, Weyerhaeuser Timber, in 1952.

**Top: An early use of accounting technology on the eve of World War II—punch card operation at the U.S. Bureau of Census, 1939.**

**Middle: Early consulting client Southern California Edison helped light the postwar economic boom in California.**

**Bottom: Tennessee Gas Transmission Co. workers laying a pipeline. Joe Glickauf moved his family to Houston for a year to lead the consulting team on the Tennessee Gas project, a harbinger of the energy-related projects that would fuel the growth of the Houston office.**

Following the founder's death, some auditors felt that they had enough to handle in restructuring the partnership and in making multiyear payments to the Andersen estate. It was a mistake to divert management attention by emphasizing systems work, they argued. Glickauf recalled that one partner pulled him aside after a meeting in 1947 and told him to look for work elsewhere; his obvious gifts would never be fully utilized at Andersen.

Fortunately, Glickauf ignored the advice. He had a different view of his future at Andersen, based on the work that he and Higgins were generating with Spacek's support. In mid-1951 he was named head of the newly renamed Administrative Services Division in Chicago. His friend Higgins was put in charge of the division for the entire firm. Higgins replaced Jim Campbell, who had run the division since it was formally organized in 1942.

U.S. Army Lieutenant Herman H. Goldstine (left), the wartime coordinator of the electronic computing project, and J. Presper Eckert, coinventor of the ENIAC (Electronic Numerical Integrator and Computer), holding the portion of the ENIAC needed to store a single decimal digit.

Opposite page, top: John W. Mauchly, chief engineer of the ENIAC—the first general-purpose electronic digital computer—prepares the device for a demonstration, February 2, 1946.

Opposite page, bottom: Mauchly, Eckert and others work on the ENIAC at the Moore School of Electrical Engineering at the University of Pennsylvania.

### UNIVAC to Glickiac

Glickauf's first stop on his quest for information about computers in 1950 was a run-down warehouse on the west side of Philadelphia. Tapping academic connections from his time at the Illinois Institute of Technology, Glickauf was one of the few outsiders invited into the lab of two computer industry pioneers, Dr. John W. Mauchly and J. Presper Eckert. They had built the ENIAC (Electronic Numerical Integrator and Computer), the first truly electronic computer, based on work in support of the war effort at the University of Pennsylvania. They were working on a next-generation computer dubbed the UNIVAC, which stood for Universal Automatic Computer. (John Vincent Atanasoff, a researcher at what was then called Iowa State Teachers' College, now Iowa State University, was later credited with performing work that Mauchly drew upon to create the ENIAC.)

Despite the duo's reputation in academe for ushering in a new era of lightning-speed computation, Glickauf's first view of the future was a letdown. "I expected to see a machine, or at least some completed prototype of same, but what I actually saw were large, heavy cables running all over the floor, and over and under sawhorses. The room looked like the gathering of a bunch of snakes rather than any kind of machine."

Glickauf didn't fully appreciate the UNIVAC's significance until the inventors invited him to store a number in its memory. Prior to that point, Glickauf said, every problem was a new problem for computers, as figures weren't stored in memory. But an addressable memory from which figures could be stored and retrieved—clearly, here was a new device far beyond supercalculators. "I immediately recognized that this device was going to revolutionize any areas involving computation and that a whole new era of running and controlling business was standing before me," Glickauf said. "I was so excited about it that...I got on a train and went down to New York City to see the partners to tell them that I had just seen the millennium. I said anything that's been done on a computing job to this minute is gone."

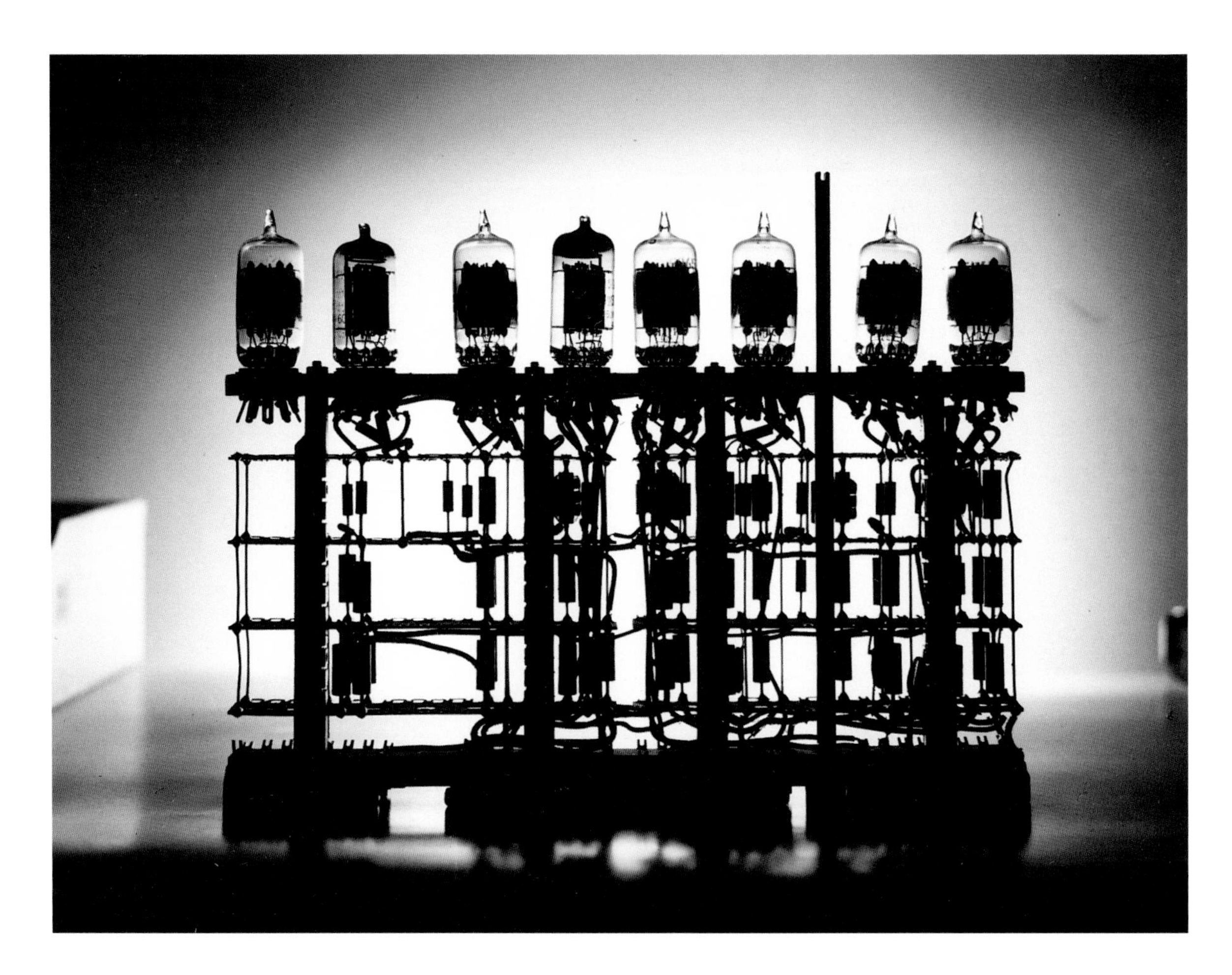



Above: The Glickiac, the model computing device built by Joe Glickauf that convinced the Andersen partners to invest in computer technology consulting.

Right: Glickauf and his creation, early 1950s.

He then rushed back to Chicago and regaled Spacek in equally evangelical terms, saying, "I've seen something just beyond anything you can comprehend, but it's something that the firm has to get into. It is the coming thing. And if we miss it, we're going to miss the boat."

**The Drake Hotel, at lower right in photo, at the foot of Chicago's Michigan Avenue. Here, the Andersen partners first saw the possibilities of digital computing as a result of Joe Glickauf's demonstration in January 1951.**



Spacek was sold on the concept, but both he and Glickauf agreed that, in order to sway the partners and get them to fund research, they needed to demonstrate the computer's potential. Glickauf, drawing on his love of gadgets, volunteered to build a small-scale replica of the Mauchly-Eckert machine in his basement. Glickauf brought the device to Chicago's Drake Hotel for a special partners' meeting called by Spacek in January 1951. Small lights on the machine blinked faster and faster as the machine's computation speed increased. Glickauf explained how the memory worked, and the partners were hooked. The device was officially called the Arthur Andersen Demonstration Computer, or AADEC, but quickly became known as the Glickiac.

A former partner remembered the meeting years later as a watershed event in the history of the partnership. "As part of our examination of the relationship of electronics to business and accounting, Joe demonstrated the speed of his model and described the potential of electronic computers in business," the partner recalled. "The ideas we were wrestling with were truly revolutionary at that time and, as we soon learned, very few people outside of Arthur Andersen & Co. were ready to buy them. But our partners grew so excited about the potential that they voted there and then to devote whatever resources were required to develop a broad base of competence in this exciting new field."

### Spacek's Folly

Spacek, with Higgins and Glickauf, selected five of the brightest young people in the firm to form the nucleus of a group to study computers. The five were lead manager John Spellman, Joe Carrico, Gene Delves, Sidney Lyons and Bill Matter. All were Phi Beta Kappas with strong mathematical skills and all but Spellman were certified public accountants. Spacek picked up the phone and convinced Eckert and Mauchly to let him send members of his team to spend time with the inventors and try to soak up what knowledge they could. "I assured them that our people would do anything—cook the meals, wash the dishes, mop the floors—just so they could trail them around and learn all there was to know about computers," he recalled. Joe Carrico ended up making the trip to Philadelphia.

Eckert and Mauchly, better scientists than businessmen, were perennially short of cash. By mid-1951 they had sold their business to Remington Rand, which continued development of the UNIVAC. After working alongside Eckert and Mauchly for six months, Carrico traveled from Philadelphia to New York, where he and the group received several days of programming lessons at the Remington Rand offices. One of the program instructors, Grace Hopper, soon became one of the best-known computer programmers in the world. Her work in the development of an English-based programming language, FLOW-MATIC, was a forerunner of the COBOL programming language. She later became head of computer systems operations for the U.S. Navy with the rank of captain (making her the highest-ranking woman in the Navy at that time).

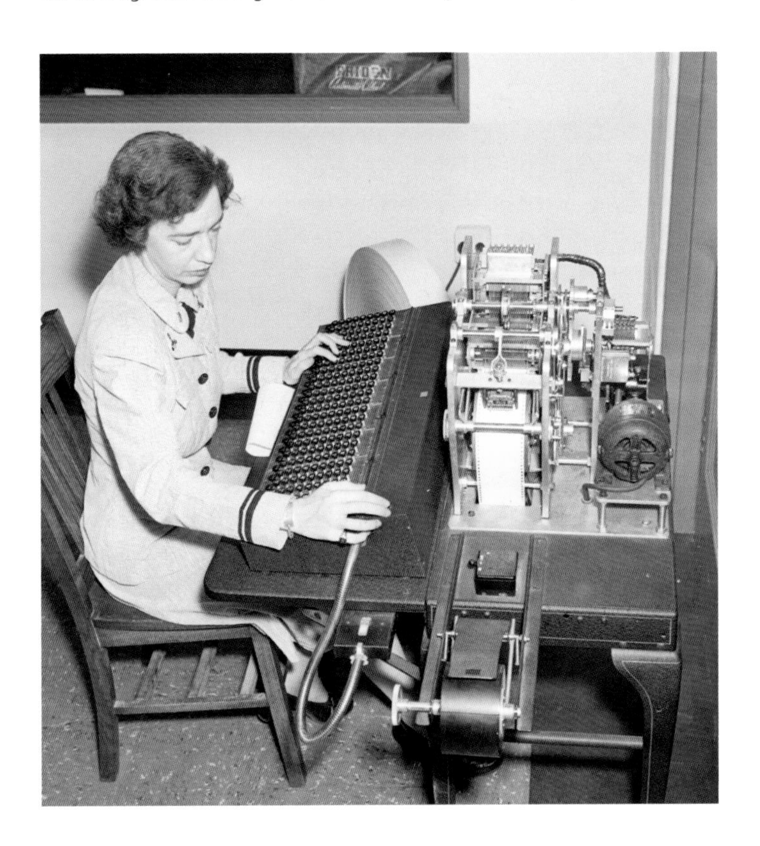

Computer software pioneer and U.S. Navy officer Grace Hopper, 1944. She retired from the Navy in 1986 with the rank of rear admiral.

Three other team members, Lyons, Matter and Delves, also spent time in 1952 and 1953 studying computers with the technical staff at Commonwealth Edison in Chicago. They didn't even have a computer. They learned the rudiments of programming using manuals for the UNIVAC and a manual from IBM for its promised, but-yet-to-be-produced electronic computer, the tape processing machine (TPM). Spacek kept Commonwealth Edison Chairman and CEO Willis Gale abreast of developments in computer research, with both agreeing that joint research was a worthwhile endeavor.

The budding computer experts also visited several academic computer installations around the United States and in Europe during this period. Writing from a European conference including U.S. and European computer experts in October 1952, Carrico told his colleagues, "You might be interested in the reception I have received here. Everyone seems to be amazed that a public accounting firm would have the foresight to get into this field at this time....Professor Aiken [of Harvard University] summed it up pretty well when he said that I must work for a pretty wonderful organization if it is progressive enough and has the vision and foresight to realize the important place electronics will play in the future of American business."

Sidney Lyons, 1950. Lyons was a member of the first group chosen by Spacek, Higgins and Glickauf to study computers.



## The Offer of a Lifetime.

When Gene Delves was summoned to Leonard Spacek's office at 5 p.m. one Friday afternoon in 1952, he assumed he must have done something wrong and that his brief career at Andersen was over. He bid his fellow recent hires goodbye and took the long walk to Spacek's corner office. Instead of being dismissed, Delves quickly realized that Spacek was offering him a chance to join the computer study task force. Spacek was flanked by Higgins and Glickauf. They were all talking at once, which they always did, about computers. Glickauf had the Glickiac beside him and gave Delves a demonstration. "You don't have to do it if you don't want to," Spacek said. "It won't affect your career if you say no, but we all think you should." Spacek then told Delves he'd give him some time to think about it—until 5:30, as the group was expected to start work at Commonwealth Edison the following Monday morning.

Delves walked around the office (it was built around a central light court) and came back and said he'd take the position. "So I went home and told my folks, 'I think I've changed my career today. I don't know what I'm going to do, but it has something to do with light bulbs,'" Delves recalled.

**Gene Delves, a member of the initial Andersen team studying computers, led the latter phase of the trailblazing computer installation for General Electric at its Appliance Park facility.**

Even though the Andersen partners had enthusiastically supported the effort to study computers in the wake of Glickauf's presentation at the Drake, it wasn't long before there was grumbling among the ranks. The cost of the endeavor was mounting, and there didn't appear to be a commercial customer in sight. Spacek himself felt the pressure. When he walked down the hall in the Chicago office he would hear partners talking, only to have them stop the minute he appeared in the door of a particular office. "This was when the idea of a systems practice came to be known as 'Spacek's Folly,'" he recalled. "Even after agreeing to the investment, a number of partners complained that all the training we were providing was awfully expensive in view of the fact that very little was coming in the way of fees for systems work."

### General Electric: A Pioneering Partner

The computer systems team got its first big break in the fall of 1952 when John Higgins received a call from a General Electric executive. GE was building a new facility called Appliance Park, outside Louisville, Kentucky. It was to be a showcase for the latest in manufacturing technology. GE officials also had been researching the use of an electronic computer to upgrade its payroll and other back-office functions. The official told Higgins, "We found that everywhere we went to learn about computers, Arthur Andersen & Co. had been there ahead of us."

Top: A 1957 aerial view of General Electric's trendsetting postwar facilities at Appliance Park, near Louisville, Kentucky.

Bottom: A GE Appliance Park billboard stressing the role of electrical appliances in improving America's quality of life.

Higgins told GE officials during a subsequent meeting that Administrative Services was so interested in doing a feasibility study of applying electronic computers to business applications that Andersen would do it for no charge. GE turned the offer down, saying it understood the importance of research and would at least expect to pay Andersen's costs. But the goodwill the offer generated, which Administrative Services would sorely need as the pioneering engagement progressed, was beyond calculation.

Administrative Services proposed on March 27, 1953, to do the feasibility study for $64,000. GE agreed. On July 15, 1953, the firm recommended the installation of a UNIVAC I computer at the GE site, including a 600-line-per-minute printer still being developed by Remington Rand. The latter was an important innovation, in that lack of speedy output had hindered earlier Mauchly-Eckert computers. GE agreed, and retained the firm to assist in the design and installation of the system. Parts for the $500,000 computer, a significant capital expenditure for that era, arrived at the Louisville site beginning in January 1954.

The GE project was the first installation of an electronic computer for commercial use in the United States. The UNIVAC I was only the eighth such computer built, the seventh one having just been installed in Remington Rand's sales offices in New York as a



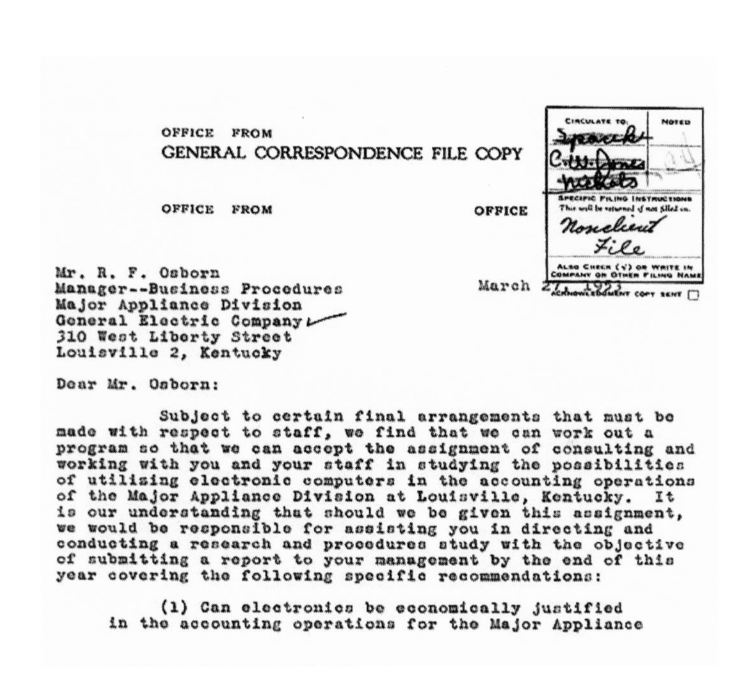
OFFICE FROM
GENERAL CORRESPONDENCE FILE COPY

OFFICE FROM OFFICE

CIRCULATE TO: | NOTED
Spaeck
C. W. Jones
Nickols
SPECIFIC FILING INSTRUCTIONS
This will be returned if not filled in.
Nonclient File
ALSO CHECK (✓) OR WRITE IN COMPANY OR OTHER FILING NAME
ACKNOWLEDGMENT COPY SENT ☐

Mr. R. F. Osborn
Manager--Business Procedures
Major Appliance Division
General Electric Company
310 West Liberty Street
Louisville 2, Kentucky

March 27, 1953

Dear Mr. Osborn:

Subject to certain final arrangements that must be made with respect to staff, we find that we can work out a program so that we can accept the assignment of consulting and working with you and your staff in studying the possibilities of utilizing electronic computers in the accounting operations of the Major Appliance Division at Louisville, Kentucky. It is our understanding that should we be given this assignment, we would be responsible for assisting you in directing and conducting a research and procedures study with the objective of submitting a report to your management by the end of this year covering the following specific recommendations:

(1) Can electronics be economically justified in the accounting operations for the Major Appliance

In its memo outlining the GE Appliance Park engagement, the firm noted that it accepted the project "in full recognition of the difficulties in such an undertaking."

demonstration model. Earlier UNIVACs were being used primarily in academia and by the U.S. federal government, including one purchased to process data collected during the 1950 census. (In Britain, building on work done at Cambridge University during the war, The Lyons Tea Co., a regional retailer, started running its payroll on an electronic computer, dubbed the LEO, in 1952.)

## Building and Sharing Knowledge.

In January 1953, John Higgins laid the foundation for a crucial element in the history of consulting at the firm—creating, building and sharing knowledge. He opened a new heading for Administrative Services in the Subject Files, which were distributed to each office.

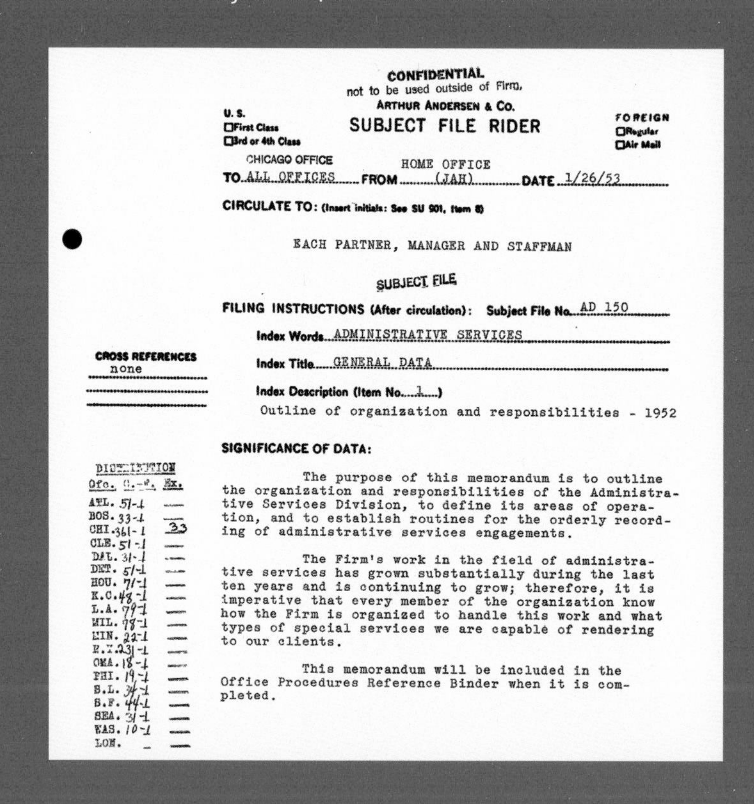

CONFIDENTIAL
not to be used outside of Firm.
ARTHUR ANDERSEN & CO.
SUBJECT FILE RIDER

U. S.
☐ First Class
☐ 3rd or 4th Class

FOREIGN
☐ Regular
☐ Air Mail

TO ALL OFFICES FROM CHICAGO OFFICE HOME OFFICE (JAH) DATE 1/26/53

CIRCULATE TO: (Insert initials: See SU 901, Item 8)

EACH PARTNER, MANAGER AND STAFFMAN

SUBJECT FILE

FILING INSTRUCTIONS (After circulation): Subject File No. AD 150

Index Words ADMINISTRATIVE SERVICES

Index Title GENERAL DATA

Index Description (Item No. 1)
Outline of organization and responsibilities - 1952

CROSS REFERENCES
none

SIGNIFICANCE OF DATA:

The purpose of this memorandum is to outline the organization and responsibilities of the Administrative Services Division, to define its areas of operation, and to establish routines for the orderly recording of administrative services engagements.

The Firm's work in the field of administrative services has grown substantially during the last ten years and is continuing to grow; therefore, it is imperative that every member of the organization know how the Firm is organized to handle this work and what types of special services we are capable of rendering to our clients.

This memorandum will be included in the Office Procedures Reference Binder when it is completed.

DISTRIBUTION

| Ofc. | [illegible] | Ex. |
|---|---|---|
| ATL. | 51-1 | — |
| BOS. | 33-1 | — |
| CHI. | 361-1 | 33 |
| CLE. | 51-1 | — |
| DAL. | 31-1 | — |
| DET. | 51-1 | — |
| HOU. | 71-1 | — |
| K.C. | 48-1 | — |
| L.A. | 79-1 | — |
| MIL. | 78-1 | — |
| MIN. | 22-1 | — |
| N.Y. | 231-1 | — |
| OMA. | 18-1 | — |
| PHI. | 19-1 | — |
| S.L. | 34-1 | — |
| S.F. | 44-1 | — |
| SEA. | 31-1 | — |
| WAS. | 10-1 | — |
| LON. | – | — |



The first item was an outline of organization and responsibilities for the Administrative Services Division. It stated, "In each office a qualified individual will be designated to assume responsibilities of manager in charge of Administrative Services." The following were identified as home office area representatives for the division: Joe Glickauf, Chicago-Midwest Area; Bob Lawrence, Houston-South and Southwest Area; Tom McDaniel, San Francisco-West Coast Area; and Ken Wulff, New York-East Coast Area.

The memo also said, "In order to achieve the maximum benefit for our combined experience, it is necessary that we provide a systematic method of recording and indexing our firmwide experience on Administrative Services engagements....Effective with the date of this release, all Administrative Services engagements will be written up and placed in the Subject File under the appropriate classifications." Spacek had created Subject Files in 1941, but they previously had been used mainly to note technical data and machine specifications. With the new Subject Files, Higgins created a crucial forum that division members would use to share knowledge and build expertise in systems installations and other engagements.

## Commitment to Education

With commercialization of the electronic computer at hand, Spacek, Higgins and Glickauf realized that it was time to formalize their previously catch-as-catch-can approach to computer education. Even before the GE installation began, Administrative Services conducted its first computer programming and installation school in September 1953. The firm's first-generation computer team members were

now considered veterans, so Joe Carrico, who studied with Eckert and Mauchly in Philadelphia, did most of the lecturing. He worked with Gene Delves in the evenings to go over the next day's material so they could keep one step ahead of the students. The classes met for 16 weeks at the downtown Chicago campus of Northwestern University, and were repeated annually for the next several years.

Twenty-six of the audit division's brightest recent hires were selected for the training. Most came from Chicago and New York, but Spacek sent out a request strongly suggesting that several other offices should send at least one candidate. His intention was that the systems installation business be spread across the organization, not based in Chicago and New York, the firm's largest offices. Boston responded by sending Bill Ingersoll, Atlanta shipped off Gordon Hamrick and Don Dixon arrived in Chicago from Washington, D.C. Each became a partner in future years. Ingersoll went on to lead the Administrative Services Division in the late 1960s. In all, 16 offices sent recent hires to the class. In fact, the quality of the first-year class, and the central role computer systems installations would play in the growth of Administrative Services, is confirmed by the fact that 19 of the 26 went on to become partners.

Photo from the Home Office Electronics School, 1953, Chicago, featured in the Arthur Andersen publication *The Chronicle.* Front row (left to right): James Paulos, Herbert Seidensticker, Harold White, Culver Floyd, Robert Zolad, William Scott, William LaBaw, Don Young. Second row: Claude Onxley, Lee Carter, Don Dixon, Bill Ingersoll, Robert Josephson, Arthur Voight, Joe Carrico (instructor), Lawrence McGaughey, John Pardee. Back row: Maurice Simpson, R.F. Lindquist, Warren Morgan, Bill Ellingson, Arthur Berger, George Murray, Howard Tomlinson, William Bell Jr., Leighton Smith, Gordon Hamrick.

**The Remington Rand UNIVAC, successor to the ENIAC, and printer, 1952. Improving printing speeds was vital to the acceptance of early electronic computers.**

Twenty-six may seem like a fairly modest number of programmers, but according to Remington Rand officials who met with Spacek in October 1953, there were only 400 to 500 computer programmers in the United States. Many worked for universities or the government. The computer manufacturer was concerned that there might not be enough qualified installers for its equipment to meet future corporate demand. According to Spacek's Subject File notes of the meeting, Glickauf told the Remington Rand officials, "The number of programmers would increase in geometric proportion to the number now existing, and that even in our own shop we intend to train as many as 200 people who could understand and program on electronic computers."

Remington Rand was fully committed to adapting the electronic computer, used mainly for military purposes during World War II, for commercial use. It recruited some of the country's top military brass to lead the charge. General Douglas MacArthur, who until recently had been head of American forces in Korea (and who was lionized by much of the public despite being dismissed by President Harry S. Truman), signed on as chairman. General Leslie Groves, who helped develop the atomic bomb as head of the Manhattan Project, was recruited to serve as chairman of the administrative committee. Spacek recorded in his notes of the meeting that Groves considered commercial demand for electronic computers nearly limitless.

In focusing on education, Administrative Services was drawing on another of Andersen's deeply ingrained traditions. Arthur Andersen himself had been an accounting instructor at Northwestern University and was the founder of its accounting department. He continued to teach even after opening his own firm. The upstart firm distinguished itself from the leading East Coast accounting firms in subsequent decades by emphasizing professional education, something virtually unheard of in the profession. The classes instilled a culture of ethical behavior and professionalism as much as the nitty-gritty of accounting. "We were the only firm that had the training, an audit training school," Gene Delves recalled. "So there was a three-week indoctrination period in there when it was beat into your head that you were the best and best trained. We only hire the best people, you're with the best firm, and don't forget it."

It's one thing to study cutting-edge technology; it's another to apply it. As the months passed, cutting edge quickly became bleeding edge in the hands of the Andersen-GE team trying to automate the Appliance Park payroll process. The extent of their initial failure became clear by October 1954 when they ran the first payroll through the computer. "When we first started off, we thought this was a machine that could run a payroll the size of GE's at that time—10,000 employees—in two hours," Glickauf said. "As it turned out, the first time it was programmed, after 40 hours it still hadn't completed a payroll." In other words, it took the UNIVAC I longer than a 40-hour workweek to produce the weekly payroll.

**UNIVAC, 1954. The machines eventually were used extensively in public and private applications ranging from the U.S. Census Bureau and the Department of Defense to corporations across America.**



Software, or rather, the lack of software, was a major hurdle in working with the UNIVAC I. Strange as it may seem to contemporary users who interact with an operating system from the moment they turn on a computer, there was no operating system for the UNIVAC I. Nor was there even a programming language in which to write instructions. The team had to write operating instructions using a letter code for operations, such as "A" for add. Finally, they had to add an address that "identified where in the memory device the operation should be performed," Glickauf said. The programs ran slowly and were very difficult to modify.

The hardware itself also presented the team with some unique challenges. The memory of the UNIVAC I consisted of mercury delay lines. These were three-foot-long tubes of mercury with a crystal at each end. Electronic impulses hit the crystal and were converted to sound waves that traveled through the tube at the speed of sound—not electricity. So, if the program accessed a word just as it entered the tube, the computer would idle until the word came out the other end of the tube. As Delves said, "We ultimately learned how to cope with this, but until we did, it was a major contribution to the slowness of the programs."

Compounding the problem was the complexity of the GE payroll. The software had to account for union wages, piecework, salaried employees and different pay scales. Multiple data validity checks, tape-to-tape controls and other features later incorporated into mainframe operating software also slowed the process. "One of the basic things that we didn't recognize was that we couldn't just drop input into the computer and let it run, because it would recognize an error and then stop," Glickauf said. "Then all the work had to be done to make the correction [and rerun the program]."

### Commitment to Client Service

Glickauf was devastated. He called a meeting with the GE vice president in charge of finance at Appliance Park, who reported to Roddy Osborn, the GE executive who ultimately was responsible for the installation. Glickauf took full blame for the failed installation and, without checking with Spacek, demonstrated Administrative Service's commitment to client service by offering to reprogram the entire system at no additional cost to GE. Glickauf recalled that the vice president smiled and said, "You have to appreciate that GE has problems like this all the time. We recognize that there are difficulties with innovation and development, so we wouldn't expect you to do this for nothing. We'll arrange to have you do it on a cost-plus basis. The main thing is that we don't want to lose the experience that you already have, knowing where the problems are."



The installation team worked nearly around the clock for another seven months rewriting the payroll software before attempting a second runthrough. The nationwide community of computer programmers was so small at the time that a number of programming pioneers from academia and government, including Grace Hopper, stopped by the site to lend a hand. During this period, Joe Carrico wrote the first programming manual for the UNIVAC I. At the same time, Administrative Services employees Bill Ingersoll and Bill Ellingson wrote the first general software programs for the UNIVAC I—programs that would come to be known as the General Run. The programs provided prepared coding for operating instructions, including input-output requirements and read-write instructions, which became mainstays of the computer programming industry. The second try was a dramatic improvement on the first, but it wasn't until well into 1956 that the team had the computerized payroll, materials handling and other systems fully functional on the UNIVAC I.

The GE installation was so important to the Administrative Services Division's future that Spacek himself traveled to Louisville in 1954 to check on his team and meet with GE officials. He also promoted the seniors on the team, Carrico, Lyons and Matter, to the rank of manager while he was there. Delves was a year or two behind the others in terms of seniority, but Spacek promoted him anyway, even though his assistant hadn't prepared the necessary paperwork. As a result, Spacek couldn't even tell Delves what his new salary would be. "He gave me a field promotion, as it were," said Delves.

A Pennsylvania Railroad sleeper car similar to the one Gene Delves took from Chicago to Louisville in 1953 to work on the GE assignment.

## All Aboard.

Travel has been an unavoidable part of most consultants' lives at one time or another. Gene Delves was among the first group of technicians to arrive at the GE installation site near Louisville in 1953. As head of the second portion of the installation, he was the last to leave in mid-1956. Delves and the other employees who were married moved their families to Louisville for the duration of the project. When they returned to Chicago headquarters for a meeting and then needed to return immediately to Louisville, they caught the Pennsylvania Railroad sleeper that left Chicago at 10 p.m. and arrived in Louisville at about 8 a.m., then headed straight for the work site. Some may have had a clearer head than others, especially those traveling on Saturday nights. "It was all through Indiana, and Indiana was then dry on Sundays," Delves said. "So as soon as you got on the train, the porter would make everybody about five drinks" while the train was still in Illinois.

Delves frequently got calls at his home from night managers at the site who were having problems. They tended to be recurring problems, and Delves patiently gave the same answer over and over. One evening he was in Chicago on business and his wife Sue answered the phone in Louisville. It was a night manager with a problem. Sue had heard her husband on the phone so often that she simply repeated what she had heard him say time and again. The manager's problem was solved.

## Progress.

Corporate America's desire to boost productivity by paring labor costs was one of the reasons most often cited to justify the time and expense of installing an electronic computer in the early years of the industry. Administrative Services estimated that GE could save $500,000 a year by installing a UNIVAC computer to handle payroll, material scheduling and inventory control, commercial service (order processing) and general cost accounting. Trimming labor costs had become a very sensitive issue by the mid-1950s, however, with the AFL-CIO increasingly active in unionizing efforts, and labor strife in the steel and transportation industries from the early 1950s still fresh in the minds of most corporate executives.

**The entrance to one of the administrative buildings at GE Appliance Park site near Louisville.**



To counter the impression that the principal impact of installing computers would be lost jobs, many companies, including GE, went on the offensive. They launched public awareness campaigns stressing that computers would lower the cost of production, expand business and generate more jobs in the long run. A GE radio spot that ran in Louisville captures the tenor of the times:

> Announcer: Friends, do you know how a giant electronic brain is helping GE's tremendous payroll operation?...UNIVAC, as you know, is an electronic computer that compiles data in hours rather than days. It accumulates, summarizes, budgets and organizes plans for future operations. It removes much of the drudgery from clerical work, and at the same time, contributes to greater job stability. For UNIVAC, like other mechanized production, enables appliances to be made at a lower cost and stimulates expansion of business which, in turn, provides more jobs. General Electric is proud to have been the first industry, and the first company in all the world, to use UNIVAC for business purposes. For...better production is achieved through progress...and at General Electric and at Appliance Park, "Progress is our most important product."

Higgins and Glickauf didn't waste any time marketing the group's newly minted systems installation expertise. Even before they realized the extent of the problems they would face with the GE payroll system, the duo jointly published "Electronics Down to Earth," a landmark article in the March-April 1954 issue of the *Harvard Business Review*. The magazine's editors declared, "No two men are better qualified, on the basis of experience with the problem of installing and operating the new digital computer." The opening paragraphs of the piece delivered a clear message to business leaders: A new era was dawning.

> If you are an executive of a moderately large enterprise, you should be aware of the fact that electronics for business is not something which must wait to be developed in the future, but that it is here now—today. No longer is the development of electronic equipment for business just an engineer's dream on a drawing board.
>
> The year 1954 will see at least one and possibly several installations of large-scale digital computers for accounting and business operations. In January of this year a large-scale digital computer was delivered to the General Electric Company's Major Appliance Division in Louisville, Kentucky, for use in accounting and in related operations. Several other companies have ordered such equipment, and many more are in the process of studying the economic effects of utilizing such equipment in their operations.
>
> Thus, at last, the machine which has probably had as much advance publicity, which has been the subject of as much speculation, and around which has grown as fancy a crop of misconceptions as has ever been seen or heard will make its opening bow on the American business scene.

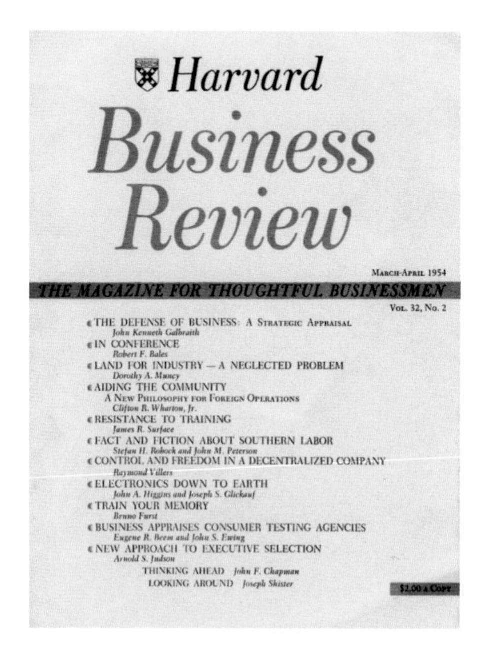

Harvard Business Review

March-April 1954

THE MAGAZINE FOR THOUGHTFUL BUSINESSMEN

Vol. 32, No. 2

THE DEFENSE OF BUSINESS: A Strategic Appraisal
*John Kenneth Galbraith*

IN CONFERENCE
*Robert F. Bales*

LAND FOR INDUSTRY — A NEGLECTED PROBLEM
*Dorothy A. Muncy*

AIDING THE COMMUNITY
A New Philosophy for Foreign Operations
*Clifton R. Wharton, Jr.*

RESISTANCE TO TRAINING
*James R. Surface*

FACT AND FICTION ABOUT SOUTHERN LABOR
*Stefan H. Robock and John M. Peterson*

CONTROL AND FREEDOM IN A DECENTRALIZED COMPANY
*Raymond Villers*

ELECTRONICS DOWN TO EARTH
*John A. Higgins and Joseph S. Glickauf*

TRAIN YOUR MEMORY
*Bruno Furst*

BUSINESS APPRAISES CONSUMER TESTING AGENCIES
*Eugene R. Beem and John S. Ewing*

NEW APPROACH TO EXECUTIVE SELECTION
*Arnold S. Judson*

THINKING AHEAD *John F. Chapman*

LOOKING AROUND *Joseph Shister*

$2.00 a Copy

**The Higgins and Glickauf article "Electronics Down to Earth" made quite a splash in the March-April 1954 issue of the *Harvard Business Review*.**

As part of a campaign to drum up corporate interest in electronic computers, about 18 months earlier Administrative Services had produced a film, *Electronics in Accounting and Business*, that it showed to groups of business leaders around the country. The computer scenes in the film were shot at the University of Illinois Computer Center in Champaign-Urbana using the university's computer, called the ILLIAC. Many of the executives who came to see the presentation were clients of Andersen's audit side. But over the next few years, as word of the film spread in business circles, executives from companies that weren't already clients started to attend. Rival accounting firms learned of the interest, and several contacted Spacek, claiming that Andersen was using unethical means to lure away their audit clients. Spacek, perhaps recognizing the film's value in differentiating Andersen from its rivals, didn't pick a fight over the issue. Instead, he directed Administrative Services employees to invite the auditors of the companies who were scheduled to view the film to join their clients and see what Andersen was up to.

**The ILLIAC was an early computer built at the University of Illinois Computer Center, Champaign-Urbana. The U.S. government encouraged and funded early academic research in electronic computers at several locations.**

Leonard Spacek was a tireless worker and advocate of workplace equality.

### Spacek's Legacy

Few individuals did as much to shape Andersen's future as Leonard Spacek. Though only 39 when he assumed the top post at the firm, he picked up founder Arthur Andersen's banner of industry and firm integrity and carried it forward until the end of his career in the early 1970s. He ensured that the old Norwegian dictum, "Think Straight, Talk Straight," which Arthur Andersen first heard on a farm from his immigrant mother in the final years of the 19th century, would remain a firm motto into the final decades of the 20th century. He often testified before congressional committees and regulatory bodies on issues confronting the accounting industry—always calling for greater public accountability—and became a pillar of Chicago's business and charitable communities. He insisted that avoiding even the appearance of impropriety was crucial to Andersen's ability to sustain the public's trust. Fearing that the organization's integrity might be compromised, he summarily fired two staffers in the early 1950s for making weekend trips to Las Vegas to gamble, even though they were traveling on their own time, recalled Glickauf.

Spacek was also focused on developing the careers of Andersen personnel at all levels. Arthur Andersen, an aloof, imperious leader, maintained sharp distinctions between partners and more junior professionals. He personally held a majority of the equity in the

## Walk Briskly.

Leonard Spacek always was motivated by his strong feelings about workplace equality and hard work, but he did have his share of quirks. In 1954 he issued a memo to the staff that almost immediately became known as the "walk briskly" memo. He didn't want clients to see employees standing about each others' offices or desks and chatting. Like Arthur Andersen, Spacek had been raised on a Midwestern farm during tough economic times and was taught the value of hard work from an early age. When in the office, employees were to "walk briskly" through the halls with a sense of purpose, his memo decreed. When at their desks, they were to be engaged in client work, not reading newspapers. Shortly after the memo was distributed, Delves was carrying a stack of documents down the hall. He rounded a corner and ran straight into Spacek's secretary Mildred "Mel" Baker Heskett, who also was carrying an armful of files. As the two bent down to retrieve their work, Heskett looked at Delves and said, "Don't worry, I'll tell him that we were walking briskly."

Time wasted drinking coffee was another of Spacek's pet peeves. He complained to John Higgins one day that employees always were leaving the office to have a cup of coffee. (Needless to say, he forbade coffee at office desks.) To prove his point, Spacek strode down the hall with Higgins to the first partner's office he came to, stuck his head in and demanded, "Do you drink coffee?" To which the startled partner responded by jumping out of his chair and saying, "Just a minute, let me get my hat." Spacek went storming back down the hall and slammed his door. Glickauf, an inveterate coffee drinker, managed to avoid Spacek's wrath by removing the files from one of his desk drawers and having his secretary put in a thermos of fresh coffee each morning, from which he would surreptitiously pour a cup or two when Spacek wasn't looking.

**Shown with Spacek are Beatrice Olsen (left) and Mildred "Mel" Baker Heskett.**

## Big Blue Sees Red.

In retrospect, the UNIVAC's potential might seem obvious. In fact, few at the time grasped the significance of the electronic computer. Thomas Watson Sr., chairman and CEO of IBM, famously observed during this period that given the computer's immense size, he thought corporate America would only need five such machines. Many, including Spacek, thought IBM was using such statements to protect its market dominance in the punch card field. IBM officials told Spacek during an October 1953 meeting that IBM had surveyed 24 of its major corporate clients and found no demand for electronic computers using magnetic tape, as opposed to existing IBM punch card machines. As Andersen's research had unearthed quite the opposite, Spacek pressed IBM to share at least some of the surveys. Watson promised to forward some reports to Spacek, but they never materialized.

Not surprisingly, IBM executives were furious with Andersen for steering GE toward a Remington Rand UNIVAC, rather than wait a year or two for IBM to deliver its first electronic computer. IBM questioned how Administrative Services could make such a judgment and presume to know more about IBM computers than IBM itself. Spacek assured Watson that while IBM experts might know more about the detailed workings of its computers, his systems staff was well qualified to recommend whose machine was best

**IBM's 705 computer, an upgrade of the short-lived 702, its first real competitor to the Remington Rand UNIVAC.**

suited to a client's particular needs. The firm wasn't biased against IBM, Spacek noted; the choice for GE was driven mainly by the fact that the UNIVAC was in production, while IBM's TPM computer existed only on paper. (In fact, it would never be produced.)

Watson made a point of telling Spacek that IBM had been offered the opportunity to buy Eckert and Mauchly's company in 1951 before it was offered to Remington Rand, but had passed, reasoning that the technology was too limited in scope. His son and successor at the helm of IBM, Thomas Watson Jr., admitted two decades later that it was a missed opportunity, "Many people in our industry, and I was among them, had seen the [Eckert and Mauchly] machine, but none of us foresaw its possibilities."

partnership until his death, and refused to name a successor. "When Mr. Andersen was head of the firm, the partners had roughly one-half of the floor with offices of substantial size," Glickauf recalled. "They had desks that were purchased separately and made for them by Marshall Field & Co....They had their own bathroom. Then between the sections of the partners and the next lower stance, which were the managers, there were swinging doors. The swinging doors were made of leather with brass knobs on them....Almost the first thing that Leonard did [as head of the firm] was to take those doors down."

Spacek, a commanding presence in his own right, also led the restructuring of the partnership in 1947. He rescued it from a succession crisis and created an organization owned by its active partners, who thought of themselves as owner-operators. And he promoted the "one firm" concept, in which partners made decisions in the best interests of the entire organization, not just their offices or countries. That concept drove growth for decades, helping support Andersen's investment in its systems installation and consulting businesses within the Administrative Services Division during lean years.

Despite the setbacks at GE's Appliance Park, the hands-on experience Administrative Services gained established the division as the leader in installing electronic computers for business use. International Shoe Company in St. Louis retained Andersen for what would be the firm's next major installation. After hearing a review from Carrico and others of the lessons learned at Appliance Park, the president of International Shoe said he would award the business to Andersen, "because it looked to me like you have made all the mistakes, and you won't have to make them again here."



It wasn't long before Administrative Services gave the nod to an IBM computer. The division continued to work closely with the technical staff at Commonwealth Edison during these years, and in 1953 was engaged to recommend what type of computer the utility should use for its business applications. Administrative Services recommended the newly released IBM 702 computer (later upgraded to the 705) for customer billing and related applications. The installation of the massive computer, which required a room of 2,400 square feet and 75 tons of air conditioning, began in 1954 and was completed on January 1, 1956, making Commonwealth Edison the first utility in the country to operate billing functions on a large-scale, general-purpose computer.

Other early installations suggest how quickly IBM made up for its slow start in the field and indicate that the systems installation effort at Andersen spread rapidly beyond its birthplace in the Chicago office. Teams from Chicago handled IBM 705 installations for International Shoe in St. Louis, Pure Oil Co. and Chicago-based Field Enterprises, which distributed World Book encyclopedias.

## Does ERMA Take Visa?

Bank of America* jumped on the computer bandwagon in 1957 when it commissioned a computer to be built by the Stanford Research Institute, with assistance from GE. The computer, named ERMA (Electronic Recording Machine, Accounting), was to be used for deposit accounting for the bank's roughly 600 branches as well as other bookkeeping requirements. Reasoning that the computer would have plenty of excess capacity, bank management commissioned Administrative Services to suggest other applications.

A team including Chuck Hemphill, who recently had moved from Chicago to the San Francisco office to help build its Administrative Services practice, suggested the concept of a universal credit card.

**Left: The Pleasures of Plastic. A woman holds a recently introduced credit card in the 1950s.**

**Right: Members of the Stanford Research Institute team that took part in the development program on ERMA.**

There were nearly 60 smaller banks in the United States offering such credit card plans, but Bank of America would be the first large bank to do so. Another unique feature of the San Francisco office's recommendation was that the card could be used as a regular charge card or a revolving charge card.

Like anxious Broadway producers, Hemphill and his team decided to try out the new product in a smaller market before launching it in the big city. "Since nothing quite like this had ever been done, the new credit card system was introduced in Fresno in 1958 on a trial basis using familiar punched card technology before moving on into a computer installation," Hemphill recalled. "After a few short months of experience, however, the bank moved quickly into [the] major metropolitan center of San Francisco and Los Angeles, and the BankAmericard, later to become Visa, was on the way."

* The Bank of America client of 1957 was a far-distant predecessor of the Bank of America of 2005. The Bank of America of 2005 was formed in 1998 by the merger of BankAmerica Corporation and NationsBank Corporation.

Electronic Recording Machine, Accounting, better known as ERMA. Creator Ken Eldridge at the controls of the check sorter in 1957.

These engagements were followed by installations of IBM 650s at Combustion Engineering Co. by the New York office, and the installation of a 650 system at Consumers Power Co. by the Detroit office.

The corporate demand for UNIVAC and IBM computers by the mid-1950s spurred production from several rivals. Within a few years, Administrative Services was weighing the relative merits of new computers from RCA, GE, NCR, Datamatic (later taken over by Honeywell) and Electrodata (which became Burroughs). The new players introduced several innovations, many addressing the pressing need for more storage capacity. In some cases these new entrants hired Administrative Services personnel as consultants, given their unparalleled installation experience. Joe Carrico and Leighton Smith reviewed proposed equipment for NCR, and Dick Nerad consulted with Raytheon. One of the executives Nerad worked with there, Harold Geneen, later headed the global conglomerate ITT and retained Administrative Services for future projects.

## Number One

Administrative Services struggled with the installation of major computer systems and the continuing need to improvise software during the late 1950s. But John Higgins, who in 1957 was named to the newly created position of director of administration under Managing Partner Leonard Spacek, and Glickauf, who succeeded Higgins as head of the Administrative Services Division, never wavered in their commitment to this new technology. In the span of a single decade, Administrative Services, which numbered about 150 people by the end of the 1950s, or barely 5 percent of the entire firm's personnel, went from nothing to No. 1 in commercial computer system design and installation—an industry that it created virtually from scratch.

ENIAC and UNIVAC inventors J. Presper Eckert (left) and John W. Mauchly flank Arthur Andersen Managing Partner Leonard Spacek at a reception honoring their contributions to the development of the computer industry.



**That commitment kept Andersen at the technology consulting forefront and ready to capitalize on its investment as a new generation of easier-to-use, more affordable computers sparked renewed business interest in mainframe systems. The wrenching experience of the Appliance Park team blazed a path for Administrative Service's subsequent technological success. The consultants took a tremendous amount of satisfaction from the fact that they were succeeding with computer installations when virtually everyone else was failing. Though, as team member John Spellman put it, "Pioneering is painful."**

# Late 1950s–Late 1960s

## Coming of Age

POWER
ON
POWER
OFF

INSTRUCTION ADDRESS - ROS ADDRESS
LOAD UNIT
DATA
F
G
H
J
SYSTEM
MAN
WAIT
TEST
LOAD
INTERRUPT
LOAD

BASE V PROGRAM TAPE
Copyright
©ARTHUR ANDERSEN & Co.
1969
OS BASE V
9-TRACK
1600 BPI
STANDARD LABEL
DATA SET NAME = BVMACRO
RELEASE—
04-06-74
UPDATE—
SGBV11
TAPE VOL1 SERIAL NUMBER
UNLOADED PDS

"That was where the firm pioneered, in developing systems software. We did that all during the 1950s, and in the early '60s, had our library of software tools, which was unheard of. IBM didn't have anything like it. We were able to get systems in and running where nobody else was able to do it."

Dick Nerad

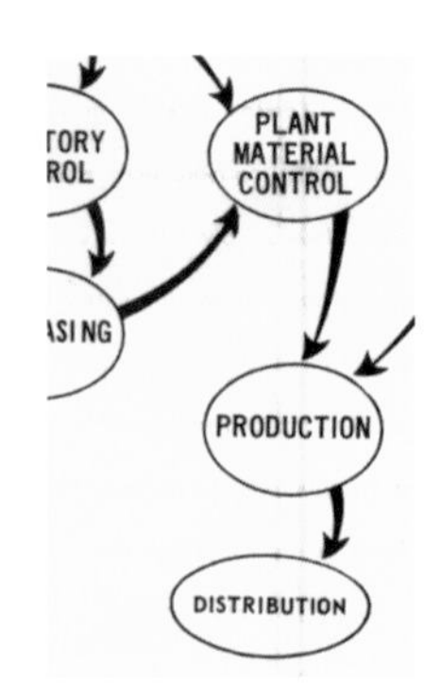

# Late 1950s–Late 1960s
# Coming of Age



**Anything seemed possible at the dawn of the Computer Age, but companies and governments needed experts who could tell them how to benefit from a succession of new technologies. Consulting played an increasingly important role at Arthur Andersen as pioneering partners focused on using computer technology to improve both the efficiency and effectiveness of their client's management systems. As the firm began building practices around the globe, it achieved efficiencies for clients across a variety of industries. The firm focused on transforming its own approach to business as well, constantly implementing new ideas as it developed a global "one firm" concept.**

Chapter opening image: Base V Software tape, developed by the firm's consulting division.

## Art Welby thought he must be dreaming. He was just regaining consciousness after being anesthetized for minor surgery in July 1956 and there, standing over him, was Basil Regione, head of Administrative Services in the Chicago office.

What did Welby, who had been with Andersen for five years on the audit side, think about moving to Milan, Italy, and running Administrative Services there, Regione asked. Welby, who had served in the U.S. Army Air Force in World War II and whose wife was a "war bride" from Italy, liked the idea, as did his wife. Within a month, the young couple had sold their suburban house, which they had just purchased, back to their contractor, and were on the Twentieth Century Limited overnight train bound for New York. The next day they caught a boat headed for Genoa, Italy, and then boarded yet another train bound for Milan.

Welby was in the vanguard of Administrative Service's first sustained effort to expand internationally. In many ways he personified the ethos of Administrative Services during this period—he was young, a little impetuous and ready for a fresh challenge.



Arthur Andersen Annual Partners' Meeting, 1954.

From the late 1950s through the late 1960s, Andersen took its "one firm" concept, which was proving phenomenally successful in the United States, around the world. In many offices outside the United States a significant portion of the work involved consulting services. American corporations were expanding rapidly overseas, and Andersen was determined to keep pace with—and in many cases anticipate—the growth, especially compared with rival U.S. accounting firms.

At the same time, the U.S. computer systems installation business and related consulting activities were growing rapidly. Offices across the country engaged in major installations. By the end of the 1960s, Andersen made its most significant investment in training by paying just under $4 million for its own training facility in St. Charles, 35 miles west of the Chicago Loop on the banks of the Fox River. Considering the contribution the training facility would make to the firm's success, it was the bargain of the century.

### Continental House Cleaning

Andersen had affiliated with a handful of non-U.S. accounting firms in the 1930s, mainly in Europe and Latin America. The Great Depression, followed by World War II, limited growth opportunities overseas, however. The non-U.S. business grew slowly in the postwar years, but by the mid-1950s sustained global recovery had revived Spacek's interest in global growth. First, he had to address mounting U.S. client complaints about the quality of service they were receiving from Andersen's overseas affiliates.

One day in 1957, Forrest Mars, the mercurial son of the founder of the Mars candy empire who had moved to London to start his own candy company, came storming into Spacek's Chicago office. "I want you to go to London and check on the work your people are doing for my company. The service is lousy," Mars shouted at Spacek, who recalled the conversation years later in an interview. Spacek retorted that Andersen provided clients the same services overseas as it did in the United States. "That might be the plan," Mars responded, "but the plan is not working. The service in London is bad and you don't know a damn thing about it!" Spacek conceded that he had never been to London, and promised to make the trip as soon as possible.

Mars was right. Andersen had been affiliated with Turquand, Youngs, one of the oldest accounting firms in London, for more than a quarter century. The contract extended to the United Kingdom, continental Europe and South America. Andersen audit clients with overseas operations received auditing services from Turquand, Youngs' offices in those overseas countries where it had offices. Within 24 hours of arriving in London, Spacek could see that the British partnership was putting its clients first and servicing Andersen clients as time allowed.

**Top: Basil Regione, 1962. Regione was named a partner in 1954 and headed the Administrative Services Division of the Chicago office.**

**Bottom: Art Welby would play an instrumental role in building the firm's European consulting business.**

Spacek canceled the business relationship with Turquand, Youngs on the spot, resolving to build Andersen's own network of offices in Europe. He wasn't willing to make a similar investment in South America, however. Spacek offered to buy Turquand, Youngs' business there, but none of its partners could tell him the extent of the firm's holdings. "But they knew how much they wanted—$100,000," Spacek recalled. "Well, I said, 'If you want $100,000, that probably means it's worth $50,000. But I don't have time to haggle. Let's make it $75,000 and I'll write you a check.'" The offer was accepted, and Spacek phoned Higgins back in Chicago, "I just bought the Turquand, Youngs operations in South America. Go down there and find out what we've got."

Spacek began reconstituting offices in London, Paris, Brussels, Milan and Oslo. Americans came over for brief periods to "seed" overseas office growth in subsequent years, but the firm emphasized hiring nationals to run these offices once they had been trained in Andersen's procedures and "one firm" ethos. "We sent Americans overseas to open offices, but we hired locals, raised them under the Andersen system and sent the Americans back to the States," noted William Hall, an Andersen partner. "We had a policy of, 'Yankee go home.'"

### Talent Search

Art Welby had been in Milan for less than a year at the time of the Turquand, Youngs purge. The systems and responsibility reporting jobs he was overseeing were staffed mostly with American imports. Europe in the mid-to-late 1950s was several years behind the United States in embracing computers, even the most up-to-date punch card tabulating systems, so the pool of local talent was fairly shallow. Welby and others always were on the lookout for promising nationals they could send to the United States for a year or two of training. Pierre Reveillion, who would later head Administrative Services in France, started in an entry-level position in the Paris

**European Pioneers.** Early European partners Guy Barbier (left) and Pierre Reveillion (middle), who played leading roles in building the practice in France, and Manuel Soto (right), an early partner in the Madrid office.

office in the mid-1950s. Other European consultants who later played key leadership roles joined Andersen in the late 1950s, including Reveillion's predecessor as head of the Paris office, Guy Barbier, and Ian Hay Davison and Martin Vandersteen in London.

## Stewardship and Sacrifice.

Investing for the future, be it in terms of training or new offices, has always been a part of firm culture. But this concept of stewardship was sorely tested in the late 1950s. International expansion was a considerable drain on partners' profits. Andersen was opening new offices in the United States at a rapid pace, investing heavily in training and still making annual payments to the Andersen family estate.

Matters came to a head in early 1958 at the Annual Partners' Meeting. "I heard it from overseas that a number of partners were unhappy that the firm had dropped a cool million dollars in getting Europe and South America established," Welby recalled. "Leonard stood up and said, 'This is the way we're going, and there's no more discussion.'" Spacek demanded a vote of confidence in his leadership and received overwhelming support.

"Keep in mind that at that time, I purposely allocated one-third of all earnings of the partners to developing other offices," Spacek later recalled. "The reason why is we had to be able to serve clients around the world. There seemed to be no alternative to that kind of conclusion....The whole partnership sacrificed tremendously. All these men that lived at that time sacrificed tremendously."



Other overseas offices that later expanded rapidly opened at this time or shortly thereafter. In Spain, Manuel Soto started in the Madrid office in the early 1960s. He was an accounting partner, but he played a significant leadership role in building the consulting practice. In Asia, the Tokyo office opened in 1962.

Welby's main problem during his first few years in Europe was lack of manpower. He was crisscrossing the Continent, usually by train, and making frequent trips to the United Kingdom to meet with clients. "I was used to the times in the Chicago office, as small as it was then, when you could walk down the hall, and if you had a problem, somebody in the office at one of those doors could help you with it, and you could learn from it," he recalled. "But when you're over there making those decisions...I used to kid people. I'd say, 'Well, there were really three of us—me, myself and I—and boy did we ever talk to each other a lot.'" Welby convinced Joe Glickauf to find someone to help manage the expanding European practice, and in a little over a year Frank Dwiggins was brought in from Chicago to head Administrative Services in the United Kingdom.

Initially, the consulting and systems installation client roster was mainly audit clients based in the United States with operations in Europe, including Texaco, Colgate-Palmolive, Getty Oil and Kraft. Kraft, the Chicago-based food products company, hired Administrative

Top: In July 1961, Administrative Services held its first training outside the United States in Bad Homburg, West Germany. Six of the firm's offices were represented by the faculty members (left to right): John Biella, Harford Robb, Charles Jewell, Joe Glickauf, Richard Eichner, Ernst Schoepe and Guy Barbier (not pictured: Frank Dwiggins and Rolf Handschin).

Bottom: Twenty students from eight countries attended the 1961 Basic Systems training school in Bad Homburg.

Services to create mechanized inventory control systems for its business in Germany, which consisted mainly of delivering cheese to small warehouses around the country. Forrest Mars, apparently satisfied that Spacek had put his European business in order, continued to retain the firm for various consulting assignments.

The Administrative Services leaders in Europe quickly realized that if the practice was to grow, they couldn't rely solely on work from audit clients. Nationals being hired and trained at the time were even more convinced. Martin Vandersteen was typical of the future European leaders who joined Andersen in the late 1950s. He was recruited by the London office in 1958 and initially worked out of the Paris office, then spent much of 1959 training in Chicago and Cleveland. He worked with Administrative Services in the San Francisco office before returning to Europe, initially to work on Rust-Oleum and Penn Controls engagements in Holland. By the early 1960s, "It became very clear to us that the only way we were going to build the practice was not on the back of audit clients," Vandersteen recalled. "Because most of the audit clients were referred from the United States and every time a decision needed to be taken, it had to go back to the United States to be taken, and you could sit there for ages waiting for a decision. We had to build the practice by focusing on British clients and that became very, very clear, and that is what we did."



## "Leaking" Oil.

Consultants expect the unexpected when they embark on assignments that take them into a new field or practice. Welby and a few others were brought in by the eccentric entrepreneur J. Paul Getty in the late 1950s to convert handwritten record-keeping systems to a mechanized system at an oil refinery Getty recently had purchased from a syndicate of Italian businessmen. At that time, Italy didn't tax the oil being refined at such facilities, as long as it was shipped to another country after refining. The tax authorities, however, suspected that a certain amount of the oil was "leaking" out of the refinery and being sold tax free in Italy. On the morning Welby and his team were set to convert to the mechanized system, the doors of the refinery flew open and in rushed armed revenue agents. They seized all of the group's flow charts and other working papers, paying particular attention to any records pertaining to inventories. No one associated with the project was accused of any wrongdoing, however, and the conversion eventually was completed successfully.

Though never an audit client of the firm, Ford Motor Co. retained Administrative Services in the United Kingdom to consult on the redesign and operation of its expanded Dagenham, England, assembly plant in the early 1960s. The assignment would lead to punch card systems work at 11 Ford locations in the United Kingdom and greatly enhance the firm's standing as a global leader in systems design and installation.

The development of Arthur Andersen audit practices in Europe varied country by country. In the United Kingdom, there already was a large established audit profession and the upstart "American" firm never really was able to gain entrance to this exclusive club. The firm had to prospect for its own consulting clients, nearly all of whom were not audit clients. The situation was similar in France and Germany. However, in Italy and Spain there was not an established audit profession, and leaders from Arthur Andersen helped create a strong leadership position in local audit—indeed, they created a modern audit profession in those countries. For this reason, there initially was more work done by consulting for audit clients in those two countries.

One of the largest U.K. consulting clients during the early 1960s was Ford Motor Co. Ltd., based in London, even though its Detroit parent was never an audit client. Ford brought in a team led by Frank Dwiggins and Ian Hay Davison in 1962 to install an IBM computer to handle purchasing, receiving and accounts payable for its Dagenham, England, auto manufacturing facility. The success of the Dagenham engagement led to the design and installation of a punch card system in 11 Ford locations in the United Kingdom, involving 120 Ford personnel, and additional engagements with Ford's U.K. unit in the 1970s. It also greatly enhanced Administrative Services' standing as a global leader in systems design and installation.



Another major U.K. client relationship began in 1961 when Cummins Engine Co. retained Administrative Services to convert manual procedures to machine accounting at its engine plant near Glasgow, Scotland. That work led to a much larger engagement two years later at the newly built Chrysler-Cummins plant in county Durham. The project involved a dozen Administrative Services personnel—marking it as a major engagement for the period—and spanned inventory control, parts requirements, scheduling, product costing and cost accounting.

Cummins Engine Co. retained the firm for systems work in the United Kingdom during the early 1960s, which led to an expanded engagement with Chrysler-Cummins two years later in county Durham.

Another consultant reviewed this system several years later for Chrysler-Cummins and gave it a "AAA" rating, the top ranking the consultant granted.

While Andersen began featuring nationals in its overseas offices in the late 1950s and early 1960s, and increasingly was foraging for non-audit, overseas clients, it still remained true to its "one firm" approach to client service. As Vandersteen recalled:

> We are "one firm" and that is why we are different from everyone else. Everyone else has a separate British firm and an American firm and a French firm. We are "one firm"...That was drilled into me from almost day two and it struck me as being the source of enormous competitive advantage. It was not without its trials and tribulations from time to time. I mean, you sit here occasionally and say, "You know those bloody Americans are driving us nuts." But the "one firm" concept is something which has stood us in good stead all these years and it is still there. And no other firm has it like we do.

### Competitive Advantages

In the United States during the late 1950s and early 1960s, the Administrative Services Division was enhancing its reputation to handle big systems jobs. The work often sprang from comments included in "blueback reports" issued in conjunction with an audit. Named after the color of the paper cover and first used in the late 1930s, the blueback included comments concerning how a company might change different procedures to improve its performance. A multiyear engagement with Mutual of Omaha beginning in 1958 grew out of

Chicago & Northwestern Railroad was an industry leader in incorporating computers into its operations.

just such comments. "The engagement originally was obtained during the audit as a result of pointing out to management the possibilities of cost reductions in their existing 705 [IBM] installations," the Subject File chronicled. "This work in conjunction with audit personnel was done by Administrative Services personnel with electronics background concentrating on the company's electronic procedures."

This was also the first job in which Administrative Services completely redesigned a computer system that it hadn't installed. Administrative Services personnel quickly identified the problem with the existing system, one that probably could have been avoided if the original installer had adopted the firm's comprehensive approach. As the Subject File noted, "The company in developing its existing computer system had used individual programming efforts which resulted in a great variety of techniques in the actual operation of the system. We illustrated the use and purposes of the programming concepts which we have developed which would provide better control over operations and also reduce programming efforts."

The Car-Fax System allowed Chicago & Northwestern Railroad to organize and manage each of its nearly 75,000 freight cars.

Already, Administrative Services was extending its competitive advantage with pathbreaking work in software and standardizing procedures. "The machines were a lot simpler than they are today as far as capability is concerned, but you didn't have the software aids," recalled Dick Nerad, who was an Administrative Services manager working on the Mutual of Omaha engagement in the late 1950s. The engagement required more than 100 people working for almost two years. "That was where the firm pioneered, in developing systems software," Nerad said. "We did that all during the 1950s, and in the early '60s, had our library of software tools, which was unheard of. IBM didn't have anything like it. We were able to get systems in and running where nobody else was able to do it."

Nerad said that the Mutual of Omaha job was concluded, "one month ahead of schedule and on budget." That performance laid the groundwork for a relationship that lasted more than 25 years as Mutual of Omaha upgraded additional systems, and also brought Administrative Services back to update its own work as more powerful generations of computers were introduced. Indeed, the likelihood that the firm would be called back for upgrades and related work put constant pressure on the systems design and installation teams to maintain the high standards set by the group from its inception, and its willingness to go the extra mile to satisfy a client.

### Growth on Track

Administrative Services' work in responsibility reporting often led to systems installation engagements. In the mid-1950s, the Minneapolis & St. Louis Railway Co. retained the division to redesign its financial reporting and controls. Lead partner on the project was John Higgins, who had a close working relationship with the railroad's Chairman and

CEO Ben Heineman. So did Larry Provo, an audit manager supervising the project. Heineman wrote to Leonard Spacek on November 30, 1954, "I would be remiss if I failed to write and tell you how superbly John Higgins and his associates presented the report to the board of directors, and how deeply appreciative I am of the interest taken by you and your entire organization in the preparation of your report."

Shortly after the project was completed, Heineman became president of the much larger Chicago & Northwestern Railroad (C&NW); he brought along Provo, who was named chief financial officer. He also hired Administrative Services for a much more comprehensive review of the railroad's systems needs. Out of this initial engagement came one of the largest Administrative Services assignments of the late 1950s and early 1960s. At various times, it included the majority of the Administrative Services staff in the Chicago office. When the firm upgraded the system from mechanical punch cards to an electronic computer in the early 1960s, it became the first computer installation for a railroad.

We've Been Workin' on the Railroad. The firm's work for the Chicago & Northwestern Railroad was featured in the June 1959 issue of *Modern Railroads.*



At the core of the C&NW engagement was a system called Car-Fax, designed to keep tabs on every one of the railroad's nearly 75,000 freight cars on a 24-hour basis. Sixty-eight reporting stations across the Midwest, equipped with IBM transceivers, read special ID tags on each car and transmitted the data back to Chicago via dedicated phone lines. As Higgins noted in the Subject File, "A number of railroads have extensive mechanized car reporting systems; however none have integrated the data from these systems with traffic requirements for 'sales analysis' or revenue estimating, or controls to any significant extent."

C&NW promotional material from the era focused on the benefits the system delivered for its customers, marking the engagement as a forerunner of jobs in subsequent decades that would help transform the way clients do business. "The watchful eyes of this electronic marvel overlook nothing!" the material promised. "Faster turnover of loads and empties means the right cars at the right place at the right time. It means more cars to serve Northwestern shippers." Administrative Services produced a film of the new system, and in showing it to business groups stressed, presciently, that a similar concept could be used in the trucking industry.

### John Higgins' Charismatic Leadership

John Higgins died unexpectedly in October 1965 at age 52. He was serving as the chief operations officer of the entire firm at the time, but he had remained a tireless booster of Administrative Services and helped ensure that the division's growth wasn't shortchanged during slow periods. While Glickauf was the technical guru of the consulting division's immediate postwar years, Higgins was the organizational genius. "John was probably one of the most brilliant men I have ever

## Get Him to the Church on Time.

John Higgins was considered the best salesperson in Administrative Services, and his salesmanship didn't just extend to winning over clients. Si Moughamian recalled working for Higgins on the Minneapolis & St. Louis Railway engagement fresh out of punch card school in the mid-1950s. Moughamian was planning to get married the following February, in the midst of the first month's closing of the railroad's books following conversion to a mechanical system. Higgins said it wouldn't look good to the client, even though Moughamian was "pretty far down the ladder" at the time. The groom-to-be complained that his future bride, a Teletype operator who also worked at Andersen, already had made all of the church and hotel arrangements, and wasn't the type to change her mind. Moughamian said that if Higgins could convince her to delay the wedding for the sake of the project, it was okay with him. When Moughamian got back to Chicago his fiancée met him at the train station. "Guess what?" she said. "We have a new wedding date."

**Si Moughamian. His bride-to-be decided the wedding could wait.**



met in my life," Glickauf recalled. "He was meticulous in everything he did. Time meant nothing to John. It was either going to be right or not at all."

At the same time, Higgins was a charismatic leader and salesman who forged the consultants into a cohesive group. "He had a sense of where technology was going," recalled Si Moughamian, who himself led the consulting practice from 1983 to 1988. "And he was trying to take this small band—I could say group, but we were almost a small band of people—and have them follow him in this direction that he wanted to go....I just think we all just lined up and charged right up the hill with him."

John Higgins, 1960s.

Partners in the decades following Higgins' death in 1965 often referred to the consulting group's "special sauce" (a term borrowed from a heavily advertised key ingredient in McDonald's Big Mac sandwich). It was a mixture of moxie, drive and the willingness to commit the necessary resources. The phrase was widely used in the 1970s and 1980s, though no one could say exactly when it became part of the consulting culture. While Higgins clearly didn't coin the phrase "special sauce," his strong leadership provided all the key ingredients for the recipe.

The Empire Strikes Back. IBM was slow to introduce computers for business use, but its System/360 computer (above) rapidly became the de facto computer standard for many industries in the 1960s.

## Next Generation Hardware

The rise of rival computer makers was putting pressure on IBM. By the early 1960s, Andersen "recognized that several manufacturers had produced equipment capable of handling business applications effectively, and on a price/performance basis were more attractive than IBM's computers," noted Chuck Hemphill. The Chicago office, in fact, was running its payroll on an RCA computer well into the mid-1960s. Indeed, the willingness of Administrative Services, particularly the Chicago office, to recommend non-IBM computers led to periodic accusations that the Chicago office was "anti-IBM." The New York office, operating in the shadow of IBM's headquarters and its high-powered sales efforts, tended to recommend IBM solutions more frequently.

The office's decisions also were strongly influenced by George Trentin, head of New York's Administrative Services, who was known to favor IBM systems. At that time, however, Trentin headed a major assignment at Travelers Insurance Company that involved UNIVAC hardware. The job had great significance in the insurance industry because it was the first success in automating the issuance and maintenance of automobile policies. It was followed by the building of the Travelers' Data and Computer Center. New York partner Tony Abbott led the system installation. This engagement was followed by a new expense management system, using variable budgeting, which was so enthusiastically supported by Sterling Tooker, the CEO, that he produced a film about the use of computers to be shown throughout the company.

IBM responded to the competitive pressure by unveiling its System/360 line in April 1964. This line was considered the first of a new generation of computers to incorporate the latest developments in solid-state circuitry with multiprogramming and other features to increase processing speeds. The System/360 also held out the promise of easy modular upgrading and, therefore, a certain amount of technological stability.

Thomas Watson Jr., who had replaced his father at the helm of IBM, bet the company on the new computer and won. The improved performance and relative ease of use attracted a much broader universe of corporate customers. At the same time, the U.S. economy was gathering steam for a period of sustained economic growth (fueled partly in later years by spending tied to the nation's escalating involvement in the Vietnam War). The new model also provided a more versatile platform for Administrative Services to use in new systems installations, and for upgrading older systems using punch card equipment.

IBM's reinvigoration of the mainframe computer industry was part of a tremendous technological boom in the 1960s. As the decade began, U.S. President John F. Kennedy instilled a sense of drive and idealism against a backdrop of political and technological competition

Thomas Watson Jr., CEO of IBM, with an IBM System/360 computer in September 1966.

from the Soviet Union. The United States was still scrambling to recover its postwar technological edge following the launch of the Sputnik satellite in 1957 by the Soviets. The Apollo Program to land a man on the moon, and massive funding for technological research, more than recovered the lead for the United States by the end of the decade. It also spurred the private sector to invest in computer systems, driving a portion of the consulting practice's business.

## Leadership Changes, But Not Client Focus

Andersen has been influenced by a number of very strong leaders over the decades, none more so than Leonard Spacek. But the constant, overarching driver of its success has been its unwavering commitment to client service. On the firm's 50th anniversary, December 1, 1963, at Spacek's request and with the approval of the partnership, Wally Oliphant was named managing partner. Oliphant had worked closely with Glickauf and Higgins in the U.S. Navy during World War II, and

played an important role in persuading the two to join Andersen, not IBM or AT&T, after the war. He was promoted to partner in 1952 and worked on several major engagements during the following decade, and was a consistent advocate for the growth of Administrative Services. Spacek assumed the newly created position—chairman of the partnership—and was expected to focus on external issues while Oliphant effectively ran the firm. At least, that was the plan.

Spacek, still only in his mid-50s at the time, wasn't prepared to take a backseat to anyone, on any issue. While remaining as active as ever in the public sphere, he also worked closely with many partners who brought client-related issues to his attention. Many partners at the time thought that Spacek's larger-than-life personality must have made it difficult for Oliphant to function as head of the firm. Oliphant didn't complain. "Many things changed, some subtly and some drastically, when I succeeded Leonard, but there were a number of constants as well," Oliphant recalled 25 years later, reflecting on his seven-year term as managing partner. "One of those was the shared attitude that we could never compromise on quality. We all recognize that changes in the profession, the overall business environment and now in the competitive marketplace can change a firm's emphasis and approach. But any approach that does not focus heavily on quality of service is surely foredoomed to fail."

Top: NASA used IBM System/360 computers to give it a leg up in the 1960s "space race" with the Soviet Union as both countries vied to be the first to land a man on the moon.

Bottom: Wally Oliphant succeeded Leonard Spacek as Arthur Andersen managing partner in December 1963. He would serve in that position until 1970.

## Working for Uncle Sam

Prior to the mid-1960s, Andersen had been wary of becoming entangled in government engagements. Spacek, among others, had taken repeated potshots at the U.S. federal government's accounting shortcomings when it came to budget projections and other issues. Still, the sustained growth of public-sector spending in the 1960s presented a clear opportunity for Administrative Services to apply its expertise to increasingly complex government problems.

Left: The Pentagon placed a heightened emphasis on systems planning in the 1960s as the Vietnam War escalated. That focus on systems quickly would spread to other branches of U.S. government.

Right: U.S. Secretary of Defense Robert McNamara in 1967. He and his staff were aided by the firm's application of systems technology.



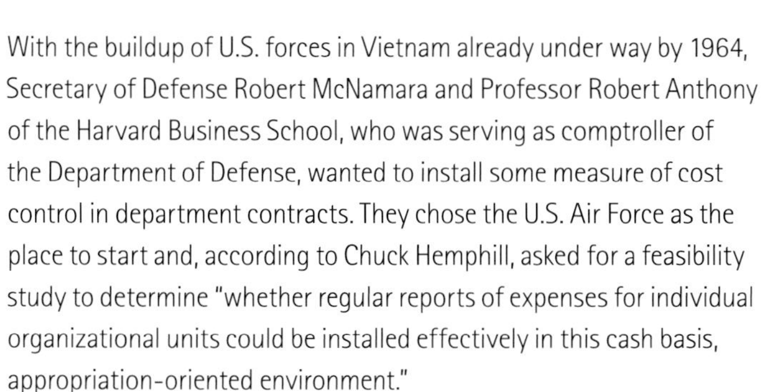

With the buildup of U.S. forces in Vietnam already under way by 1964, Secretary of Defense Robert McNamara and Professor Robert Anthony of the Harvard Business School, who was serving as comptroller of the Department of Defense, wanted to install some measure of cost control in department contracts. They chose the U.S. Air Force as the place to start and, according to Chuck Hemphill, asked for a feasibility study to determine "whether regular reports of expenses for individual organizational units could be installed effectively in this cash basis, appropriation-oriented environment."

Hemphill's proposal noted that the Department of Defense was asking for an accrual accounting system that closely resembled responsibility reporting systems Andersen had been installing for years. Hemphill learned later that when the Administrative Services' proposal was being discussed, one officer said, "They talk like they invented responsibility reporting." To which Defense Department Comptroller Anthony replied, "They did!" Administrative Services eventually won the four-year contract.

## Big Iron Age

The widespread adoption of mainframe computers, referred to as "Big Iron," powered the growth of the consulting practice through the balance of the 1960s. Indeed, the business generated

In 1966, *Forbes* described the growing importance of consulting to the major accounting firms in the United States.

*"Well, the efficiency consultants you retained have tracked down what's wrong around here, J.B., and . . . well . . . I'm afraid you aren't going to like this . . . but . . ."* Leo Garel—From Roth Agency

**Are CPA Firms Taking Over Management Consulting?**

**Not yet, but their consulting practice is booming. In seeking to expand beyond their traditional auditing function, CPAs are increasingly competing with regular management consultants.**



by Andersen and other accounting partnerships during the decade was attracting broader notice. In 1966, *Forbes* ran an article titled, "Are CPA Firms Taking Over Management Consulting?" The article concluded that, "One thing is clear: The old image of the accountant as a silent, grim-faced man in a green eyeshade sitting apart from the mainstream of business is completely out of date. He's now a top management consultant and that role is going to grow."

Andersen officials often were called upon to explain, and at times defend, the growing Administrative Services business. As early as March 1962, Patrick Rivett, a member of the London Administrative Services staff, wrote in the British publication *The Statist* that, "Such [accounting] advice is intimately bound up with the accounting systems used by a client and it is not possible to give advice on an accounting system without at the same time advising on the way in which masses of data are to be processed, handled and presented to management...These management services may amount to as much as 20 percent of the accounting firm's total fee-paying business. In the fierce competition prevailing in American accountancy the development of this complete range of services is necessary to survival and growth."

The textile industry's need for better communication and coordination among its mills and other facilities led to several major client engagements in the 1960s.

One of the major installations of the mid-1960s was for Deering Milliken, one of the world's largest textile companies. The Administrative Services staff in Atlanta, under the direction of Gordon Hamrick, worked with the company to develop a long-range plan for a management information system. The innovative system, unique for its time, provided real-time information on the company's far-flung network of plants, and also enabled company managers to look five years into the future in each of the company's functional areas.

A July 1965 Subject File entry conveys a sense of the Deering Milliken's significance and the state-of-the-art in systems installations at the time:

> This engagement is unique in that the approach to a Management Information System which the Company has adopted is predicated upon the capture of essential input data; the transmission of such data to a central facility; and the storage and processing of such information on an immediate or "real-time" basis. Output from such a system would be produced on a selective basis and other information would be made available by interrogating the system through the use of remote inquiry stations.

If there were any doubt that this was a plum assignment, a note in the same Subject File points out that Administrative Services was chosen over several high-profile rivals—information that rarely found its way into the firm's records. The also-rans included the Stanford Research Institute, the consulting division of General Electric and RCA, "who had proposed staffing the engagement with top corporate officials." Administrative Services even bested Arthur D. Little, despite the fact that Deering Milliken President Roger Milliken was on Little's board of directors. With continued hard work, particularly from Andersen's Don Dixon, who took the client relationship with him when he transferred to Charlotte, North Carolina, Deering Milliken became one of the Charlotte office's core clients.

FIN-PAC, the firm's first significant applications software package.

### Filling the Software Vacuum

Computer experts across the country assumed that IBM would develop operating systems for the new System/360 generation of computers. When nothing appeared by 1967, an Administrative Services team of programmers led by Bill Ellingson, Gresh Brebach and Charlie Balch developed Base V. Not just an operating system for the System/360, it was designed as a program generator consisting of a shell into which interchangeable parts could be inserted to produce a variety of operating systems needed by the user. The name referred to the five runs in a typical computer system: input validation, sorting, file posting, file reading and output formatting.

In the early1970s, the Houston office developed Administrative Services' first significant applications software package, based on Baker McAdams' work installing computerized general ledger systems at a number of companies. McAdams, with the assistance of Jesse Tutor and others, developed the standardized package, dubbed FIN-PAC. The product was an instant success, with about 200 companies using it in the United States and Europe. Unfortunately, this early success may have encouraged Administrative Services to engage in later software development—from which it would eventually pay dearly to extricate itself.

### Picture-perfect Results

Another milestone engagement of the late 1960s was a systems integration project for Zenith Corp.'s quality-plagued television picture tube business. The project continued into the early 1970s, and portions the system created by the firm are still in use. Jack Butts, a partner who worked on the project for five years, recalled that it was the largest project of its kind at the time. By 1971, Administrative Services had more than 60 employees on the job. "We tied together systems in production, inventory control, shipping, procurement and cost management," Butts recalled. "On the materials side we put in a significant portion of what would later come to be known as enterprise resource planning, or ERP, systems."

The results were spectacular. At Zenith's Rauland subsidiary plant in Melrose Park, Illinois, the number of TV sets assembled jumped from 220 to 650 per line per shift, recalled Jack Garrahy, another partner who worked on the project as a manager. Even more impressive, the percentage of good tubes skyrocketed to 95 percent from a paltry 15 percent prior to the adoption of the integrated systems plan.

The engagement marked a number of impressive firsts for Administrative Services, including being one of the first large-scale uses of CRTs, or cathode ray tubes, for online data access. At the same time, the nitty-gritty reworking of the shop floor at the Rauland plant marked



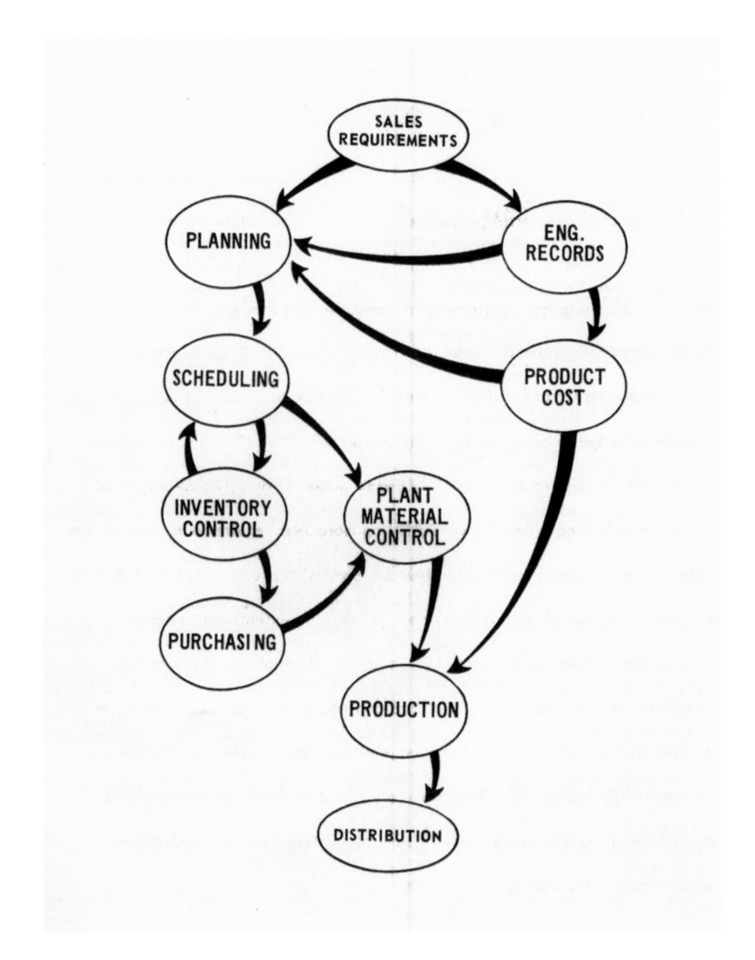

Zenith Corp. Manufacturing Information and Control Systems diagram (left) and manual cover (above), 1969. This type of systems installation was a forerunner in many ways of contemporary enterprise resource planning, or ERP, systems.

The picture looked bright for Zenith in the late 1960s, thanks in part to systems work by the firm's Administrative Services Division.

a first that partner Garrahy hoped would also be a "last" in his career. Looking at data from the plant, it wasn't clear why 85 percent of the picture tubes were bad. A quick visit to the shop floor yielded at least one reason. Unbeknownst to senior Zenith management, plant managers were "busing in winos from skid row on Chicago's west side to move the tubes around," said Garrahy. Not surprisingly, a lot of the tubes were damaged when entrusted to the temporary employees' less-than-steady hands. "We told them to hire permanent staff," Garrahy said, which went a long way toward increasing the quality level of TV tube production at the plant.

### Big Apple Versus Big Potato

Chicago remained the largest Administrative Services office during this period, but New York was growing its business rapidly. Major New York clients included International Paper, ITT and Travelers Insurance Co. A mostly friendly rivalry between the two offices resulted.

The International Paper engagement, overseen by New York partner John Stephens, grew to be one of the largest engagements of the period. Stephens, who joined the firm from U.S. Steel, supervised work at International Paper mills across the United States where comprehensive cost accounting and manufacturing control systems were installed. Teams of consultants from across the Administrative Services Division were assembled to tackle the multiyear project. New York partner

## Women Join the Ranks.

In 1965, Susan Butler became the first professional woman hired by Administrative Services. She also was in the first class of hires that didn't do audit work. Although she had dropped her only computer programming course while a senior at Purdue University, she began learning programming on a new IBM System/360 at American National Bank in Chicago. Butler eventually worked on a series of major engagements in Chicago, Detroit and Houston. While a manager in Detroit, she was encouraged by Gale Hitchcock, head of Administrative Services in the office, "to seriously consider going for partner." Butler took her mentor's advice and became the first female consulting partner in 1979, and later served as "chief of staff" under George Shaheen, John Kelly and Joe Forehand. In 1995, she became the first woman in the consulting practice to be named an office managing partner. She was active in the mid-1990s as a mentor to many, including other women rising through the ranks.

**Susan Butler broke new ground in 1965 as she became the first professional woman hired by Administrative Services.**



Reg Jones ran the portion of the job that dealt with capital budgeting, which was a new discipline for the consultants. The International Paper engagement formed the basis for the comprehensive systems that would be installed at Hershey Foods and other process manufacturing clients in the 1970s. Jones led the Hershey engagement after Stephens left the firm to join International Paper as a senior vice president in 1969. Reporting to Jones were partners Kurt Schaffir and Gran Gargiulo, as well as managers Peter Fuchs, Joe Carr, Neil Doppelt and Steve Zimmerman, all of whom would later become partners.

As mentioned, George Trentin, head of consulting for the New York office, tended to prefer IBM systems over rival hardware makers, compared with the Chicago office's more catholic view. At a more technical level, the New York office advocated the newer, real-time, disk-oriented systems versus Chicago's preference for tape-based batch processing.

New York personnel tended to think of their work as more varied, exciting and cutting edge, reflecting the city's cosmopolitan milieu. To what extent that judgment reflected reality or was a defensive posture in response to Chicago's brawn was almost beside the point. If New York was the Big Apple, then straightlaced Chicago was the Big Potato. Not to be outdone, Don Baker, the head of Administrative Services in Houston in the early 1970s, the third-ranking office in the division at the time, had a sign on his wall that read, "Take a Bite Out of the Big Apple."

Consulting grew on an office-by-office basis during this period. Among the five major U.S. consulting offices at the time, Chicago, Detroit and Milwaukee dominated the manufacturing and utility industries. Houston developed strong oil and gas, and financial services practices. New York dominated in financial services. Other practices were emerging in Charlotte, Atlanta, Dallas, Boston, San Francisco and Los Angeles. Overseas, London and Paris were the dominant players. By 1969 the U.S.-based consulting staff had grown to 752, while the European consulting staff numbered 147.

### Basic Training

The rapid growth of Administrative Services put increasing pressure on the division's traditional hiring approach. Prior to the 1960s, nearly every new hire, with a few notable exceptions such as Joe Glickauf, had been an accountant by training—or had studied accounting and then worked for a year or two as an auditor. But as the decade progressed, the increasing demand for more technical skills led the division to start hiring significant numbers of engineers and those with technical degrees. The audit side of the firm complained that they and the consulting partners were competing on campuses for the same accounting students, putting pressure on Administrative Services to look beyond its traditional talent pool. By the second half of 1965, Administrative Services dropped the requirement that new hires work on an audit. But that didn't lessen the need for on-the-job training.



In 1964, the Administrative Services leadership asked Art Welby to move back to Chicago from Cincinnati and assume overall responsibility for the training program. In the late 1950s and early 1960s, Administrative Services classes had been held at Northwestern University and at various hotels around Chicago. Welby centered the training program at Chicago's Knickerbocker Hotel, and by the end of the decade, firm trainees accounted for 45 percent of the hotel's occupancy.

**West Coast Administrative Services Basic Training School, 1959. Chuck Hemphill is in the front row, far left.**

Welby helped keep Administrative Services at the forefront of computer installation training, maintaining its competitive advantage over accounting firm rivals, most of whom did little in the way of formal training. And the training regimen remained cutting edge. Glickauf and Welby implemented a training course on installing and programming IBM's new System/360 computers in 1965, less than a year after the computer was introduced. IBM personnel taught the first class until Andersen's own experts got up to speed, which they did in a matter of months. Also in 1965, the organization agreed to subsidize transportation costs for far-flung offices so it wouldn't cost them more to send personnel for training than it did for those offices only a few hours away.

Continued demand for more training pushed Welby's program to the breaking point by 1969. At decade's end the training program called for 40,000 class days annually, with Administrative Services classes accounting for 60 percent of the total. Andersen looked at building its own training facility on Chicago's near north side on a parking lot it had purchased from Northwestern University, but balked at the cost. While crowding was an issue at the Knickerbocker, the hotel also may have fallen out of favor with Andersen management, if not many

### The 1959 West Coast Administrative Services Basic Training School

The third Home Office Administrative Services Basic Training School was held at the Olympian Motor Hotel in Los Angeles, California, August 17 to 29, 1959. This two-week course was conducted by the Firm for the first time on a regional basis for men from the West Coast offices. The Denver, Los Angeles, Phoenix, San Francisco and Seattle offices were represented by the twenty-one men attending the school.

The course itself consisted of an introduction to administrative services work, covering the fundamentals of the entire field. Those attending the school engaged in a tight schedule of lectures, class problems, equipment demonstrations and evening assignments.

A comprehensive training manual in the form of a Firm reference binder had been prepared prior to the course to serve as a basis for reference and reading assignments. Each subject was covered first by assigned reading and then by a lecture and a related working problem. Office equipment was demonstrated in the classroom and also at the offices of the manufacturers.

All students displayed an unusually keen interest in the course case study on order-billing procedures. As a result, they devoted several evenings to the design of improved order-billing procedures and the preparation of a report to management on their findings. Judging from the results of these efforts, the school accomplished its primary objective of providing those attending with a sound background in the principles and techniques of office methods, systems and procedures.

The instruction, as well as the organization and administration, was carried out by a faculty consisting of B. M. Crawford of San Francisco and S. A. Clarke and R. E. Karrenbrock of Los Angeles. In addition to presentations made by C. E. Hemphill (in charge of administrative services for the West Coast region), lectures on special subjects were handled by J. H. Bergstedt, J. E. Ingalls, D. G. Johnson, D. J. Kevane, R. E. McIntire, L. A. Moody and J. E. Sylie, all of Los Angeles.

29

West Coast Administrative Services Basic Training School article in *The Chronicle*, December 1959.



## Sign of the Times.

On the cultural front, the 1960s were a time of tremendous upheaval in the United States. The war in Vietnam. Student protests. Race riots. Assassinations. The 1968 Democratic Party National Convention in Chicago. The sexual revolution. Woodstock. It seemed to many that America, and much of the rest of the world, was coming apart at the seams. How to stitch it back together was anybody's guess.

For the newly hired Administrative Services staffer, on the other hand, cultural change came a bit more slowly. The trademark Andersen hat for men—felt in the winter, straw in the summer—was a thing of the past by the mid-1960s for new hires. But the surge of students into and out of the Knickerbocker training classes was still a sea of dark suits, white shirts and ties. Women wouldn't have dreamed of wearing anything but a conservatively cut suit. And 12- to 16-hour days didn't leave a lot of time for leisure pursuits or protests. Hairstyles for men had expanded a bit beyond the close-cropped 1950s, but not by much. One young man in the Atlanta office in the late 1960s asked his manager if he thought it would be alright if he wore a beard. "Sure," the manager said, "just not to the office."

Chicago's Knickerbocker Hotel, the site of extensive Administrative Services training courses from the mid-to-late 1960s. Playboy Enterprises arrived as a major tenant just as the firm was making plans to relocate training to its newly purchased facility in St. Charles.

of the trainees, in light of the fact that it had been announced that *Playboy* magazine's headquarters would be located in the building, which would bear the Playboy name.

The partnership initially rejected purchasing St. Dominic College in St. Charles, Illinois, in part because of its distance from downtown Chicago. But the logic of converting the recently closed campus, which consisted of a classroom building and residence hall on 57 acres, eventually carried the day. Andersen agreed to purchase the school for just under $4 million. The firm took possession of the property in October 1970. The last class was held at the Knickerbocker Hotel in November 1970, and the first training class was held in St. Charles in March 1971.



The end of the decade also marked the beginning of a new era for the Administrative Services Division. In 1969 Joe Glickauf turned over responsibility as leader of the group to Bill Ingersoll, who had been technical director of data processing. Glickauf continued to consult with the division until his retirement in 1972.

End of an Era. Joe Glickauf turned over leadership of the Administrative Services Division to Bill Ingersoll in 1969, though he would continue to consult with the division until his retirement in 1972.

**The Administrative Services Division was positioned for a new burst of growth. The new training facility provided the infrastructure the division needed to create a platform for future expansion. A new generation of leadership—including Ingersoll's replacement as technical director of data processing, Vic Millar—spearheaded the use of the St. Charles facility to standardize teaching methods and leverage the firm's employee base much more effectively. An agglomeration of consulting practices—each reporting to a different office location lead audit partner—would slowly be shaped into a cohesive unit.**

# Late 1960s– Late 1970s

## Setting Standards

"We refused to be beaten, and having challenges like that is what pulled us together. And it made barriers drop. Doing things that had never been done before is exactly what we wanted to do."

Jim Fischer



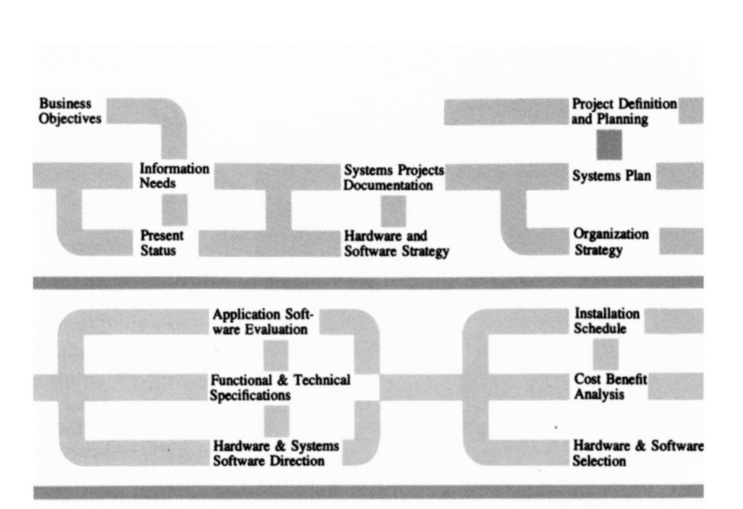

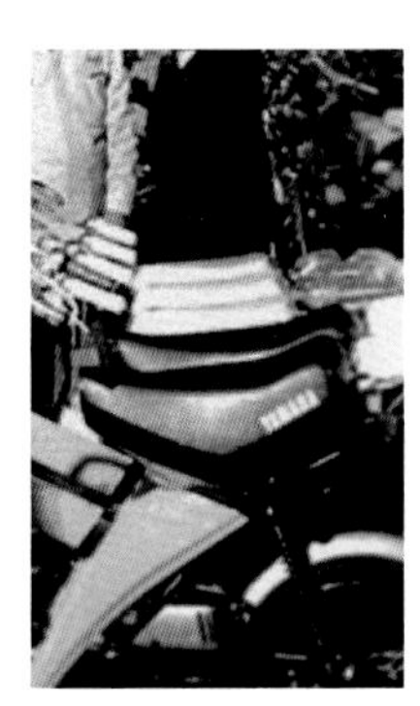

# Late 1960s–Late 1970s
# Setting Standards



**By the late 1960s unprecedented changes were buffeting societies and businesses around the world. Arthur Andersen's entrepreneurial culture helped produce new ways of creating and measuring business success. The consulting division's rapid growth, coupled with changes in technology and a tumultuous world economy, created new challenges for partners. Innovative consulting leadership enabled Arthur Andersen to emerge as a dominant global consulting firm by the end of the 1970s, and assured that the consulting practice would play an increasingly important role within Arthur Andersen.**

Chapter opening image: Arthur Andersen's training facility near St. Charles, Illinois, early 1970s.

**Vic Millar was sitting calmly in the back of the Knickerbocker's conference room one morning in 1968, waiting to make a presentation to a group of fresh-faced recruits. If anyone had been able to peer inside the mind of the coolly analytical Administrative Services veteran, however, they might have seen the equivalent of a light bulb switching on. Millar's insight that day, drawing upon earlier teaching stints as well, was that the division needed to produce uniform approaches to systems installations and other major engagements to reach its true potential.**

The era of pioneering artistry that began in the early 1950s was over, Millar concluded. The consulting practice was getting too big and customer demands were becoming too complex to support that approach any longer. Millar was convinced that it was time to reinvent Administrative Services and leverage its tremendous collective know-how. The firm needed to standardize installations step by step so that personnel could move easily among major jobs. This type of reinvention would enable the firm to employ a greater number of people working under each partner to maximize profits per partner.

Vic Millar played an instrumental role in standardizing the firm's approach to systems installations, paving the way for significant growth in the 1970s.

As no one else appeared willing to take on the job, Millar, a senior manager based in Chicago, decided to do it himself. Thanks to his initial efforts, Administrative Services embarked on a decade of significant growth—despite two international oil crises, a recession and persistent stagflation—based on encapsulating and standardizing its consulting expertise. The firm's Electronic Data Processing (EDP) practice, one of it's seven practice competencies in the late 1960s, would overshadow all other consulting businesses a decade later.

Millar's insight wasn't that his peers were teaching inaccurate techniques or glossing over the complexities inherent in the installation business. The problem was that each was teaching differently, depending on the techniques developed in a particular office. Partners from New York preached one approach, from Chicago a second, and from Houston or Paris, yet another. The recruits didn't know enough to pick up on the differences until they found themselves on a job where the manager or partner was doing something one way and they had been taught another.

Art Welby agreed with Millar, but he and others leading the education effort were stretched to the limit simply trying to find big enough rooms to accommodate the ever-growing classes. (The St. Charles campus was still a pipe dream at that point.) And they weren't in a position to criticize partners who took time out of their hectic schedules to fly to Chicago and share their insights with new hires.

In November 1968, Millar put his thoughts in a memo to Bill Ingersoll, the technical director for data processing. Ingersoll, based in New York, disagreed with Millar's approach. He argued that differences between office methods were too wide to bridge, and that Millar wanted to effectively straightjacket their creative installation experts who, everyone agreed, were the best in the business. Joe Glickauf, in one of his last official acts as head of Administrative Services before Ingersoll succeeded him in 1969, agreed with Millar. He called a meeting in Chicago where computer experts from around the organization met to debate the issue.

The meeting began with the partners sharply disagreeing on the wisdom of trying to standardize the firm's practices. Gene Delves proposed that instead of taking an "all or none" approach to the issue, they should instead discuss the issue point by point. As Chuck Hemphill recalled, "When the group focused on each step in

Bill Ingersoll, who was a member of the first computer programming and installation in 1953, succeeded Joe Glickauf as head of Administrative Services in 1969.



## Who's Who.

The November 1968 meeting called by Joe Glickauf to debate the issue of uniformity in the practice drew 12 of consulting's top computer installation experts. Attendees represented a who's who of leading computer installation experts in the United States at the time, given Administrative Services' predominance in the field. The offices represented at the meeting also underscored the truly national scope of the consulting practice. (For expediency's sake, partners from London and Paris weren't included in the meeting.) Those attending included:

Don Anguish (Atlanta)
Don Baker (Houston)
Gene Delves (Chicago)
Bill Ellingson (Chicago)
Clark Higgins (Cleveland)
Bill Ingersoll (New York)
John Kindt (Los Angeles)
Vic Millar (Chicago)
Dick Nerad (Chicago)
Ed Schefer (New York)
Art Voight (Detroit)
Art Welby (Chicago)

the new planning chart format and considered specifics rather than generalities, to the amazement of all, agreement was reached on one point after another, and ultimately a consensus was resolved." These "planning charts" became crucial documents in spawning the success in the division in the 1970s.

The task of gathering and documenting the information fell to a handful of meeting participants. It included Millar, who was named the following year to replace Ingersoll as head of EDP. The effort benefited from a slowdown in the economy at decade's end, freeing up additional people to work on the project. It eventually involved 60 partners and managers. While initial materials were used in training classes fairly quickly, it took more than two years to write all 90 chapters and publish the collection of loose-leaf binders. The final product became known as "The Binder of Firm Practices in EDP."

Other teams at the firm also were using the downtime to encapsulate knowledge. MAC-PAC was developed out of Administrative Services' work with manufacturing clients. Lexicon, a data dictionary and database management tool, was put together by a team working in extra space at the recently opened education center in St. Charles.



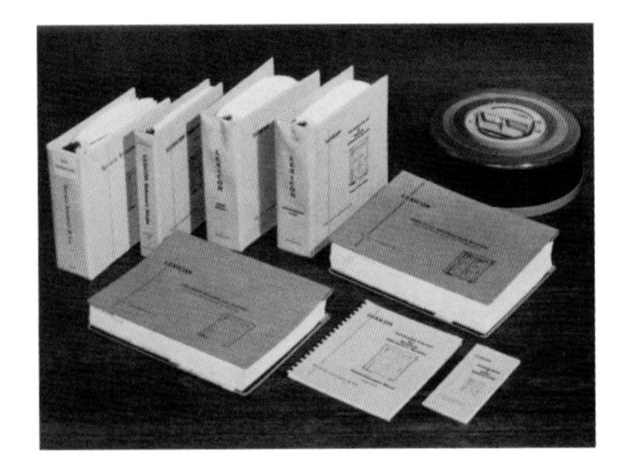

Lexicon binders (above) and diagram (right), early 1970s. Lexicon was an early example of the firm's success in standardizing and packaging systems installation knowledge.

Opposite page: The firm's planning charts were crucial documents in the effort to standardize systems installations.

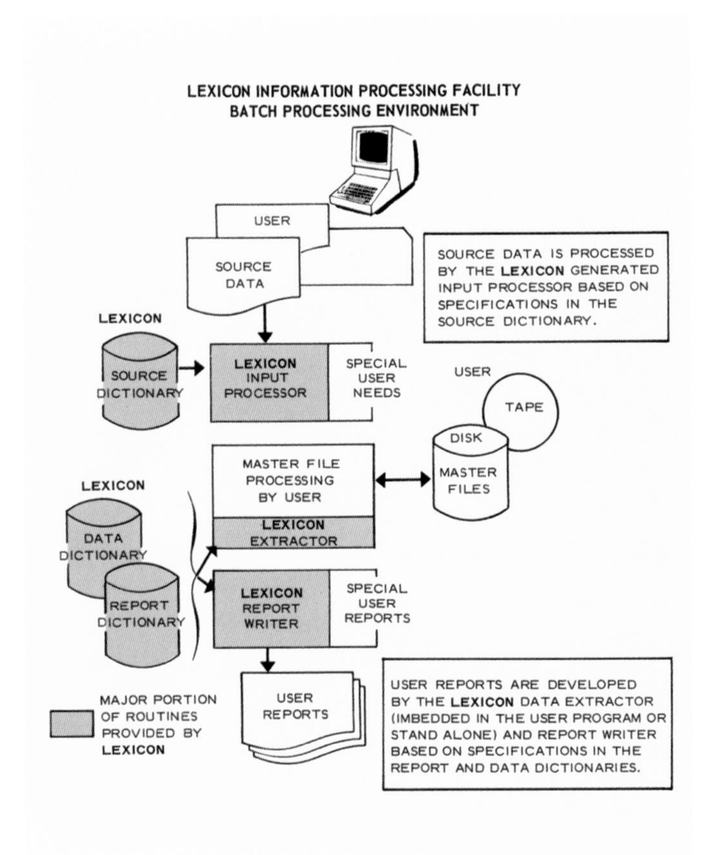

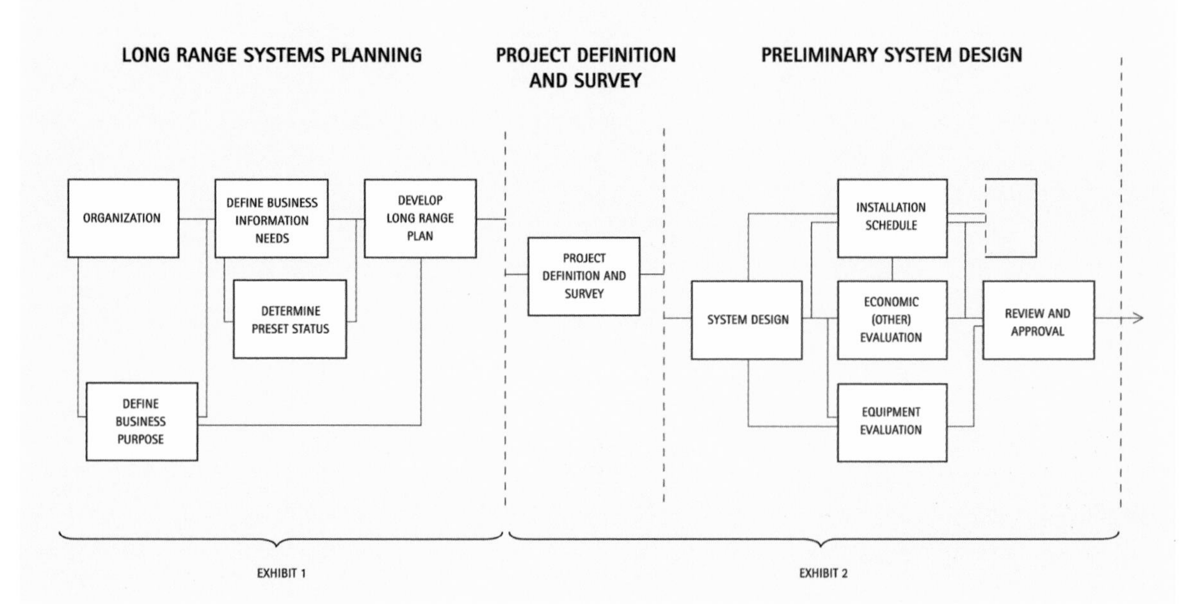
LONG RANGE SYSTEMS PLANNING
PROJECT DEFINITION AND SURVEY
PRELIMINARY SYSTEM DESIGN
ORGANIZATION
DEFINE BUSINESS INFORMATION NEEDS
DEVELOP LONG RANGE PLAN
DETERMINE PRESET STATUS
DEFINE BUSINESS PURPOSE
PROJECT DEFINITION AND SURVEY
INSTALLATION SCHEDULE
SYSTEM DESIGN
ECONOMIC (OTHER) EVALUATION
REVIEW AND APPROVAL
EQUIPMENT EVALUATION
EXHIBIT 1
EXHIBIT 2



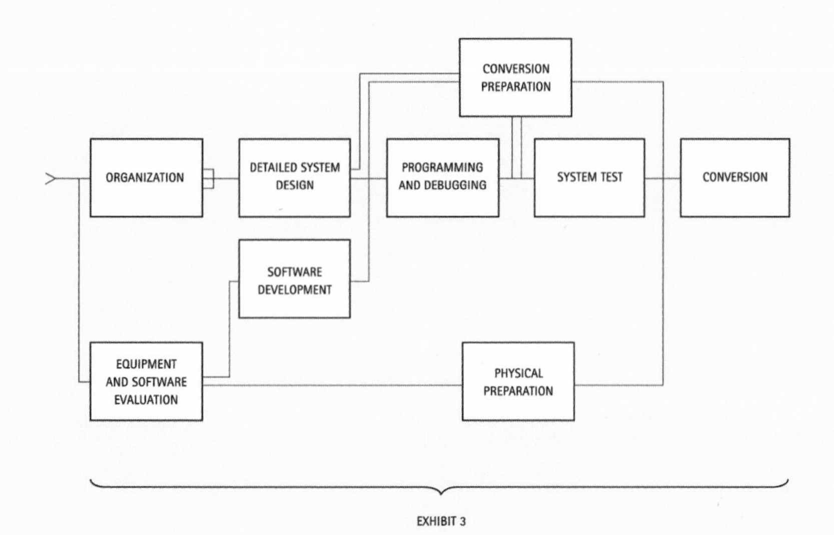
SYSTEMS INSTALLATION
CONVERSION PREPARATION
ORGANIZATION
DETAILED SYSTEM DESIGN
PROGRAMMING AND DEBUGGING
SYSTEM TEST
CONVERSION
SOFTWARE DEVELOPMENT
EQUIPMENT AND SOFTWARE EVALUATION
PHYSICAL PREPARATION
EXHIBIT 3

## The St. Charles Experience

Beginning in the early 1970s and for nearly a quarter century (after which regional training became more prevalent as the firm mushroomed in size), a trip to the St. Charles campus was a rite of passage for newly hired consultants. Young men and women from around the world spent a few weeks in the office where they were hired, then off they went, typically for a three-week stay at the converted, and eventually greatly expanded, Catholic women's college campus. The intense training in computer programming and other skills could be nerve-racking, but what consultants tend to recall most vividly is being exposed to the true breadth and depth of the consulting practice, and the friendships forged over punch cards or late-night drinks.

Joe Forehand was among the first wave of students. "I think it was maybe the second year that we had established St. Charles," he recalled. "I can remember going to that first basic Administrative Services school, the old Suburban Pump case study. And what was striking to me was how many smart people that this firm had. That was one of the first things that stood out—the quality and the talent and the people that were your peers [were] extremely impressive. I think St. Charles itself and how we went about training was one thing that really struck me as something early on that was very different and was very important in terms of what it meant to be able to build the business."

Opposite page, top: The St. Charles training facility offered a self-contained, campus atmosphere conducive to intensive learning sessions, far from the "distractions" of Chicago's Rush Street nightclub area.

Opposite page, bottom: Will That Be on the Test? A typical St. Charles lecture classroom during the 1970s. New hires were expected to absorb a tremendous amount of information during all day and evening "basic training" computer courses.

Gill Rider (second from right) and colleagues in the London office, in the late 1970s. Also pictured is John Skerritt (center), who would go on to lead the worldwide Financial Services industry group.

Gill Rider recalled her first visit to St. Charles in 1979, shortly after being hired in the London office. "It was this coming together of people, like-minded people, from all over the world," she recalled. "And spending three weeks trying to learn something that I'd certainly never done in terms of computer programming and dealing with the boxes of cards. You know the work was one thing, the learning was another and the people were just tremendous." Rider, named chief leadership officer in 2002, said that she remained close to several of the consultants who attended her initial St. Charles class.

### Pyramid Power

Millar's insight into the importance of standardization laid the foundation for the rapid scaling up in terms of revenue. Millar's goal was to have the EDP practice grow 15 percent a year, or double every five years. As he later noted, the standardized training allowed the division to "think very logically about what size of a pyramid we could have on a job by shoving more work down. The pyramid idea gave rise to the understanding that a very broad-based pyramid gave us more [resources] for growing future managers and partners, which we needed to grow. And it also provided extraordinary profitability, after we'd gotten all we could out of pricing and productivity. So that was really the core [model] that led to a lot of the things that took place in structuring for growth."

Millar moved to head the Washington, D.C., practice in 1973, and later had different regional management responsibilities, but he retained a strong influence on the EDP practice throughout the decade.

The economic slowdown that began in 1969 gave the EDP team a chance to write many of their practice binders, but it also turned the heat up on Bill Ingersoll, head of the consulting business. The consulting unit was barely turning a profit, and despite Millar's efforts at standardizing teaching and practices, the business was run without much sense of a guiding business plan. Shortly after Harvey Kapnick replaced Wally Oliphant at the head of the firm in 1970, he named Bill Mueller, an audit partner in the merchandizing practice, to replace Ingersoll as head of Administrative Services.

Harvey Kapnick (above) succeeded Wally Oliphant as head of the firm in 1970 and played the leading role in raising the firm's national and international profile by the end of the decade.

Opposite page: Administrative Services head Bill Mueller (middle) was known for his keen business skills. He piloted the division through the early 1970s downturn and the strong growth that followed, despite the uneven economic performance experienced by many U.S. and European industries during this period. Pictured with Mueller are Gale Hitchcock (top center), and Bill Ingersoll (bottom left) and Don Thiry (bottom center).

### "Bad and Getting Worse!"

Kapnick was concerned that the audit and consulting practices were drifting apart, due mainly to the consulting side's focus on technology and non-audit clients. For that reason he was attracted to Mueller, who was known for his strong business skills and savvy appreciation of technology. He advocated the widespread use of information systems by audit clients. In his 1971 long-range plan for the consulting business, Mueller didn't mince words: "By and large, relations of the Administrative Services division with the Audit division are bad and are getting worse, and it has to stop—right now!" He wanted the consulting staff to work more closely with auditors, and held up the example of the Detroit office, where Gale Hitchcock, head of the consulting practice there, worked closely with the audit partners to coordinate work with major clients.

Mueller also created two new positions for directors of professional competence—Vic Millar was put in charge of the newly renamed information processing unit, and Don Thiry was put in charge

of the other six practices: cost controls, manufacturing controls, performance standards, marketing systems, application software and modeling. At the same time, Mueller named regional practice directors in Administrative Services in an attempt to break down the office-by-office approach. The newly defined Administrative Services regions and their practice directors were: Chicago-Joe Carrico; South-Gene Delves; Central-Gale Hitchcock; West-Bill Ingersoll; Southeast-Vic Millar; Northeast-Dave Sullivan; and New York-Reg Jones. Practice directors were identified later for the United Kingdom, Europe, Japan, South America, Australia and Mexico. The practice directors, who generally were the heads of the major practices, were to play a major role in the pooling of resources and ensuring the quality of work and partner admissions over the years ahead, particularly outside the United States.

Mueller may have talked tough, but he quickly became a strong advocate for Administrative Services and provided some much-needed business guidance. And not a moment too soon. The business went from bad to worse in 1971, the first year in the history of the young computer industry that annual shipments of new equipment decreased in the United States. The total headcount in consulting declined modestly in 1972. But Mueller had the consulting business back on a sound path of growth by the following year, and he kept recruiting through the downturn to take advantage of the coming economic rebound.

Industrial Strength. Gale Hitchcock (left), partner in charge of Administrative Services in the Detroit office and later named head of the Central region, was credited with a close working relationship with the audit partners in the office. In 1971, partner Don Thiry (right) was put in charge of the practices other than information processing, which reported to Vic Millar: cost controls, manufacturing controls, performance standards, marketing systems, application software and modeling.



In Europe, the Paris office was the standard-bearer in computer systems installations during this period, under the leadership of Pierre Reveillion. Reveillion and Millar had attended the same computer school in Chicago in 1960 and remained close throughout their careers. As Millar recalled, "Pierre took the [computer systems] message home and really led France in that direction."

London was focused more on financial reporting and manufacturing management in the 1970s, although it did handle several leading-edge systems engagements, including British Airways, Standard Telephones and Cables, Cummins, Chase Manhattan, Willis Faber and F. W. Woolworth. In 1973 Martin Vandersteen became head of the U.K. practice. The other consulting partners at the time were Roy Chapman, Leon Fuller, David Kaye, Kevin Lavery and Graham Reddish.

Several key U.S. partners were sent to London in the mid-to-late 1970s. John Kelly, Larry Levitan, Bill Bramer and others who followed helped encourage and support the development of an information technology practice. They helped build the skills that enabled the London office to play a leadership role in handling some of the firm's largest and most significant engagements of the following decade. This expertise was carried to many other of the firm's locations. In 1979 and 1980, for example, U.K. partners and managers provided leadership assistance to more than 100 projects in 40 different countries.

Opposite page: From the mid-1960s until the late 1970s, St. Alphage House housed the firm's London office.

al Westminster Bank

In the meantime, senior U.S. consulting partners who had groused about having their division run by an auditor were won over by Mueller's business acumen and enthusiasm for promoting major consulting projects. By the time Mueller had the consulting business back on track in 1973, the EDP practice binders that provided a common platform for the consultants to leverage their work also were being widely disseminated. That platform paved the way for the group's next growth phase, ushering in the era of big installations that established Administrative Services as the undisputed leader in the field.

Mueller started his term as head of Administrative Services berating consultants for not effectively leveraging the business generated by the audit practice. In fact, audit clients continued to be a significant source of new business for the consultants for much of the 1970s. Many consultants maintained friendships and close working relationships with the auditors they had "grown up with" in the firm in their early years and at various training schools. In cities such as Atlanta, where the audit side of Andersen had a 50 percent local market share, it behooved consultants not to slight that sizable client base, noted Joe Forehand, who joined the Atlanta office in 1972. But with each major new installation it became increasingly clear that Administrative Services was creating a new business model that was tied less and less to the audit business, and one that was contributing significantly to Andersen's bottom line.



The recession of 1973-74, precipitated by the Arab-Israeli War and the subsequent Arab oil boycott, was especially hard on the audit side of the firm, which had grown rapidly in the 1960s as the economy expanded in the United States and much of the rest of the world. "When the stock market crashed and the fuel problem emerged, we

Exporting Expertise. Andersen representatives arrive in Moscow to present a seminar in 1973 on the firm's services to Russian officials: (left to right) Jeffrey Hertzfeld (firm legal counsel), Bob Jones, Bill Mueller, Claude Remy, Bob Prince, Martin Vandersteen, Gordon Nicholson, Dick Nerad and Jim DePauw.

suddenly realized that a lot of the growth in the audit practice was not auditing, it was special work," Vic Millar related. "When all that special work went away, the practice declined very, very rapidly. And the auditors did what we knew they shouldn't have done; they retained partners, stopped recruiting in large numbers. And the profitability of the audit practice, which up until that date had carried the consulting practice, suddenly diminished. So we had a role reversal in about 1973. Our methodology and growth was kicking in while the audit pyramid was going down. And while we didn't realize it at the time, [the consulting practice] became more profitable [than the audit practice] in about 1973."

In the early 1970s, Administrative Services undertook a unique engagement for Kraft North America, based in suburban Chicago, to combine online and database systems. Mel Bergstein, an industrial engineer who joined Administrative Services in 1968 and became a manager while working on the 18-month project, recalled, "That was the first time that, from a software standpoint, CICS [Customer Information Control System], which was then the important online system, and IMS [Information Management System], which was the important database system, had been put together...We were too young to know what we couldn't do."

IBM, which had developed both pieces of software, flew developers to Chicago to rewrite code to fix glitches that had been uncovered during the installation, Bergstein added. It was also one of the first major projects in which large numbers of employees from the New York and Chicago offices worked together to pool their expertise.



## Strains.

Consultants often found themselves enduring considerable stress and long hours, and the combination could strain relationships. "I became an expert by working 18 hours a day," Mel Bergstein said. "My wife and I have been married for 39 years. We've only discussed divorce twice. Once was when I wanted to join an all-men's golf club. And the other was at Kraft." In order to get some free time to run programs on Kraft computers, he said, "We worked the midnight shift because all the other programmers were working during the day, and I noticed that the development machine had nobody on it at night...I would go to work at 8 in the evening and I would typically return the next day at noon. And we got it done. But my wife and I had a serious chat about that."

### Big Jobs Foretell Future

Thanks to its reputation for tackling big, difficult jobs, the systems installation business was growing so rapidly by the early-to-mid 1970s that it regularly was installing larger IBM systems than IBM itself. Its track record also made it a favored choice of governmental and non-profit bodies that were struggling to modernize antiquated systems in response to growing demands for services as the population increased. One of the highest-profile megajobs during this period was a project for the Chicago Board of Education. It was the first truly "mission-critical" systems upgrade among the major installations of the period, and was a precursor of the many large government jobs that would follow from the mid-1970s through the 1980s.

The City of Big Shoulders was running a big school system with big problems by the early 1970s. The Chicago Board of Education operated the third-largest public school system in the country with more than one-half million students, more than 600 schools, nearly 49,000 employees and an annual operating budget of more than $1 billion. Because politics had driven much of the decision-making process at the board for many years, its financial reporting systems were unduly cumbersome. And the systems provided little control over costs, which were escalating rapidly.



Administrative Services was called in to revamp the board's payroll and personnel systems as well as financial and reporting processes without shortchanging day-to-day educational needs. Consultants determined that the basic unit level for reporting was each individual school, with reports formatted so that they could be understood easily by nonfinancial personnel. The consultants made accounting codes translatable into those required by the state of Illinois, so data for the annual report required by the state could be accumulated automatically. The engagement used IBM System/360 computers initially, and added the 370 model after it was introduced. Chicago partner Bob Ahern recalled, "The scope and complexity of the Chicago Board of Education engagement—including more than 40 of our people for one-and-a-half years—made it one of our most important engagements of the '70s."

The engagement helped Administrative Services broaden its scope of work to systems that were critical to the client's survival. "This engagement foretold the future," said Susan Butler, who worked on the project. "Yes, it was very large, but was very complex and mission critical because of the need to integrate operational systems with the financial systems on a daily basis. We did the things we're doing today. Reengineered and integrated processes. Trained over 2,500 personnel. Implemented an online school systemwide network. And did this with teams composed of Board of Education and Andersen personnel...We were on time and under budget."

## Schooled in Software.

One of Administrative Services' more significant software innovations grew out of its work for the Chicago Board of Education, according to Jim Fischer, one of the young technical experts on the project. (He later led the Technical Services Organization, or TSO.) The board had selected control program software that it wanted to use on the project. Fischer and others on the team considered that program to be a starting point, and came up with their own innovation that not only better suited the immediate client's needs, but would be applicable to many subsequent engagements:

> We had to learn how [the control program] worked. I mean, we did things with it that, actually, should have never been done, but we built a middleware framework around it that became the hallmark of our business. That is something that's continued all the way through to this day. We have a middleware separation between the actual physical hardware and the operating software, and the user functionality. And, if you write that middle layer, then you can allow things to change on both sides without having to make dramatic changes. We built a middleware layer for the Chicago Board, and we implemented those systems successfully.



### Reviving a Troubled Client

If the systems at the Chicago Board of Education were in serious need of revamping, problems surfacing at one of the state of Illinois' largest agencies indicated a system in collapse by 1975. The state was hit with a class-action suit and faced near-riot conditions on the sidewalks outside its Bureau of Employment Security as a result of its inability to issue unemployment checks on anything approaching a timely basis. Unemployment remained stubbornly high that year, following the 1973-74 recession. Combined with shifting federal mandates, it was more than the bureau's 1950s vintage computer system could bear. Illinois was ranked 48 out of 50 states in terms of timely payment. The state mandated that Administrative Services convert the bureau to a new system within nine months of the start of the engagement in mid-1975. Otherwise, the state would incur hefty fines, imposed as part of the resolution of the class-action suit.

The engagement, under the direction of lead partner Gresh Brebach, was a first in terms of size and speed of implementation required. "I believe it was the real first time that we had put together an integrated program for change at a client on an absolute mandate by the client that we had to do it in a very, very narrow period of time," recalled Jim Fischer, who joined the project in 1975 as soon as he finished work on the Chicago Board of Education engagement. "And to be quite frank, all odds were against us."

No one at the firm had any experience working with unemployment or similar payment programs. "So, we had to learn the application, redesign the applications, and completely get it implemented to distribute it to make it an online system in the 65 local offices and put the terminals in all the offices," Fischer said. "We were reengineering the process from a centralized to a decentralized one, and with all the educational things that that entails for the spread throughout the offices—and nine months from the beginning to the time we convert." Fischer added that the job peaked at 350 people, from the bureau and Andersen, drawn from offices around the country. It averaged about 250 people at any given time.

"This was [one of] the first IMS online system[s] we had built," noted Ann Jones, who worked at the bureau in 1979 in a follow-on engagement. "When they were doing the conversion, it was the biggest single IBM database that was ever built."

The National Railroad Passenger Corporation (Amtrak) engaged the firm to help it incorporate the systems of numerous rail lines around the country as they were merged into the national carrier in the 1970s.

### "We Refused to Be Beaten"

A key reason the engagement was a success may have been that the consultants in the trenches were too young and eager to know what they didn't know or couldn't do. "Most people were between 22 and 28," said Fischer. "But, in order to do it in nine months, we did work three shifts, and we worked three shifts continually until the thing was done. But you see, that's an important part of [the firm]. We refused to be beaten, and having challenges like that is what pulled us together. And it made barriers drop. Doing things that had never been done before is exactly what we wanted to do."



Chicago wasn't the only source of major public-sector work during the decade. Gene Delves split his time in the mid-to-late 1970s between Chicago, where he was leading a systems team working with United Airlines, and Washington, D.C., where he led a team helping to integrate systems for Amtrak, the government-owned rail system. Each time the U.S. Congress approved another private rail line addition to Amtrak, Delves and his team scrambled to integrate the new line's systems. "As soon as the railroads got rid of the passenger service [by transferring it to Amtrak], they lost total interest in it," Delves noted, and the railroads didn't maintain any of the passenger-related systems.

Mike Hill, an Administrative Services partner in Atlanta, led a systems design and installation project at the Tennessee Valley Authority (TVA), a government-created electric utility. Beginning in 1976, the TVA engagement highlighted Administrative Services' growing resource base. "It was a very large situation at that point in time, that had 150 people at its peak," Hill noted, including professionals from 32 different offices over the course of 22 months. The result was a state-of-the-art system that substantially reduced TVA's inventories, cut costs, reduced administrative workload and improved management reporting.

The State of Illinois Bureau of Labor building at 910 S. Michigan Avenue in Chicago.

## Endurance Tests.

Tales of triumphing over adversity bind each generation of consultants as they tackle their first major assignments. In the case of the Illinois Bureau of Employment Security, one particular story stands out. The Administrative Services team was working on the ninth floor of 910 S. Michigan Avenue in Chicago. As it was a state-owned building, the heat was turned off every night at 8 p.m. But the team was working around the clock, so it got very cold during the third shift, especially in December and January. The team quickly discovered that the only source of warmth was the computer room where the printer was located. One of the team members, Chuck Saddoris, realized that if he stretched out with his head next to the printer, he could get some sleep until the printer kicked in to print out a problem.

Jim Fischer arrived at 2:30 one morning and met one of the client software programmers, Bill Seidel, on his way out. Seidel was shaking his head. Fearing some new crisis, Fischer asked him if he was okay. "No," Seidel said. "I just wish when they die you'd take them home." He had just walked through the computer room and seen Saddoris and two other staffers sprawled on the floor, sound asleep.

Many personnel on the TVA project, working in remote rural locations, groused about hardship duty. But like most major engagements, TVA had a way of minting partners. Emerson Dickey and Randell Thomas each were promoted to partner while working on the project. Others promoted to partner after working on the TVA engagement were Don Warnecke, Jim Yoakum, John Robbins, Marie Campagna, Joe Carter, Jim Barney, Michael Caine and Steve Kupres.

Right: A Tennessee Valley Authority (TVA) dam on the Tennessee River. A major systems installation for the electric utility was managed out of the firm's Atlanta office.

Bottom: A TVA administrative office, 1976.

The Charlotte and Atlanta offices focused on two major corporate clients during the latter half of the 1970s. Duke Power retained Administrative Services in 1976 for what ended up being a 34-month engagement. A team led by the Charlotte office and partner John Kelly installed systems throughout the utility. Kelly later was head of the Americas practice following the creation of Andersen Consulting in 1989 and led the firm for a short time in 1999. The installations encompassed order entry, customer billing, accounts receivable, meter inventory, credit, collection, revenue reporting, large-customer billing and general ledger interface. Beginning in the mid-1970s, the Atlanta office, including partners Bob Anclien, Al Burgess and Jack Wilson, worked with Southern Company on several projects. One involved designing and installing an automated fuel reporting system to help the utility sharply reduce its nearly $1 billion in fuel expenses.

The firm also played an important role helping New York City recover from its fiscal near-collapse in the mid-1970s. The city was thrown into turmoil in 1975 when U.S. President Gerald Ford's administration refused to lend it money to see it through a fiscal crunch caused by years of poor financial management and runaway spending. The New York *Daily News* caught the mood of the moment with the famous headline: "Ford to City: Drop Dead." U.S. Treasury Secretary William Simon, who subsequently was given authority by the U.S. Congress



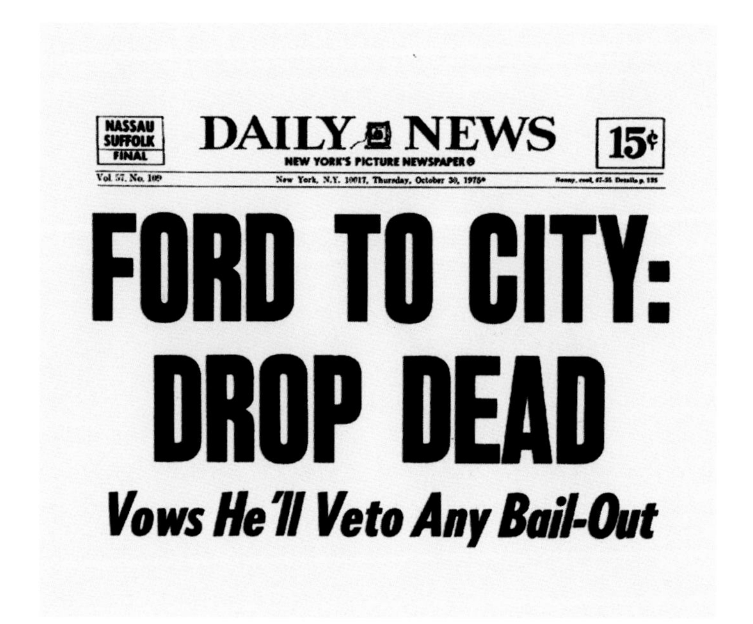

NASSAU SUFFOLK FINAL

DAILY NEWS

NEW YORK'S PICTURE NEWSPAPER®

15¢

Vol. 57. No. 109 | New York, N.Y. 10017, Thursday, October 30, 1975

# FORD TO CITY: DROP DEAD

## *Vows He'll Veto Any Bail-Out*

Famous New York *Daily News* headline characterizing the federal government's response to New York City's request for financial aid in the mid-1970s.

to make loans to bail out the city, retained the firm to advise him and review and recommend changes to the city's financial reporting systems and controls. Reg Jones was the consulting partner running the engagement, but because of its high profile, Harvey Kapnick, firm managing partner, insisted on acting as engagement partner, and moved to the top floor of the New York Hilton Hotel to oversee the firm's activities.

The depth of municipal mismanagement made it difficult for anyone to provide a clear picture of the city's fiscal condition. At Kapnick's request, Jones prepared a set of 14 key management reports to demonstrate headcount control and progress toward budget improvement, following an adaptation of organizational responsibility reporting. The following week the two met with Ken Axelson, a senior partner of Peat Marwick who had been brought in as deputy mayor of finance, and a group of city accounting and data processing personnel. When Axelson told the firm partners that there was no way the information they wanted could be retrieved from the city's systems, Kapnick told him to type on the cover of each report that the city "cannot provide this information." Kapnick paused, then added, "I will advise the Secretary not to make the loans." Suitably motivated, Axelson and his team found the information required and the loans were made to the city. Three months later, New York City Mayor Abraham Beame held up the book of reports prepared by Andersen and described them as his management control system.

### Low-hanging Blue Chips

Administrative Services' corporate work gathered momentum throughout the decade in nearly every office. Jon Conahan, who joined the division in New York in 1974 after working for Bell Laboratories, EDS and a few other companies, described the mid-to-late 1970s business environment as being close to perfection for Administrative Services, despite the troubled economy. Major corporations were convinced that they had to upgrade systems to remain competitive in a hostile business environment, he said. It wasn't the same level of frenzy as the "Y2K" build-up 20 years later in anticipation of the year 2000, but there was a sense of urgency. As one former partner said, "Every party you went to, people were talking about needing to buy new computer systems for their companies."

Conahan spent much of the second half of the 1970s working for just three blue-chip clients—PepsiCo, American Can and General Foods. Their corporate headquarters were located within a mile of each other in New York's Westchester County. After a year and a half at Pepsi installing an Employee Information System (EIS), "I went over to American Can, gave the [EIS] presentation and two days later, we had another engagement, and I was at American Can for two years," Conahan recalled. "Then I got into distribution and logistics and, you know, you just work your way through an organization. And then...we did this massive systems plan for all the divisions of General Foods." That engagement lasted until 1979, the same year Conahan was promoted to partner, at which point he sold Exxon Enterprises on a multiyear systems engagement.

George Shaheen (right), future head of Andersen Consulting (pictured in an early software brochure).



## Small Jobs, Big Experience

The firm also carried out significant work for small- and medium-sized companies during this period. While the work clearly benefited the clients, it also aided the key engagement staff, giving many of them access to senior decision makers at relatively early stages in their careers. That, in turn, helped the personnel, two of whom would later rise to the top of the consulting business, to see engagements in terms of the transforming benefits they provided to the companies.

Waste Management already was a rapidly growing medium-sized company in the mid-1970s when senior manager George Shaheen started working on what he later described as a "big design and installation of a financial information system and a custom, very complex billing system." He met regularly with senior management. "So we pulled that off quite well, the client liked me, wanted me to come to work for them," recalled Shaheen, who later became head of the consulting practice. "I had a string of pretty nice accomplishments that showed I could sell work, I could keep clients happy, I could get the jobs done." He added that the Waste Management engagement "did a lot to help me become a manager, and then served me well almost all the way up to when I was a partner."

Joe Forehand recalled the benefits of working closely with several smaller companies in the Southeast in the early-to-mid-1970s. "I met with presidents of small- to medium-sized companies in my first year," Forehand said. He worked with several regional manufacturers in Chattanooga, Tennessee, Crestview, Florida, and Albany, Georgia. His peers working on megaprojects rarely met with anyone other than information technology staff on the client side. While he never considered himself a "big systems expert," Forehand did quite a bit of "hands-on work with manufacturing clients," including setting labor standards for a family foundry, devising inventory controls and performing materials resource planning work. He rose to partner in 1982, 10 years after joining the division, and succeeded Shaheen in 1999 as CEO of Accenture.

### Harnessing Technical Know-how

As the size and scope of engagements continued to grow, Mueller, Millar and others were concerned about Administrative Services' ability to tap its expanding technical expertise and enhance the development of software. They worried that much of what was being learned and developed in various offices wasn't being fully distributed across the organization. In 1974, the firm formed the Technical Services Organization, or TSO, to provide central control over software development and enhanced technical competence for



## Tech Track.

At the CertainTeed client engagement in 1978, Glover Ferguson was part of the team that replaced a mainframe computer system with a Perkin-Elmer online system. The building materials manufacturer in Waco, Texas, was the firm's first client to purchase this 32-bit minicomputer system.

Glover Ferguson, named Accenture chief scientist in 2000, fits Mueller's description of a partner with great technical skills but admittedly little sales ability. Ferguson, who joined the San Francisco office in 1974, moved to Chicago in 1977 and joined the Technical Services Organization (TSO), reporting to Dick Nerad. He later married Nerad's secretary, Kathy Long. Under Andersen rules at the time, one of them was required to resign. After chiding Ferguson that he didn't want to lose such a good secretary and that Ferguson should consider leaving, Nerad recalled, he volunteered that it should be Long. "To this day, I still don't know if he thought that was his decision to make," Ferguson noted. He was promoted to partner in 1984, and in his career with Administrative Services he had only one client. "But hey, at least it was IBM," he said.

the entire firm. Dick Nerad, a partner in Chicago, was put in charge of the group. Stan Cornelison, who led the consulting group from 1988 to 1989, noted, "The technology was changing constantly... and it was appropriate to have a central repository of those kinds of skills." Within a few years, larger offices, such as New York, Chicago, Houston and later London, also set up local TSO groups so they could tap a well of technical expertise close at hand.

The TSO improved the firm's ability to retain people with deep technical skills and make those skills available across the division. It also allowed Administrative Services to retain technically advanced personnel who weren't adept enough at generating new business to be considered for the partnership. "It was always sort of the Andersen culture, and particularly consulting division culture, that our partners be promoters of business," Bill Mueller later recalled. "If we didn't promote business, we wouldn't have business. And so these technical guys were, frankly, not very good promoters, so we got to thinking that maybe what we ought to do is form a separate little division within the [consulting] division...and we moved these people into it. And that was, I think, a great success."

On the hardware front, by the mid-1970s minicomputers were widely used by major corporate clients. Administrative Services retained its primary focus on larger mainframe computers in systems installations. But it used minis in several engagements, especially those involving online processing, such as Kraft Foods, and was also using distributed processing. The advent of Tandem Computer's fault-tolerant computer was especially important in financial services. The devices, which literally had two computers operating in tandem inside a box, were used increasingly in financial services installations to lessen the possibility that real-time transaction data might be lost.

The METHOD/1 development team (left to right): Dick Nerad, Jack Butts, Barry Patmore, Jim Yoakum and Larry Levitan (not pictured: Ron Cullum and Peter Fuchs).

The division reached a new product milestone with the November 1979 launch of METHOD/1. Nearly two years in the making, METHOD/1 was Administrative Services' structured, systematic approach to information planning, design, installation and support. It was a major overhaul of the "client binders" developed in the early 1970s. It drew on the expertise of the leaders of practice methodologies from around the firm. "It is obvious that there has been a great deal of thought, long hours and personal sacrifice to achieve this foundation for our practice," Nerad noted in an internal congratulatory memo in November 1979. "Without Ron Cullum it would not have been the product that it is, nor would it even have been finished... Jim Yoakum headed an Atlanta team to develop the Production Systems Support manual; Peter Fuchs headed a New York/Stamford team to develop the Systems Planning manual; Barry Patmore spearheaded the Preliminary Systems Design (PSD) and Installation manuals, and the overall strategy on the manuals. Partner Jack Butts and Larry Levitan [who would later lead TSO] provided counsel and critical review of the manuals as they were being developed."

**METHOD/1**
**Systems Development Methodology**

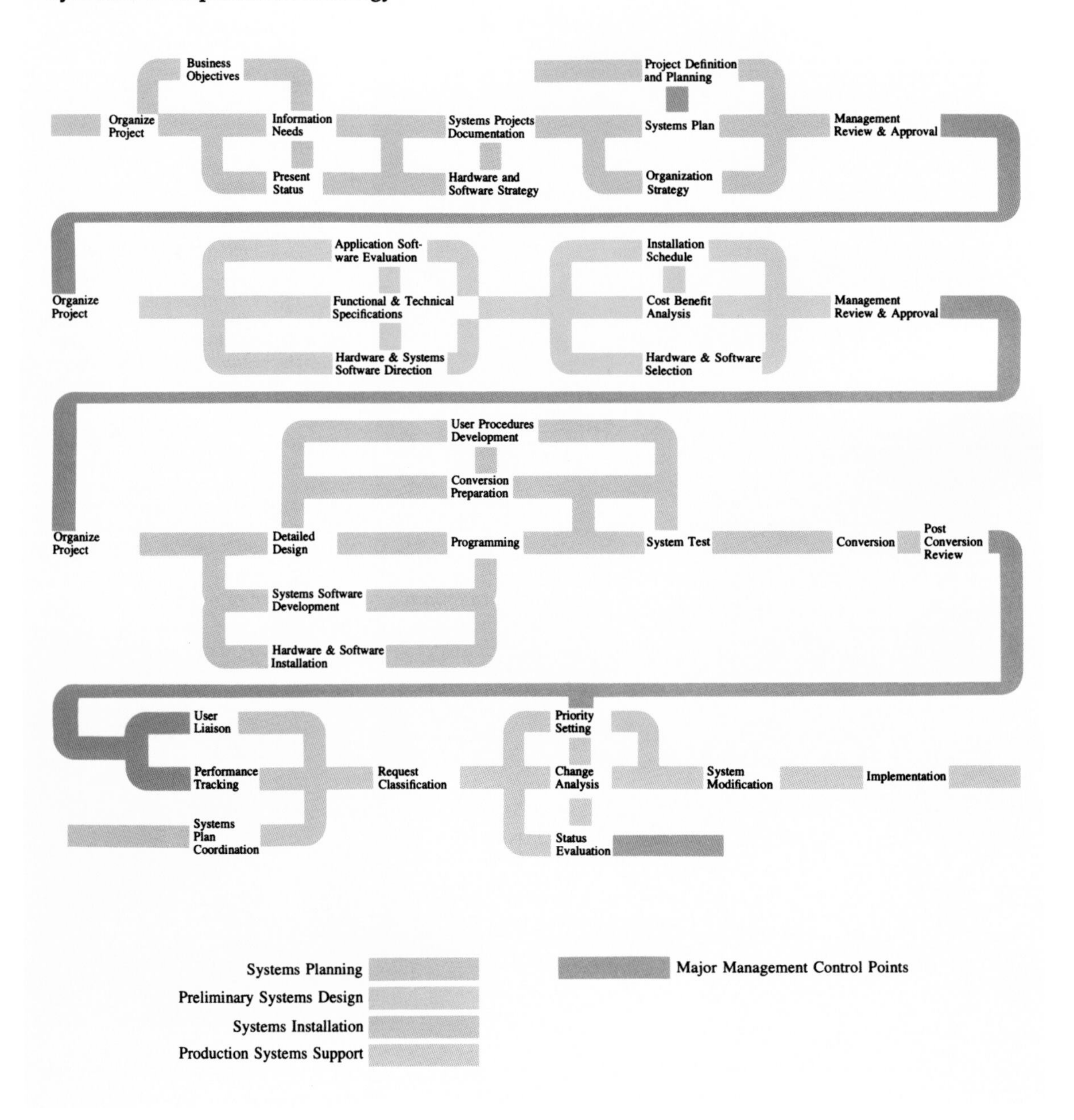


METHOD/1. This 1979 approach to information planning, design, installation and support was a major upgrade of the client binders introduced in the early 1970s.

METHOD/1 represented a high-water mark of the consultants' leadership in systems design and installation. In the subsequent decade, it was used with enormous success to guide clients from Illinois Power to the Bank of California in the United States, to Bank Simpanan Nasional in Malaysia and a host of others worldwide. "I could not think of any hang-ups I have had in the past that would not have been covered by following this methodology," a client noted to Levitan after evaluating the binders. "We must not underestimate the vast amount of brainpower that has obviously gone into METHOD/1, nor must we underestimate the enormous wealth of experience behind it."

### The French Connection

European offices experienced the trend toward bigger projects. In fact, in France the consulting practice escaped the early 1970s recession largely unscathed. Under Pierre Reveillion, who took over in 1967 from Guy Barbier, the consulting practice built its reputation working for major corporate clients. They included local computer industry leader Bull-General Electric and the French insurer Gan. (Bull-GE was renamed Compagnie Honeywell-Bull, CHB, in 1970 when GE sold its computer division to Honeywell.) According to a French partner, who had joined the office in 1965, the momentum carried into the early 1970s. "In '71 we had an airline I was working for," he said. "We

Left: French Connection. Administrative Services partners Pierre Reveillion (left), Claude Remy (center) and Michel Falcotet (right) in the Paris office, 1975.

Right: Administrative Services was retained to study the integration of online reservation and other systems relating to the 1974 merger of British carriers that created today's British Airways.



had our first manufacturing engagement, and those were big jobs at the time. And so we really surfed over the recession." Beginning in May 1973, the Paris office designed and installed a comprehensive management information system for La Société des Ciments Francais, the cement manufacturer's first companywide use of computers.

By 1975, the Paris office's Administrative Services Division accounted for 40 percent of the fees generated by the entire office. That ranked it third, behind only Chicago and New York, in terms of total Administrative Services fees. "Quite an achievement for a division which began in 1957," noted an article titled "Our French Connection" in the December 1975 issue of *The People of Arthur Andersen*, the firm's in-house publication. In addition to Reveillion, the consulting partners in the office at that time included Serge Audouin, Michel Falcotet, Alain Legendre, Claude Remy and Gerard Van Kemmel. Also in the office were 22 managers and 45 staffpersons.

The London office may not have had as broad-based a focus on major systems engagements as the Paris office, but it did land a major project that raised Administrative Services' European profile. In 1973, shortly after Britain entered the Common Market, the British government merged British European Airways and British Overseas Airways Corp. into a single British Airways, effective April 1, 1974. Administrative Services was retained to study the integration of online reservation and other systems. A major job in its own right, the integration was made even more difficult by the fact that one airline used a UNIVAC computer, while the other used IBMs. Administrative Services recommended going with IBM for the combined system.

The job underscored the depth of the division's global talent. Steve James, future chief operating officer of Accenture, was a manager in the Houston office at the time and played a leading role in advising on the systems integration work. Also drafted to work on the British Airways engagement were Declan O'Riordan, then a manager in the Chicago office who would join TSO, and Chicago's Gene Delves. Maurice Blackman, an early pioneer in the development of real-time, online systems from London, also was on the project. That global mix turned heads in the consulting world, according to Brian Wilson, an Australian staffperson on the job at the time. "It was unusual for a firm to do this sort of thing," he said. "These people assembled from around the world. They showed up and worked on this job."

In Italy, the Milan office began a multiyear relationship with Italian automaker Fiat in 1973. Fiat became the first and largest non-U.S. user of the Lexicon data dictionary and database management system. For the balance of the decade and into the 1980s, Administrative Services worked with Fiat to install new systems and implement effective

Fiat retained the firm in 1973 for a multiyear engagement to install new systems and management control procedures.

management control procedures. "Prior to our engagement," noted Milan office head Bruno Ricca, "the client had virtually no significant data to direct its sales effort, financial controls and marketing activities, and was hardly able to price his invoices on a timely basis."

### Just In Time

One of the most significant non-U.S. engagements of the 1970s helped introduce new manufacturing methods to the United States. Within a few years, those methods revolutionized the way America's leading companies approached manufacturing.

The diversified Japanese manufacturer Yamaha wanted to improve its engine manufacturing processes, so it turned to the firm's Tokyo office in 1977 to tap the best expertise in the West. Yamaha also turned to Toyota, known as a leader in just-in-time manufacturing, to capture the best manufacturing practices in the East.

The engagement, which lasted until 1985, merged materials resource planning systems, such as the division's MAC-PAC software, with Japanese just-in-time manufacturing. The result translated into millions of dollars of savings from material cost reduction, improved inventory investment and more efficient use of plant workers. "That's where we created the Japanese practice in manufacturing," noted Masakatsu Mori, a member of the consulting practice in the Tokyo office at the time. "That's a real start. It was a big job," he said, one that included the design of an integrated manufacturing planning and control system for five major plants. Mori later led the Japanese practice and was a member of the Accenture board of directors.

Left: Brainstorming in the Tokyo Office, 1978. Leighton Smith (center) led the Tokyo practice in the late 1970s and early 1980s.

Right: Just in Time. Beginning in 1977, Yamaha tapped Administrative Services expertise to help improve its engine manufacturing processes. Masakatsu Mori (right) worked on the engagement, which sparked the growth of the firm's manufacturing practice in Japan and led to the firm's importing of just-in-time manufacturing methods to the United States.

The Yamaha engagement made a significant contribution to consulting's global knowledge capital base. "What we did during that time was learn how Toyota was manufacturing and organizing the plant differently," noted Leroy "Pete" Peterson, a partner in the manufacturing practice who went on to help Nissan Motor Manufacturing Corp. set up its first automobile manufacturing plant in the United States in the early 1980s. "So, the [MAC-PAC] software got us into the Japanese manufacturing environment. We learned [just-in-time]. When we

## Hog Heaven.

Masakatsu Mori, a member of the Administrative Services Division in Tokyo at the time of the Yamaha engagement, would later lead the Japanese practice and serve on the Accenture board of directors.

Motorcycle maker Harley-Davidson was one of many U.S. companies feeling the full effect of the just-in-time onslaught from Japan. Yamaha, Suzuki and Honda were producing big bikes that matched or outperformed Harley's big bikes, and they were producing them much more efficiently. By 1979 Harley's market share had plunged to less than 30 percent of the market, from nearly 100 percent at the start of the decade. Roy Harmon, Pete Peterson and others saw just-in-time manufacturing as a perfect fit for Harley, and perhaps the only thing that could save the Milwaukee company from bankruptcy.

First, they had to clear exporting the just-in-time approach with Yamaha, a direct Harley competitor. Yamaha, like most Japanese manufacturers at the time, was keenly aware of the mounting pressure in the United States for retaliatory trade measures. Such protectionist talk was aimed at stopping, or at least slowing, the flood of Japanese products coming into the United States, many of which critics claimed were unfairly priced in order to gain market share. The company realized that it was in its, and Japan's, best interests not to be blamed for putting a well-known American brand out of business. "The vice president of Yamaha told us, well sure, Harley was in trouble, almost bankruptcy," Mori recalled. "So he said, 'You know, if Harley went out of business, that would become more of a trade problem with the U.S. government,' so they were happy that we [wanted to] help Harley in Milwaukee."

Harley officials attended a consulting seminar on just-in-time manufacturing in 1981. The following year Harley retained Administrative Services to begin a multiyear engagement using just-in-time techniques to restructure manufacturing processes. For the balance of the decade the firm organized tours of the Harley plant to showcase its just-in-time expertise for prospective clients.

came back we put on seminars about Japanese productivity. That started our manufacturing productivity practice." Others who played a leadership role in the Yamaha engagement included Leighton Smith, Dave Nellemann and Roy Harmon. (Harmon would later collaborate with Pete Peterson on *Reinventing the Factory*, the business bestseller.)

Administrative Services was among the first to bring just-in-time concepts to the American market at a time when U.S. manufacturing was just beginning to realize it needed some serious retooling. The Japanese had shown American automakers that it was possible to make smaller, affordable cars with good gas mileage appeal to American consumers. The 1979 oil crisis served to strengthen the Japanese automakers' hand. Other manufacturing industries quickly realized that Japanese competitors were producing better, more affordable products. While many industries tried to get the U.S. government to enact punitive trade measures against the Japanese, most came to realize that if you can't beat 'em, you'd better join 'em in embracing just-in-time manufacturing.

### Geneva Headquarters

As Andersen continued to expand internationally, it became increasingly cumbersome to legally and structurally weave the various national offices into a cohesive global unit—the "one firm" that Spacek worked so hard to create—while complying with all the national

**The Zurich Assurances building in Switzerland, where Harvey Kapnick wanted to relocate the operations of Arthur Andersen & Co., Société Coopérative, which had been created in the mid-1970s to accommodate international expansion.**

regulatory regimes. Harvey Kapnick, who some partners felt was trying to establish a legacy for himself that would rival those of Spacek and Andersen, decided in the mid-1970s to form an international umbrella organization in Geneva to accommodate international expansion. Each partner became a partner in the Geneva-based organization, which was called Arthur Andersen & Co., Société Coopérative, as well as in their own locally owned country partnership. The partners saw the value in such a plan and endorsed it. But they balked at Kapnick's grandiose plans for a global Andersen headquarters in Geneva, one of the most expensive cities in the world. The new organization would have to operate out of leased space and never achieved the scope of operations in Geneva originally contemplated.

Above: Harvey Kapnick testifying on Capitol Hill. The Arthur Andersen managing partner testified frequently on accounting issues in Washington, D.C., and was an outspoken critic of government accounting practices.

Right: Vox Populi. New York audit partner Brian Peoples spoke out at the 1979 Annual Partners' Meeting against Harvey Kapnick's demand for an immediate yes or no vote on Kapnick's stunning proposal to split the firm into audit and consulting halves. The vote was deferred, setting in motion events that would lead to Kapnick's retirement within a matter of weeks.

On the U.S. front, Kapnick spent a considerable amount of time testifying on Capitol Hill and giving speeches concerning accounting standards—an issue that was also a Spacek favorite. Kapnick made the official rounds in Washington, D.C., and at business forums across the country, assuring listeners that Andersen could operate audit and consulting practices side by side. He repeatedly advocated self-regulation for the accounting industry, an issue debated intermittently in Congress and by the U.S. Securities and Exchange Commission (SEC) since the mid-1960s.

### Independence Issues

The accounting industry's Public Oversight Board in mid-1979 rejected a board committee's report recommending that accounting firms sharply limit non-audit functions. Possibly in response to that action (or inaction, depending on one's point of view), the SEC issued an Accounting Series Release, or ASR, that rattled the accounting industry, and no player more so than industry leader Arthur Andersen. ASR 264, as it was known, dealt with "scope of services by independent accountants." While worded in general terms, ASR 264 suggested that a "global test" be applied by each public company using public accounting firm services to determine what portion of an accounting firm's aggregate fees stem from non-audit engagements. If a substantial portion of an accounting firm's fees from a particular client were from non-audit activities, the SEC suggested, then clients could consider the firm as lacking independence. A year earlier, ASR 250 required public companies to make certain disclosures in their proxy materials when fees for non-audit services provided by their auditor amounted to 3 percent or more of the audit fee.



The double-whammy of ASR 250 and ASR 264 convinced Kapnick by early fall 1979 that something had to be done. He was confident that Andersen's audit independence wasn't threatened by the consulting practice. But he was certain that it was only a matter of time before Congress and/or the SEC took measures forcing Andersen to sever its audit and consulting businesses. After meeting with the chairman of the SEC in Washington, D.C., Kapnick set in motion a series of meetings with partners and the board. At the partners' meeting that September, he stunned the nearly 1,100 partners present by first asking them to approve the board's decision to select him for another term as managing partner, with a hefty raise. Then he argued that Andersen should split into two separate firms, along audit and consulting lines, before Congress forced its hand. What's more, Kapnick proposed that he and a handful of audit partner lieutenants should lead the consulting business, arguing that the consulting partners lacked the requisite business and management experience.

Brian Peoples, an audit partner in the New York office, broke the stunned silence by telling Kapnick it was unfair to spring such a group of proposals on the partnership and expect them to give him an up or down vote. Weeks of additional meetings and flurries of memos followed. Some partners accused Kapnick of misrepresenting what the SEC chairman had told him. The audit and consulting partners thrashed out what it meant to be a partner of Arthur Andersen and weighed other contingencies. The consultants also pondered what a split would mean to their lives and livelihoods.

While the board of directors and several senior consulting partners initially supported Kapnick's proposal, the tide quickly turned against the proposal, among the consultants as well as auditors. That was especially so when memos from Kapnick indicated that he didn't appreciate the extent of the resistance. The vast majority of both groups of partners voted it down. Kapnick, in total defeat, retired on October 29, 1979, after 10 years at the Andersen helm. As Martin Vandersteen, head of the London consulting practice at the time, recalled, "It was a classic illustration of rank-and-file partner power and stewardship over the assets of the firm."

### Regrouping

The partnership quickly put in place a nominating commission to choose leadership candidates for the board. To dilute the power of the chief executive, they voted to split the role of chairman and CEO. Dick Boland, an audit partner from Cleveland, served as acting CEO until the firm installed Duane Kullberg in February 1980.



**In responding to Kapnick's attempt to split Andersen, the consulting partners clearly stated that they saw themselves as part of the "one firm," Arthur Andersen. But it was a mistake—a mistake made by some members of the audit leadership in the decade ahead, unfortunately—to assume that the consultants weren't interested in acting more autonomously. The Administrative Services Division had grown tremendously, totaling 3,261 people by 1979, more than three times as many consultants as were employed at the start of the decade. In 1970 only the Chicago and New York offices had more than 100 consultants, and only four other offices had 50 or more. By 1979, seven offices had more than 100 consulting professionals and nine others had more than 50. The growth of the EDP business in particular and a series of increasingly large and complex engagements made the consulting partners confident that they deserved a greater say in running their business, and the firm as a whole.**

# Late 1970s – Mid-1980s

## Shifting Competition

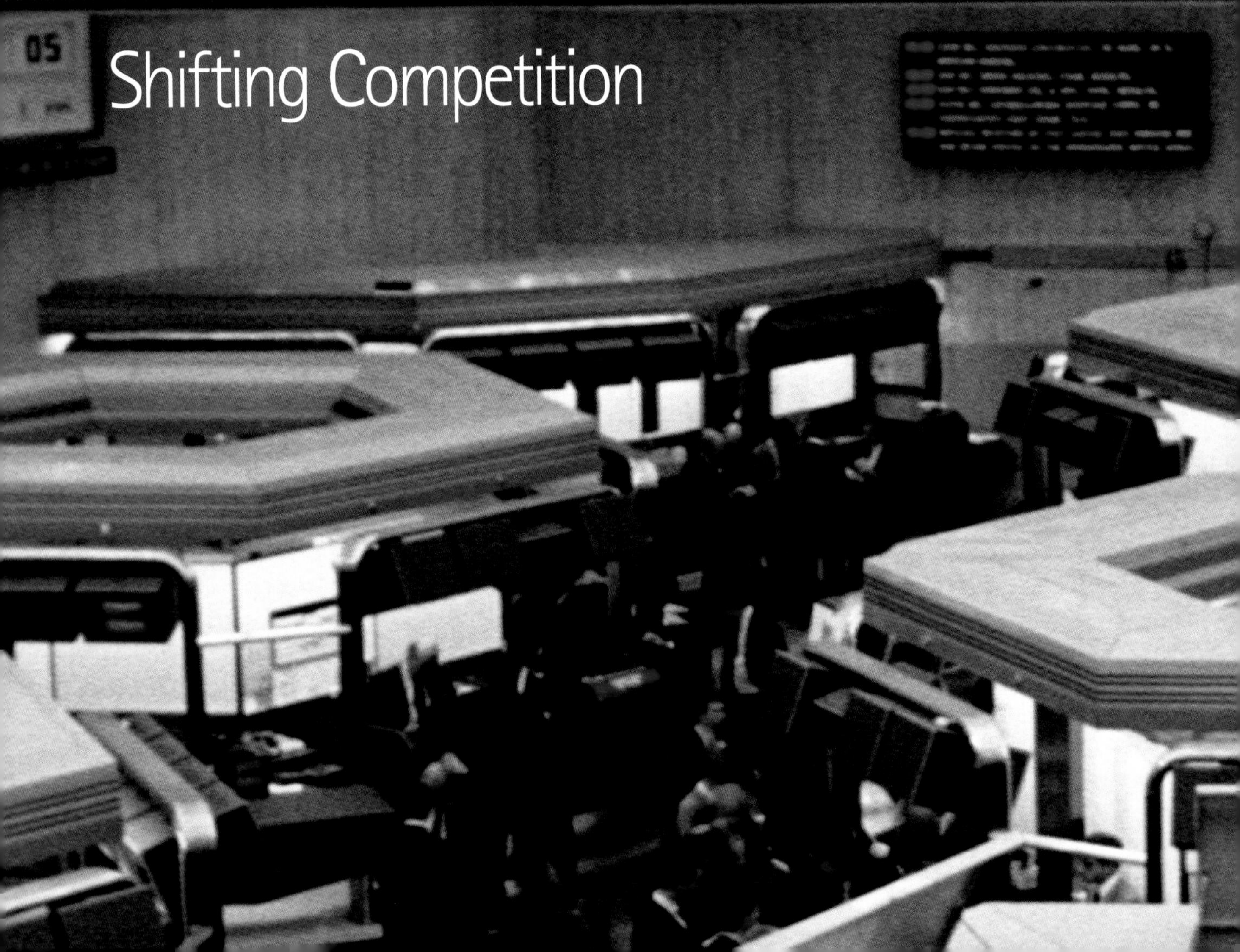

14 05
17 05
EXIT

"We wanted to become the leaders in the information industry. And the whole dialogue about the Information Age was emerging. We wanted to ride that horse forward. And that's what we did, beginning in the early '80s."

Vic Millar

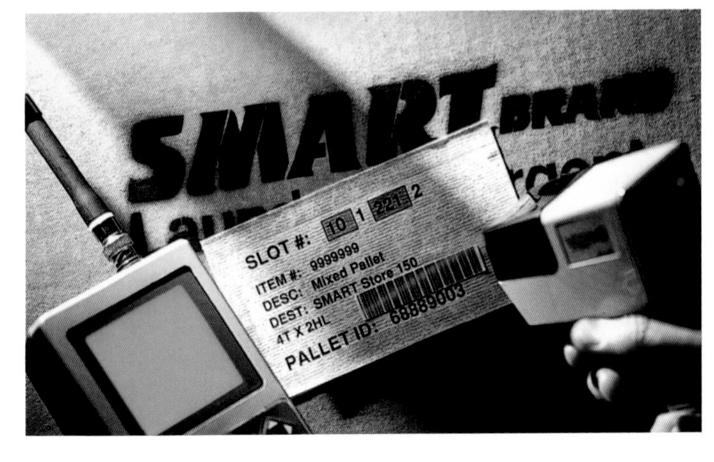

# Late 1970s–Mid-1980s
# Shifting Competition



**The global spread of technology by the early 1980s raised the competitive pressure on companies across a wide range of industries. In addition to their success in using computer technology, Arthur Andersen consultants played a leading role in applying new management techniques, such as just-in-time processes to manufacturing clients, serving as a model for truly integrated business solutions. Given the potential of business consulting, new players emerged to challenge Arthur Andersen's dominance in the field and compete for top talent.**

Chapter opening image: The London Stock Exchange, a major financial services client in the early 1980s that involved dozens of personnel from both the London and New York offices.

**Eyebrows arched, Vernon Ellis gazed intently at Bill Mueller, head of the firm's worldwide consulting practice. Mueller was visiting the firm's London office one afternoon in the late 1970s and giving a group of consulting managers and partners a combination business update and pep talk. The firm he described was very much in the mode of big systems installations and pyramid-based profitability put in place earlier in the decade. So far, so good, thought Ellis, who would be promoted to partner in 1979.**

But that wasn't really a complete picture of the U.K. practice. "[Mueller] was saying we don't do strategic planning. It's not in our scope of practice," Ellis recalled years later with a chuckle. "And I remember some of us looked at each other—well, you may not think we do, but we do here. We didn't tell him, of course."

The discrepancy between Mueller's view and the work actually performed to meet clients' needs by the London office underscored one of the key trends that dramatically reshaped the firm's business over the next several years. While megajob computer systems installations remained the core of the increasingly profitable and rapidly growing practice, offices in different regions and countries were responding to clients' more complex needs by offering solutions that went beyond just installing and integrating systems. In fact, the London office took the lead beginning in the early 1980s with a systems update for the U.K. Department of Health and Social Security's outmoded benefit disbursement process. In many ways a harbinger of the firm's Business Integration Model that wouldn't be fully realized for nearly a decade, it tied together capabilities in strategy, technology, process and change management. The multiyear engagement drew in as many as 150 personnel from across the firm, who returned to their offices with a new appreciation of how to meet clients' evolving needs.



At the same time, the consultants realized that their competitive landscape was changing, and that the firm needed to change with it. By 1986 the consultants realized that while Administrative Services was growing at roughly 20 percent a year, the industry was growing even faster, and, therefore, the consultants were losing market share. A new breed of non-accounting firms, led by IBM and EDS with practices coming from their IT outsourcing roots, was emerging, initially in the United States, and in Europe and Asia by the end of the decade. These competitors were not only more closely identified with the information technology sector than were rival accounting firms, they were much bigger. General Motors' agreement to buy EDS for an eye-popping $2.5 billion in 1984 only heightened the sense that

Andersen's consulting practice needed to grow to remain competitive. And it rekindled a sense among much of the consulting leadership that they needed to take greater control of their destiny, rather than continue to be dominated by the audit leadership. A key firm leader's defection to build a consulting practice for the global advertising and marketing services firm Saatchi & Saatchi in 1986 strengthened demands for dramatic change.

### Consensus Management

When Duane Kullberg was ratified as CEO in February 1980 by 96 percent of the partners, there was a palpable sense of relief felt throughout the firm. Kullberg, who had risen through the audit ranks from running the Minneapolis office beginning in 1970 to running the entire audit practice by 1978, was known for his consensus-style management. His approach was especially appreciated following the final years of Kapnick's heavy-handed rule. "The ground that Kullberg had to plow was very different from the ground that Kapnick had to plow when he took over," recalled Skip Battle, a consulting partner at the time who would go on to lead the industry program and Marketing & Communications under George Shaheen beginning in 1989. "What Kullberg had to do was to heal the firm. And he was brilliant at that. He gave the partners the sense that it's important to be a partner." Kullberg sent just such a message through the ranks by giving the heads of functional, geographic and practice units the common title of managing partner, and changed the name of the board of directors to the board of partners.

**Duane Kullberg, named Arthur Andersen CEO in February 1980, rose through the audit ranks to run the Minneapolis office beginning in 1970, and as of 1978 was leading the entire audit practice out of Chicago.**

The firm also dropped the Administrative Services label for its consulting business in favor of the more descriptive Management Information Consulting Division, or MICD. Consulting employees had argued for years that the Administrative Services title was outmoded, or worse. Mike McGrath, who became Accenture's chief financial officer in 1997 and again in July 2004, recalled arriving on site for an engagement with the J. I. Case division of Tenneco in the mid-1970s in Racine, Wisconsin. "I walked down the hall of this rather antiquated office building into the back hall, and I saw a sign up on the wall that said 'Administrative Services,'" he said. "It was a nicely painted sign, and I thought to myself, 'Gee, we've arrived. We have our own sign on the place.' And so I turned right...and found myself in the janitorial section of the Case organization."

One of Kullberg's first acts was to name Vic Millar to replace Mueller as head of the consulting practice. At the time, Millar was Mueller's deputy for the consulting division and practice director for the Southeast. He reinvigorated the push for productivity using the pyramid approach, training recruits so that partners would have more staff reporting to them, and drove that model throughout the consulting practice.

Larry Levitan, head of the firm's Technical Services Organization from 1979 through mid-1985, noted, "Millar drove that concept throughout the organization, and we started measuring it, and we started rewarding it." He added, "Through the first half of the '80s, that drove very, very significant growth of the Management Information Consulting Division. It also started to drive us toward more profitability and started to make us a lot more profitable than the audit practice."

### Information Age

Millar also concluded that by the late 1970s the consultants were in danger of progressing from job to job and not focusing adequately on trends in their market. "My thought at the time was to put together a five-year plan to allow everybody to get their eyes off of their shoes and look out at the horizon about where this thing was heading," Millar recalled. He retained management consultants Peter Drucker, Michael Porter and the Boston Consulting Group to advise the consulting division. One of the major ideas to come out of this process, Millar said, "was to stop referring to ourselves as being systems people, and focus on information, the deliverable. That allowed us to talk more to the senior client about what he was interested in." This work also paved the way for the consulting group's name change in 1980 to Management Information Consulting Division.

Vic Millar was tapped by Duane Kullberg in 1980 to run the consulting practice, replacing Bill Mueller. Millar was instrumental in boosting productivity and broadening the scope of the consulting practice, as reflected in the 1980 name change to Management Information Consulting Division.



"We wanted to become the leaders in the information industry," Millar recalled. "And the whole dialogue about the Information Age was emerging. We wanted to ride that horse forward. And that's what we did, beginning in the early '80s."

### Government Work

Millar and the consulting practice leaders positioned the division for success heading into the 1980s. But first they had to work through a pronounced business slowdown in the first few years of the decade, precipitated in part by the second Arab oil boycott of the 1970s, which had occurred in 1979. A relatively strong U.S. dollar through much of the first half of the 1980s also made American products more expensive compared with similar European and Asian goods. Born of necessity, a renewed focus on government clients helped diversify the consulting partnership's practice. The government work accelerated the trend toward a broader range of services for clients, and further lessened the consultants' reliance on audit clients for new business. It also led the consultants more directly into competition with a new group of rivals, such as IBM, EDS and CSC, that already were established players in the government arena. The government practice built expertise that helped the firm land ever-larger government contracts in the future.

No office was immune to the effects of the slowdown in corporate spending—not even the Chicago and New York offices, which had the deepest roster of consulting clients and experienced professionals. As partner Jon Conahan recalled, "In the early '80s, the New York

## Software Leverage.

In the process of bidding on a systems upgrade for the New York State Department of Taxation and Finance, Mel Bergstein realized that the consultants could leverage software they had developed for an earlier, corporate project. "When I went to the bidder's conference, they started talking about the kind of architecture they wanted...and I realized we had the software," Bergstein recalled. "And so we were able to get a pricing advantage when we did the work and we were able to explain our approach...in a way you could only explain it if you really understood it in depth."

Bergstein and others built on that experience to encapsulate the firm's knowledge in software architecture that could be used as a template in a variety of jobs. He added, "We built a programmer's workbench...a start at automating the approach...to essentially give us the productivity to meet the goals, which were very ambitious." That experience became the basis for building a designer's workbench tool as well, and eventually formed the basis for the firm's FOUNDATION software package.

By the late 1970s, the Technical Services Organization (TSO) staff in Chicago were suffering constant jet lag from being called for help on jobs across the country and, increasingly, around the world. To try and reduce turnover in the group, Millar and other senior managers decided to decentralize the firm's technical expertise, starting in New York. Bergstein was the obvious choice to head the New York TSO given his software expertise. He initially resisted the move, he said, but acquiesced when he was told that the group would report to the New York office, not Chicago, and that he could operate near his home out of an office in Stamford, Connecticut. Bergstein later moved to Chicago and formally took over the global TSO from Larry Levitan in mid-1985. Levitan would later run the St. Louis and Washington, D.C., consulting practices and the first global market unit, Communications. By the time Bergstein left New York, the TSO staff there had grown from zero in 1979 to more than 80, and were in such demand by clients that the New York office was billing clients a premium rate for their services.

**Mel Bergstein opened the New York Technical Services Organization (TSO) in the late 1970s and moved to Chicago to run the global TSO as of mid-1985.**

Computing Revolution. IBM ushered in a new era in computing with the launch of its PC (personal computer) in 1982. The PC-XT followed in 1983, and the AT personal computer pictured here was introduced in August 1984.

## Computers Get Personal.

The introduction of IBM's first personal computer in 1982 supplied critical mass to the nascent PC industry. The consulting group was still focused primarily on mainframe and minicomputer systems in the mid-1980s, but PCs were starting to have an impact. "They were still individual personal computers, and we hadn't started to link them up into networks, which has really created the explosion that we're seeing in today's technology," Larry Levitan, head of the Technical Services Organization at the time, recalled. "But we were starting to move toward using PCs as tools, as actually putting applications on them. And we were starting to see them replace the dumb workstations that we had previously developed systems for." Marketing literature from the period also proudly notes that the consultants were early adapters of the recently introduced computer disc, or CD, technology for data storage.

office struggled...and Reg [Jones, head of consulting in New York] came under a lot of pressure to lay off people." According to Conahan, Jones removed some underperforming partners and pushed some of the younger partners into leadership positions, including Conahan, Mel Bergstein, Steve Zimmerman and Gerry Rydberg.

With corporate clients slashing their information technology budgets until they saw signs of an economic upturn, the consultants started to focus more attention on government contracts at the city, state and federal level. Bergstein had spent the first 12 years of his career with the firm on the Kraft and other corporate engagements, and didn't have any experience handling government clients. Reg Jones was hardly an expert on government work, either, though he did play a leadership role in the mid-1970s working with the New York City Financial Control Board. Nevertheless, one mild fall morning in the early 1980s the two roared up the New York State Thruway in Jones's blue Mustang convertible, top down. They were headed toward Albany and a bidder's conference for an extensive systems upgrade at the New York State Department of Taxation and Finance. Jones had convinced Bergstein that pursuing government work was the only way for the consultants in the New York office to make up for the falloff in corporate engagements.

Reg Jones ran consulting in the New York office from the mid-1970s until his retirement in 1984.

Jon Conahan's pursuit of the government market led to a breakthrough engagement that he described as his first megajob. The firm won the bidding for a Port Authority of New York and New Jersey system that would manage all the cargo that came into the region's airports. The system "connected airlines around the world, the U.S. Tax Service, Immigration and Customs, all the brokers, the distributors and the banks," he said. "It was a massive application."

"We bid a very unusual technical architecture, very unusual high-speed operating system that very few people used," Conahan noted. "But it allowed us to use a very small mainframe that made our price very attractive at the end of the day to the client. And we won it, we executed it and it was an $18 million dollar job. Now, that was a mega, mega-engagement. I mean that was a blip on everybody's radar, including Millar in Chicago and anybody else," he added.

David Hunter recalled landing a "huge, complex system" upgrade for the Texas Comptroller of Public Accounts in January 1980 that involved 50 people in the firm's Austin office (at the time a satellite of the Houston office). Hunter had joined the firm in Sydney, Australia, in 1973 and moved to the United States in 1978, initially to work in the TSO in Chicago. He noted that government work in the early '80s in some ways hastened the firm's transition from working primarily on back-office and support systems to tackling more mission-critical systems. "For the first time, I think, in the '80s we were taking on mission-critical systems of clients," Hunter said. "I mean, you can't get much more mission critical than a state taxation system. And at that particular time I think that system was a sales tax system, representing something like 60 percent of the state's revenue. If you screw it up you're in a lot of trouble." Hunter was named global managing partner of the Government industry group in 1997.

### U.K. Milestone

If the U.S. economy was weak in the early 1980s, the British economy was on life support. Following a succession of Labour Party governments and labor disputes in the 1970s, the country was in a state of virtual economic collapse by the time the Conservative Party came to power in 1979 under the leadership of Margaret Thatcher. Keith Burgess, who led the consulting group in the United Kingdom from 1989 through 1995, had done some work for the Treasury Department and other arms of the British government during the 1970s. But it was the group's engagement with the U.K. Department of Health and Social Security (DHSS) beginning in the early 1980s and lasting for several years that "proved to be a milestone event in the development of the U.K. practice," noted Martin Vandersteen, who was the European practice director at the time.

By the time Burgess and his team were called into the DHSS, the country's social security system was on the verge of collapse. Antiquated systems, including paper ledgers, were hopelessly outdated

The United Kingdom would adopt a decidedly pro-private enterprise stance under the leadership of Prime Minister Margaret Thatcher who, as the head of the Conservative Party, was elected in 1979 and would serve for three consecutive terms.

and poorly synchronized, and the additional demands put on the system by double-digit unemployment levels created a crisis atmosphere. "Major investments had to be made because the social security system would crumble unless something was done," Vandersteen noted. "I mean, it had old-fashioned systems. The service to the public was terrible. The morale in that department was rock bottom."

The firm helped transform the practices of the entire organization, including building a nationwide computer network with 41,000 terminals linking 80,000 employees in 1,800 locations. The firm's Change Management Services practice helped plan the rollout, redefine jobs and train 34,000 employees over a two-and-one-half-year period. In an innovative approach to problem solving, the consulting group helped the agency develop a holistic approach to providing and tracking benefits by integrating on one terminal a complete picture of each person's situation, including all benefits and payments. As Burgess recalled, "The challenge was to help deliver better benefits, faster, at a lower administrative cost, using fewer employees—through information technology."

"The technical infrastructure was laid down and that was the beginnings of what we now regard as good, best practice and program management," Vandersteen added. "A lot of our thinking came out of the Department of [Health and] Social Security and got transported from there on to a series of other very big jobs in the United Kingdom." Examples included the firm's work with the London Stock Exchange, which after several chief executives is still an Accenture client, and with several major international banks in London to upgrade their systems in preparation for the "big bang" of deregulated trading in late 1986.

The floor of the London Stock Exchange, 1982. The floor was closed and all trading was carried out electronically as of 1986 as part of the deregulation of the British securities markets. The exchange remains a client.



## Big Deals, Black Holes.

Nearly every consultant can recall a major engagement, usually during the early years of his or her career, that earned the reputation as a "black hole" into which colleagues seemed to disappear for years on end. So the DHSS job appeared, at least at first. It proved to be the largest assignment ever carried out by the firm, and remained so into the 1990s, with consultants from around the world helping staff the project. In 1985 alone, the engagement was the sixth-largest in the global consulting business, generating $4.6 million in fees that fiscal year.

Martin Vandersteen noted, "Everybody got called to the colors and there were loud mutterings and shouts from the other divisions in the practice that they had to give up people." But as the magnitude and pathbreaking significance of the engagement became clear, staff attitudes began to change. Added Vandersteen, "We even had people coming through to become partners who had spent most of their management career on that job, and it gradually became viewed as being something that would be extremely beneficial to your career. And, of course, we all learned a lot from that job about large-scale programs of change." Key consultants involved in the project included Mark Otway, Dave Clinton, Ian Watmore, Al Donald, Philippa Reid and many others who subsequently became partners.

## Audit Slump

The audit side of the firm also went into a slump in the early 1980s. It proved to be a downturn in profitability from which the audit practice would never fully recover. As the decade progressed, the importance of audits would be downgraded by most corporate clients and considered a cost with limited business value, to be minimized and priced as a commodity. Litigation costs, virtually a nonissue a decade earlier, were becoming an increasing concern as companies and shareholders became more likely to sue auditors over financial irregularities.

Si Moughamian, who had been Southeast practice director in consulting, was named head of the consulting division in 1983, following Vic Millar's promotion to the newly created position of managing partner–Practice.

In 1983 Vic Millar was named to the newly created position of managing partner-Practice, with oversight responsibilities for the audit and tax as well as consulting practices, and reporting to Kullberg. This marked the beginning of efforts by the audit practice to find future sources of growth and profitability, though it would take several years before such efforts, including a foray into consulting, yielded significant results. Frank Rossi, an audit partner, was named to the post of managing partner-Operations, and had all offices reporting to him. Si Moughamian, who had been Southeast practice director in the consulting division, replaced Millar as head of the consulting practice, based in Chicago.



## Economic Rebound

The economy started to recover by the early to mid-1980s. The stock market anticipated the rebound when it began what would become a historic rally in August 1982. Business picked up initially in the United States, with a strong recovery in Europe following a few years later. And with the recovery came reduced tensions, at least initially, on the consulting, audit and tax sides of the firm.

During the first half of the 1980s, the firm's U.S. consulting practice expanded dramatically. Barry Patmore helped develop the firm's systems design and installation segments of METHOD/1 and eventually would head the Seattle and Los Angeles practices. He was the second consulting partner in Seattle when he arrived in 1978, working with a total consulting staff of 27. The group grew rapidly, installing and upgrading information systems for numerous clients, including Weyerhaeuser and other forest products companies, the state of Washington and telecommunications companies, so that by the end of the decade the consulting staff in Seattle had swelled to 160. In the mid-1980s, Patmore and the partner team initiated a major effort directed at getting to know executives at a rapidly growing company in the area—Microsoft Corp. In 1988 Patmore received a memorable call. He said it was the only time in his career that a company called and said, "We have decided to make [your firm] our strategic systems partner and we want you to come over next week and start three major projects." Microsoft has been a client ever since and a major strategic partner.

The San Francisco office performed an extensive systems upgrade for that city's Bay Area Rapid Transit (BART) in the early 1980s.



Similar growth patterns emerged around the country. In San Francisco, the consultants took on a massive systems engagement for the Bay Area Rapid Transit, or BART, which involved most of the people in the office during the early 1980s. This engagement was led by Bill Van Lieshout, who later headed the Minneapolis, Detroit and New York consulting practices. Several consultants did work for bank and credit card companies, an outgrowth of the San Francisco office's early expertise with Bank of America's BankAmericard, the forerunner of the Visa card. Pittsburgh, Detroit (with engagements at major utility client Consumers Power) and Milwaukee (with its high-profile Harley-Davidson engagement) continued to be instrumental in the growth of the firm's utility and manufacturing practices.

In the Houston office, growth slowed somewhat as oil and gas prices peaked in the early 1980s and then declined for much of the decade. But in San Antonio, the firm was engaged in a major systems upgrade, led by Steve James and Tom Skelly, for the rapidly growing insurer USAA. As noted, the Austin office, led initially by Warner Croft, expanded rapidly with systems upgrade engagements for various branches of the Texas state government. In the Southeast, business also was picking up in Atlanta and Charlotte in manufacturing and retailing, as well as for regional utilities such as Duke Power and Southern Company. Charlotte's status as regional banking center led to several key consulting engagements, including one for NCNB, which would later adopt

Financial services client Goldman Sachs, 1983. As Goldman and other investment banking firms expanded globally during the 1980s, consulting personnel traversed the world to help install and link trading and information systems.

the name NationsBank. After merging with BankAmerica Corporation nearly two decades later, the combined financial services powerhouse would take the Bank of America name but remain based in Charlotte.

Growth in the Northeast during the 1980s was powered by an upswing in financial services engagements in New York, notably for the New York Stock Exchange and several leading investment banking firms including Salomon Brothers, Goldman Sachs and First Boston. The exchange and the investment banks scrambled to upgrade systems to handle rapidly growing securities trading volume, and, for the investment banks, a growing array of financial products that increasingly were being traded on a global basis.

Sandwiched between the fiefdoms of New York and Boston, the Hartford office nevertheless grew dramatically during the 1980s under the leadership of Dick Boyle and Bill Stoddard. The office expanded from fewer than 20 people in the mid-1970s to more than 400 by 1990. Growth was driven partly by defense-related projects, which benefited from the Reagan-era emphasis on federal defense and weapons-system spending, and systems upgrades for a number of insurance companies, including Travelers Insurance, Aetna and The Hartford. And for the first time since the pioneering Louisville engagement in the mid-1950s, General Electric was once again a major consulting client, this time of the Hartford and New York offices.

Bill Green, a future leader of the firm, joined the Hartford office in 1977. A self-described "plumber's son from western Massachusetts," Green was seen by Boyle, who ran the consulting practice there, as a good fit with the blue-collar crews working at General Dynamics' Electric Boat division. Electric Boat had retained the consultants to help boost productivity and set up systems to produce 18,000-ton, Ohio-class submarines for the U.S. Navy. After helping successfully apply project management skills that helped transform General Dynamics' shipbuilding processes, Green also worked on projects in aerospace and defense industry-related areas, including Dexter Corporation, and later Pratt & Whitney, Textron Lycoming, Sikorsky Aircraft and Raytheon. Green became a manager in 1981 and partner in 1986. He left Hartford in 1990 to run the consulting practice in the Boston office, greatly expanding its presence in mutual funds and other financial services.

This snapshot of the consulting business in the mid-1980s provides several insights into the changing nature of the practice. Underscoring the extent to which the consultants were building a stand-alone business, it's worth noting that among these top 10 clients in 1985, only two, Mutual of Omaha and Georgia-Pacific, were audit clients of the firm. Among the top 25 consulting clients that year, only six were audit clients. The growing importance of government clients, in the United States and abroad, is evident. The practice's geographic diversity also is clear, given the number of major clients handled by offices other than Chicago and New York.



It was becoming clear to the consulting leadership in the United States that their business was not being well served by the firm's office-based organization. The consulting division was operating, at least on a de facto basis, as a nationwide practice organized around industry groups with extensive sharing of staff among offices to meet client needs. As indicated by the growth in the government business, it was also expanding into new business areas and facing new competitors that had little if anything to do with the firm's regulated audit roots.

### U.S. Consulting Fees by Industry Group, 1985

| Industry | Fees (in millions) | % of Total |
|---|---|---|
| Manufacturing/Construction | $72.5 | 20.4 |
| Financial Services | 70.0 | 19.7 |
| Government Services | 59.3 | 16.6 |
| Distribution Services | 39.8 | 11.2 |
| Regulated Industries | 34.2 | 9.6 |
| Health Care | 28.5 | 8.0 |
| Oil and Gas | 15.6 | 4.4 |
| Communications and Entertainment | 9.8 | 2.7 |
| All Other | 26.4 | 7.4 |

Note: Comparable non-U.S. fee information not available. In Europe, major banks and other financial institutions were the largest source of fees.

## Tangled Up in Blue.

IBM and the consulting practice alternately competed and cooperated on a number of engagements during the 1980s. As by far the largest supplier of computer hardware in the world, IBM was a tremendous influence on the information technology sector. The Andersen consultants naturally worked closely with IBM experts, designing and installing systems using IBM equipment and software. And IBM retained Andersen consultants in the New York office for several engagements during the 1980s that, as of 1985, made IBM the consulting division's single-largest client, generating $14.9 million in revenue for the consulting practice that year (see table below). At the same time, IBM was expanding into the IT services business and increasingly positioning itself as a consulting industry rival.

**Top 10 Consulting Clients in 1985**

| Client | Fees (in millions) | Office |
|---|---|---|
| IBM | $14.9 | New York |
| Federal National Mortgage | 8.8 | Washington, D.C. |
| U.S. Federal Government | 6.4 | Washington, D.C. |
| U.S. Department of Agriculture | 6.3 | Chicago |
| USAA | 5.0 | San Antonio |
| U.K. Department of Health and Social Security | 4.6 | London |
| State of New York | 4.4 | New York |
| Mutual of Omaha | 4.2 | Omaha |
| State of New Jersey | 4.1 | New Jersey |
| Georgia-Pacific Corp. | 4.0 | Atlanta |

**International Growth**

In 1986, a group of Swiss futures and options exchanges dubbed SOFFEX retained the firm to design an "electronic trading floor" that would accept buy-and-sell orders that exchange members entered at computer terminals. The system would go "live" in 1988. The firm was retained to create a similar system for the German automated exchange Deutsche Terminbörse, which also formed the basis for the Eurex automated trading system.

The SOFFEX engagement drew on more than 100 experts from firm offices around the world. In that sense it was typical of the major engagements of the period, especially in financial services. Since the late 1970s, the New York and London offices had been exchanging financial services experts on jobs. Carol Meyer, for instance, was promoted to manager in the early 1980s working on a massive trading systems upgrade for the New York Stock Exchange. She also worked on engagements for several of the largest global financial services firms based in New York, including Salomon Brothers, Goldman Sachs and First Boston. As these firms expanded into London and Tokyo beginning in the mid-1980s, Meyer and other consultants went with them to set up trading systems. Meyer was later named Accenture managing partner of Human Resources and then head of Investor Relations.

An engagement to design an electronic trading floor in 1985 for the Swiss futures and options exchanges dubbed SOFFEX drew upon the talents of more than 100 firm consultants from around the world.

In London, John Skerritt was leading major engagements to help the newly emerging capital markets institutions prepare for open, global competition. One of the most significant engagements was National Westminster Bank in the run-up to the "big bang." To reflect the global nature of the financial markets, an international team of 110 people from New York, London, Sydney, Tokyo, Singapore and Hong Kong worked to install global trading and investment management systems. Skerritt later relocated to New York to head the global Financial Services industry group.

While Chicago and New York battled stateside for bragging rights in terms of the size and prestige of their clients, the intramural action in Europe mainly was between London and Paris. There was a close rivalry between the two in the 1970s, but the multiyear U.K. Department of Health and Social Security and numerous financial services engagements helped put London in the lead by the mid-1980s. The firm dominated the consulting field in the United Kingdom when it came to financial services, with engagements for Girobank, Lloyds Bank, Barclays Bank, TSB Trust and others, in addition to National Westminster Bank and its merchant banking subsidiary NatWest.

The Paris practice wasn't about to cede European leadership if it didn't have to. The British clearly had pulled ahead in quantity of business by the mid-1980s, but the consulting leaders in Paris argued that they were the quality leaders as often as the British, at least in terms of profits. "During those 10 years, '79 to '89, we were probably more profitable than they were," a former partner in the French practice recalled. "But in terms of growth and size, we pretty much were known at the same level. And I remember I was, during all those years, asking myself, 'Are those Brits going to be over us? Are we going to pass them this year or are they going to pass us this year?'"



The Italian practice was also coming on strong. Even though Art Welby had worked out of Milan in the late 1950s as he helped build the European consulting practice, the Italian practice languished for much of the 1960s and 1970s. But under the leadership of Bruno Ricca, and with a renewed focus on recruiting from Italian universities, it blossomed in the 1980s. From roughly 80 consultants in 1980, the practice grew to nearly 900 by the end of the decade, recalled Diego Visconti, who took over the practice in 1991. Visconti and Marco Vigorelli were instrumental in growing the Italian banking practice. They led an installation of billing and other systems for Credito Romagnolo in 1984 and 1985 that involved nearly 150 personnel.

During the 1980s, growth accelerated in Spain as the practice was buoyed by major engagements for several large banks and other financial institutions, many under the direction of partner Carlos Vidal. In fact, the firm's Spanish banking software solution Alnova was first delivered in 1989 and was employed across Europe during the following decade, as the European practice became more integrated. The Spanish practice also benefited tremendously from building up Coritel, a relatively low-cost technical programming capability borrowed from the French practice in the 1980s. Vic Millar and certain other firm leaders opposed the Coritel approach, arguing that it effectively bifurcated the practice by creating a classification of technical employee not necessarily on the partner track, and ran counter to the "one firm" ethos that was driving much of the consulting practice's success. But the Spanish partners resisted calls that they jettison the highly profitable capability. It's not hard to see why.

At one point in the 1990s, Spanish partner José Luis Manzanares boasted that he had roughly 1,000 employees reporting to him via Coritel, giving him the largest "pyramid" of any partner in the global firm.

The drive for larger systems jobs spread across Europe, aided by increased pooling of resources, and many European practices experienced significant growth beginning in mid-decade. Under the leadership of Bob Manion, and later Thad Perry, the German practice began to take off, with significant assignments for Volkswagen, several German banks, and the German Railways and Postal government departments, among others. Scandinavia, under the leadership of Lars Henriksen, also grew rapidly, with major engagements in Norway for Statoil and the Norwegian Savings Bank, Alfa Laval in Sweden and Statsanstalten in Denmark. Financial services engagements served as the principal drivers of growth for the firm's consulting practices in the Benelux countries, Switzerland, Portugal and South Africa during the 1980s as well.

Terry Neill led the Irish practice through a period of sustained growth in the 1980s that coincided with the beginning of sustained economic liberalization in that country. The firm landed several large engagements, including those for the Irish Permanent Building Society and the Irish National Transport Company. Neill eventually became the global head of Change Management and also served as the chairman of the Andersen Worldwide board during the period of arbitration in the late 1990s.



Larger client jobs also began to emerge outside the United States and Europe. Bank Simpanan Nasional in Malaysia became the first Asian client to get a METHOD/1 license, one of the largest contracts in Asia at that time. Andersen's consulting division, using its Lexicon data dictionary, designed a mainframe system to serve 4 million bank customers. The firm also designed an elaborate loyalty system that awarded prizes to bank customers equal to what they would accrue in interest on their accounts.

During this period the firm not only landed new clients, it expanded relationships with existing clients to add to their systems work or upgrade work done a decade earlier in response to changing client needs and improved computer technology. Clients whose systems were upgraded by the firm during the early 1980s included Mutual of Omaha, Milliken, Mars, J.I. Case, American General, Southern California Edison and Harley-Davidson.

### Reinventing the Factory

While the computer systems installation and integration business grew apace in the United States and overseas offices, the firm's manufacturing practice also began expanding rapidly in the early to mid-1980s. Once-a-week tours of the Harley-Davidson plant led to a raft of new business for the firm's Products group, which covered manufacturing. The consultants demonstrated that

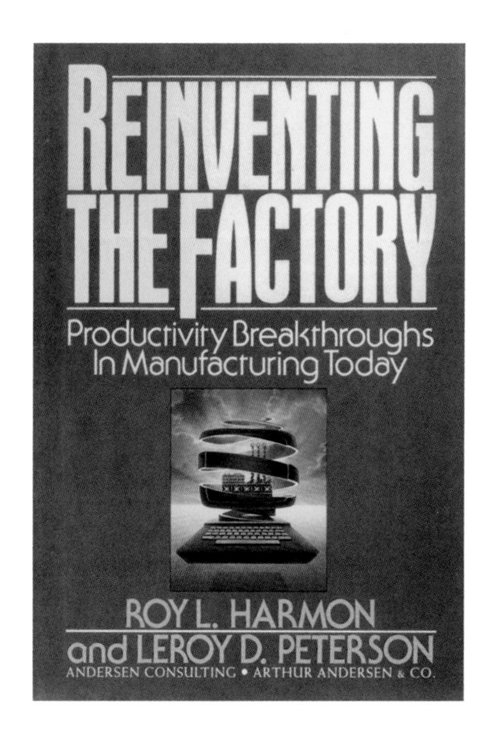


**Manufacturing Must-read.** ***Reinventing the Factory,*** **by firm consultants Leroy "Pete" Peterson and Roy Harmon, documented the firm's successes in introducing just-in-time manufacturing concepts to clients around the world.**

just-in-time techniques could yield significant results across a range of industries and companies. "We had tremendous results," recalled Leroy "Pete" Peterson. "We were reducing lead time to make something from months to days....I remember one [company] where it took them 30 days and we got them down to two hours."

Peterson and Roy Harmon wrote *Reinventing the Factory* to document the firm's many just-in-time successes. The book was an instant hit and remained on business bestseller lists for more than a year. Their efforts and those of their colleagues challenged the notion that the consulting sides of accounting firms didn't do plant layouts.

By the mid-1980s, Peterson and other consulting partners wanted to marry what the firm was doing in systems integration with just-in-time and other manufacturing applications. Peterson went to Millar in 1985 to get funding for a demonstration project that would be included in an Advanced Manufacturing Show scheduled for Chicago's McCormick Place convention center the following year. Millar wasn't enthusiastic, preferring to focus more on developing systems integration methodologies, and ended up giving Peterson only about $100,000 for his project.



With the help of other manufacturing practice leaders such as Bill Stoddard, Karl Newkirk and Carl Kilmer, Peterson went to the heads of manufacturing groups in other firm offices around the country, including New York, Boston and Milwaukee, to solicit funds. He ended up raising $1.5 million. The resulting exhibit highlighted the latest in factory technology, including robotics and voice recognition equipment. The exhibit was the hit of the show, according to many corporate executives who complimented the consultants.

The firm repeated its success at the Advanced Manufacturing Show the following year. That sparked a burst of growth in the manufacturing practice that led to the creation of systems integration centers in Evanston, Illinois, just north of Chicago, and in Dallas. Several of the firm's next generation of leaders were involved in this manufacturing practice expansion. Joe Forehand led the creation of an integration center in Atlanta. Other demonstration centers were Smart Stores in London and Chicago led by Glen Terbeek, the Retail Place (also in Chicago), the Financial Ideas Exchange in New York sponsored by John Skerritt, a Logistics Center in Atlanta sponsored by Bill Copacino (who led the Logistics Strategy practice and later Business Consulting) and the Hospital of the Future, a demonstration center led by Doug Ryckman.

**Back to the Future**

The successful execution of the Advanced Manufacturing Show exhibit underscored the significant changes under way at the firm and in the consulting industry. In addition to Millar's success in building the unified approach to massive system design and

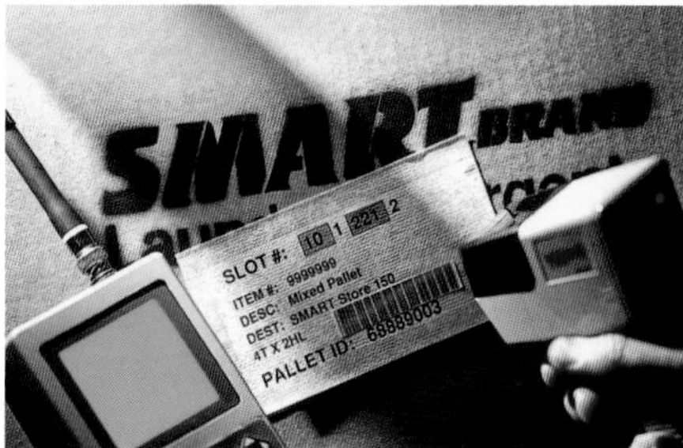

Top and lower left: The Retail Place demonstration center in Chicago highlighted trends in retailing technology during the 1980s.

Middle and bottom right: Smart technology used in Smart Stores—demonstration centers the firm developed in London and Chicago.

installation, there always had been a functional, business-strategy aspect to the consulting practice in a number of offices. This combination made for a powerful one-two product offering that, at least early in the 1980s, no competitor could match.

With Millar assuming responsibility for audit and tax as well as consulting as of 1983, a new generation of consulting group leaders was able to promote a broader-based practice in response to client needs and the changing competitive landscape. "The world was changing, and many of us that were there at the time knew we needed to be more into strategy consulting," recalled Bob Prince, who succeeded Millar as head of the Washington, D.C., practice. "That was a tough thing for Victor to relate to, because he was always used to thinking of what he used to call the 'one mainline, everything-going-to-be-the-same, teach programming to everybody.'" Millar was concerned about the potential difficulty of bringing in experienced people in a separate consulting field. Prince went on to head the firm's Human Resources, Partnership Matters and Partner Income Committee, as well as the quality and legal functions.

Peter Fuchs, who ran the consulting group's strategy practice from 1987 through 1998, and chaired the firm's nominating commission in 1999 when it nominated Joe Forehand as CEO, was among the firm's strategy pioneers. "We saw the need to diversify beyond the single mainline business," Fuchs recalled. "In some ways it was a case of going back to the future—of recognizing the need to solve both technology and business strategy problems."

Stan Cornelison, head of the Chicago consulting practice in the mid-1980s, supported George Shaheen's push for a strategy practice.

In the early 1980s, the strategy group failed two years in a row to convince the consulting management group to adopt the strategy practice, "because there was not a compelling interest or desire to mess with the model that had made us successful," recalled Joel Friedman, who eventually would lead the U.S. strategy practice and serve on the Accenture board of directors. Si Moughamian, head of the consulting practice, asked George Shaheen, who was a rising young star in charge of San Francisco's consulting practice, to lead the next push to gain acceptance for the strategy practice.

Shaheen, who was very supportive of the mainline technology practice, initially was reluctant to take on the strategy cause. But he began to see the potential power of broadening the skill set of consulting, of offering a greater array of capabilities to client executives. From late 1985 through much of 1986, Shaheen flew around the country to visit and persuade consulting practice leaders that it was time to embrace a strategy practice. Shaheen refused to be put off by partners who told him to talk to others and see what support there was, then get back to them. He confronted Stan Cornelison, then head of the Chicago consulting practice, knowing his support was crucial to the success of the proposed practice. "I said, 'I'm not going forward with this thing unless you're with me, and if you're not with me, you and I are going to go in and talk to Moughamian and tell him why this thing isn't going to fly,'" Shaheen recalled. Cornelison and others signed on. By the annual consulting management meeting in October 1986, the partners were ready to approve the creation of a Strategic Services practice on a pilot basis in New York, Chicago and San Francisco.

### Changing Competition

Despite the tremendous amount of income the consulting practice was generating by the mid-1980s, changes in the marketplace weighed heavily on the group's decision-making process. "It was the early days of IBM and EDS figuring out that the hardware or outsourcing business ran the risk of becoming commoditized," Friedman recalled. "And there was more revenue in the services side, and we saw pressures competitively that caused us to think very differently about our own model." The fact that General Motors had agreed to pay $2.5 billion for EDS in June 1984 drove home the message that the installation business was getting more competitive, and that the competitors increasingly were able to tap very large financial resources with which to finance their businesses.

The influx of giant technology companies onto the consultants' systems installation turf drove much of the strategy-related soul searching. With the consultants' mainline business increasingly technology driven, there was great concern internally that the consulting practice lacked a clear identity in the market. "In the '60s and '70s, if you want financial record keeping and you do it on computers, you would go to an accounting firm," Skip Battle recalled. "It made all the sense in the world. But would you go to an accounting firm to help you manufacture some stuff? I don't think so. To help you do marketing? I don't think so....So, as we got into the '80s, we found that there were a lot more dances to be held. At those dances accountants weren't particularly respected. We didn't have a whole lot of brand equity coming in there."

"Back in the '80s in the business we were in, which was then systems building, systems integration, there was not a dominant leader, there was not a branding," Larry Levitan noted. "We were successful, but if you sat down on an airplane next to a businessman, they wouldn't know who we were or what we did."

### A Bigger Slice of the Pie

The tremendous financial success of the consulting practice in the mid-1980s, combined with concern about growing competitive threats to its primary business, led to renewed demands from consultants for a greater say in Andersen affairs. They felt their say was critical because the nature of the business was changing rapidly and the old model, where each office managing partner decided how to run the business in his office, was no longer effective. Yet the office managing partners were unwilling to yield their power base. A series of meetings, dubbed Williamsburg I, II and III, were held among partners from the different practices. Discussions were held on the direction of the firm and the consultants' demands for more influence and a greater share of profits. As CEO Duane Kullberg noted in a November 13, 1986, memo, "One of the clear undercurrents at the present time is the strong feeling on the part of many of the Management Information Consulting partners that the strong performance in recent years of the consulting practice deserves greater recognition in the management and other aspects of our practice."

Millar and other consulting partners had been trying for years to pry figures out of Kullberg and others in the firm's leadership detailing the profits of the consulting practice. The consultants felt that the audit partners were deliberately obscuring the consultants' profits so that they would not have to dilute their control of the firm. As noted earlier, Millar suspected that the consultants had become more profitable than the auditors as early as the 1973-74 period, but he didn't have the figures to back up his suspicions. Kullberg and others in the audit leadership responded that the firm's performance was tracked historically on an office-by-office basis, not by practice. It took sustained effort from Millar and Chief Financial Officer Randal McDonald to finally produce figures.



In the 1986 memo, Kullberg also reiterated an argument that the auditors and tax partners would employ over the next 14 years as their disputes with the consultants gathered momentum: For years, the consulting business had been funded out of the earnings of the firm. Just because the consultants were becoming more profitable didn't mean that the structure of the firm needed to be radically altered, even though such a decision might seem "obvious" to the consultants. "Had our predecessors made the 'obvious' decision based on historical results," Kullberg noted, "my speculation is that we would have about six offices in the United States, none outside the United States, and clearly would not have an [MICD] practice."

### Millar Leaves, Consultants Regroup

The consultants' victory was short-lived. They were hit with another shocking bit of news circulated by Kullberg at virtually the same time he disclosed the profit figures: Vic Millar was leaving the firm. Millar was the highest-ranking consultant in the firm since John Higgins served as Leonard Spacek's chief operations officer in the early 1960s. His loss was seen by consultants as leaving them without a voice at the highest levels of management. To make matters worse, he was leaving to head a newly formed consulting division of London-based Saatchi & Saatchi, a publicly held advertising and public relations company that would compete directly with his former partners.

## More Than Money.

As much as the consultants cared about their income, their argument with the audit side of the firm always was about more than money. They saw themselves in different businesses with different economics, and they certainly didn't see the audit practice as the "core" of their business. They were angered that Kullberg and other firm leaders failed to see their side of this argument, and were infuriated that the established leadership was questioning their allegiances, rather than asking them what they needed to compete effectively in their marketplace. Eventually, Kullberg would come to appreciate the consultants' view.

Kullberg knew he could not continue sharing firm profit figures with only the small coterie of audit partners controlling the board. With further caveats about not rushing to judgment and keeping such information in historical perspective, he released, for the first time ever, the profit contributions per partner, by practice, in the 1986 memo. The results were electrifying, and the consultants felt vindicated in having argued that they were being shortchanged by the auditors who controlled the firm.

**Net Income Per U.S. Partner by Practice Area**

| Year | Total | Audit | Consulting | Tax |
|---|---|---|---|---|
| 1979 | $131,300 | $135,700 | $129,000 | $124,000 |
| 1980 | 174,200 | 173,500 | 197,700 | 154,700 |
| 1981 | 215,700 | 210,200 | 251,500 | 192,300 |
| 1982 | 235,300 | 245,700 | 223,900 | 223,900 |
| 1983 | 218,800 | 232,200 | 177,800 | 230,700 |
| 1984 | 255,500 | 246,500 | 276,300 | 253,200 |
| 1985 | 252,700 | 221,700 | 338,700 | 230,800 |
| 1986 | 284,400 | 237,100 | 442,200 | 218,000 |

Note: Figures include partner retirement and other benefits, employment taxes and return on capital.

Outside the United States, by 1986 consulting profits had soared to $241,000 per partner, compared to $223,500 per tax partner and only $148,800 per audit partner.

Kullberg and Millar insisted there was no bad blood between the two. Kullberg added in a note sent to all employees that Millar's departure didn't signal divisiveness at the top of the consulting ranks. After Kullberg said that he was running for reelection as head of the firm earlier that year, Millar had simply concluded he never would have a shot at running the organization, given firm rules putting age limitations on chief executives at the start of their terms. At Saatchi, Kullberg told the consultants, Millar would finally be able to realize his dream of running a major company.

Millar's resignation was a wake-up call for the consulting group. There was a growing sense among the consulting partners that they had to have greater control over their destiny. Many had doubted the firm's willingness to give them their say in firm affairs, even with Millar in the upper echelon and with their profits finally made available to all partners. Now they were even less inclined to give the audit partners controlling the firm the benefit of the doubt.

The consultants could afford to make deliberate plans. There was no call for a Kapnick-like insurrection. Their main systems installation practice was booming and demand appeared strong for at least the next five years, despite the increasing competition from the likes of IBM and EDS, according to a study issued a year earlier by Keith Burgess and other members of the Technology Advisory Committee. At the same time, the consultants had shown their willingness to pursue innovative solutions by agreeing, with prodding from Shaheen and others, to start a strategy practice. But more changes would be needed, they agreed, to maintain and expand their practice in the years ahead. Plans would soon be put in motion that in less than three years would lead to the creation of an autonomous consulting practice.



**The consultants were grappling with a new reality that they were just beginning to fully understand. It was becoming increasingly clear to them that they needed a new business model to deal with the situation. The office managing partner-based leadership didn't share this view and wasn't about to cede power, especially to a group of upstarts who in their view had been nurtured in their infancy by the audit and tax practices. The consultants, armed with the knowledge that they were now producing the largest share of the profits and were growing at twice the rate of the audit and tax practices, would not be denied. A period of major upheaval was in the offing.**

# 1986–1989

## Winds of Change

"The London meeting was in a sense a call to arms, a call to the issue of where consultants' future in the firm was. What are we going to be allowed to do? How are we going to operate?"

Bob Prince



I see no point
that the Firm w
proprietary or
former partners

# 1986-1989
# Winds of Change



**Economies were booming around much of the world by the mid-1980s. The Andersen consultants leveraged their market-leading position to produce record revenue and profits. The consultants as a result demanded a greater say in running their business as it continued to diverge from the more traditional and regulated audit and tax practices. Partners in the traditional divisions balked, but following a series of wrenching management summits and reorganizations they finally granted the consultants a measure of the self-governance they desired.**

Chapter opening image: London's Le Meridien Piccadilly Hotel, site of the July 6-10, 1987, consulting leadership planning meeting.

**Arthur Andersen CEO Duane Kullberg felt as if he had been blindsided one morning in late May 1987.**

**It had been nearly six months since Vic Millar, a personal friend and the former head of all practice areas at the firm, had resigned to join Saatchi & Saatchi and head up a consulting division for the giant British advertising company. Kullberg had looked forward to getting together with his old friend and confidant, at Millar's suggestion. He assumed they would talk about how Vic was faring now that he finally had the opportunity to run his own company.**

The two were heads of competing organizations, but Kullberg didn't feel threatened. The firm's consulting revenues were growing at more than 25 percent a year, more than twice the rate of the audit or tax practice, and were on track to top $800 million, more than one-third of total firm revenues, in 1987. At that rate, consulting was projected to exceed $1.5 billion in revenue by 1990 to become the largest practice within the organization. And the firm, true to its long-term commitment to education and training, wasn't just milking this cash cow. It was reinvesting for future growth, plowing $120 million of partner earnings, much of it from consulting, back into R&D and employee training—spending nearly $6,000 on each new hire annually. All of which helped rank Andersen's consulting practice the largest in the world—more than 60 percent larger than its nearest rival, and more than three times the size of Saatchi & Saatchi's consulting practice.



Industry gossip and press reports made it clear that Millar was finding it harder than he had expected to build a major consulting business. He had some success acquiring smaller consulting operations in the United States, but his momentum seemed to have stalled, despite the white-hot consulting market in the United States and Europe. Kullberg had even imagined offering Millar some friendly advice along the lines of how different the world looks from the CEO's seat, and counseling patience to his friend, who tended to be so certain of his analysis of a situation that he sometimes wasn't open to opposing views. Of course, Kullberg wouldn't mind the opportunity to get some of his frustrations with his fractious partners off his chest, either.

Kullberg was shocked when Millar revealed the real reason for their get-together: He wanted to discuss buying the Andersen consulting practice—lock, stock and partners' interests. Though no price was mentioned, Millar made it clear that Saatchi, a rapidly growing public company, had the financial wherewithal to make a hefty payment,

## Top International Consulting Firms.

### 1987 Consulting Results in Millions (U.S. dollars)

| Firm | Revenues | Number of Consultants |
|---|---|---|
| Arthur Andersen | $838 | 9,639 |
| Marsh & McLennan | 530 | 6,400 |
| McKinsey | 510 | 1,600 |
| Towers Perrin | 465 | 3,085 |
| KPMG | 438 | 4,700 |
| Booz-Allen & Hamilton | 412 | 2,075 |
| Coopers & Lybrand | 381 | 4,712 |
| Ernst & Whinney | 374 | 3,255 |
| Price Waterhouse | 345 | 4,300 |
| Saatchi & Saatchi | 267 | 1,445 |

Source: *Consultants News.*

Note: The consulting businesses of IBM, EDS and CSC are not included in the above rankings. Much of the revenues of these emerging competitors were from outsourcing.



likely to run into the billions of dollars, to the partners to get the firm to part with the consulting practice. More than a year earlier, when he was still at the firm, Millar had broached the idea of a buyout of the consulting business to Kullberg. But that had been something of an intellectual exercise, the type of mental puzzle that Vic always seemed to be turning over in his mind.

As for that day's unspecified offer, Kullberg didn't give a direct response. He said instead that he needed to think about it, while acknowledging what Millar already knew—that strains caused by the growth of the Andersen consulting practice were a major preoccupation. Their lunch ended without a yes or a no. But Kullberg had a distinct feeling as he headed back to his Chicago office that things would never be the same, either for him or the firm.

Kullberg had no way of knowing at the time just how right he would be. Andersen went through a multiyear planning process in the mid-1980s, culminating in the December 1986 meeting known as Williamsburg III, to set a path for the growth of its audit, tax and consulting practices. The accelerating growth of consulting compared to the slower growth rate for the other two practices was the key factor driving the planning process. But as always, the organization's accounting legacy formed the basis of these discussions. These discussions occurred against a backdrop of waxing and waning concern among key U.S. congressmen and regulators as to the possible negative influence the increasingly lucrative consulting business was having on the objectivity of auditors. Kullberg, in his deliberate fashion, already had said that a discussion of this issue would be the main topic at the Annual Partners' Meeting in October 1987.

The offer from Millar, which Kullberg didn't immediately share with the consulting partners, dovetailed with detailed planning already under way among the consultants. Not content with Kullberg's leisurely timetable, the Management Information Consulting Division (MICD) strategists were putting the finishing touches on a far-reaching planning document to be unveiled at a meeting of the consulting leadership in London in early July 1987. For the first time the consultants, meeting by themselves, were planning to openly consider the best way to realize the full potential of their practice, operating as part of the broader Andersen organization or as a stand-alone business. They acknowledged the organization's "one firm" legacy and the values of outstanding client service, professionalism and integrity they inherited from the audit practice. But they insisted on being treated as equals among the three practices. They particularly bridled at the office-based management system, in which their business in each U.S. office reported to office managing partners, most of whom were audit or tax partners.



The fallout from the London meeting triggered a kaleidoscopic blur of changes in the structure of the organization during the ensuing 18 months, all playing out against a background of accelerating consulting industry growth. The structural changes helped fan even faster growth in the consulting practice, which led to more meetings and more structural changes. A final round of meetings in the summer and fall of 1988 would lead, early in 1989, to the creation of a stand-alone business unit, Andersen Consulting, and the end of Kullberg's tenure as CEO of Arthur Andersen.

### Millar Rebuffed

A few days after their first get-together, Millar called Kullberg and asked for another meeting; they agreed to meet for breakfast on June 1 in Chicago. At that meeting, Millar asked to make a presentation to a group of partners about buying the consulting practice. He also requested certain internal financial data. Kullberg rejected his requests, telling Millar that the firm wasn't for sale, "in whole or in part." Again, as he said in a later note to partners, Kullberg didn't consider Millar's statements to represent an actual offer for the firm.

Kullberg thought that was the end of the matter, until he received another call from Millar about six weeks later, while the firm's board of partners was holding a previously scheduled meeting. Millar told Kullberg that he had sent him a telex a few weeks earlier.

**ARTHUR ANDERSEN & Co.**

DUANE R. KULLBERG
MANAGING PARTNER-
CHIEF EXECUTIVE OFFICER

69 WEST WASHINGTON STREET
CHICAGO, ILLINOIS 60602
(312) 580-0069

July 18, 1987

Mr. Victor E. Millar
Chairman & Chief Executive Officer
Saatchi & Saatchi Consulting Ltd.
1110 Vermont Avenue NW, Suite 710
Washington, D.C. 20005

Dear Vic:

You are well aware of the importance to the Arthur Andersen Worldwide Organization of our MIC practice. As a result of recent meetings, we are more confident than ever of the future of this practice.

I advised you when we met on June 1 that the Firm is in the process of evaluating and implementing various changes to respond to current strategic plans. I also cautioned that any further steps by Saatchi & Saatchi before our implementation and evaluation of these changes was complete would be regarded as hostile or designed to disrupt the Firm's operations.

Your telex (of unspecified date) was not received until yesterday mid-afternoon but in time for the Boards of Partners to consider it before adjourning. The Boards (with everyone in attendance and after discussing your telex) unanimously agreed that neither the Firm, nor any practice segment, is for sale. You will recall this is the same personal view I had previously expressed to you.

I see no point in our having breakfast Wednesday morning but must advise you that the Firm will not react passively, particularly if information that is proprietary or confidential to the Firm is misused (whether by present or former partners or anyone else).

Sincerely,

Duane

KF



No Sale. Duane Kullberg's July 18, 1987, letter to Vic Millar, who had earlier joined Saatchi & Saatchi to build a consulting practice for the advertising firm, reiterating that neither Andersen nor its consulting practice was for sale.

Kullberg hadn't received it, so he asked that it be resent. The telex from Millar to Kullberg read, in part: "We have now completed our business expansion plan and would like to add the [Andersen] consulting practice as our flagship member firm. We have access to the financial resources needed to consummate a transaction of this magnitude. I am available at anytime for this purpose, including this weekend if the board were to choose to remain in session."

The board discussed Millar's telex, and Kullberg informed firm partners in a July 18 telex that board members "were incensed that an outside party with a competing commercial interest had apparent access to confidential (and possibly proprietary) information about the firm. This is particularly upsetting given Vic's trusted position when he was a senior partner of the firm. After discussion, the board unanimously resolved that our firm is not for sale, in whole or in part."

"I was on the board at the time and everyone was outraged," recalled Martin Vandersteen, one of the European practice directors and a board member. "It was unbelievable. Here he is, he has just left the firm and already he is making a play for the firm."

In a letter to Millar dated July 18, 1987, Kullberg communicated the board's decision. He added, in what would prove a prescient warning, that he "must advise you that the Firm will not react passively, particularly if information that is proprietary or confidential to the Firm is misused (whether by present or former partners or anyone else)."



### London Calling

Events already were overtaking Kullberg's and the rest of firm management's ability to control them by the summer of 1987. Or so it seemed, in light of the fact that Kullberg's note detailing Millar's interest in the consulting business actually was the second part of a July 18, 1987, telex. What could be more important than a former senior partner proposing to buy the most rapidly growing practice in the firm? In Kullberg's mind, at any rate (and perhaps suggesting the failure of the firm's auditor-dominated leadership to adequately focus on external competitive and client-service issues), it was the just-concluded, unprecedented meeting of key members of the consulting practice's leadership in London.

Peter Fuchs moved from New York to Chicago in October 1986 to head up strategic planning for the consulting practice, reporting directly to Si Moughamian. He and others immediately started preparing a strategic plan that would build upon the firmwide Williamsburg planning sessions. One of Fuchs' first duties in his new role was to attend a firm Executive Committee meeting on October 8.

Fuchs and the other planners had their work cut out for them. His analysis of the meeting in a note to Moughamian dated October 16 was discouraging. Despite years of hashing over the issue, "There is not necessarily any consensus among the members of the

Executive Committee regarding the whole area of MICD growth or scope of practice and its impact on our mix of service," Fuchs pointed out. "The paper that was presented...reads as though it was written from the perspective of the audit practice and thereby seeks to establish a series of principles which encourage the status quo and validate many conventional wisdoms."

Indeed, little progress had been made on dealing with the demands from the consultants for a greater say in firm affairs. A widely distributed planning document written in February 1986 by the highly respected audit partner Robert Mednick, head of the firm's professional standards group, asserted that, "After all, we continue to claim that auditing is the core of our business—the center from which everything else emanates." An indicator of the consulting leaders' mounting frustration with what they considered such backward-looking analysis appears in the margin of Vandersteen's copy of the February memo. A penciled-in response to Mednick's assertion about audit being at the core of the firm reads, "Who says?"

Cutting to one of the core concerns of the consultants—that auditors, with their control of the board, might act to hinder their growth—Fuchs advised Moughamian in October 1986, "It may be necessary to seek agreement that our intent to maintain leadership

The program (top) prepared for the July 6-10, 1987, Management Information Consulting Practice Directors' Meeting at London's Le Meridien Piccadilly Hotel (bottom).

[in all practice areas] does not require the audit practice to be any particular percent of our total business," Fuchs noted. "Nor will it be necessary to sacrifice one segment of our business for the benefit of another. If we can't reach agreement on this principle, or the two are deemed to be mutually exclusive at some point, then some alternative form of organization or relationship may be required."

The consulting leadership chose London as the site of their planning meeting, booking Le Meridien Piccadilly Hotel for July 6-10, 1987. In a document circulated to the consulting leadership a few weeks before the meeting, Fuchs laid out the path the consultants had taken to get to this point, giving credit to the other practices for their support of consulting during its infancy and detailing what was at stake:

> Our marketplace is undergoing what are perhaps the most drastic changes since the middle 1960s. It is quite likely that some of the strategies that have placed us where we are today will not be sufficient to assure our continuing success, or perhaps even our survival. Our focus must be on what we need to do to capitalize on the opportunities and respond to the challenges of a rapidly changing marketplace and increasingly aggressive competitors. We have a unique opportunity to deal from our current strength to position the firm as a dominant participant in the information services marketplace well into the 1990s.

Martin Vandersteen, head of the U.K. practice in the 1980s and European practice director in the 1980s and 1990s.

## A Call to Arms

Back-to-back days of presentations on every aspect of the consulting practice followed at the London meeting. Even many of the consulting leadership who thought of themselves as fairly well versed in the details of the practice were impressed with the scope of the business—and its potential. "Each one of the leaders of these individual task forces presented what the future would look like in their individual segment," recalled Jim Fischer, who later led the Technical Services Organization (TSO) and served as a member of the Executive Committee under Shaheen. "What will our future be like in Government, what will it be in Financial Services, Technology, Change Management, Strategy? And as you sat back, you got a vision of what this business was going to be like." Each group also detailed the expected investment, running into the hundreds of millions of dollars in total over several years, that they believed to be necessary to put—and keep—their practice in the competitive forefront.

It was obvious to the consulting leadership that to realize their practice's full potential they had to dramatically change their relationship to the audit and tax practices. As Martin Vandersteen recalled, "There is this sort of inner circle that said if we are going to achieve this, we have got to be able to be masters of our own destiny." Bob Prince added, "The London meeting was in a sense a call to arms, a call to the issue of where consultants' future in the firm was. What are we going to be allowed to do? How are we going to operate?"

The consulting leaders present at the meeting didn't hammer out a "declaration of independence." But there was clearly a demand for greater ability to operate and invest in their own business within the existing firm structure. A separate strategic business unit, or SBU, reporting up to senior firm management was the favored option of many at the meeting, according to Vandersteen.

Kullberg, the other senior management members, and the leaders of the audit and tax practices, were not invited to attend the meeting. Kullberg did have a representative there, Thomas B. Kelly, who reported back to him on a daily basis the nature of the discussions. Kullberg was concerned that the momentum from the London meeting might spin out of control. Already, rumors were flying around the entire firm about what the consultants were up to.

That momentum led Kullberg to address the London consulting meeting in his July 18 telex to all partners. Kullberg noted that organizational issues had been discussed at the London meeting, even though the agenda initially had been limited to a discussion of the needs of the consulting practice groups. "Various options were presented," Kullberg said, "but in summary the preferred choices would tend to develop an MICD organization outside of the office, area or country organization combined with other practices as now exists." The issue would be taken up at the board's August meeting, he said.



### Semi-independence

In August, firm management, while reasserting "retention of the 'one firm' concept as the overriding principle" of the organization, adopted several significant changes, mainly in response to pressure from the consultants. The most important was that "regionalization and the creation of national practice units for our Management Information Consulting Practice are to be implemented as appropriate to respond to market conditions." The biggest impact for the consulting practice was in the United States and Canada. Most other countries already were organized along such lines, although they still reported to an overall country managing partner who was, generally, an auditor.

Si Moughamian, global head of the consulting practice, declared in a memo to consulting partners that "the changes in organization and responsibility described in this memorandum are the most sweeping and far-reaching in our history." For the first time, the U.S. consulting practice would function along countrywide lines. It would be free of what many considered the tyranny of having to report to auditors acting as office managing partners, who were tempted to maximize short-term profits at the expense of long-term growth in the consulting practice. Others in consulting groused that because consulting still reported up through the overall country managing partner, audit partner Jim Edwards in the United States, the group leaders had settled for half a loaf, and could have pressed Kullberg and the rest of firm management for true independence. Clearly, however, the majority of consulting partners at the time took the restructuring as a cause for celebration. Moughamian added that further gains might be in the offing, stating, "The process of determining if it is feasible to establish a Member Firm [a separate legal entity in the United States] to serve the Consulting Division's U.S. clients is already under investigation."

Key to the reorganization was that Gresh Brebach, who had been head of consulting in New York, was named to the newly created post of managing partner-Consulting in the United States. Five new regional managing partners and a federal government services managing partner were also named, reporting to Brebach. They were:

| | |
|---|---|
| Northeast | Jon Conahan (New York) |
| Southeast | George Shaheen (Atlanta) |
| Central | Stan Cornelison (Chicago) |
| Southwest | John Kelly (Dallas) |
| West | Mike Noling (Los Angeles) |
| Federal Government Services | Tom Ross (Washington, D.C.) |

Industry marketing heads were named as well and considered national practice heads. They reported to the regional managing partners in whose regions their offices were located. The wide geographic dispersion of the industry heads underscored the extent to which consulting had become a truly nationwide practice in the United States by the mid-1980s. And the emerging importance of industry expertise eventually was to become the organizing principle for Andersen Consulting. The industry marketing heads were:



| | |
|---|---|
| Consumer Products | Glen Terbeek (Chicago) |
| Energy & Natural Resources | Winton Starling (Houston) |
| Financial Markets | Marc Sternfeld (New York) |
| Health Care | Jay Toole (Atlanta) |
| Industrial Products | Bill Stoddard (Hartford) |
| Insurance | Tom Skelly (Philadelphia) |
| State & Local Government | Dean Nichols (Sacramento) |
| Telecommunications | Alan Burgess (Atlanta) |
| Utilities | Thad Perry (Columbus) |

### Best Face Forward

The reluctant reorganization of the firm clearly was the major event of the year—if not the decade—to date. The firm's annual report for 1987 mentioned the organizational change somewhat obliquely in the traditional letter from CEO Kullberg. But that change was the obvious, if unspoken, motivation for the theme of the annual report—competition, both with rival firms and internally among partners.

The 1987 annual report represented Kullberg and firm management's attempt to bless the growth of the consulting practice and healthy internal competition, while offering a subtle warning that these trends could get out of hand and undermine the future of the firm.

The gatefold for the firm's 1987 annual report, which emphasized the importance of the growth of the consulting practice while maintaining the "one firm" concept.

The cover of the report was adorned with drawings and quotes from historic competitors ranging from Sun Tzu to Teddy Roosevelt to Vince Lombardi. In a section titled "The Heart of Our Culture," the report noted that early generations of partners succeeded because "they didn't compete only with other firms; they also competed with one another to be the very best." Left unmentioned was that personal rivalries between Arthur Andersen and his early senior partners were so intense that he died without a succession plan, which nearly doomed the partnership.

## "Let's Go"

Gresh Brebach definitely hailed from the Vince Lombardi school of leadership. He personified the gung-ho nature of the consulting practice during this period. A cigar-chomping, aggressive leader in his mid-40s, Brebach played pivotal roles in some of the most important client engagements of the previous decade in Chicago (including the Board of Education and the Illinois Bureau of Employment Security) and in New York, where he succeeded Reg Jones as head of consulting in 1984.

He was the star of the consulting practice, having also played key roles in developing successful software products, notably Base V and Lexicon. He surrounded himself with like-minded, hard-charging marketers for whom no job was too big or too challenging. These colleagues included Jim Fischer, Chuck Peterson and John Oltman from his days in Chicago, and Jon Conahan and Steve Zimmerman in New York. For those who didn't consider themselves Brebach insiders, however, he could be a polarizing, overbearing personality. Indeed, some partners claimed that Brebach's overreaching style would be his undoing at the firm in less than a year's time, and trigger the next management crisis.

Conahan recalled a moment in Brebach's office in the mid-1980s that highlighted his bulldozer approach to business. "Gresh had this plaque on his bookcase that to me captured the essence of his management style," Conahan noted. "It said, 'A good strategy violently executed is better than a perfect strategy that's too late.' And that was Gresh's style: Give me the rough idea, and if the peg doesn't quite fit, give me a bigger hammer. I told him one time, 'Gresh, let me just sum it up for you. What you're telling me is ready, fire, aim, right?' And he said, 'Yeah, that's it. Let's just go. Let's go.'"

Gresh Brebach, as pictured in the November 14, 1988, issue of *Forbes*. Brebach, head of consulting in the firm's New York office since 1984, was named head of U.S. consulting in 1987 as part of a firmwide reorganization.



Brebach's rise to the top of consulting in the United States during the mid-1980s wasn't a fluke. This was the era of megajobs. At the same time, the consultants chafed at having to explain their business to the audit management of the firm, even though their businesses were growing less and less alike. "We were flexing our muscles and feeling our oats then because we could take on really big engagements," Conahan recalled. "Some of them were scary to the traditional audit practice, because they were huge financial liabilities....It took a lot of confidence to say, okay, we can deliver that for $30 million. I mean, $30 million, the accountants are saying, 'My God, that's 60 audits! That's equal to the 60 biggest audits. What are you guys doing?' So we still had to go explain to somebody who wasn't in our business anymore, and the explaining was hard and took a lot of time."

The consultants' "special sauce"—a mixture of confidence, drive and the willingness to commit the resources needed to get the job done that had been talked about for a decade—was at its peak during this period. It was the result of intense, collective effort and was bigger than any one partner, no matter how important his or her role, or how important the consultant considered that role. "Anyone of us could have been gone, and this thing would have kept going just because of the power of the culture," Conahan said. "The collective group of partners was so good, so motivated that anything that any one of us felt like he got credit for, there are 10 other people that deserved at least as much or more individually."

Nor was such explosive growth confined to the major Chicago and New York offices. In some regional offices, such as Atlanta, the 1980s growth rate actually was faster than in either New York or Chicago. In a September 2, 1987, note concerning the management changes set in motion by the restructuring of the consulting practice, U.S. Country Managing Partner Jim Edwards noted that under Mike Hill's seven years of leadership, the Atlanta practice "has grown from 95 to 270 personnel, and profits have increased at a compounded growth rate of 39 percent. We now have the third most profitable consulting practice in the firm." Edwards praised Hill for "leading in the development of large, complex and challenging consulting engagements."

In fact, offices around the United States experienced burgeoning growth during this period. On the West Coast, the San Francisco office, under the leadership of George Shaheen and later Bill Van Lieshout and Ed Kennedy, began a period of rapid growth with such clients as Safeway, Visa and Kaiser Permanente. The Los Angeles office, under the direction of Mike Noling, who had recently relocated from Milwaukee, challenged San Francisco for West Coast dominance based on an expanding number of engagements in the aerospace and defense industry, the utility sector, and state and county governments.

Washington, D.C., became one of the largest consulting offices during this period. Following Vic Millar's return to Chicago, Bob Prince and later Larry Levitan led Washington's growth. They produced significant growth in the private sector with clients such as Marriott, MCI, Mars, DuPont and Mobil Oil, as well as a major engagement with Fannie Mae. Continued success in the U.S. federal government practice fueled the office's growth as well.

Among other offices, Dallas also rebounded smartly from the early 1980s oil and gas industry slump. With the untimely death of Dave Ewing, managing partner for the Dallas consulting practice, John Kelly transferred to Dallas from Detroit in 1986 and led a period of phenomenal growth with major clients such as GTE and Arco Petroleum. He was named head of the Americas region following the creation of Andersen Consulting in 1989. The Minneapolis office also grew dramatically in the second half of the 1980s based on new client relationships with General Mills and 3M; Kansas City expanded to serve Sprint; and Columbus grew with engagements for Nationwide Insurance, The Limited and Dayton Power & Light.



The same can-do spirit was being expressed by offices around the world as the consultants handled more megajobs. After earning a Ph.D. in botany, Gill Rider joined the London office in 1979. She worked on several large utility industry privatization engagements in the United Kingdom. "Whatever it was that the firm said we should do, we had the entrepreneurial spirit that would say, okay, we'll go sell that to a client and then we'll work at how to deliver it," Rider said of the firm in the late 1980s. "And by the way, we will. We'll have problems along the way, but we will deliver it." Rider became a partner in 1990 and later an Accenture Executive Leadership Team member and the company's chief leadership officer.

The U.K. practice responded to the 1980s business boom in several ways. In 1986 it started an unprecedented recruiting drive under Country Managing Partner Vernon Ellis. Starting with 350 professionals and 50 from other countries working on U.K. projects, Ellis and others attended 70 recruiting events and ended up recruiting more

**As country managing partner in the United Kingdom, Vernon Ellis spearheaded consulting's explosive growth in the 1980s, beginning with an unprecedented recruiting drive in 1986.**

than 150 new hires to position the practice to handle the wave of new business. Consulting fees grew at 50 percent a year in the United Kingdom and the other large European practices, and at an even faster clip in the smaller practices.

David Andrews led a cutting-edge development project at the time in the United Kingdom when he headed the creation of a Total Support Facility computer operations center in west London in the latter half of the 1980s, originally set up to handle outsourced systems for Swiss Bank. By 1989 other contracts had been added, the center's staff had grown to 82 and the project was generating annual revenues of $5 million.

### U.K. Privatization

In the late 1980s the United Kingdom began privatizing utilities, including both water and electrical utilities. The London office won several of the largest privatization contracts written during this unprecedented effort, including major systems engagements for North West Water, Thames Water and National Power, though the majority of the fees wouldn't accrue to the firm until the 1990s. According to Rider, hours of work went into understanding the needs of the utility executives and landing the North West Water engagement. "We put together a proposal that was the vision of the future," she recalled. "And it just completely agreed with the mind-set of the chief

Privatization of utilities in the United Kingdom in the 1980s created opportunities for engagements such as Thames Water.

executive at the time, Bob Thian, because he wanted to take what was a really excellent utility in terms of public service, but actually completely lacked investment in its people, its systems, and really didn't have a vision for what a utility should be in the public sector." As many as 400 personnel worked on the multiyear engagement.

The United Kingdom's Central Electricity Generating Board was split into three parts under privatization, with National Power being the largest of the newly formed companies. The utility engaged the London office to create a new information technology system, with the goal of empowering its local operations and staff to encourage employee initiative and for-profit business judgment. The consultants created a highly distributed computer system that allowed National Power's staff seamless access to their applications from a standard PC, wherever they happened to be in the country.

### Explosive Growth

By the second half of the 1980s, the consultants' biggest problem (once they looked beyond internal disputes) was staffing the rapidly growing number of consulting engagements. In May 1988, Brebach estimated that the U.S. consulting practice was 28 partners and 55 managers under plan, compared to the number needed to meet the requirements of the pyramid model. At the bottom of the personnel pyramid, the firm would add roughly 2,000 to the consulting practice in 1988.



And by the end of 1987, the Center for Professional Education in St. Charles provided a setting for 6.8 million hours of professional education, the majority directed to consultants, compared to just 4.2 million hours in 1983. In the second half of the 1980s, an expansion plan was under way at St. Charles, now under the direction of Dick Nerad. The plan brought the firm's total investment in the educational complex to roughly $140 million over 20 years. By any measure, the firm's commitment to professional education remained unchallenged in the consulting industry.

Vic Millar (second from left), Dick Nerad (second from right) and CEO Duane Kullberg (right) take the lead at groundbreaking ceremonies for the 1986 expansion of the Center for Professional Education campus at St. Charles.

Seven months into his new position, Brebach sent a glowing status report to all U.S. consulting partners. In the May 13, 1988, memo, he detailed how the U.S. practice was exceeding expectations, even compared to the robust growth of the previous few years, and despite the stock market crash of October 1987. Chargeable hours through March of that year were 12 percent over plan and 25 percent ahead of 1987's first quarter. Major new corporate and government clients the consultants had landed since the new reporting organization was put in place the previous fall, included Sears, AT&T, the U.S. Social Security Administration, Jet Propulsion Laboratories, Boeing, U.S. Sprint and MCI.

As for what was next, Brebach said the group's mission was "to become a dominant provider of professional services through aggressively increasing our market share and investing in our future." Its second goal was "to attract and nurture the best people through competitive salaries, effective recruiting and retention strategies, and challenging, long-term careers." He added, "These objectives cannot be achieved without our continued focus on long-term success rather than short-term profitability." Brebach's note to the consulting troops didn't suggest he felt the consultants had to rely on the auditors or tax partners to execute their plan. In early May, Brebach decided to hold a meeting of a select group of consulting leaders at Manhattan's '21' Club. As it turned out, that decision cost him his job.

Opposite page: The Center for Professional Education was expanded significantly with the addition of the Tower in 1986 and 1987 to accommodate the training needs of the rapidly growing firm.

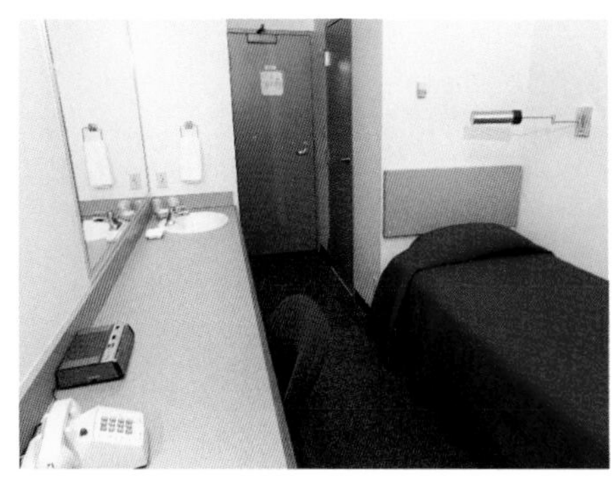

Left: During meal breaks at the Center for Professional Education, the multinational trainees gave the eating area the aura of a cafeteria at the United Nations.

Right: Individual quarters were relatively modest, encouraging trainees to socialize with their peers in the center's extensive public spaces.



Even as the consulting group was posting record-breaking results, one particular issue kept eating at them. Following the 1987 reorganization of the consulting management, the firm board passed a resolution in October 1987 that threatened to drive yet another wedge between the consultants and the rest of the firm. A handful of consultants had left to join Vic Millar, so the firm board approved what came to be known as the "bonding amendment." It stated that all partners had to sign an agreement that if they left the firm they couldn't be employed in a business that competed directly with the firm for three years. Many among the consulting leadership were outraged, arguing that the auditors in charge of the firm were trying to sharply limit the value of the consulting business and treat them as indentured servants. Many in the consulting leadership threatened to resign if the board took the bonding amendment to all the partners for a vote of approval, arguing that that was the only way they could avoid being bound by the terms of the amendment. Kullberg pulled his support of the bonding amendment after he and Larry Weinbach, chief operating officer of the firm, met with several consulting group leaders. But the episode left a bitter taste in the mouths of many consulting group leaders.

## Too Hot to Handle.

Duane Kullberg, though CEO of the combined organization, at times felt like little more than an observer as the consultants blazed new trails. Sometimes literally. Gresh Brebach suffered a serious fire at his Connecticut home in early 1988, though no one was hurt. A few months later, Peter Fuchs was en route to St. Charles to make a consulting strategy presentation to the firm's partners when his limo caught fire and had to be abandoned at a strip mall en route. When a somewhat flustered Fuchs explained the reason for his tardy arrival to Kullberg, his co-presenter on the video, the CEO looked at him with a hint of a smile and said, "Maybe the gods are trying to tell you guys something."

Larry Weinbach, chief operating officer of the firm at the time of the consultants' '21' Club meeting in 1988, would succeed Kullberg as firm CEO in January 1989.

### '21' Club

It was in the context of this just-concluded meeting with Kullberg and Weinbach that Brebach and about a dozen consulting group leaders met at Manhattan's '21' Club in the first week of May 1988. Such a gathering in and of itself was nothing new. But this time Brebach brought three outside lawyers with him to advise the consulting leadership of their legal rights in the event the firm's board of partners actually put the bonding amendment to a vote of all the partners. And Brebach prepared a one-page agenda for the meeting. "Gresh had a rough agenda," Conahan later noted. "We'd do agendas for everything. I mean, we didn't go to the john without an agenda, this place was so structured. And we had an agenda of things that were bothering us, and the bonding agreement was the cause célèbre."

It didn't take a legal scholar to conclude that the stakes had been raised in the on-again, off-again wrestling match between the consultants and firm leadership. Nevertheless, several of the consulting group leaders who were at the meeting noted that the lawyers said very little, and that the meeting didn't differ markedly from earlier "bitch sessions" at which consulting partners let off steam about firm leadership while enjoying each other's company.

The façade of New York's famous '21' Club restaurant, site of the consultants' May 1988 meeting that led to Gresh Brebach being stripped of his authority and his subsequent resignation.



Kullberg and Weinbach obtained a copy of the agenda. On May 17, The two met with Brebach in Weinbach's office in New York, and summarily relieved him of his duties as head of the U.S. consulting practice. Shortly thereafter, Brebach resigned from the firm. In Kullberg's view, Brebach had crossed the line and violated his responsibilities as a partner by preparing a plan to take a group of partners out of the firm. As managing partner and CEO, Kullberg felt it was his responsibility to take this action to protect the firm. It would have taken a vote of two-thirds of the firm partnership to remove Brebach as a partner.

The story of Brebach's ouster hit *The Wall Street Journal* on May 19 in an article written by Lee Berton, a *Journal* reporter and former accounting journal editor. Kullberg responded to the article with a telex to all partners:

> There is no single event that caused this decision. It was a series of circumstances over a period of time, culminating in a series of documents that were available at a meeting of a few of the MIC partners that essentially portrayed a plan, however contingent, to separate a part of the MIC practice from our firm. While it was reported to me that it was not a focal point of discussion, the mere existence of such a plan in its specific content brought me to the conclusion that [Brebach's] agenda for a segment of our organization was inconsistent with the overall objectives of the partnership.

THURSDAY, MAY 19, 1988

# Andersen's Chief Of Consulting Relieved of Role

## Brebach, a Partner, Denies That He Was Planning To Leave With Clients

By Lee Berton
*Staff Reporter of* The Wall Street Journal

NEW YORK—The partner who heads Arthur Andersen & Co.'s domestic consulting operation, the largest in the U.S., has been relieved of these duties for allegedly planning to leave the accounting firm and take the operation with him.

The partner, Gresham Brebach, confirmed in an interview that he had been relieved, but denied that he was trying to take away Andersen's consulting business. But he asserted that many of Andersen's consulting partners "have a major disagreement" with top management "over the strategic direction and philosophical approach" of the firm.

With consulting revenues rising at a faster pace than auditing and tax-practice

**Growth of Consulting Revenues Among Big Eight Accounting Firms**

**The big eight accounting firms are Arthur Andersen & Co., Peat Marwick, Ernst & Whinney, Coopers & Lybrand, Price Waterhouse, Arthur Young & Co., Deloitte Haskins & Sells, Touche Ross & Co.**

| | TOTAL U.S. CONSULTING REVENUE OF BIG EIGHT (In billions) | AS % OF TOTAL U.S. REVENUE OF BIG EIGHT |
|---|---|---|
| 1987 | $1.75 | 22.7% |
| 1986 | $1.46 | 19.5% |
| 1982* | $0.70 | 15.9% |

*Estimate  Source: *Consultants News*

This May 19, 1988, *Wall Street Journal* article broke the news of Brebach's demotion and highlighted tensions between the consultants and auditors at the firm.

Others among the consulting leadership who were at the '21' Club meeting, including Conahan and Shaheen, were shocked by the way Brebach had been treated. They hardly thought that the meeting was insurrectionist in nature, but at the same time they thought they might be the next to be demoted or fired. When Kullberg and Weinbach told Shaheen, who had only recently taken over as head of consulting in the southeast, they wanted to meet with him shortly after pushing Brebach aside, Shaheen thought that his career might be over. Instead, they offered him Brebach's position as head of the North America consulting practice. Kullberg and Weinbach didn't see Shaheen as being among the most aggressively divisive consulting leaders. After all, he had played no role in planning the London meeting.

Shaheen initially demurred. "I said, very simply, it's not clear to me that the consulting partners want me to be their leader," he recalled. "And I'm not going to step into those shoes unless I'm convinced that they want me to be their leader. After all, this is a partnership." He insisted that firm leadership poll consulting partners in the different regions to confirm that they supported him. When word came back from each region that Shaheen had their support, he agreed to take the post. At about the same time, Moughamian, whose role had been diluted to a large degree by Brebach's appointment as head of U.S. consulting, agreed to step down from his post as head of consulting firmwide. He was replaced by Stan Cornelison.

While Shaheen was well respected by the consulting partners, his promotion hardly quelled the sense of outrage that was widely felt among consultants over Brebach's removal. Most assumed that it was only a matter of weeks or months before Brebach joined Millar in some fashion to compete with the firm, and many were prepared to follow their leader wherever he chose to take them—something they would've considered unthinkable only days earlier. Conahan was among those ready to jump ship. He recalled shouting at Weinbach, whom he had considered a friend, during one meeting, "You've just blown it apart, Larry. Man, how could you do that unilaterally? You weren't even there. You could've at least come [to] ask somebody what happened [at the '21' Club dinner]."

Mel Bergstein, head of the Technical Services Organization in Chicago at the time, was outraged by the way Brebach was summarily demoted. Bergstein unloaded on Kullberg. What did he expect was going to happen? Bergstein asked Kullberg, after the auditor-controlled board had kept the consulting leadership out of the office managing partner position for so many years. The consultants were bound to rebel against their lack of representation in management at some point; it was a question of when, not if, Bergstein said.

### "You Better Have an Answer"

In what was probably the single-most important decision of his career, and the one that convinced most of the consulting leadership to at least stick with the firm for the next few months, Kullberg created a Change Management Task Force late that summer to find some solution to the audit-consultant conflict that would be mutually agreeable to a majority of partners. A crucial part of his decision, and one that would serve as a model for subsequent planning task forces, was to exclude existing senior management and choose members from the next layer of, presumably, future leaders. As Conahan, who was tapped to serve on the task force, recalled, Kullberg "picked six from the consulting practice, five from audit and four from tax. And so there were 16 of us, including Kullberg, and he said, 'You guys go get locked in a room.' It was September. 'We've got a board meeting and a partners' meeting in November. Don't come out until you've got an answer, but you better have an answer by the board meeting and the partners' meeting.'" Kullberg subsequently decided to push the partners' meeting back to January 1989, so that the partnership would have time to consider the task force's recommendations before voting.

| Change Management Task Force | |
|---|---|
| Jon Conahan (New York) | Consulting |
| Celso Giacometti (São Paulo) | Tax |
| Mike Hill (Chicago) | Consulting |
| John Jasper (Minneapolis) | Tax |
| Utomo Josodirdjo (Jakarta) | Tax |
| Alain Legendre (Paris) | Consulting |
| John Oltman (Chicago) | Consulting |
| Brian Peoples (New York) | Audit |
| David Phillips (San Francisco) | Audit |
| Joe Reichner (Philadelphia) | Audit |
| Marzio Saa (Milan) | Audit |
| John Skerritt (London) | Consulting |
| Jesse Tutor (Houston) | Consulting |
| Jose Luis Vazquez (Bilbao) | Audit |
| Barry Wallach (Chicago) | Tax |
| Duane Kullberg – Chairman | |



Shortly after Brebach left the firm, he made contact with Millar and Gene Delves (who had taken early retirement from the firm and joined Millar at Saatchi) about creating a new, stand-alone entity to replicate the Andersen consulting practice. They contacted key consulting partners and managers about joining their new firm. Shaheen and Cornelison both rebuffed such overtures in the weeks that followed, as did Conahan. Many consultants remembered this period as one of the darkest of their professional careers. It created rifts among former friends and associates that in some cases never healed. "I called Gresh," Conahan recalled. "We had dinner. I said, 'Gresh, you know I can't do it. These partners have asked me to do this job [on the Change

Management Task Force]. I feel like it's my responsibility, and I'm going to do it, and I can't do both.' And he said, 'Fine. I understand your logic. Thanks very much.' I have never seen him or spoken to him since. And I'd say he was one of my two or three best friends in the firm."

Rumors swirled in the following weeks that offers to follow Brebach were made to as many as 20 Andersen partners. None of this group took the bait, at least not initially. And that was in spite of the fact that Brebach was reportedly offering signing bonuses of up to $1 million.

The task force members spent months wrestling with governance and profit-sharing issues. Kullberg served primarily as a mediator, not an active participant taking sides on any particular issue. Members recalled an intensity driving their deliberations, a feeling that this was the firm's last, best chance to find a solution to the centrifugal force that seemed to be pulling apart their practices. They probed each other for compromises, while at the same time assuring members of their respective practices that they weren't giving away the store. A major recommendation of the Change Management Task Force was that the board be elected by representation, divided by practice and geography, to ensure that minorities would be represented and further reduce the U.S. audit dominance.

The new logo represented the consulting group's desire to boost its independent brand image.

### Andersen Consulting

Even while the task force was deliberating, Shaheen was charging ahead as the new leader of the North American consulting practice. One of his first efforts was to complete the name change initiative for the consulting group. For months, many senior consultants had argued a name change was imperative to boost the group's brand image in the marketplace. Shaheen took charge of the initiative and brought it to completion. The consultants kicked around various combinations of the terms *information*, *technology* and *consulting*, and reviewed market research data compiled by a Young & Rubicam team under the leadership of Jim Murphy, who was chairman and chief executive officer of Burson Marsteller, Americas (a Y & R unit), and later would lead the firm's Marketing & Communications organization. The consulting leadership eventually went with what many considered the simplest, most elegant solution: Andersen Consulting. A mid-October 1988 launch date was set for unveiling the new name and an unprecedented, at least among accounting firms, $10 million TV and print ad campaign to boost the new brand.

Unfortunately for the consultants' image mavens, the news of the name change and advertising campaign received second billing on the day of the planned launch. *The Wall Street Journal* and other papers led their October 17, 1988, coverage of the consulting practice with news that four consulting partners had decamped over the weekend to join Brebach in his much-anticipated new firm, Information Consulting Group. The new venture had financial backing from Millar at Saatchi & Saatchi.

## Four Consulting Partners Quit Andersen To Join New Venture Backed by Saatchi

By Lee Berton
Staff Reporter of The Wall Street Journal

"as far as this putting a crimp in our consulting practice, no way." He added that

The consultants' unveiling of their new identity as Andersen Consulting, scheduled for October 17, 1988, was somewhat dampened by published reports that same day of four consulting partners leaving the firm to join Information Consulting Group, former Andersen partner Gresh Brebach's rival venture.

As the Change Management Task Force reached the end of its deliberations, the participants agreed that they had to present a unified front to the partnership. Otherwise, their recommendations quickly would be picked apart and their months of deliberations would have been for naught. Nothing short of a unanimous vote by the group would suffice. "We said if we get there none of us can break, because we're going to get pressure from the board, we're going to get pressure from the Executive Committee, we're going to get pressure from the partners," Conahan said. "But once we go through all of this, if we come out of here united, then we're going to stay united."



## Professional Images.

For decades, professional ethics rules barred accountants from advertising. But accountants and other professionals such as lawyers dropped such bans in the late 1970s under pressure from the U.S. Federal Trade Commission and the U.S. Justice Department. Print ads for accounting firms initially appeared in 1978, but they were relatively few and far between. Arthur Andersen took a stab at a print ad campaign late that year, but it was shelved by the board, in part because it appeared to focus too directly on Managing Partner Harvey Kapnick. The $10 million 1988 campaign for Andersen Consulting, developed under the leadership of Jim Murphy, represented the firm's first real foray into advertising and set the tone for subsequent campaigns.

The group did, in fact, come out with some major recommendations. The first was that the practices be divided into two separate global business units, one for the Arthur Andersen audit and tax partners, and one for the Andersen Consulting partners. The Arthur Andersen & Co., Société Coopérative, in Geneva, Switzerland, would serve as a coordinating administrative framework for member firms around the world. The second was a worldwide board of partners, but with seats on the board to be allocated proportionately to the number of partners in each business unit. For the first time, Andersen Consulting partners were guaranteed proportionate representation that would grow as they grew relative to Arthur Andersen. Only the partners of Andersen Consulting would vote for their board representatives, as would Arthur Andersen partners for their board representatives. All major decisions that the board was authorized to make required a super majority vote of either the board members or all the partners. The consulting partners on the Change Management Task Force insisted on a provision: Even though the head of each new business unit would report to the CEO, the CEO could not remove the business unit heads from office without the approval of the elected board members from that business unit. This organizational design, a legacy of the Brebach affair, effectively bulletproofed the head of Andersen Consulting from being unilaterally removed. Equally important, this overall organizational design put the new Andersen Consulting on equal footing relative to Arthur Andersen.



One of the most important by-products of this recommended structure was little understood or appreciated at the time. The implementation of this recommendation by the Arthur Andersen & Co., S.C., legal group established separate legal entities (called member firms) for each business unit in every country where they did not already exist. This act effectively placed ownership of Andersen Consulting firms with the Andersen Consulting partners, separating the combined ownership of the member firms that historically had been controlled by the majority audit and tax partners. This separate ownership became a key foundation of Andersen Consulting's claim in the International Chamber of Commerce arbitration almost 10 years later. Arthur Andersen never fully understood the significance of this structure until the result of the arbitration was announced.

Another crucial recommendation was known as the "income model." Previously, earnings per partner in Andersen Consulting were much higher than in Arthur Andersen, although the earnings were not distributed in those proportions. The earnings recommendation provided that each business unit got to keep a lot more of its earnings for its own partners. The practical effect would be a big pay increase for the Andersen Consulting partners and a reduction for the Arthur Andersen partners, even though Andersen Consulting would continue to provide a significant subsidy to Arthur Andersen. No one really expected at the time that the subsidy, or "transfer payment" as it became known, would grow to $300 million by the end of the 1990s. Nor did anyone expect that the very success of Andersen Consulting would drive Arthur Andersen leadership into competition with Andersen Consulting in the consulting business.

After members of the task force and firm management made presentations to partners around the world to explain the recommendations, they were adopted at the Annual Partners' Meeting held in January 1989 at the Anatole Hotel in Dallas. The vote was a watershed event in the history of the partnership, recalled task force member Mike Hill. "The vote was more to keep the firm together under a revised organization, than it was a continuation of the past," he said.

# Andersen's Chief Will Step Down

## Move Is a Surprise; Partners Back Plan For 2 Separate Units

**By JULIA FLYNN SILER**

Special to The New York Times

**CHICAGO, Jan. 6 — In an unexpected move, Arthur Andersen & Company said today that Duane R. Kullberg would relinquish the title of term was scheduled to expire.**

**Andersen, the world's largest accounting and consulting firm, has been shaken by disputes between its accounting operations and its consulting side. A number of consulting partners have left in the last six months.**

**The firm said today that its partners had overwhelmingly approved a previously announced plan to revise its compensation system and restructure its business into two separate operating units.**

Above: The agenda for the Annual Partners' Meeting in Dallas, Texas, in January 1989 that led to the creation of the two separate firms, Andersen Consulting and Arthur Andersen (audit and tax), under the Arthur Andersen & Co., S.C., umbrella.

Left: *The New York Times* termed Kullberg's retirement announced at the Dallas meeting a surprise, but it was clear to many partners that he had lost his formerly widespread support as a result of the tumult at the firm.

Fallout from the Change Management Task Force and the firm's turbulent recent history went far beyond the group's specific recommendations. Sensing that he had lost the support of many board members as a result of the months of turmoil, Kullberg retired as CEO, even though he had two years remaining in his term. His consensus style of management had left him ill prepared to deal forcefully with many of the crises of the previous few years, many partners believed. At the same time, it was precisely this impulse to find a broad consensus that led him to create the Change Management Task Force, which many felt saved the firm as they knew it and enabled the creation of Andersen Consulting. Kullberg said later that he didn't think that either business unit was ready to go off on its own at that point—something with which many consulting partners at that time probably agreed.

The Anatole Hotel in Dallas, site of the historic January 1989 Annual Partners' Meeting.

Kullberg was succeeded by Larry Weinbach, who moved up from the COO post to the newly defined position of head of Arthur Andersen & Co., S.C. George Shaheen and Dick Measelle were named head of Andersen Consulting and Arthur Andersen, respectively. The agreements that led to the creation of the two separate businesses were referred to as the Dallas Accords. The consultants finally were united as a single global business unit (although local country partnerships would remain) with complete responsibility for shaping their business.



**The consulting leadership regrouped following the Annual Partners' Meeting in January 1989 to plan their future. While they had agitated for years to be masters of their own fate, they realized that they hadn't invested much time and effort in providing a basic business infrastructure. At the same time, they knew that their rivals hadn't been sitting on their hands while the Andersen Consulting partners were wrestling with their audit and tax peers. Millions of dollars would need to be invested in short order in hardware, software and training if the group was to make good on its plan to strengthen the firm's position as one of the dominant players in the information technology field.**

# 1989–1997

## The Consulting Firm of the Future

"Our mission essentially is to help our clients rethink and reshape their businesses as single, interconnected entities—not just collections of individual parts and processes. We embrace business integration because we want to be strategically relevant and offer our clients high-value solutions."

George Shaheen

# Merger Blues

While Andersen Consulting is expected to continue under that name, the name of the combined firm is more contentious.

Andersen loyalists are quick to note the advantages of the Andersen name when firms are listed alphabetically.

# 1989–1997
# The Consulting Firm of the Future



**The birth of Andersen Consulting as the 1980s drew to a close was a major breakthrough for the consultants, but further challenges lay ahead. The firm needed to create its own operating infrastructure at the same time as the world economy swooned in the early 1990s. As the global economy recovered, Andersen Consulting once again led the industry both in terms of operating performance and innovation, its success driven by concepts such as system integration and business process outsourcing. Success gave consultants the confidence they needed to continue their growth—and their need for full independence from Arthur Andersen's tax and audit partners.**

Chapter opening image: Andersen Consulting's highly effective ad campaigns of the 1990s, including the "Constellation" ad, helped the firm distinguish itself as a creative, innovative industry leader.

**Skip Battle had always considered his friend George Shaheen a tireless leader. But he didn't realize just how tireless until he worked closely with Shaheen in early 1989. Their task was to fashion a management structure and systems to operate the newly separated Andersen Consulting. "I said to Shaheen, 'I have got to sleep six hours,'" Battle recalled. "I said, 'You can have me until midnight, and we can start again at 6:30 a.m., but I can't do any more than that.'"**

George Shaheen led Andersen Consulting during one of the most dramatic periods of growth in the firm's history.

Shaheen, who was named to head the consulting practice by Larry Weinbach and ratified by the board of partners in April 1989, knew he didn't have any time to waste. The hard-driving 44-year-old was the consensus choice among the next generation of consulting leaders, and had been anticipating what steps the group should take next. But even he was stunned by the challenge facing Andersen Consulting. For professionals known as premier systems installers and integrators, they were sorely lacking in basic management experience of their own. "It hit me that we had no future if we couldn't manage our business, and we had no way to manage our business," Shaheen recalled. "We had no systems, we had no management structure, we had no process to make decisions."



Fashioning an organizational and management structure separate from Arthur Andersen was the first of many challenges that faced Shaheen and other consulting leaders on the eve of the 1990s. The economy and their consulting business, following Iraq's invasion of Kuwait in 1990 and the Gulf War that followed, was about to suffer through the toughest economic downturn since the 1973-74 recession. Even while structuring its own management and coping with the downturn, Andersen Consulting embarked on a series of planning and strategy sessions that reshaped the practice and set the course for dramatic growth once the economy rebounded in 1993. The group's Business Integration Model—combining strategy, people, process and technology—formed the basis for the next surge in growth. The newly created outsourcing business, which began in earnest with major engagements for Salomon Brothers in 1988 and British Petroleum's North Sea operations in 1990, further drove a dramatic increase in the consultants' operations, as well as providing an important new resource for clients.

Rapid growth, in turn, attracted increased competition in consulting from the newly separate Arthur Andersen audit and tax practice. That competition seriously eroded even the modicum of cooperation between the two business units that existed when they were created. By 1997, relations between the businesses had deteriorated after almost three years of failed negotiations to such an extent that the consultants felt they had no choice but to file an arbitration claim against their audit and tax sibling, and the Andersen Worldwide organization.

### Going Global

From observing how the firm leadership functioned during his early days as a partner, Shaheen vowed that he would do things differently if and when he had the chance. "It seemed like [the leadership] only talked to themselves," he noted. "I always said when it's my turn to run the firm, I'm going to be out and about."

To make the firm less "U.S.-centric" and embrace leadership from outside the U.S., Shaheen said, it was no longer realistic to ask people to move to a world headquarters. Instead, in May 1989, he named a 12-member Executive Committee to work with him to lead Andersen Consulting. Rather than congregate in one central headquarters, the committee, with members based in the United States, Europe and Asia Pacific, would meet six to eight times a year at locations around the world.

The step toward global management was a courageous one, given the sweeping organizational issues with which the consulting group was dealing at the time. The prudent thing would have been to put off the shift to global management until basic systems were fully in place and tested. But Shaheen and his management team insisted that beginning to put the practice on a global, industry basis over the next few years was as high a priority as any issue facing the business unit. The extent to which this global approach helped the consultants capitalize on the tremendous growth opportunities of the 1990s—for several years revenue growth in the smaller European and Asia Pacific business regions exceeded that of the Americas—was a testament to their wisdom. By the end of the decade, the consultants tried to balance local geographic and global industry management, but there was no question that the global focus had served the consultants well.



### Recession

The consulting business weathered a significant economic slowdown in the early 1990s, as it has at several points in its history. Consulting revenues increased at a 30 percent clip in 1989 as well as 1990, so the full impact of the recession that began in 1990 wasn't immediately apparent, at least in terms of the group's top-line growth. But there were signs of trouble brewing. While consulting revenue increased 30 percent in 1990 to $1.9 billion, revenue per partner grew by a more modest 10 percent to $2.6 million. Costs in many areas seemed to be out of control. For instance, Technical Services Organization (TSO) spending in fiscal 1989, mainly on software projects, was $5.7 million over budget, while revenues generated by the technology unit were $4.4 million below plan. To rein in technology spending, Shaheen installed Jim Fischer as head of TSO in 1989, a position he held until 1994.

During this period, client spending on technology declined around the world. Companies sought to absorb the capacity that they had acquired in the second half of the 1980s. IBM, which had boldly set a revenue target of $100 billion by the mid-1990s, started a decline that led to layoffs of tens of thousands of workers and took most of the next 10 years to reverse.

At Andersen Consulting, successive rounds of belt-tightening in all business lines helped keep costs under control until the global recovery began in earnest in 1993, led by the United States. But one consequence of the slowdown was that the leadership asked some partners who were admitted to the partnership during the booming late 1980s to leave Andersen Consulting. That, in turn, put pressure on Shaheen and his management team to demonstrate to the consulting partnership that they had a strategy for the newly created business unit, and weren't just focused on short-term cost controls.

### Saatchi Stumbles

As the Andersen Consulting partners were coming to grips with the management issues facing them, Vic Millar was having difficulty achieving his goals for the consulting division of Saatchi & Saatchi. In March 1989, Saatchi & Saatchi indicated that its pro forma operating results from consulting for the fiscal year ending that September would be lower than comparable results from the previous fiscal year. In press interviews Millar attributed the shortfall to greater-than-expected expenses from retooling existing consulting businesses and spending in anticipation of new business "a little before" it materialized. In addition, the Saatchi brothers had made a variety of investments that resulted in financial strains on the organization. The advertising firm said it was considering the sale of its consulting business, and Millar told *The Wall Street Journal* that he most likely would leave the firm. By mid-1989, as all lawsuits stemming from the defection of the consulting partners who had left to join Millar or Brebach were settled, Saatchi & Saatchi and Millar effectively fell off the Andersen Consulting radar as rivals.



### Business Integration

In the fall of 1989 key consulting partners met northwest of Chicago in Lincolnshire, Illinois, to hold their first strategy meeting as a separate business unit. Different groups of partners in different offices around the world had been wrestling with forming a new strategic approach for the consulting group for several years, as was apparent at the London meeting in July 1987. There was widespread concern that the consultants needed to expand their strategic approach beyond such an overwhelming reliance on the mainline technology systems business. But it wasn't until the Lincolnshire meeting that these different threads were brought together in the Business Integration Model.

## Price Waterhouse.

The consulting leadership was presented with a fresh challenge even while sorting out the basic organizational issues of running the day-to-day business. Arthur Andersen & Co., S.C., disclosed in early July 1989 that it and fellow Big Eight accounting firm Price Waterhouse were discussing a possible merger and had agreed to a 60-day period during which to decide whether the two firms could become one. Mergers were sweeping the accounting industry during this period as firms sought economies of scale in a slow-growth industry.

Many in the consulting industry predicted that one outcome of such a merger would likely be the spinning off of the combined consulting businesses of Andersen and Price Waterhouse. That would leave the merged accounting firms free to concentrate on their traditional audit and tax businesses. Andersen Consulting insiders were also confident that they, as the larger, more aggressive business unit, would dominate a combination that included Price Waterhouse's smaller consulting business. The merger talks were called off in late September, as the two parties could not reconcile differences in their partner retirement programs. Andersen Consulting partners speculated that the inability of the two firms to agree on who would run the combined accounting firm also contributed to the collapse of the talks.



# Price Waterhouse-Andersen Merger Blues

**By ALISON LEIGH COWAN**

**The accounting giants must still settle tough issues.**

With less than a month before the deadline for completing their proposed merger, Arthur Andersen and Price Waterhouse are still trying to iron out wrinkles in the plan to form the world's largest accounting firm, one with more than $5 billion in annual revenues.

On paper, the deal has much to commend it, many outsiders say. But thorny issues remain, including how to accommodate the strains between consultants and auditors, potential conflicts of interest involving important clients and even the delicate matter of choosing a new name. If the negotiators are not careful, fallout could haunt the combined firm for years to come.

"The question of who is going to run which office and who is going to be head of the various technical issues are difficult issues, as are seemingly simple things like the name of the firm, which can prove very emotional," said Donald J. Kirk, a Columbia Business School professor and former Price Waterhouse partner.

The battle for certain symbolic trophies has already become fierce. While Andersen Consulting is expected to continue under that name, the name of the combined firm is more contentious.

Andersen loyalists are quick to note the advantages of the Andersen name when firms are listed alphabetically. A former Price Waterhouse professional cited the subliminal marketing value of "price" in the name, for cost-conscious clients. Outsiders are betting on an acronym, like PWA.

Officials of the two firms declined to discuss the merger's prospects because of a confidentiality agreement they signed before beginning 60 days of formal talks on July 6.

But former partners, competitors

*Continued on Page D4*

An August 7, 1989, *New York Times* article notes the difficulties involved in potentially merging Arthur Andersen and Price Waterhouse. The exploratory merger talks were later called off.

Keith Burgess, who served as managing partner for the U.K. practice from mid-1989 through mid-1994, first articulated the business integration approach at the Lincolnshire meeting, according to many of his peers. "It was really the point where we collectively concluded that being a technology organization in its own right wasn't going to get business results and wasn't going to get us there," Burgess recalled. "We actually started saying we've got to take this larger view, essentially what we now know as business integration: strategy, people, process and technology. And all of those needed to be addressed to get business results."

Shaheen made certain that the partners did not view what came to be known as Lincolnshire I as an exercise in navel-gazing. They reasoned that as clients' needs became more complex in the 1990s, Andersen Consulting had an opportunity to redefine management consulting along lines that played to its multiple strengths. Traditional firms such as McKinsey and Boston Consulting Group were too narrowly focused, Shaheen argued. "At the time there was a tremendous opportunity, there was a changing of the guard in leadership in the consulting profession," he later said. "We decided we were going to take that mantle and we decided that we were going to redefine it on our terms. And we did. We wrestled it away from the traditional consulting firms. What they allowed us to do is redefine management consulting along the lines of our view of business integration."

This illustration of the Business Integration Model formulated at Lincolnshire I, became an Andersen Consulting icon for much of the 1990s. Reproduced endlessly within the company, it was an easily grasped and powerful statement of the combined expertise that only Andersen Consulting could deliver for clients.



Shaheen saw business integration as the latest evolutionary step in the consulting group's willingness to adapt to serve clients' needs. "Our mission essentially is to help our clients rethink and reshape their businesses as single, interconnected entities—not just collections of individual parts and processes," he declared in the Arthur Andersen Worldwide Organization 1990 Annual Report. "We embrace business integration because we want to be strategically relevant and offer our clients high-value solutions. We were the first to build systems for business use. We were the first to blend industry and technology skills to create a business perspective. And we are the first to recognize that companies need to move beyond systems integration and embrace business integration."

### Florida Accords

Less than a year after the formation of the separate Andersen business units, friction between the two groups led to a January 1990 meeting in Florida. Business unit management teams as well as those of the umbrella organization, Arthur Andersen & Co., S.C., attended. The meeting was called in response to repeated claims from consulting partners that audit partners engaged in consulting were violating the letter as well as the spirit of the Dallas Accords that embraced the recommendations of the Change Management Task Force and led to the creation of the separate businesses. Specifically, the consultants complained that the newly established audit and tax unit's Business

**The first issue of *Outlook*, Andersen Consulting's magazine for clients, 1990. The magazine, still published today, continues to focus on business issues and leading trends.**



Systems Consulting division, which was supposed to serve the consulting needs of small- to medium-sized audit clients with consolidated revenues of less than $175 million, was going beyond that arena to compete directly with Andersen Consulting for larger clients. The audit and tax partners, in turn, alleged that Andersen Consulting was ignoring their clients' consulting needs and wasn't cooperating on jointly servicing clients.

The Florida meeting resulted in the restatement of the principles behind the creation of the separate businesses in 1989, and pledges of greater cooperation from both business units. Shaheen and other consulting leaders continued to argue, however, that it was a mistake to have any consulting competition between the units, even if it might enable the audit and tax partners to drum up additional revenues on a short-term basis. Shaheen argued at the time, and again in a lengthy December 1991 memo to Arthur Andersen Worldwide Organization CEO Larry Weinbach, that the competition for consulting business was blurring the separate identities of the Andersen units in the minds of corporate clients. And he argued presciently that the ill will generated by the competition would only get worse and could eventually threaten the life of the combined firm.

## SEC Loosens Restrictions

In the spring of 1990, the chief accountant of the U.S. Securities and Exchange Commission (SEC) issued a landmark decision that had a significant impact on the consulting practice. He agreed in a "no-action letter" that Andersen Consulting could enter into certain types of business relationships with Arthur Andersen audit clients registered with the SEC, as long as those relationships were not material to either Andersen unit or the audit client. The SEC agreed that such relationships would be indirect and would not in themselves impair the audit unit's independence. The unprecedented ruling, which both the consulting and audit and tax sides of the firm had argued in favor of relentlessly, enabled Andersen Consulting in the United States to compete on more of a level playing field with rivals such as EDS, IBM and CSC—firms that weren't associated with a public accounting practice.

## BP Outsourcing Milestone

As the firm entered the 1990s, the emergence of outsourcing as a major area of growth quickly became apparent. Not that Andersen Consulting hadn't been involved in outsourcing efforts. Indeed, independent industry analysts The Yankee Group ranked Andersen Consulting third among U.S. outsourcing vendors in 1990. A project with the investment banking firm Salomon Brothers, an Arthur Andersen audit client, was the firm's first major outsourcing engagement.

The firm's work for British Petroleum set the standard for industry outsourcing solutions.

Engagement partner Joellin Comerford, who would later lead all of the company's outsourcing operations and serve on the Executive Leadership Team, recalled, "In the case of Salomon Brothers, they really needed to concentrate very scarce management skills in trying to recreate a new world, and they wanted someone to run their existing world, and the client said, 'I want you to outsource applications management.'"

The consultants also extended the number of their strategic alliances for bidding jointly with computer manufacturers on large outsourcing projects. Among the companies with which the consultants shared such alliances were IBM (a rival on consulting projects as well), Digital Equipment Corp., Tandem Computers and Amdahl Corp.

In 1990, the consultants inked a 10-year, $200 million systems management contract with Sun Refining and Marketing Co., purchasing its Dallas computer center and hiring its employees. The group also signed an agreement in the emerging Canadian market for systems management services, reaching a $50 million, five-year agreement with the Province of Alberta's Workers' Compensation Board and hiring 36 of its systems developers. However, the consultants didn't get a real taste for outsourcing's potential until the following year, when they unveiled a first-of-its-kind business process outsourcing (BPO) arrangement with British Petroleum (BP).

For years, London-based consulting partner Tim Forrest worked closely with Colin Goodall, BP's chief financial officer of upstream operations in the North Sea. So it wasn't a surprise to Forrest when Goodall made a lunch date at London's Savoy Hotel in July 1990. What was a surprise, bordering on shock, was Goodall's proposal. BP wasn't interested in Andersen Consulting advising them on how to make their North Sea back-office operations more efficient. With the price of a barrel of North Sea oil having plunged from $25 in the early 1980s to nearly $10, and with production costs having tripled during the same period, BP wanted a more radical solution. Goodall proposed that Andersen Consulting take over BP's entire North Sea finance and accounting function. Following a recent acquisition, BP had staff scattered across six separate locations. A year later, Andersen Consulting opened a new facility in Aberdeen, to which nearly 320 BP staff transferred.



At that time, and even today, the BP engagement was seen as leading industry outsourcing developments. Until this deal, business process outsourcing tended to be confined to such functions as payroll, cafeteria support, building services or IT functions. For the first time, a corporation proposed outsourcing an entire business-critical function to a third party. The BP engagement set the standard for outsourcing in the North Sea oil industry and ushered in several similar opportunities for leading North Sea oil producers. And as BP saw how much it was saving via the outsourcing engagement, it gradually increased the amount of outsourced services to total nearly $1 billion a year.

Senior executives from both BP and Andersen Consulting spent a year hammering out how the revolutionary arrangement would work. In addition to Goodall, the BP team was led by Alan Eilles, who became CFO of BP's downstream operations. The Andersen Consulting team was led by Forrest, Mark Otway and David Andrews in London, who developed a close relationship over the years with John Browne, later

Lord Browne, who at the time was running exploration and production for BP and would later serve as CEO. Ed Fikse, a senior partner in Dallas and the head of the Energy industry group, was another Andersen Consulting team leader.

### Rapid Results

BP services and productivity were stabilized within nine months. The staff, now part of Andersen Consulting, made rapid progress in transitioning from an internal BP support function to a client-focused service delivery team. The change of focus, combined with the ability to leverage the Andersen Consulting global resources and knowledge base, along with the deployment of an SAP system, led to a greater than 50 percent reduction in costs for BP. That superior performance led to contract renewals in 1994, 1999 and 2005. Within a few years Andersen Consulting also attracted several other North Sea oil industry clients anxious to pare their costs as well, including Talisman U.K., Conoco U.K., Elf/Total, Lasmo and Britannia Operator. By the end of the decade Andersen Consulting would handle 40 percent of the North Sea oil industry's back-office functions.

Larissa Koudeleva, accounts assistant, and Mubbasher Khanzada, junior systems engineer, at the Accenture multiclient outsourcing center in, Aberdeen, Scotland, 2001.

The Aberdeen engagement demonstrated that Andersen Consulting's outsourcing ability was second to none. BP was so enthusiastic that it expanded outsourcing to include U.S. operations, beginning in 1995 with 60 people in Houston providing accounting and financing services to its downstream business in the United States. Over the following decade, that business grew tenfold to include 600 personnel and integrated processes from BP's acquisitions of Amoco and Arco. Alan Eilles, BP's CFO for downstream operations, noted that this outsourcing relationship "has broadened over the years from what was essentially a financial transaction around accounting outsourcing to now encompass everything from systems and technology to e-business, logistics and supply, and most recently, our retail business."

Joellin Comerford would eventually lead all of the firm's outsourcing operations.

Comerford pointed out that the tremendous outsourcing success flowed from the dramatic shift in firm strategy as the consultants embraced business integration. "Our skills and strength lie in trying to understand what a client's competitive positioning is, helping them improve it, and helping them run big, complex change," she noted. "When we started with the notion of business integration—which was all about helping clients recognize what they needed to do to be successful and the things they had to change—then our business process management business emerged as an engine for helping them change."

The U.K. practice launched another significant engagement in the early 1990s when the London Stock Exchange brought in Andersen Consulting to revamp the trading and information systems that had been cobbled together in anticipation of the deregulatory "big bang" of 1986 in the U.K. securities markets. Under the leadership of Vernon Ellis, David Andrews and Cherine Chalaby, among others,

## Building a New Order.

Following the collapse of the Berlin Wall and communist dictatorships in the Soviet Union and much of Central Europe beginning in 1989, Andersen Consulting quickly established itself as the leading Western consulting firm operating in the region. Led by partner Les Bergman, who was based in Vienna, and supported by the U.K., German, Italian and Spanish practices, consultants lined up major engagements in the key finance, manufacturing and transportation sectors. Clients included Komercni Banka in Prague, where consultants introduced concepts such as identifying bad loans and credit analysis to the Hungarian State Railways and Poland's Bank of Pekao. The Moscow City Council retained the firm to work with 50 large bakeries that were having trouble

**Kneading Advice. Keith Burgess, managing partner for the U.K. practice from mid-1989 through mid-1994, visiting a Moscow baker as part of an engagement with the Moscow city council to advise dozens of local bakeries on distribution logistics.**

distributing bread in the capital. Work on the project was delayed for a few months as a result of a coup in the fall of 1991. As *Crain's Chicago Business* noted in its December 9, 1991, issue, "In the politically unstable and risky Central European market, the Chicago-based consulting firm has managed to snag eight large contracts in former Eastern bloc countries over the past two years." Capturing the sense of exhaustion and exhilaration that accompanied such pioneering work, Vernon Ellis summed up the firm's early efforts in Central Europe in the November-December 1991 issue of *Dialogue*, the firm's internal publication: "The work is often frustrating, the working conditions are awful, the change management issues form an enormous challenge—but the rewards of building a new order are satisfying indeed."

Andersen Consulting entered into an innovative five-year business transformation outsourcing arrangement with the London Stock Exchange. The money saved from rationalizing staffing and systems architecture paid for a state-of-the-art trading system. The London Stock Exchange has remained a consulting and outsourcing client through several subsequent changes in its management and major contract renewals.

Trading Technology. Monitoring markets at the London Stock Exchange.



### Strategic Horizons

A group of consulting partners involved in strategic planning gathered in the fall of 1991 at the historic Coronado Hotel, just outside San Diego. That meeting became known as Lincolnshire II, reflecting that in important ways it was a continuation of the 1989 discussion in Lincolnshire that led to the formulation of the Business Integration Model. Many of the partners at Lincolnshire II were concerned that the partnership's long-term interests were being ignored as the leadership coped with shorter-term business and management issues. In many ways, they were tested by an economic downturn similar to the downturns that broadsided the consulting practice about once a decade. While no two downturns are alike, Andersen Consulting leaders were learning important lessons about surviving and investing for the future. They discussed the need to agree on a vision to ensure that their guiding values and beliefs, based around the Business Integration Model, were included in a strategy for the future.

That meeting set in motion a yearlong strategic planning process that came to be known as Horizon 2000. One goal was to get as many of the partners as possible to buy into the Business Integration Model and feel they had a stake in the consulting group's direction. Shortly before the San Diego meeting, Shaheen named Jon Conahan chief strategy officer. Conahan, assisted by Skip Battle and Jim Fischer, led a

## Global Management Council.

As part of its increasingly global focus, the firm formed its first Global Management Council in 1992 to ensure that Andersen Consulting leadership was focusing on global issues. In 1993, the Council included (from left to right):

First row: Bob Anclien, Steve Zimmer, Bob Prince, Al Burgess, Steve James, Charlie Paulk, George Shaheen, Skip Battle, Masakatsu Mori, Martin Vandersteen, Diego Visconti, John Gullo, Jesse Tutor, Baker McAdams

Second row: Larry Levitan, John Kelly, Alain Legendre, Jim Fischer, Mike Hill, Bob Manion, Doug Ryckman, Vernon Ellis, Peter Fuchs, Pedro Navarro, Miguel Tobio, George Hill, Tom McCarty

Third row: Dave Rey, Jon Conahan, Keith Burgess, Jack Wilson, Leroy "Pete" Peterson, Don Monoco, Stan Cornelison, John Skerritt, Mike McGrath, Gerard Van Kemmel, Brian Wilson, Thad Perry, Chuck Winslow

Executive Committee members Skip Battle (left) and Jim Fischer.

process of drawing out and categorizing the partners' concerns. They came up with 14 strategic categories, such as training and growth, and then named a team of partners from each global region—the Americas, Europe, Asia Pacific—to each category, which they dubbed paradigms. By the 1992 Annual Partners' Meeting, as many as 225 partners from around the world participated in the process. As Martin Vandersteen recalled, the process "promoted an enormous feeling of teamwork, because rank-and-file partners were pulled in from all over the world. The younger, the better, because it was their future we were talking about." Some of the future leaders who played a prominent role in Horizon 2000 were Mike McGrath, Joel Friedman, Jim Fischer, John Skerritt, Keith Burgess, Larry Gan, Gill Rider and Joellin Comerford.

The central theme that came out of the Horizon 2000 process was the consensus that the consultants had survived the industry shakeout of the early 1990s—now it was time to execute a breakaway strategy to leave the rest of the consulting pack behind. To do that they agreed on three major points: To deliver on the promise of business integration; to recognize that knowledge capital was the future of the firm and build a knowledge exchange; and to reignite the growth engines of Andersen Consulting. On the issue of growth, the partners sought balanced growth, emphasizing four specific growth targets: income per partner, number of partners, margin per employee and investment per partner.

### On a Mission with a Vision

As part of the Horizon 2000 process, Shaheen directed his leadership team to address the creation of mission and vision statements for Andersen Consulting that would capture much of the new strategic direction in a few simple phrases. Shaheen had an inspirational moment one evening in Boston. "I was by myself in a restaurant," he said, "and I remember seeing this older, heavyset businessman and saying to myself, 'What would I say if he asked me what our firm does? I'd probably tell him that our firm helps our clients to be better.' So I said to myself, that's a pretty good mission statement—to help our clients become better." He bounced the idea off of Jon Conahan, and Conahan talked with U.K.-based Vernon Ellis, area managing partner of Europe, Middle East, Africa and India (EMEAI). After a few more rounds back and forth they agreed on the following mission statement: "To help our clients change to be more successful."

The genesis of the firm's vision statement followed a similar route. Conahan refined some initial phrasing from Shaheen, who had been asked during a leadership meeting for his vision of the firm. While not quite as pithy as the mission statement, the vision statement helped drive the Horizon 2000 strategy throughout the organization. And it was a particular favorite of Shaheen's. Senior partners recall Shaheen



## A Strategy by Any Other Name.

Shaheen and Conahan met in St. Charles in the fall of 1992 to present the design of the yearlong strategic planning effort to a group of partners. There was just one problem. They didn't have a name for the strategy development process. Shaheen was convinced that they had to have a name that would give partners something to remember; simply calling it "the strategy project" wasn't going to stick in anyone's mind for long. "I was in the limo coming out to St. Charles and I'm staring out the window," Conahan recalled. "I'm saying to myself, 'What am I going to tell George to call it?' I found myself staring at these flat cornfields going way out to the horizon. I said, 'That's it, the horizon.' I needed something more, so 2000 was an easy subscript. I told George Horizon 2000 and he thought about it for about two seconds and said, 'Great. Let's do it.' And he stood up there five minutes later and said it as if we had been working on it for five years."

## Core Values.

The consulting practice had been guided by a fairly consistent set of values and beliefs, many drawn from principles laid down by Arthur Andersen himself, since its founding. By the time of the Lincolnshire II meeting and the Horizon 2000 strategic planning process, the consulting leadership felt it was important to spell out these values that "form the foundation that supports our mission and vision," as George Shaheen said.

Coming out of the Horizon 2000 process, the consultants committed themselves to six core values: Quality Client Service, One Global Firm, Integrity, Stewardship, Best People and Respect for the Individual. Nearly a decade later, when the firm was in the process of moving to public ownership, it would recommit itself to its core values, which had changed little, despite the enormous changes the company went through in the interim: Client Value Creation, One Global Network, Integrity, Stewardship, Best People and Respect for the Individual.



expecting them to be able to recite the following vision statement on command: "One global firm committed to quality by having the best people with knowledge capital, partnering with the best clients to deliver value."

### Operational Excellence

Even as the firm was forming and executing its latest strategic objectives, on the operational side it was going from strength to strength coming out of the early 1990s recession. And it showed: Consulting revenues jumped from about $1 billion at the time Andersen Consulting was formed to $5 billion by 1996. Shaheen always had been known for his operating prowess as he rose through the organization, and as CEO he drove a relentless focus on client service.

From 1989 through the mid-1990s, the firm maintained its traditional geographic focus, with operations following national boundaries. The operating units reported to the three area managing partners: John Kelly in the Americas, Vernon Ellis in EMEAI and Tom McCarty in Asia Pacific. They worked closely with Shaheen in allocating resources and making related decisions to fuel the rapid-fire growth during this period. In 1994, in an effort to spark higher growth rates and to be more effective in sharing skills across the Continent, Ellis instituted a regional organization in Europe. Jim Fischer moved from the United States to lead the Maritime region (the United Kingdom and Scandinavian countries), David Andrews led the West Europe region and Pedro Navarro was in charge of South Europe. As part of this reorganization Keith Burgess, who had been responsible for consulting in the U.K., took global responsibility for all of the competencies (Strategy, Change Management, Process and Technology) and Business Process Management (BPM). Bob Prince and Carol Meyer worked closely with Shaheen on human resources matters during this period, while Mike Hill implemented firmwide financial controls and maintained a sense of operational rigor.

Leaders of the Asian Dynasty helped focus firm attention on the growth potential in the Asia Pacific region.

Beginning in August 1995 in the United States, and over the next two years around the world, the firm began to adopt an industry-focused organizational structure. This shift acknowledged what many of the firm's largest clients already were experiencing—leading businesses increasingly were operating on a global basis, and they needed consulting and related services delivered accordingly. As John Kelly recalled, "I sat in front of major clients with worldwide operations, and basically they couldn't understand that we hadn't been operating that way all along. That if you were serving DuPont, the people serving DuPont out of Wilmington, Delaware, should be able to manage the account relationship and provide client service on a consistent basis around the globe."

Shaheen identified the telecommunications industry, one of the fastest-growing global industries, as the first that the firm would treat on a global basis. Larry Levitan was asked to lead this group, thereby becoming the first global industry managing partner. As Fischer related at the time, the telecommunications industry is "'global in itself. It is not part of any of the areas—they've taken all the clients in telecommunications, they've put them in one industry segment, and said go out and make money.'" Fischer added that the goal of the shift to an industry focus was to "help ensure that we can make the firm truly global and have virtually no limit to its size and what it accomplishes."

The transition to a full global industry organization in 1997 also brought a new group of partners into senior leadership roles. Jack Wilson was put in charge of the industry groups, while Fischer assumed responsibility for the vast majority of personnel and competencies, and Keith Burgess was put in charge of global outsourcing. Those with geographic responsibilities also retained their responsibilities and were key members of Shaheen's senior management team.

### Asian Dynasty

The Horizon 2000 strategy incorporated input from teams in all three global regions—the Americas, EMEAI and Asia Pacific. But it was easiest to implement in the more established practices of the Americas and EMEAI, which had the longest track record of major business integration engagements. To stimulate growth in Asia, especially in light of the 1990 bursting of the speculative "bubble" economy in Japan, the consulting group leadership reasoned that a more regional identity specifically geared at Asia was needed.

Just as the partners funded growth of the European practice more than 25 years earlier, the leadership agreed to a multiyear plan. Dubbed Asian Dynasty, it took the themes of Horizon 2000 and built on them as the basis for a quantum leap in growth. Tom McCarty (head of the Asia Pacific region at the time), Brian Wilson (who had run the consulting practices in both Australia and Southeast Asia) and other regional leaders met in Bangkok in 1993 to formulate the basis for Asian Dynasty. "The idea was, let's try to go after a much higher growth rate for Asia Pacific to make that a larger part of the practice, recognizing the future of Asia as being a very big part of the world economy," Wilson recalled. "And so we set off with this goal to increase our growth rate. That became Asian Dynasty. Asian Dynasty was the first time [Andersen Consulting] really invested in a geographical initiative, in Asia Pacific in this instance, to achieve a higher growth rate."

McCarty asked Wilson if he would be willing to lead the Asian Dynasty project. Wilson quickly realized that if the region was going to achieve significantly higher growth, Andersen Consulting needed to focus on China, the emerging growth engine for the region. "I began looking at what was required to really grow in Asia and quickly recognized that the place we were underrepresented and missing an opportunity was in the greater China region," he said. "And so I moved to Hong Kong in 1993 and began again what I'd been through twice before, in Southeast Asia and in Australia, to build a practice." The growing importance of the region and China to the world economy—and to the consultants—underscored the wisdom of the partnership's investment in Asia in the early 1990s.



### Software, Hard Lessons

To truly capitalize on the growth opportunities of the 1990s, the consultants first had to confront a problem that had been brewing for years. From its pioneering years writing systems software programs for the UNIVAC I computer at General Electric, the consulting group had been in the software business. Within a few years, enterprising consultants were packaging software, such as FIN-PAC and MAC-PAC, developed for one client or groups of clients and selling it to others. Later, they sold FOUNDATION, based on METHOD/1 and early versions of automated tools.

But for almost as long, key partners warned that focusing on software was a mistake waiting to happen. The consultants were in the business of advising clients and implementing the best solutions to their problems. Selling software as a stand-alone offering might create a conflict if some consultants wanted to sell the firm's software, while others thought the best solution was to use software from another vendor. In addition, the consultants didn't have necessary depth of experience developing and maintaining software packages as a real business. Software was something the firm backed into and built into a success, but it wasn't a core competency.

## Putting Principles into Practice.

By the early 1990s, a growing number of partners worried that the firm was becoming "too corporate." At the 1993 Annual Partners' Meeting in London, discussions were held on what it meant to be an Andersen Consulting partner. In a follow-up memo, Shaheen singled out five younger partners—Benoit Genuini, John Craven, Tom Fox, Joel Friedman and Gill Rider—as facilitators, who "shared our vision of the partnership." A Partnership Success Steering Committee, including those five and partners Jane Hemstritch and Ann Jones, was formed to develop the ideas expressed at the London meeting. Shaheen served as chairman.

After several meetings, the committee developed the following Partnership Principles: mutual respect, performance commitment, stewardship, interdependence, honesty and integrity, social responsibility, and shared rewards. To put these principles into practice, the committee also championed an Empowerment Credo by which the partners could fully harness the power of being both owners and operators:

> Trust each other to make intelligent decisions and communicate openly when we don't.
>
> Expect each individual partner to take responsibility to check his/her judgment with appropriate individuals.
>
> Design decision-making processes to be value-added, simple and nonhierarchical.
>
> Each partner has the responsibility to step forward and correct that which is not working in this way.

The principles and the credo would serve as a common touchstone for the partners as they wrestled with divisive governance and growth issues in the years ahead.

At the same time, a new generation of software vendors had emerged, including SAP, PeopleSoft, Oracle and, a few years later, Siebel Systems. They were creating a new type of enterprise software with which the consultants would find it difficult to compete. Within a few years, the firm embraced the more effective strategy of becoming highly knowledgeable implementers of the new software offerings and creating alliances with the key players.

One of the greatest software challenges the firm faced involved MAC-PAC/D, a version of the group's popular MAC-PAC software targeting the defense industry. The software turned out to be riddled with software bugs that resisted fixing. The consultants—true to their core value of delivering quality client service—were forced to spend roughly $75 million over two years to stabilize the product and eventually withdraw it from the marketplace.

The U.K. financial services group led a major customer relationship management (CRM) project at Barclays, one of the largest banks in the United Kingdom.

Shaheen asked Mike Bass to solve the problem. Bass did so, but the cost, at a time when the firm was still being buffeted by the recession, surprised nearly everyone. "Mike was given an unlimited check to solve the problem and he exceeded it," Shaheen would later note with a chuckle. But he underscored how important Bass' software fix was to the firm. Shaheen added, "To his credit, [Bass] assured me that he could get it done, and we listened to him. And without a lot of day-to-day supervision and without a lot of detailed direction setting, Bass stepped up to that and hit that one over the outfield wall for us. Without that, I don't know what could have come out of the woodwork at the firm."



If they had refused to fix the problem, the consultants could have faced a bevy of lawsuits, not to mention a crippling blow to their reputation. The MAC-PAC/D experience convinced Shaheen and the rest of leadership that the consultants should exit the application software business and leave the field to true software companies. By the mid-1990s, Andersen Consulting had accomplished this objective.

Shaheen managed to find a silver lining in the software debacle. "That gave me a lot of confidence as a leader that I had an organization that could respond to the tough situations that were right for our clients, right for our firm and right for our partners," he said. "Although this situation was quite expensive."

### Spending Recovers

Corporate spending on business integration projects was beginning to rebound by 1993-1994. Companies increasingly were embracing major software applications from the likes of SAP to help solve their enterprisewide needs for streamlined operations and greater productivity. Andersen Consulting revenues jumped from about $1 billion when the separate business unit was formed to $5 billion by the end of 1996, largely as a result of the firm's market-leading role in implementing business integration strategies based on these complex software applications.

## The Virtual Water Cooler.

Sharing knowledge freely among professionals has been a value of the consulting practice dating back at least to the Subject Files created by Leonard Spacek in the 1940s. Indeed, it was preached and practiced by founder Arthur Andersen. By the 1990s, with consultants taking an increasingly global focus, firm leadership recognized consultants had to communicate and share knowledge seamlessly as the size and scope of the practice evolved. "Knowledge capital is our most valuable asset and it drives our organization," Shaheen said. "It's what we sell, and what we must continue to protect and perfect. Our people should diligently find new ways to share and reuse information and deploy it around the world."

In 1993 the firm launched its Knowledge Xchange, an outgrowth of the Horizon 2000 initiative that enabled personnel to share information globally using personal computers and Lotus Notes—at that time cutting-edge technology. Millions of pages of information eventually would be included in the shared databases. The initiative was led by Charlie Paulk, who had been named the firm's first chief information officer the previous year.

**The Knowledge Xchange enabled the global sharing of information within Andersen Consulting, continuing a tradition dating back at least to John Higgins' first Subject File in 1953.**



Giant enterprise resource planning (ERP) and customer relationship management (CRM) projects drove much of the growth for the balance of the decade. At Barclays, one of the United Kingdom's largest banks, the firm installed the most advanced CRM system available at the time. It was also one of the largest client/server implementations of the era. In fact, Andersen Consulting became the largest installer of Siebel CRM systems in the world. It also led the industry in SAP installations during this period. And that was even before the tidal wave of systems business driven by fears that the millennium, Y2K, would wreak havoc with older legacy software systems that wouldn't be able to make the transition from 1999 to 2000.

### Innovative Image Campaign

Andersen Consulting single-handedly created the professional services advertising category beginning with its 1989 ad campaign, and it did so with eye-catching style and attitude. Jim Murphy was determined to counter the ho-hum image that dogged much of the consulting industry. Murphy and Young & Rubicam, Andersen Consulting's advertising agency, had their job cut out for them. A sampling of *FORTUNE* 500 executives had described the firm in 1987 market research sessions as "stodgy," "inflexible" and "old-fashioned," despite its success. While most rivals still focused their marketing efforts on trade shows and client brochures, Andersen Consulting formally launched its new brand with a New Year's Eve television ad. Advanced computer graphics depicted a future New Year's in 2000. A voiceover predicted:

> One night, not too many years from now, some companies will have cause for celebration. They'll be the ones who used information and technology not merely as a way to compute, but as a way to compete. Andersen Consulting would like to help you be one of them.

The reaction among clients and competitors was electric. The TV ads, followed by a print campaign, turned conventional wisdom about consulting firms on its head. One early print ad, titled "Map," depicted a reconfigured map of the United States with the headline, "Sometimes success requires a little reorganization." The ad copy pointed to information technology as a way to transcend the restrictions imposed by geography.

The ad campaign reinforced Andersen Consulting's image as the creative, innovative industry leader, and in its first year accounted for fully 50 percent of all professional services advertising. Rivals stepped up their own image advertising over the next few years, but none had the same impact or wry, stereotype-shattering effect of the Andersen Consulting campaign.



By 1994, the firm boasted a globally integrated advertising program. Ads appeared in 18 countries, up from only five the year before. Senior executive awareness, which the firm carefully tracked from the first days of planning its image campaign, soared on a global basis to 79 percent by the beginning of 1994, from just 32 percent in 1990. Clients were describing the firm as "creative and innovative," "visionary" and a "leader."

### Outsourcing Gathers Steam

The consultants continued adding to their roster of outsourcing clients as the decade progressed. In June 1997, the group signed its largest business process management job to date—a 10-year, $500 million-plus engagement with DuPont. The engagement included the transition of about 500 DuPont employees into Andersen Consulting. Earlier that year, the firm began an engagement with another global chemical industry leader, Dow Chemical, to form a global alliance to develop and support all software applications globally. By the end of the decade, the alliance included 350 Andersen Consulting personnel and 200 from Dow.

Also in 1996, the consulting group announced a multiyear, multimillion dollar contract that foreshadowed what would become an increasingly common practice in the outsourcing world: design/build/run. The engagement called for Andersen Consulting to design, build and then maintain business information systems for Texas Instruments. Andersen Consulting developed client/server software for use in key business processes, and ultimately integrated and maintained

**Opposite page, top: One of the most memorable of the early Andersen Consulting ads featured a "reorganized" map of the United States.**

**Opposite page, bottom: Andersen Consulting single-handedly created the professional services advertising category beginning with its 1989 ad campaign to establish the firm as a technology and consulting leader.**

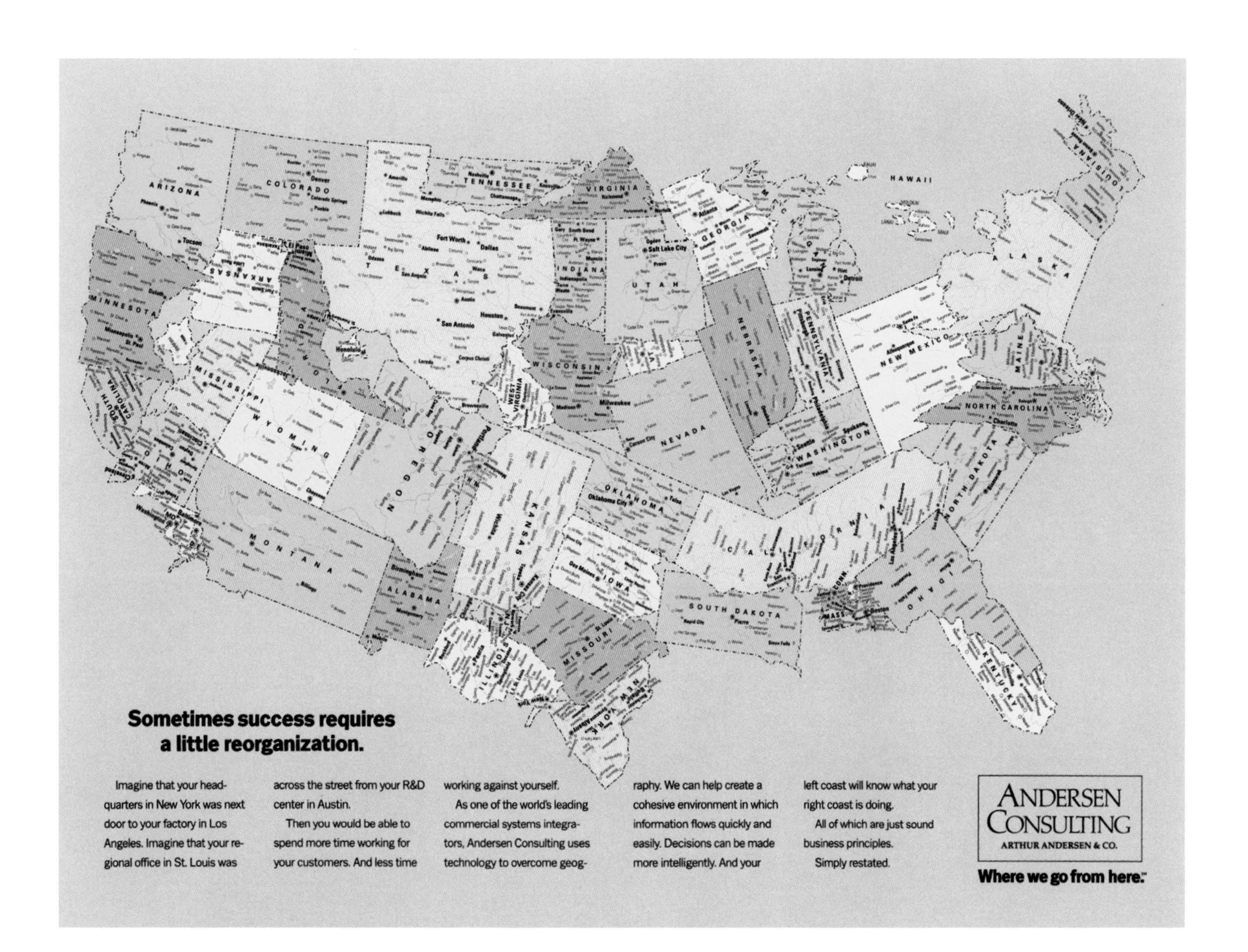

A

B

**We sell straight lines.**

These days, companies are being forced to draw the line.

Frustrated by mounting competitive pressures and nagging productivity concerns, they are reexamining their fundamental business approaches.

They are realizing that information technology can shorten the distance between themselves and their goals.

And Andersen Consulting is helping them connect the dots.

By combining business intelligence and technological command, Andersen Consulting can offer strategic solutions that help drive a company forward.

And that's not just some promising theory. Our techniques have already tangibly improved company performance in industry after industry.

At Andersen Consulting, it's what we call thinking straight.

**Where we go from here.™**

# Just don't expect it to roar.

These days, organizations are seeking to become swifter and more ferocious.

But superficial changes are unlikely to produce results. Especially when information technology is part of the plan.

Which is why Andersen Consulting helps companies link technology to the heart of their business. Their strategies, business processes and human resources.

Because today, winning often means transforming the organization. Not just hopping on a technological bandwagon.

their client/server systems. About 250 TI employees transferred to Andersen Consulting as part of the engagement. And as Shaheen told TI's partners in a January 1997 note announcing the agreement, "Our compensation will be tied directly to delivering measurable results and achieving specific service levels during the five years."

Strategy and Change Management practices around the world expanded existing engagements and added scores of new global clients during the mid-to-late 1990s. In the United Kingdom, the relationship with the Department of Social Security (formerly known as Department of Health and Social Security) was extended beginning in 1993 into major new change management work reforming welfare benefits and the national insurance system. By the end of the decade, the firm agreed to provide ongoing services to the Department of Social Security in a collaborative effort with Fujitsu/ICL and Microsoft. Also in the United Kingdom, a four-year engagement with the London Stock Exchange reached a climax in August 1996 when electronic trading was conducted for the first time on an entirely new system.

In the United States, longtime client Harley-Davidson officially unplugged its last mainframe computer in 1995 as part of a conversion to client/server computing. While the firm worked with Harley-Davidson on more than 100 projects, the motorcycle maker boosted its big-bike market share to 60 percent by the late 1990s, from 30 percent in the early 1980s.

In 1994, Accenture helped Malaysia Kuala Lumpur Options & Financial Futures Exchange (KLOFFE) set up the exchange infrastructure for trading. The technology platform chosen by KLOFFE was the Deutsche Terminbörse exchange trading and clearing system. The project was executed on a fast track approach over a 14-month period with KLOFFE launching the exchange in December 1995. And in Latin America, consultants from 15 countries worked together in Argentina in 1993 to assist in the privatization of YPF, S.A., Argentina's giant oil and gas company. It became one of the largest public offerings in the history of the New York Stock Exchange.

### Government Practice Problems

An exception to the consulting business boom of the mid-to-late 1990s was the government practice. While it wasn't widely known at the time, in 1997 the consulting leadership came close to getting out of government work while reorganizing the practice along global lines. A handful of engagements had difficulty in the previous few years, and the government practice was losing money at the time, recalled Steve Rohleder. Rohleder was named to head the U.S. federal government practice in 1997, and later would be named global government head and then chief operating officer.

Opposite page: Andersen Consulting's 1992 ad campaign included the "Tiger Bunny" ad, highlighting the firm's ability to create transformational change for its clients.

Top: Major corporate clients, such as DuPont, turned to Andersen Consulting during the 1990s for strategic advice and continue to maintain close working relationships with the company.

Bottom: Members of the Andersen Consulting team on the U.K. Department of Social Security project, 1995. The team created a new way to gather and store information about the insurance contributions and benefit entitlements for every U.K. citizen. Standing, left to right: Kurt Moreby, Sean Prince, Faith Guest, Mark Goodyear and Simon England. Seated: Amanda Miller, Kate Weatherly and Doug Stoddard.

David Hunter was group chief executive for the global Government operating group and later was named senior partner for strategic programs.

Shaheen challenged the leadership team of the government practice, led by David Hunter, to demonstrate why the firm should continue that part of the business. It was a galvanizing moment for the government practice. In 1997, Hunter assembled his leadership team, including Rohleder, Marty Cole and Kevin Dixon, in their first global meeting in Sydney, Australia. Hunter made it clear that they had two years tops to prove themselves. "The feeling around that table was, look guys, we have one or two years to prove the firm wrong," Rohleder recalled. "It was really a catalyst to pull that team together. I really view that as a launching point to where we are today [in the government practice]."

With a renewed focus on bold decision making coupled with disciplined execution, the group had its first score with a U.S. Postal Service contract in 1997, followed by U.S. Department of Defense contracts in 1998 and 1999. The true turning point came in 2000 with a $390 million, multiyear contract with the Defense Logistics Agency that later was extended and increased in scope.

### Spanish Revolt

With consultants around the world encouraged to repeat Shaheen's vision statement as often as possible, the firm evolved more of an industry, and less of a geographic, bias during the 1990s. However, national and regional identities remained important. Spain was a case in point. A crisis erupted in Spain in 1990 as the country managing partner resisted attempts to knit the highly successful Spanish practice more closely into the context of the broader European, and global, consulting practices. By 1990, Vernon Ellis, in charge of the European practice, was negotiating terms of the country managing partner's resignation when that partner launched a surprise bid to take over the Spanish practice and run it as a separate entity.

The country managing partner had nearly lined up a majority of the ownership of the Spanish practice to back him, when Ellis and several senior partners in Madrid convinced other partners that they were

José Luis Manzanares (left) and the Coritel executive committee, 1991. Manzanares served as the managing partner for Coritel, Spain's Technology Solutions unit, from 1990 through 1997.

being misled into believing the takeover was a fait accompli. Managers in the practice also lined up against the country managing partner, arguing that they had joined the international consulting firm of Andersen Consulting, not a Spanish practice. Despite lawsuits and countersuits that would drag on for months, the country managing partner was replaced by Pedro Navarro, a senior partner in Barcelona at the time.

With Navarro in charge, the Spanish practice grew at an accelerated rate in the 1990s, benefiting from the firm's established position as the leading consultant in Spain with deep ties to the country's banking and manufacturing sectors. The consulting practice also expanded heavily into telecommunications and other sectors as Spain's rate of economic growth quickened in the 1990s. As Spanish banks and telecom companies expanded in Latin America, so did demand for the firm's expertise and solutions. The shift in Europe in the second half of the decade to a more regional focus, joining Italy, Spain and Portugal in the southern Europe region, accelerated demand for the Spanish practice's expertise, especially in financial services. Indeed, by the end of the decade, financial services software and solutions developed by the Spanish practice were being used in client engagements around the world. In addition to Navarro, senior partners who led the expansion of the Spanish practice during this period included Carlos Vidal, José Luis Manzanares, Basilio Rueda and Raúl Alvarado (who, though based in the United States, twice worked in Spain for extended periods during the 1980s and 1990s).

Top: Pedro Navarro was country managing partner for Spain in the 1990s.

Bottom: Mike McGrath led the Italy practice in 1990 and later became the company's CFO.

### Italian Renaissance

An equally important leadership transition went more smoothly in Italy. The Italian practice had grown rapidly during the 1980s under the leadership of Bruno Ricca, but not in terms of profitability. Ricca stepped down in 1989 and was replaced by Mike McGrath, who had been head of the St. Louis office. He stayed until 1991 when Diego Visconti, an Italian partner with expertise in the banking sector, stepped up to run the country practice.

France, the United Kingdom and then Spain had taken turns leading Europe's growth during the previous two decades. In the 1990s it was Italy's turn. Visconti, who later led the global Communications & High Tech operating group, launched a program called Italian Renaissance. Building on changes instituted by McGrath, it brought discipline to the Italian practice. It was, according to Visconti, "pretty important for really transforming the Italian practice into a much more disciplined type of an organization leveraging the Italian creativity, entrepreneurial spirit and so on, but also putting together some more of a disciplined approach."

Visconti put a renewed emphasis on broadening relationships with longtime Italian clients such as Fiat. The Italian practice helped Fiat capture knowledge, document processes and package best practices to build a global business model by 1998. With the help of Marco Vigorelli, Visconti also worked with several of the nation's largest banks. He broadened the practice's reach into other major sectors of the Italian economy, including communications, with a multiyear engagement with Telecom Italia led by engagement partner Michele Liberato.

### European Reorganization

Vernon Ellis facilitated globalization in 1994 by reorganizing Europe into three major regions—Maritime, West Europe and South Europe—and a smaller region, Central Europe. The controversial move sharply reduced the authority of individual country managing partners at a time when national identities were still deeply entrenched in many offices. The Harvard Business School conducted a case study on the reorganization in 1995, and a follow-up study in 1998. While the reorganization irritated some partners, it ultimately contributed to the doubling of European consulting revenue—to $2.1 billion—by 1998.

"Profitability and growth, though higher than in the U.S., were both falling badly," Ellis recalled of that era. "This was partly due to market conditions, but I used the financial challenges as a 'burning platform' and argued that Europe, as a collection of varying-sized, varying-quality insular country practices, was suboptimal. We had to get critical mass and sharing of skills across borders at a higher level."



## Culture Clash.

Long-standing cultural differences in Europe and Asia also presented occasional hurdles on the path toward globalization. Such differences lessened dramatically by the end of the decade as more partners relocated within regions and more clients adopted English as the global language of business. Nevertheless, during the early 1990s the firm extensively used training specialists to discuss cultural awareness as well as the behaviors and sensibilities of different nationalities.

George Shaheen and Vernon Ellis were meeting with veteran consultant Chris Van Aalst in the early 1990s to discuss who would succeed him as country managing partner for the Netherlands. The fact that there was no clear local candidate made the choice more difficult than usual. "How about Spanish?" asked Shaheen. "Oh no," Van Aalst replied. "They would be totally unacceptable." Shaheen, taken aback, asked, "But why?" After a pause Van Aalst answered, "Well, you know how the Spanish once ruled the Netherlands." Shaheen said, "When?" The answer: "About 400 years ago."

## Conflicts Come to a Head

As in earlier periods of strong economic growth, increased global revenues during the mid-1990s tended to paper over intramural tensions between the consulting and audit and tax sides of the practice. But this time, things were different. The audit and tax leaders were making a concerted effort to expand their scope of practice to compensate for the slow growth in their traditional businesses. And consulting was squarely in their sights.

One of the first serious fissures occurred in late 1994, when the audit and tax practice combined two service lines into a unit called Arthur Andersen Business Consulting. Contrary to the spirit and intent of the Florida Accords, the new unit pursued services that were strikingly similar to the technology expertise, strategic planning and business transformation services offered by Andersen Consulting. In January 1995 and again in September, leaders of the two groups met to iron out their differences, but each time their talks ended in stalemate.

The consultants' sense of outrage was further stoked in 1996 by a series of rapidly unfolding events. In May, Arthur Andersen's consulting business opened a technology park that bore a striking resemblance to Andersen Consulting's own Technology Parks and Business Integration Centers. Shaheen related to his partners that Andersen Worldwide CEO Larry Weinbach, who was supposed to be

The Executive Committee in 1994 on the steps of the firm's Palo Alto office, which served as a showcase for firm efforts in cutting-edge technologies during the 1990s. First row: Tom McCarty, Jim Murphy, Carol Meyer, George Shaheen and Ann Jones. Second row: Jack Wilson, Vernon Ellis, Jon Conahan, Bob Prince and Charlie Paulk. Third row: Keith Burgess, Mike McGrath, John Kelly and Mike Hill.

enforcing the agreements between the two units, upon learning of the auditor's technology park, said he was "shocked." (Note: In 1995, Andersen Worldwide was introduced as the new name for the global coordinating entity, previously known as Arthur Andersen & Co., S.C.)

In July 1996, Arthur Andersen CEO Dick Measelle stated his intentions to encroach on Andersen Consulting turf when he wrote to his audit and tax partners that, "The three critical, immutable interests of Arthur

Andersen that I have identified throughout this process [are] to pursue unconstrained growth, to provide consulting services, either directly or indirectly to all markets, and to have the technology we need to compete." An Arthur Andersen ad that ran several times in a Silicon Valley magazine in 1996 even appeared to co-opt the consultants' heritage. The ad copy read, "Arthur Andersen's commitment to high technology goes back to 1954. That's the year we installed the first electronic computer-based information system used in a business application."

Adding insult to injury was the fact that Andersen Consulting, under the terms of the 1989 separation, paid close to $282 million to Arthur Andersen from 1990 through 1996. The consultants estimated that, based on trends at the time, the consultants would pay an additional $1 billion to the audit and tax partners during the next five years. As unfair as the payments might have seemed to the consultants, Shaheen noted, in light of Arthur Andersen's consulting forays, "These numbers raise an even greater question: Are we financing a competitor? We should either provide the payment to Arthur Andersen or engage in competition, but not both."

### Booming Growth

Driving the size of the payment, of course, was that the consulting business in the late 1990s was experiencing the most explosive growth it had ever seen. Corporate clients around the world were racing to upgrade or replace legacy computer systems so that they could handle the transition to the year 2000. The biggest problem for the consultants was staffing engagements, not drumming up clients. At the same time, the advent of the Internet and corresponding growth of e-commerce were driving fundamental changes in the way companies did business, and creating a new industry led by Amazon.com and eBay. Clients flocked to consultants for help in designing and implementing online strategies to complement and interact with their existing operations. From 1994 through 1998, Andersen Consulting revenues soared to $8.3 billion from $3.4 billion, and personnel more than doubled to 65,000 from 32,000.

Despite the record revenue and profits, many among the consulting leadership felt as if they were involved in a slow-motion train wreck with Arthur Andersen, and it was too late to get off. Throughout much of 1996 and into early 1997, leaders from both the consulting business and audit and tax business met repeatedly in a process known as Andersen 21. Once again, different proposals were put forward to try to resolve the impasse between the businesses. But with each meeting the leaders of the business units seemed to get more entrenched. Andersen Worldwide CEO Weinbach tried to come up with a "third way" to resolve the deadlock by breaking up and reshuffling the units, and giving himself more authority in the process. Both sides rejected his proposal, which he took as a vote of no confidence. Weinbach let it be known in early 1997 that he would not run for reelection at the next partners' meeting. Increasing acrimony between the leadership groups set the stage for the Andersen Worldwide Annual Partners' Meeting in Paris in April 1997.

The 1997 Annual Partners' Meeting, held in Paris, became increasingly polarized as the consulting and audit partners butted heads over who would be the firm's next leader.

### Paris Meeting

As the partners convened in Paris, at the top of everyone's agenda was the question: Who would replace Weinbach? A flurry of firmwide e-mails sent in the weeks preceding the meeting indicated that a growing number of the audit partners might favor Shaheen. The audit and tax leadership scrambled to dampen any pro-Shaheen sentiment, but their actions seemed to have the opposite effect. Audit partners were impressed with Shaheen's clear sense of vision. And who could argue with 25 percent increases in annual revenues for the previous four years?

A nominating commission formally recommended two CEO candidates to the board: Shaheen and Jim Wadia, tax partner and lawyer by training who was head of the Arthur Andersen practice in the United Kingdom. The bylaws of Andersen Worldwide required that they nominate at least two candidates for the board to consider. Reflecting the broad sentiment among the partners, which had surfaced in a straw poll of all partners in which 69 percent favored Shaheen, the commission then said that they preferred Shaheen, even though their mandate was to simply propose two candidates. The board couldn't agree on a candidate, even though it was controlled by audit and tax partners. The partners' meeting ended after both Shaheen and Wadia had made presentations to the partners.

Over the weekend, a glimmer of hope appeared for Shaheen to get the board's support to run Andersen Worldwide. On Saturday, he met with Weinbach and Wadia, and the three came to a verbal agreement: Weinbach and Wadia would support Shaheen as the candidate to be CEO of Andersen Worldwide if Shaheen in turn would support Wadia as head of Arthur Andersen, replacing Dick Measelle, who would retire. Shaheen met Conahan in his hotel on Saturday and told him the good news. But early Sunday morning, Conahan got a call from a furious Shaheen. Wadia had reneged. The deal was off. Only days later, Shaheen and Conahan learned that the reason Wadia reneged was that the U.S. Arthur Andersen partners on the board refused to back Wadia on the deal.

The board met again to try and get the two-thirds majority required to recommend a candidate to the partners. Wadia supporters could muster only 16 of the required 17 votes that would give him the support of two-thirds of the 25-person board. Weinbach previously stated that, as a board member, he would never cast the deciding vote if the vote was along business unit lines. However, he finally relented and voted in favor of Wadia, making him the board's official candidate.

In an unprecedented rejection of the board's recommendation, the partners, more than 60 percent of whom were still audit and tax partners, gave Wadia barely 51 percent of the vote, far short of the two-thirds majority needed to win the post of CEO of Andersen Worldwide. Shaheen's name, representing the only other candidate presented to the board, was then put before the partners. He received more than 60 percent of the vote, but fell roughly 100 votes shy of the required two-thirds majority.

The board met once again and eventually appointed Bob Grafton as interim CEO, adjourning without a plan to field another candidate for the CEO post. Shaheen thought he had suffered a defeat, but he would concede that it was probably the best possible result for himself, and for Andersen Consulting, given the unbridgeable gulf between the consulting and audit and tax practices. "The Paris partners' meeting was a seminal event in the beginning of the end, because we had nowhere to go," Shaheen recalled. "There was not a reasonableness in the mix anymore."

Jon Conahan was tapped by Shaheen to lead the planning for the eventual arbitration filing in December 1997.



### Arbitration

In the weeks leading up to the Paris partners' meeting, Shaheen directed Conahan to immerse himself in the reams of pages comprising the Andersen Worldwide and Andersen Consulting legal documents. His goal was to see what leverage—if any—the consultants might have over the audit and tax unit, or Andersen Worldwide, if they couldn't work out their differences. Shaheen insisted that the only way the consultants would prevail would be to stick to the terms of the interfirm agreements.

Shaheen and Conahan determined, and lawyers from the New York law firm of Simpson, Thacher & Bartlett, which had been retained earlier by the consultants, agreed that their best option would be to seek international arbitration to settle their differences with the accountants, as allowed for in the interfirm agreements. They further decided to hold firm and demand a single arbitrator, as described in the interfirm agreements. Shaheen and Conahan agreed to keep their arbitration strategy to themselves at the time, rather than tip the other parties about what might be a legal strategy worth pursuing.

The Simpson, Thacher team confirmed that, contrary to the conventional wisdom among Andersen Worldwide and Arthur Andersen partners, the firm was not owned "jointly and severally" by all the partners as a group. Instead, the attorneys pointed out to the consulting leadership, the consultants in each country owned their own practice, and the accountants owned theirs, based on the ownership structure insisted upon by the Andersen Worldwide management following from the Dallas Accords in 1989. This insight would be disputed by the accountants and Andersen Worldwide, but eventually upheld in arbitration.

Following Shaheen's defeat, he and Conahan focused on the details of arbitration, all the while keeping their interest secret from all but a handful of consulting leaders. That summer, half-hearted attempts at yet another compromise between the business units were made by the board of Andersen Worldwide, but they went nowhere. Meantime, the Simpson, Thacher attorneys proposed running mock arbitrations, always in secret but with real arbitrators, to learn how the process worked and to try out different strategies. One of the attractions of the arbitration process was that, according to Simpson, Thacher, arbitration was likely to last about two years, compared to an estimated five to six years if the partners sought to fight it out in court. Most important, a decision by an International Chamber of Commerce (ICC) arbitrator was final and could not be appealed in any court in the world.

That fall, Shaheen announced to the Andersen Worldwide board that he was calling an unprecedented meeting of only the consulting partners for December in San Francisco. The Arthur Andersen board members at first said that Shaheen couldn't hold such a meeting. Shaheen, his voice dripping with sarcasm, said that technically it wasn't a meeting of consulting partners, it was a meeting of his 1,000 closest friends. Shaheen wasn't revealing the agenda for the meeting, only saying that the partners were going to discuss the deadlocked state of affairs at the firm. Jim Wadia then demanded that he be allowed to address the consulting partners. Shaheen and Conahan initially resisted the idea, but the more they realized what a polarizing effect Wadia was likely to have, the more inclined they were to invite him to speak.

San Francisco, site of the unprecedented meeting of the consulting partners in December 1997.

Jim Wadia appeared confident that he could talk some sense into the consulting partners as he mounted the stage at the San Francisco Hilton & Towers on the morning of December 15, 1997. He used the opportunity to present a summation of the dispute between the consultants and their fellow partners. In his opinion, there really wasn't any basis for a dispute. The consulting practice belonged to all the partners of Andersen Worldwide, and that was that. Auditors earlier had bandied about figures as high as $15 billion as the price they would have to be paid over several years by the consultants in order to leave Andersen Worldwide. Wadia reiterated that the firm had supported the consulting practice for decades, although he granted that lately it had been on a tear.

Shaheen and Conahan were incredulous. Wadia had done much of their job for them. They were just that day about to brief the Andersen Consulting partners on the strategy of ICC arbitration they had developed over the previous six months. Now Wadia made it clear that the audit leadership was never going to compromise. The two had hoped for a unanimous vote, but would have settled for a very significant majority of the partners voting in favor of arbitration. After Conahan and other leadership partners went over the ramifications of filing for arbitration, how the International Court of Arbitration worked, the leadership's thinking on the subject and other options they had considered, the issue was put to a vote of the partnership on December 16. The vote, held by secret ballot via a computer system, was unanimous in favor of arbitration. The 150-page claim against Arthur Andersen and Andersen Worldwide was filed the next morning in Paris with the International Chamber of Commerce Court of Arbitration, without any warning given to either Arthur Andersen or Andersen Worldwide. As Shaheen was unable reach him, Bob Grafton, the interim CEO of Andersen Worldwide, learned about the arbitration filing when he picked up *The Wall Street Journal* in O'Hare International Airport.

### Terra Incognita

With that December vote, the consulting partners embarked on a new phase in their careers and the life of the firm. Their lawyers couldn't assure them of any particular outcome. There were few, if any, road maps to follow. Disputes that could involve billions of dollars changing hands were rare for the ICC. What made the case truly unprecedented was the number of parties involved. The multiparty arbitration involved more that 40 Andersen Consulting firms from 36 countries and more than 90 Arthur Andersen firms from 57 countries.

The consulting partners showed tremendous faith in their leadership, and the strength of their partnership, in voting for arbitration. They were determined to be masters of their own fate and not sacrifice what they felt was the potential of the consulting business to avoid what they were convinced was unfair interference in their affairs. Few could have imagined then that the path toward arbitration would also lead them to the equally radical step of converting to public ownership within a few years.



**Of more immediate concern, however, was the charge Shaheen gave them before they left the meeting: Leave the arbitration process to the leadership team. The partners' job was to keep Andersen Consulting operating as the world's premier consulting firm. And that is just what happened. Andersen Consulting generated record revenues and income up to the millennium. And Shaheen, Conahan and the lawyers, with the advice of the board members and Shaheen's leadership team, drove the arbitration process.**

# 1997–2001

## Becoming Accenture

accenture
NYSE
The world puts its stock in us.
Now it gets interesting.}
ACN
LISTED
NYSE
NYC
accenture
accent

"We continue to stare change in the face every day and continue to challenge ourselves with, 'What do we have to do to remain relevant to our clients?'"

Joe Forehand

# 1997-2001
# Becoming Accenture



**The late 1990s witnessed a surge of entrepreneurial risk-taking unleashed by the growth of the Internet. Andersen Consulting pursued its entrepreneurial destiny as well by filing, and winning, an arbitration case against Andersen Worldwide. The fully independent firm established its own identity with the adoption of its new name, Accenture, and a successful IPO, despite the bursting of the dot-com bubble. The company adjusted to new realities brought on by economic recession and the war on terror.**

Chapter opening image: Accenture's listing of its stock on the New York Stock Exchange on July 19, 2001, was a cause for celebration.

## Jon Conahan felt like a high diver whose feet had just left the platform. After Andersen Consulting's mid-December 1997 arbitration filing against Arthur Andersen and Andersen Worldwide, there was no going back. All he could do was execute the arbitration strategy that he and CEO George Shaheen had worked out with the consultants' legal team at Simpson, Thacher & Bartlett.

Shaheen, Conahan and the rest of the consulting partners had no way of knowing that they had just embarked on the most intensive four-year period of career- and life-changing events in the firm's history. Even before the arbitration case was resolved, in 1999 the firm would lose its high-profile CEO of 10 years to an e-commerce startup. Despite the unexpected departure, the consultants promptly tapped a new CEO in a nearly seamless leadership transition. Then, as part of the arbitration award in 2000, the consultants were required to stop using any form of "Andersen" in their name by the end of the year. That forced the firm into a flurry of rebranding itself as Accenture in a little over four months and at a cost of nearly $200 million.

The firm refreshed its brand in 1998 with the debut of its "A to the Power of C" logo. The logo retained the letters AC of Andersen Consulting, but raised the "c" as an exponential notation to convey a sense of energy and high-tech savvy.

With the ink barely dry on the new Accenture name, the firm took the historic step of a massive reorganization, followed by selling shares to the public in July 2001 in an Initial Public Offering (IPO) to raise much-needed permanent capital. Two months later, Accenture and the world were shocked by the terrorist attacks on the Pentagon and the World Trade Center, where 12 Accenture employees perished. Even while coping with that loss, the consultants rallied to fund and construct a Family Assistance Center in downtown Manhattan where families of September 11 victims could seek information about loved ones and emergency aid. And within months, the Accenture leadership was grappling with what would turn out to be one of the worst economic downturns since the Great Depression of the 1930s.

The company's values of caring for its clients and employees, while building a new professional services firm that features both consulting and outsourcing, would be tested during these years. Despite the frenzied rate of change, however, Accenture remained true to its roots. Rather than resist change, its employees proved willing to make the kind of bold moves that characterized Accenture's strategy over the years, and that kept Accenture in the vanguard of the global technical services industry.

### Arbitration Strategies

Following the arbitration filing, Conahan divided his time between working closely with the legal team and traveling around the world to brief consulting partners on the progress of the arbitration effort. He approached the arbitration process the same way any of his partners would approach a major engagement. "I know how our partners think," Conahan said. "They are fanatic about systems testing. So I wanted to be able to stand up in front of them and tell them that I had tested this."

**Employees from the Minneapolis office form the new logo.**

Months before Shaheen revealed to his partners that the consulting leaders were considering arbitration, the Simpson, Thacher legal team hired six different international arbitrators to weigh the consultants' case in mock arbitrations. The arbitrators didn't know whether they had been hired by attorneys for the consultants or the accountants. They not only wanted to try out the arguments before a selection of arbitrators, they hired potential arbitrators with a reputation of being especially tough on financially successful parties such as Andersen Consulting. By doing so, they disqualified them from hearing the Andersen case once it was actually filed in Paris with the International Chamber of Commerce's International Court of Arbitration.

The international lawyers hearing the mock arbitrations offered valuable advice, but a judge from Nigeria made what would turn out to be the singlemost important observation: The attorneys had planned to file the consultants' claim solely against Arthur Andersen, saying in essence that it was competing with the consultants in violation of the 1989 agreement forming the separate business units, as well as acting contrary to the 1990 Florida Accords. The Nigerian judge said that the consultants should file the claim against Andersen Worldwide. "That's the bad person," Conahan recalled the judge saying. The judge observed that the consultants should make the claim that Andersen Worldwide had failed to fulfill its responsibilities as the coordinating entity to manage conflict among the various firms; therefore, it was in breach of its contractual relationship with Andersen Consulting.

Based on the mock arbitrations, Shaheen, Conahan and the attorneys refined their approach. They agreed to file arbitration complaints against the member firms of the audit and tax business unit, as well as the Andersen Worldwide umbrella organization. Despite pressure from Andersen Worldwide to have the case handled by three arbitrators from highly developed countries, Shaheen insisted that the letter of the interfirm agreements be followed, which called for one arbitrator from a country where neither Arthur Andersen nor Andersen Consulting had a member firm. Moreover, he urged that Andersen Consulting should push for a well-educated arbitrator from a developing country. He wanted someone judging the case who would be put off by Arthur Andersen's claims that they were owed billions of dollars by the consultants. Shaheen wanted an arbitrator who thought of his country's gross national product when he heard the phrase "billions of dollars." Conahan added, "You get three high-flying attorneys from New York, Paris or London, and billions would mean nothing. They would say sure, we can handle billions." The consultants got their wish, and the judge selected to hear the case was a Harvard University-trained, respected Colombian lawyer from Bogota named Dr. Guillermo Gamba.



As expected, Arthur Andersen responded to the arbitration claim with a claim of its own, saying that the consultants would have to pay them $14.6 billion to go off on their own. The audit and tax partners also were adamant that they owned the consulting practice.

Shaheen and Conahan reassured the partners that the auditors were misreading the legal documents. As part of the 1989 agreement creating the separate business units, the Andersen Worldwide leadership and Larry Weinbach directed the creation of a separate legal entity in each country to house the consulting practices. Each of these entities was owned by the consultants in that country, while the audit and tax firms were owned by their partners.

The first 18 months of the arbitration process were concerned mainly with the issue of jurisdiction. Arthur Andersen and Andersen Worldwide argued that the case shouldn't be in the international court of arbitration, citing the fact that few of the Arthur Andersen country partnerships had up-to-date, signed agreements with Andersen Worldwide. Dr. Gamba ruled in June 1999 that the standard agreement that Andersen Worldwide used applied to all the partnerships, even if their paperwork wasn't up to date. He also ruled that he did indeed have jurisdiction. A subsequent attempt by Arthur Andersen and Andersen Worldwide to have the case moved to Switzerland was also defeated in a separate legal battle in Geneva.

With those challenges behind them, the Andersen Consulting team engaged in the pitched legal battle of asserting and proving claims, fending off counterclaims and preparing for the actual hearing portion of the arbitration process that would be conducted before the arbitrator, Dr. Gamba. An important Andersen Consulting tactic was to call principally Arthur Andersen and Andersen Worldwide partners as witnesses. The logic was that it would be far more powerful if the Arthur Andersen and Andersen Worldwide leadership partners could be forced into admissions detrimental to their defense, than to have Andersen Consulting witnesses simply asserting those statements.

This bold tactic meant that the Andersen Consulting team would have to work tirelessly to develop an evidentiary discovery process. The team constructed a paper trail of documents and memos that would back up every one of the assertions they would make in questions directed to the Arthur Andersen and Andersen Worldwide partners. When the actual hearings and cross-examination of witnesses began, Simpson, Thacher didn't ask a question if they didn't have a piece of paper or a video clip to back up what they knew was the correct response. Arthur Andersen witnesses quickly realized that if their recollections of events differed from the paper trail, they risked appearing to be trying to put too much "spin" on past events and damaging their credibility with the arbitrator. The hearing portion of the arbitration process ended with the consultants feeling confident about their case, but realizing that it would be months before the arbitrator was likely to render a decision. It was also clear to them that the Arthur Andersen team felt equally confident about their case at the same point in the battle.



### New Economy

Shaheen was convinced that the consultants couldn't afford to wait for the arbitration case to be resolved to move forward with the next iteration of their evolving global structure and strategy: organizing the business around industry groups, instead of by geographic regions and countries. As part of that reorganization Jack Wilson became head of the Market Unit organization, which had responsibility for revenue generation and client management. Several of the next generation of leaders, including Joe Forehand, Steve James, Bill Green, David Hunter and Gregg Hartemayer, took on significant responsibilities running industry groups. In addition to Wilson, Jim Fischer, Jesse Tutor and Keith Burgess assumed roles as leaders of the firm's operations. This organizational change, while logical and consistent with the overall business strategy, created considerable stress with the firm's historic geographic focus, a pull and tug that continued in subsequent years as the leadership tried to strike the correct balance.

Cover Story. Andersen Consulting CEO George Shaheen was featured on the cover of the March 8, 1999, issue of *Forbes*.

In the meantime, partners remained focused on "attacking the marketplace," just as Shaheen had asked them to do at their San Francisco meeting in December 1997. There was a tremendous amount of work to be done. The economy was booming, especially the information technology sector. In fact, Andersen Consulting dominated in providing

## Boom and Bust.

The technology sector, as represented by the NASDAQ Composite Index, soared to record heights by early 2000, then would plunge by more than 80 percent in value after the dot-com bubble burst.

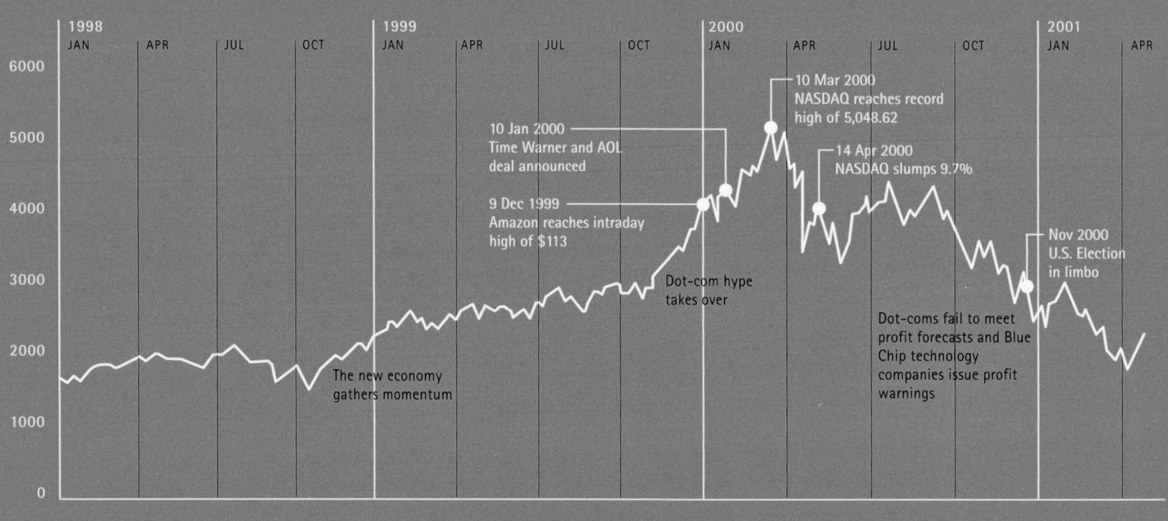


Source: Four Corners, Australian Broadcasting Corporation



consulting services to the soaring communications and telecommunications sector, overseen at the time by Managing Partner Joe Forehand. Eighteen of the top 20 communications companies worked so closely with Andersen Consulting during the late 1990s boom that they rarely sought competitive bids on new projects. The consultants were so focused on major clients, however, that they trailed some rivals in serving the soaring e-commerce sector in the Americas and other regions in the early days of the dot-com boom.

Andersen Consulting responded quickly to the Internet's impact on clients of all sizes, and by 1999 was offering a full complement of e-commerce services. Several months earlier, Hewlett-Packard asked Andersen Consulting to "create a more integrated and satisfying customer experience" across its Internet presence. And for the French bank Credit Agricole, Andersen Consulting introduced the first banking service delivered via interactive digital television using a simple remote control. In Canada, the firm was working with the Canadian Imperial Bank of Commerce (CIBC) to use Internet-based procurement to slash acquisition costs for non-strategic goods, and to use the Internet to identify approaches to new markets.

While Andersen Consulting's balanced mix of businesses may have appeared downright stodgy to some consulting upstarts that focused on cutting-edge Internet strategies, it served the firm well when the

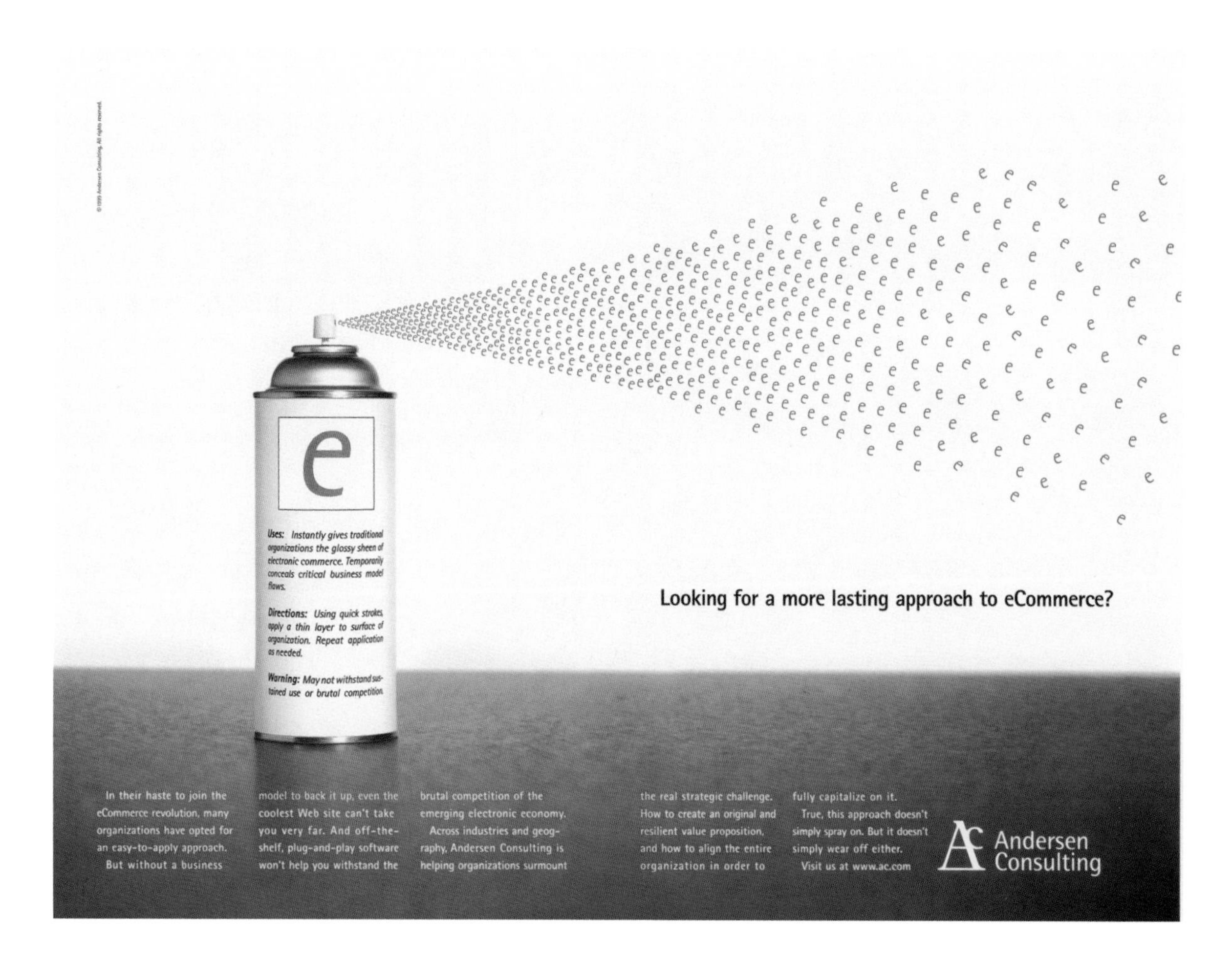




dot-com boom was followed by the inevitable bust. That said, the firm made an ill-timed foray into venture capital investing in the late 1990s. While some investments succeeded dramatically, such as an early investment in Siebel Systems, other investments yielded widely varying results and the portfolio was sold in 2002.

E-commerce was a major focus of Andersen Consulting's advertising campaigns by the late 1990s. The firm continued to push the advertising and brand-building envelope. What started as a $10 million annual campaign in 1989 blossomed into a $100 million "advertising and marketing blitz" (as described by *The Wall Street Journal*) by 1998.

## Shaheen Bows Out

Nearly every time a client or member of the public heard about Andersen Consulting, they heard about George Shaheen. As peripatetic as he was photogenic, Shaheen was the public face of the firm, and generally considered the best-known consultant of the era. Internally, while not all of his partners agreed with him all of the time, Shaheen had built a tremendous reservoir of support, thanks to his unremitting hard work on behalf of the firm. And he delivered. "George had the enormous trust of his partners," Conahan said. "He'd led them from a $1 billion business in 1990 to $8 billion and the top of the business world by 1999. He was a very straight shooter."

Shaheen's unusually high profile made what happened next a potentially devastating development for the firm. Like many prominent corporate leaders, Shaheen received his share of job offers over the years. But in each case he turned them down, concluding that he couldn't do better than continue as CEO of the world's top consulting firm. These rejections were also a testament to Shaheen's commitment and loyalty to his partners. He placed a very high premium on the loyalty he expected from his partners and he behaved accordingly. Then he heard the siren song of e-commerce: The dot-com grocery delivery company Webvan wanted him as its CEO, and offered him a very lucrative total compensation package.

Conahan was shocked when Shaheen first told him of the Webvan offer. "You're the heart and soul of Andersen Consulting," Conahan recalled telling Shaheen. "We're in the middle of arbitration. I can't think of anything that would make Arthur Andersen happier, that would give them more of a shot of confidence and adrenalin, really ignite their fire, than for you to resign." He added, "The partners will never understand it. They will regard it as an act of disloyalty. You have a reputation that any chief executive would kill for."

Shaheen thought it over for three weeks, then by mid-September told Conahan that his decision was made. Shaheen later said that as far as the arbitration process went, "I was convinced we were going to prevail, but for the most part there was nothing else we could do." He also reasoned, correctly as it turned out, that Dr. Gamba wasn't the type to be influenced by his resignation. Besides, Shaheen was coming up on his tenth anniversary as CEO of Andersen Consulting, and had long felt that a decade was probably the maximum amount of time any one person should run an organization like Andersen Consulting. The latest long-term planning process that was just getting under way, Horizon 2010, ought to be driven by the next generation of leadership, he argued.

Peter Fuchs, managing partner-Strategy, presents the results of Horizon 2010 at the November 1999 Partners' Meeting.

Conahan contacted Peter Fuchs, chairman of the Andersen Consulting Oversight Committee of the board of partners (the committee had responsibility for approving the appointment of the CEO of the consulting business unit), and other board members to schedule a meeting for the following day in Chicago. The group met and decided not to leave the room until they had a process in place to select the next CEO. They nominated John Kelly, managing partner for the Americas region, to serve as interim CEO, then contacted Bob Grafton, acting CEO of Andersen Worldwide, to get his formal ratification for the decision. They also set in motion steps that would lead to the consulting partners' vote in early November to approve Joe Forehand, who had been serving as managing partner of the Communications & High Tech global market unit, as the new managing partner and CEO of Andersen Consulting.

### Forehand Steps Up

As expected, the audit and tax leadership portrayed Shaheen's decision to leave the firm as a body blow to the consultants' arbitration case. The Arthur Andersen leadership appeared to believe that Shaheen single-handedly had been the source of the general conflict of the last decade between Arthur Andersen and Andersen Consulting, and with him out of the way the consultants were likely to lose their will to fight. The audit and tax partners clearly underestimated the consulting group culture. Within a few weeks, Forehand assembled a management team, met with Conahan to review the strategy and the status of the arbitration, and gave him the green light to continue.

**Firm Hand.** As CEO, Joe Forehand led the company through one of the most tumultuous periods in its history as it converted to public ownership and transformed its business to ride out the steep economic downturn in the early years of the decade.

The transition from Shaheen to Forehand, while potentially disruptive, proved to be one of the partners' finest hours. As they had in previous decades when faced with a crisis in leadership, the partners rallied in support of their collective destiny and reached into their ranks to choose a leader to meet the challenges facing the firm. In choosing Forehand, the partners bypassed a handful of Shaheen's lieutenants who were closely identified with the former CEO's management style. They also, perhaps unfairly, may have been blamed by partners outside the Americas for troubles the firm was having integrating global industry groups across national boundaries, particularly in Europe.

Forehand had a great reputation as a team leader and nurturer of talent. From his early years after being promoted to partner in 1982 in Atlanta, through a period in which he rebuilt the Dallas office in the early 1990s, Forehand had been pegged as a rising star. He then piloted both the Products and the Communications & High Tech global market units, having run 11 of the consulting practice's 18 industry groups by the time he was named CEO. He later asked one of his protégés, Bill Green, to run the Communications & High Tech unit.

Forehand didn't have the luxury of a leisurely transition. Within six days of his selection, he presided over the consultants' Annual Partners' Meeting and decided which of the recommendations coming out of the 18-month Horizon 2010 strategy effort to recommend to the partners. He also needed to reduce the tension surrounding the implementation of the global organization structure, which was frustrating the partners and leaving them feeling stripped of their prerogatives to make day-to-day decisions.

The meeting was an unqualified success, and a tribute to Forehand's ability to inspire the firm to pull together, much the way Duane Kullberg did in 1980 following Harvey Kapnick's resignation. Many partners commented that it was the best partners' meeting they had ever attended. It also featured the firm's first live global broadcast, introducing Forehand to all employees, marking the first time employees participated in a portion of a partners' meeting. Forehand was off to a rousing start with an enormous reservoir of goodwill, which was something he would need to call on repeatedly during the next four years.

Forehand spent much of his first few months as CEO traveling to offices around the world. He removed some organizational barriers that were coming between partners and their clients, especially concerning geographic issues outside the Americas. He advocated more contact between firm leadership and younger hires, partly

After his first 100 days as CEO, Joe Forehand shared his vision for the firm's future via a global broadcast to Andersen Consulting people.

in recognition that the firm's workforce was more diverse than in past years when the current leadership was rising through the ranks. Forehand also was reacting to the fact that annual staff turnover had spiked to 28 percent, compared to 15 to 20 percent in earlier years, as employees left for dot-com startups.

### Arbitration Anxiety

By the summer of 2000, Forehand and his team knew that an arbitration decision was imminent. The consultants rejected an overture from the audit and tax side, channeled through Andersen Worldwide officials, that Arthur Andersen might accept a compromise payment of $6.5 billion to $7 billion to settle their dispute.

But Forehand felt they had to make some offer of settlement. In late 1999, Forehand held a meeting with the Simpson, Thacher legal team to review the arbitration process to date, where he was told for the first time that the consultants had a 30 percent chance of losing the decision. "I never heard it in those words before," he said. Conahan remained confident of their chances, but Forehand was looking for an "insurance policy," given the consultants faced a 30 percent chance that they might be hit with a $14.6 billion decision or other scenarios that would represent a significant loss. The Andersen Consulting Executive Committee agreed to offer $2 billion paid over four to five years, including payments already held in escrow. But they didn't make the offer until the arbitrator had turned in his sealed decision. Only two to three weeks remained before it was to be ratified by the international court. The consultants reasoned that the time limit would force the audit and tax leadership to focus on the prospect that they might come away empty-handed.



The two sides held what would turn out to be the shortest meeting in the history of either Andersen Consulting or Arthur Andersen. Attending the meeting for the consultants were Joe Forehand, Jon Conahan, Jack Wilson and Barry Ostrager, the lead litigator from Simpson, Thacher. Representing Arthur Andersen were Jim Wadia, Joe Berardino, who would succeed Wadia as CEO of Arthur Andersen following the arbitration decision, and their lead outside attorney from Weil, Gotshal & Manges. Forehand looked at Wadia and said, "Jim, we're here to make an offer to settle. We're not negotiating. This is take it or leave it." Turning to Conahan he said, "Jon, make the offer." Conahan spent about 90 seconds describing the components of the proposed $2 billion settlement offer.

Wadia looked at his attorney, didn't say anything, then looked at Conahan and said, "That's a non-starter." Berardino smiled and added, "I think we'll keep our lottery ticket and the arbitrator." Conahan turned to Forehand and said, "Joe, they said no. Let's go." Conahan was confident that the arbitrator's decision would leave the consultants in a better position than the $2 billion offer, and didn't want to give the Arthur Andersen team another second to reconsider.

## Decision Time

There was nothing unusual about the sight of senior executives filing into Andersen Consulting's midtown Manhattan offices on the morning of August 7, 2000. What was unusual was the hour, even for a company and a profession known for encouraging workaholic tendencies. By the time Jon Conahan, managing partner-Arbitration, arrived in the office at 4:30 a.m., Andersen Consulting CEO Joe Forehand and John Kelly, head of the Americas for the global consulting firm, already were nursing coffees in one of the conference rooms. They had worried that they might not even make it to New York that morning, scrambling the day before to rebook flights to avoid a line of major thunderstorms blocking their path to Manhattan.

**Savoring the Moment.** Conferring in the wake of the arbitration decision (left to right): Susan Butler, Joe Forehand, Barry Ostrager, Jon Conahan and Jim Murphy.



They gathered in advance of a 5 a.m. deadline, the time at which the decision of an international arbitrator was to be released in Paris. The decision would mark the end of the contentious, two-and-one-half year international case between the consultants and Arthur Andersen. Forehand hadn't called a formal meeting for that morning, but invited executives who were going to be in the New York area to come to the office to hear the news. Other Andersen Consulting leaders, including Jim Murphy, Carol Meyer, Jack Wilson, Pedro Navarro, Karl-Heinz Floether, Gregg Hartemeyer, Doug Scrivner and Joel Friedman, congregated in the New York office to hear the arbitrator's decision. Murphy arranged to have the historic event captured on film.

Conahan sat in his office with Barry Ostrager, the lead litigator on the arbitration case from Simpson, Thacher & Bartlett, the consultants' law firm. Another Simpson, Thacher attorney, Peter Thomas, stood at the International Chamber of Commerce's International Court of Arbitration in Paris, mobile phone in hand. In the cold, dark office, Conahan glanced at the bottle of rare, 25-year-old, single-malt Bushmills Irish Whiskey on his desk. If the call was good news, he would bring the bottle down to the conference room where the rest of the Andersen Consulting leaders were waiting. If the decision went against them, he would slip the bottle into his briefcase and take it back to his home in Montclair, New Jersey.

WORLD BUSINESS NEWSPAPER

US EDITION

# FINANCIAL TIMES

www.ft.com | Tuesday August 8 2000 | USA $1.00 Canada C$2.00 Bermuda $2.00

CONSULTING ARM SEPARATES FROM ACCOUNTING FIRM AND ESCAPES $14.5bn PENALTY FOR SPLITTING UP

## Court rules on Andersen break-up

**By Michael Peel**

Andersen Consulting yesterday walked away from its estranged partner Arthur Andersen, the accounting firm, after a court in Paris ruled that the two should separate due to irreconcilable differences.

The judgment, which ends an acrimonious two-and-half-year divorce case, means Andersen Consulting has avoided paying damages of $14.5bn cited by Arthur Andersen as a penalty for separation.

Jim Wadia, Arthur Andersen's chief executive, announced within hours of the decision that he would resign and retire early from the firm.

Mr Wadia, 52, denied his resignation was a sign that Arthur Andersen had been defeated, although he admitted it could be "read that way". He said it was a logical time for him to go, as he had taken over in 1997 as a "tough negotiator" for the battle with Andersen Consulting.

In a judgment running to more than 100 pages, the court ruled that Andersen Consulting would have to give up its name to Arthur Andersen. The judgment adds to turmoil in the professional services industry undergoing sweeping change due to commercial and regulatory pressures.

A number of big firms have decided to sell or spin off their consultancy arms to free them from constraints on raising capital and conflict of interest rules imposed by US regulators.

The Andersen judgment, from the court of arbitration at the Paris-based International Chamber of Commerce, ends a process begun by Andersen Consulting in 1997.

Andersen Consulting, which specialises in management consultancy and technology, sought separation without penalty, the right to retain use of its name and up to $1.1bn in damages. It cited a breakdown in the relationship between the two firms, which became operationally autonomous in 1989 but continued to share revenues and governance structures under an umbrella organisation, Andersen Worldwide.

Andersen Consulting said its partner had begun to compete for big information technology contracts, contravening an agreement that barred it from doing so. Arthur Andersen denied the claim.

Andersen Worldwide launched a counter-claim citing a rule that any firm wishing to leave would have to pay an exit fee equal to one and a half times its annual revenues. Andersen Consulting had revenues last year of $8.9bn. The arbitrator found that Andersen Worldwide had failed in its duty to co-ordinate the practices of the two firms, meaning that Andersen Consulting should be released without penalty.

Joe Forehand, Andersen Consulting's chief executive officer, described the judgment as a "total win". He added: "This is a great day. A clear and decisive victory."

Mr Wadia admitted the decision to allow separation without penalty was disappointing, but said he was pleased with the ruling that Andersen Consulting would have to give up its name to Arthur Andersen.

The arbitrator also ruled that Andersen Consulting would have to pay almost $1bn it owed to Arthur Andersen under a revenue-sharing agreement.

**The cost of divorce, Page 11**
**Lex, Page 12**
**Joe Forehand profile:**
**http://people.ft.com/people/**

### KPMG reveals details of shake-up plans

KPMG joined in the upheaval in professional services by announcing yesterday that its consultancy arm would be a public company worth up to $5.6bn when it is sold this year.

The details of KPMG's separation, filed with regulators yesterday, show that the company hopes to raise between $2.2bn and $3.3bn from the offer. **Report, Page 13**

News of the arbitration decision hit the front page of the *Financial Times*, August 8, 2000.

After a few minutes that seemed like hours, the phone rang in Conahan's office. He punched the speakerphone button so Ostrager could also talk directly with Thomas. Thomas, his voice calm, started reading the major findings by the arbitrator. Arthur Andersen got the money the consultants already had paid into an escrow account to cover payments owed under the interfirm arrangements. And the contract between Andersen Consulting and Andersen Worldwide had been breached by Andersen Worldwide, and was therefore null and void.

Conahan cut in. "What's the amount of money? How much do we have to pay?" Thomas started screaming into his cell phone in Paris, "There's no money! There's no money!" At first, Conahan and Ostrager couldn't believe it. The firm had just been told that they were free to go on their own, without paying any more than the escrow money, as Andersen Worldwide had failed to ensure coordination and cooperation among the business units. But freedom came at a price: Andersen Consulting had to give up all rights to and use of the Andersen name by year-end of 2000.

Conahan slipped the bottle of Bushmills behind his back as he and Ostrager walked to the conference room. Before Conahan could finish saying, "Ladies and gentlemen, it doesn't get any better than this," and plop the whiskey bottle down on the conference table, everyone in the room was cheering and hugging. Champagne, which Murphy's staff

# Andersen Consulting Wins Independence

## Arbitrator Tells Firm to Pay Auditing Arm $1 Billion; Parent's Role Criticized

By Ken Brown
*Staff Reporter of* The Wall Street Journal

Amid significant changes in the accounting and consulting industries, an international arbitrator broke up **Arthur Andersen** and **Andersen Consulting**, ending one of the bitterest corporate disputes in recent memory.

The arbitrator ordered Andersen Consulting to pay about $1 billion to Arthur Andersen and to give up its name. But the payment will be far less than the $14 billion that could have been awarded to the

**Family Feud**

**Read the arbitrator's decision in the Andersen case in the online Journal at WSJ.com.**

1,900 partners at Arthur Andersen, one of the Big Five auditing firms.

The biggest loser in the nearly decade-long dispute was **Andersen Worldwide**, the parent company of the two firms, which was strongly criticized by the arbitrator for failing to supervise its units. In fact, the ruling said Andersen Consulting could leave the firm with only minimal penalties because the parent firm's poor performance had voided the contract that tied the companies together.

Despite the blame placed on the parent company, the first casualty was Jim Wadia, Arthur Andersen's chief executive, who resigned about four hours after the ruling was issued yesterday by the International Court of Arbitration in Paris, although he said his move had been a long time in coming and wasn't related to the decision.

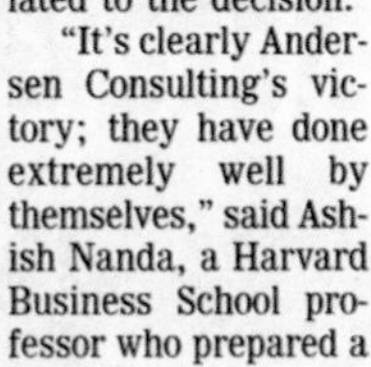

*Joseph Forehand*

"It's clearly Andersen Consulting's victory; they have done extremely well by themselves," said Ashish Nanda, a Harvard Business School professor who prepared a case study on the dispute that students began dissecting this year.

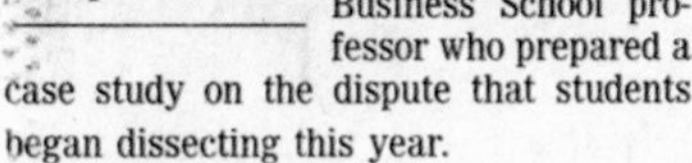

### Tumultuous Changes

While the ruling applies only to the two Andersen companies, it comes as tumultuous changes already have forced other Big

## Going Their Separate Ways

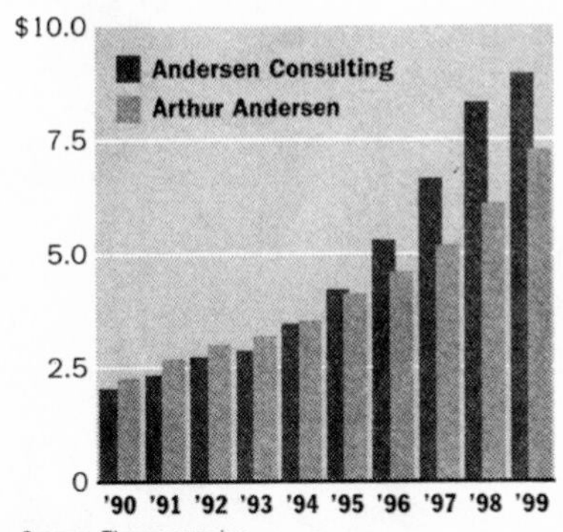


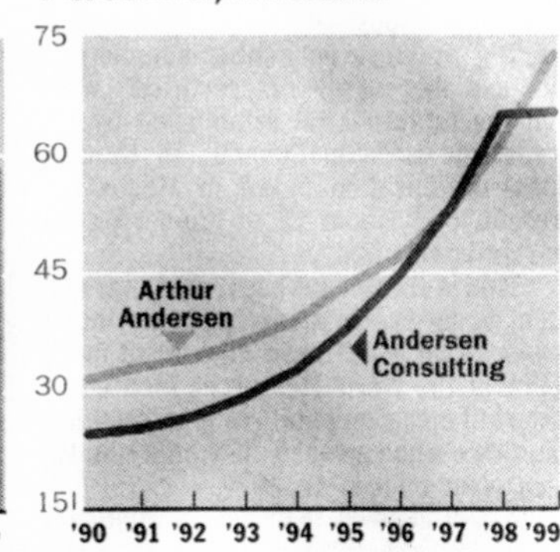


Source: The companies

Five accounting firms to shed their consulting businesses, and more changes could be in store. The firms face possible new rules from the Securities and Exchange Commission that would dramatically curtail their ability to conduct audits and consult under the same roof, on the theory that doing other work for an audit client could compromise the integrity of the audits.

*Jim Wadia*

The ruling by Colombian lawyer Guillermo Gamba granted Andersen Consulting its immediate independence and will let it keep its name until the end of the year. The $1 billion that he ordered Andersen Consulting to pay represents regularly scheduled payments to Arthur Andersen that the firm had been putting into escrow since the arbitration was filed in December 1997.

Those payments were at the core of Andersen Consulting's gripes. They were part of the agreement reached in 1989 that split Arthur Andersen's auditors from its consultants. The auditors retained the Arthur Andersen name, and the consultants became Andersen Consulting and both companies were overseen by Andersen Worldwide.

### Escalating Bitterness

But the two sides began bickering almost immediately, and the bitterness escalated in 1994 when Arthur Andersen started its own consulting business and soon was competing for clients with its sister company.

That might have been annoying enough for Andersen Consulting, but it came on top of the annual payments, which were mandated by a provision in the 1989 pact under which the more profitable of the two firms paid a portion of revenue, capped at 15%, to the less profitable firm. Partners at Andersen Consulting felt they were subsidizing the competition even as Arthur Andersen was breaking the pact with it by competing for consulting clients.

Mr. Gamba said in an interview from Bogota that Arthur Andersen hadn't violated the contract because it was never told what to do by Andersen Worldwide, which is based in Geneva. "Andersen Consulting was right in my opinion when they claimed that the Swiss corporate entity was not performing its coordinating obliga-

*Please Turn to Page A8, Column 1*

had kept discreetly on ice in anticipation of good news, quickly filled every available glass. (Conahan never found out what happened to his bottle of whiskey.)

The mood in the Arthur Andersen offices that day was much more somber. The audit and tax partners would be left with only the payments from the consulting practice that already were held in escrow. Adding to the sense of loss, Jim Wadia, the head of Arthur Andersen, resigned shortly after the arbitration decision was announced.

A few years later, Conahan and Wadia participated in a Harvard University Graduate School of Business case study of the arbitration. Before one of the sessions, Conahan asked Wadia why he rejected the $2 billion offer out of hand. Wadia told Conahan that he didn't have a choice. The Arthur Andersen board had passed a resolution that said he had to get a minimum of $4 billion as a settlement offer from the consultants or via arbitration, or resign.

### What's in a Name?

Even though it remained a closely held secret at the time, Forehand decided months before the arbitration decision that the Andersen name had to go. He knew that regardless of how many millions of dollars the consultants spent on advertising and golf tournaments, people were still going to confuse them with the audit firm. He and

Opposite page: Independence Day. *The Wall Street Journal*'s coverage of the arbitration decision, August 8, 2000.



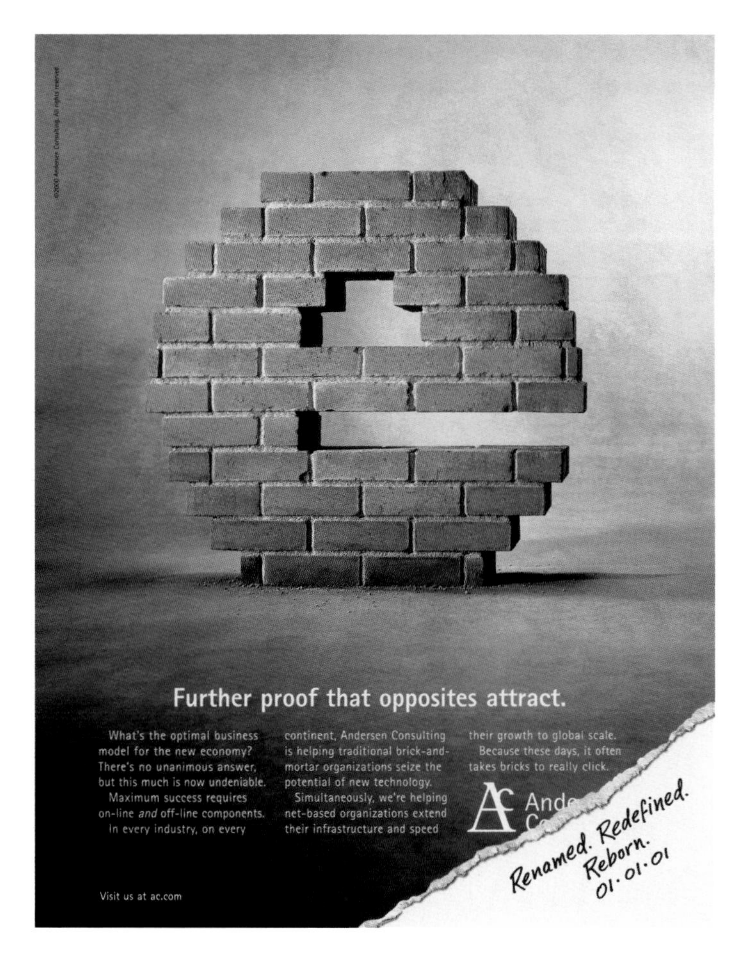

Above: Introducing Accenture. CEO Joe Forehand and Kim Petersen (right), senior manager-Resources in Oslo, Norway. Petersen won the internal contest to come up with a new name for the company by thinking of "accent on the future."

Left: In October 2000, the "Renamed. Redefined. Reborn. 01.01.01" tagline and torn signature treatment marked the first phase of the strategy to rebrand and reposition the firm.

Top: In with the New. Chris Wearing, location lead partner in New York, reveals the new Accenture sign at the New York office. The Accenture name debuted on New Year's Day, 2001.

Left: Spreading the Word. Accenture's new signature rolls off the assembly line.

Right: Company offices around the world helped promote the new 01.01.01 change to the Accenture name. In Prague, the famous "dancing building" was decorated to announce the new brand.

John Kelly were at the final round of the Andersen Consulting Match Play in Carlsbad, California, in February 2000. "That's when tournament winner Darren Clarke thanked 'Arthur Andersen' in front of millions of people watching on TV around the world. I about fell off a cliff," Forehand recalled. Shortly thereafter, he asked Jim Murphy, leader of Marketing & Communications, to start looking into a name change, realizing that it was going to be a very hard sell in light of the historical attachment so many partners had to the Andersen Consulting name.

In one very important sense, the arbitration decision made the rebranding process easier. Forehand, Kelly and Murphy no longer had to "sell" anything. They were merely following the order of the arbitrator. There still was the challenge of generating buy-in on the part of the firm's more than 70,000 employees, and doing so in the space of 147 days. One of the first steps was to inform the employees of the decision. As part of that effort, Murphy, who was already working with branding experts, created an internal process called "brandstorming" in which employees from around the world were asked for name ideas.

"In the internal process, we asked each person who submitted a name to write a brief essay on why that worked for our strategy," Murphy recalled. "So we turned it into sort of a little educational process, too. They had to know our strategy, you know, to get it right. And we had 2,677 candidate names. We got down to the end and we had 10 available that passed trademark, taste, appropriateness to our positioning." The winner, Kim Petersen, senior manager-Resources in Oslo, Norway, came up with Accenture by thinking of "accent on the future."

Consulting analyst Shamir Shah is shown with one of the taxis in London that were branded with the Accenture signature.

Joe Forehand announced the new name in a firmwide webcast on October 26, 2000. From that point forward, it was a race against the clock to effect the monumental changes required. The biggest challenge, however, involved transitioning brand equity to the new name. Starting in October, Andersen Consulting's ads included a "tear-away" corner, with the message "Renamed. Redefined. Reborn. 01.01.01." To manage logistical aspects of the change, each organization in the firm, as well as each office and client site appointed a rebranding coordinator. A direct mail campaign, complete with a capabilities brochure that outlined the organization's breadth of capabilities, was prepared and then sent to more than 40,000 clients (and prospective clients) in January. The firm also worked with more than 165 alliance partners to rebrand their materials, brochures and websites. And "day one" kits were created for internal distribution, so that as employees arrived back to work in January, they were prepared to champion the new brand. Plus, there were myriad necessary physical changes, from creating new building signage for more than 300 locations to printing 7 million new business cards. More than 2,000 people on 56 teams put in some 40,000 hours of work to ensure that the organization's new name met the arbitrator's deadline. To celebrate the launch of the Accenture name, Forehand hosted three live global webcasts—appropriate to different time zones—for employees around the world.

All told, the firm spent roughly $200 million rebranding itself, including signage, logos, paper products and databases. Some scoffed at the new name at the time, but at the end of calendar year 2001, one year after the launch, awareness for the Accenture name remained at or above the awareness level for the Andersen Consulting name. "Our brand positioning helps ensure our leadership position in the marketplace," Joe Forehand noted. "By strongly managing our brand, we can shape the way clients and potential clients perceive Accenture. This will inevitably benefit our bottom line."

### Going Public

Like the rebranding, the impetus for an initial public offering (IPO) came in early 2000, well before the arbitration decision came down. Forehand and Conahan were discussing what their options might be, given different potential outcomes. If they were hit with a multibillion-dollar arbitration decision or the global structure of the country partnerships was broken up, they might need to pursue an IPO. Forehand asked Conahan to assemble a team and start researching what steps the group would need to take if it wanted to pursue an IPO. To help with the process, Conahan, who initially had planned to retire following the end of the arbitration but agreed to stay on through the IPO process, recruited three veteran partners nearing retirement age—John Skerritt, Terry Neill and Pedro Navarro—to "stick around and help me do this." Also included in this group were Carol Meyer, head of Human Resources and later head of Investor Relations for Accenture, Accenture General Counsel Doug Scrivner, John Kelly, Mike Emmons (head of the Accenture internal tax group), Jamey Shachoy (a partner in the Accenture internal tax group) and representatives from the financial advisor Evercore Partners and the Simpson, Thacher law firm.



One of the ironies of the arbitration process was that it showed the consulting partnerships just how much power they had. All legal ownership of Andersen Consulting businesses was held by the locally owned partnerships. It became clear to the IPO team and Forehand that they needed to reestablish the "one firm" ethos if Accenture was going to continue as an industry leader. Accenture could have continued to survive as a network of national partnerships working together, as it had done since 1977, but it would have been cumbersome legally and financially. This form of governance first designed for Swiss dairy farmers wasn't especially well suited to meet the needs of a modern, global enterprise. Accenture was a $10 billion global enterprise, but with a fragile and complex legal structure that made normal corporate matters, such as borrowing, difficult.

With Accenture bidding on more multiyear, multibillion-dollar business outsourcing engagements all the time, the ability to borrow money and raise capital was key to the firm's success in the future. "The stakes were getting much higher," recalled Bill Green, at that time head of global Communications & High Tech. "The nature of the contracts [was] get-

## Partner Culture.

The real hurdle for many partners was cultural as much as financial. If Accenture did an IPO they would be giving up the only form of collective ownership and voting rights that most of them had ever experienced. Their identity as partners was crucial to who they were. It was difficult for many to conceive of having equity owners of Accenture, outside shareholders, who weren't as emotionally tied to the firm as were they, the owner-operator partners. "The men and women of this firm love this place," Conahan said. "They love the feeling of the partnership—of each of us having a vote, the camaraderie, the sense of owning something that we can control and deliver to the next generation, just as the last generation handed us the sense of control—that'll come together at a partners' meeting."



ting much more complex. And it was clear that we weren't going to be able to continue operating with roughly $500 million in partners' paid-in capital and be a player in the game [in which] we were facing off."

### Building Support

As happened at other crucial junctures in the firm's history—including the decision to file for arbitration in 1997 and the vote to create separate business units in 1989—the leadership went to great lengths to inform partners of the issues involved and make the process as transparent as possible. And to ask for their overwhelming support. At the October 2000 Annual Partners' Meeting in Miami, the leadership presented the partners with the general framework for an IPO and sought support for proceeding with a full design process. The leadership followed up with an extensive briefing book on the IPO for each partner and made trips to offices around the world to explain the IPO process and related issues.

Steve James, COO, leads a panel discussion during the 2001 Annual Partners' Meeting in Dallas, at which the partners voted overwhelmingly in favor of the public stock offering.

One of the most important aspects of the potential IPO was the financial impact on individual partners. To create a corporate income stream that could be independently valued by the marketplace, each partner had to forgo in the future as much as half of his or her historical annual compensation. In lieu of their member firm interests, they would receive shares of Accenture stock. The distribution formula for those shares was a weighted combination of seniority and years

## When the Going Gets Tough.

Bill Green, head of global Communications & High Tech at the time, was giving a presentation on the outlook for his business unit during one of the road shows. He had just finished detailing how dominant Accenture was in the sector when one of the securities analysts in the audience turned the tables on him. "The communications industry looks like it's headed into the tank, and you're saying this is the centerpiece of your store," the analyst pointed out. Didn't that mean Accenture was primed to lose a lot of business if this sector suffered economically?

Green walked over to the lectern, looked the analyst in the eye and said, "What you're asking is, 'What do we do if it gets tough?' I'll tell you what we do." The audience fell silent. They could tell from Green's tone of voice and demeanor that they weren't hearing a rehearsed answer. The usually self-contained executive growled, "We grab the bayonet and we snap it off the end of the rifles and we put it in our teeth and we get down in the mud and the grime in the jungle and we kick and scratch and we stop at nothing. That's what we do when it gets tough. And we won't lose!" A stunned silence followed. Then everyone started talking at once. Jon Conahan, who was part of the Accenture road-show team, said Green's from-the-gut response "was a real defining moment. People were saying, 'Boy, this is a special management team that they have here.'"



to retirement so that younger partners actually got more shares than if seniority were the only basis. The future would depend for a long time on these younger partners. Finally, the shares distributed to the partners could only be sold in limited amounts over the first eight years and even then, only if they remained working at Accenture. This restriction was necessary so that public investors in Accenture could be confident that the partners responsible for its success would work hard to deliver and share in that success.

The final vote of the more than 2,300 partners on the IPO was set for the April 2001 Annual Partners' Meeting in Dallas. The leadership decided that this was to be an all-or-nothing vote. They didn't want partners voting "no" on this round to hold out for a sweeter offer down the road. And they decided that they needed a supermajority of 85 percent for there to be an IPO. That by itself still wouldn't be enough to push through the IPO; the leadership decided that if just one of the top 10 largest country partnerships voted against it, the IPO was off as well. Lastly, they decided that they needed to get 90 percent of the vote of the remaining partnerships.

Despite having such high hurdles to clear, the proposal passed overwhelmingly at the April meeting. Over the next several months, all country member firms were reconstituted legally to reflect the new corporate structure. Meantime, the leadership switched into

overdrive to prepare for the anticipated July IPO date. After an extensive selection process, Accenture chose Goldman Sachs and Morgan Stanley to act as co-lead underwriters for the IPO. And to gain some insight into the challenges of running a publicly held company, Forehand spent a considerable amount of time meeting with Goldman CEO Henry Paulsen and United Parcel Service CEO Jim Kelly, who had taken their companies public a few years earlier.

Three leadership teams, led by Forehand, Chief Operating Officer Steve James, Chief Financial Officer Harry You and Jack Wilson, corporate development officer and managing general partner-Accenture Technology Ventures, would travel around the world for three weeks beginning in late June to present the Accenture story to prospective institutional investors in what was known as the "road show." The pace was grueling. In light of the then-weak stock market and the uncertain outlook for the information technology and consulting industries, questions from potential investors and Wall Street analysts were often pointed, to say the least. But the three teams successfully drummed up interest in Accenture stock despite the economic outlook. Once all the indicated orders from institutional investors around the world had been collected the day before the stock offering, the underwriters were able to advise the pricing committee to price the stock at $14.50 a share on July 18. That enabled Accenture to raise a greater-than-expected $1.67 billion to help support its future growth.

Top: Accenture celebrates its initial public offering, including Joe Forehand and the leadership team ringing the opening and closing bells at the New York Stock Exchange.

Bottom: Joe Forehand and Steve James outside the New York Stock Exchange.

The New York Stock Exchange's exterior was draped with a huge Accenture banner on the morning of July 19 to celebrate the new stock listing. Forehand rang the opening as well as the closing bell that day, a rare event for a CEO of a newly listed company. He also bought the customary first order of 1,000 shares of Accenture stock. The stock exchange listing marked one of the most significant milestones in Accenture's history. As a public company Accenture ranked among the

At a reception on the floor of the New York Stock Exchange, July 18, 2001, Jesse Tutor (left), managing partner-Partner Matters, and John Kelly, former managing partner-Legal & Arbitration, toasted the Accenture initial public offering that was scheduled for the next morning.



200 largest companies listed on the New York Stock Exchange in terms of revenues. No one involved in the process could have had any idea how important the timing of the stock sale would be, in light of the events that would stun the world less than two months later.

### Keeping an Eye on Clients

Even while much of Accenture management's time was consumed by the arbitration, rebranding and the IPO during much of 2000 and well into 2001, the firm remained focused on its primary objective: serving clients. In August 2000, just weeks after the arbitration decision, the firm announced a seven-year outsourcing deal with the U.K. supermarket chain Sainsbury's to take over its information technology functions and 800 of Sainsbury's employees.

Johnson & Johnson, the global health care products and services provider, credited its reduction of clinical supply costs by 12 percent in 2001 to work by an Accenture team. Accenture had overhauled the client's supply chain processes and systems, which was just one of several Johnson & Johnson projects with Accenture that year. And less than two weeks after the Accenture IPO, the company announced an unprecedented 13 1/2 year contract with a consortium of four California counties to design, build and operate a "next generation" welfare system.

Top: Bold Accenture ads challenged clients and potential clients to consider how technology might change the world.

Bottom: The "I am your idea" advertising campaign, launched in 2002, focused on the importance of developing ideas and teaming to bring them to life.

### September 11, 2001

Forehand and the rest of the Management Committee were meeting in Copenhagen, Denmark, on September 11, 2001. As news of the terrorist attacks in the United States reached them that afternoon, they were as stunned and shocked as most people around the world. But there was also a sense of frustration at being so far removed from their operations in the United States. Unable to fly back, they coordinated the company's response from afar. Within days, Accenture confirmed that the company had lost 12 employees, killed while at client work sites or meetings in the World Trade Center.

Forehand proceeded with a previously scheduled town hall meeting with company employees in Copenhagen the following morning. "There must have been maybe a hundred, a hundred fifty people, and there was not a dry eye in the group," he recalled. "It was a moving experience to see our people and their reactions in Europe and the sense of loss that our people had all around the world."

### Lending a Hand

New York City Mayor Rudolph Giuliani (center) paid tribute to Accenture employees' work in setting up a Family Assistance Center to serve family members of the victims of the terrorist attacks.



David Moskovitz, a partner in Government, received a call at home from a client two days after the attacks. Not just any client, he was a representative of the New York City Mayor's Office, asking if Accenture could help set up a Family Assistance Center for family members looking for information on loved ones killed in the attacks or other assistance. Within 72 hours, Moskovitz and more than 300 other Accenture volunteers, many working with little sleep, led the transformation of an empty, 130,000-square-foot warehouse on a Hudson River pier north of the World Trade Center site into a fully furnished facility with more than 250 personal computers and 300 phones. It also included 140 interview stations, a child-care center, multiple first aid stations, offices and conference rooms.

New York City Mayor Rudolph Giuliani was in demand 24-hours-a-day for weeks following the attacks. But he made it a point to attend the October 8 memorial service Accenture held in Madison Square Garden for its 12 employees killed in the attacks, a service that thousands of Accenture people around the world attended via an audio webcast. Giuliani said he wanted to honor the tremendous contributions made by the Accenture employees who had built the Family Assistance Center, saying they "helped to perform a minor miracle in the wake of the tragedy." Giuliani also spoke at the 2002 Annual Partners' Meeting, where he again praised the efforts of so many Accenture employees.

In the days following the attacks, 10 of Accenture's *FORTUNE* 500 clients, as well as the city of New York, asked Accenture for space or help in finding a place to set up temporary offices. "This is not the kind of thing we're used to doing," said Ed Lally, director of facilities-New York. "But when our clients turned to us, of course we were willing to do anything we could to help."

## Colleagues Remembered.

Twelve Accenture employees (named below) perished in the terrorist attacks on New York City's World Trade Center the morning of September 11, 2001. Each had been at a client work site or meeting at the time of the attacks. Candles were lit at a touching memorial service held on October 8 to commemorate their lives.

Donna Bernaerts-Kearns
C. Arron Dack
Jeffrey M. Dingle
Thomas Farrelly
Lyudmila Ksido
Christine McNulty
John Moran
Thomas Polhemus
Faina Rapoport
Rufino C. Santos III
Mary Rubina Sperando
Sanford Stoller

## Looking Ahead

The sense of accomplishment that came with the rebranding and stock listing was tempered by the sense of loss in the wake of September 11. And from a business perspective, it became clear within a few weeks that the company had been fortunate to go public when it did. With so much uncertainty in the world concerning security and the outlook for the economy, it was unclear how long the company might have had to wait to raise permanent capital, and whether it would have been able to raise anywhere near the amount it did in July 2001.

A sharp falloff in business spending was felt especially in the information technology sector in the final months of 2001. While engagements already under way continued to move forward, new business trailed off and the company adopted the first of several rounds of belt-tightening. Business process outsourcing remained one of the strongest performers among Accenture's businesses as corporate and governmental clients sought to cut their operating costs.

**Accenture not only had survived the previous four years of dramatic change, it had thrived, and remained in the forefront of the global consulting industry, even though the prospects for the industry were far from certain. However, the company once again would find its values of superior client service, long-term commitment to personnel development and the willingness to embrace change tested over the next few years as it weathered one of the most severe economic downturns since the Great Depression of the 1930s. It would face the challenge of meeting the performance expectations placed on public companies to deliver short-term results while also investing for future growth. Accenture would prove more than capable of meeting those challenges in the years ahead, but it wouldn't be easy.**

# 2002 to Present

## Building High Performance

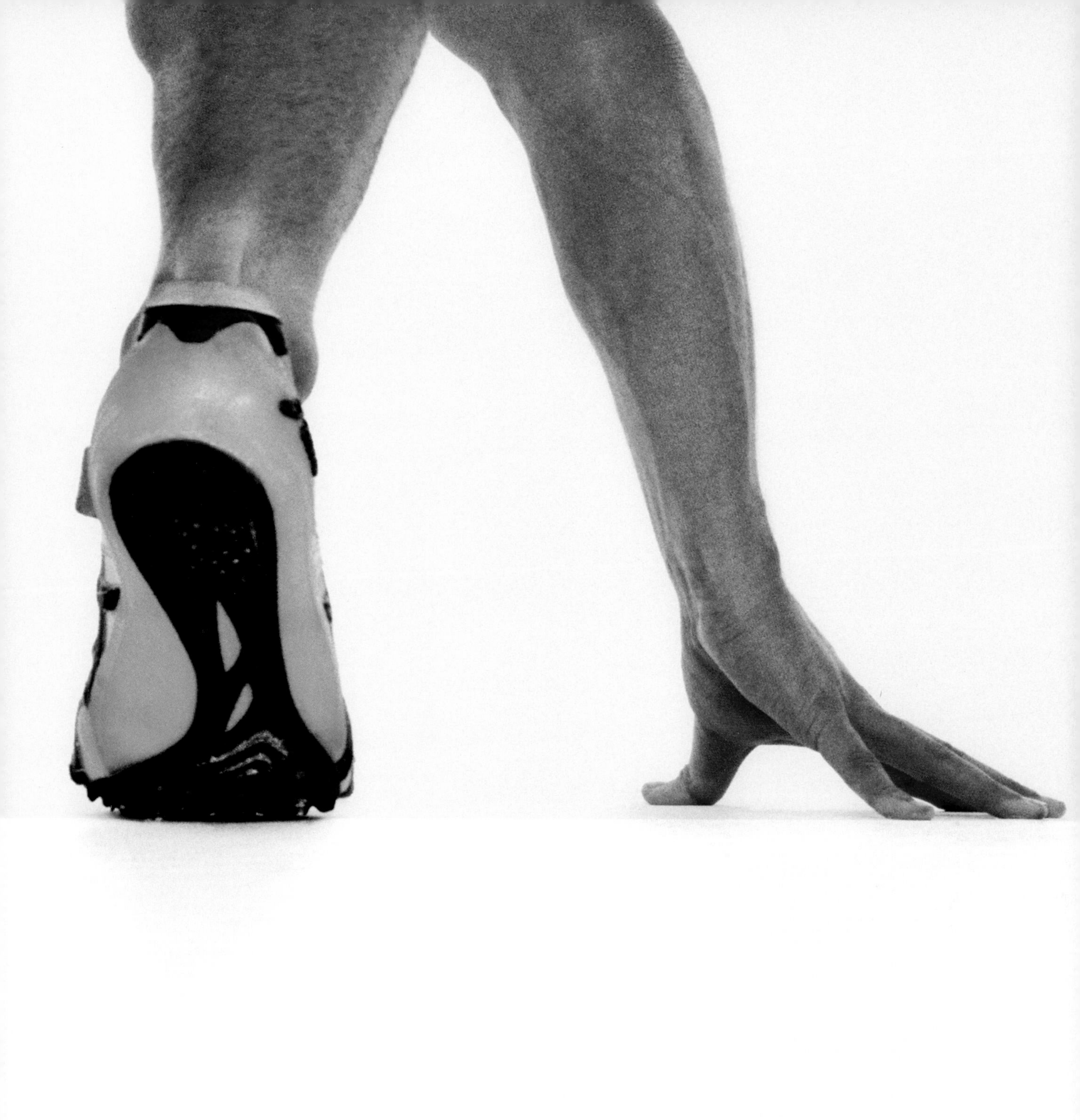

"Maybe titles will change, maybe compensation will change, maybe career paths will change. But the principles, what have historically been the partnership principles, as we call them, are precious, and every day we have to work to make sure that those never change."

Bill Green

# 2002 to Present
# Building High Performance



**Accenture responded to adversity in the post-September 11 world by once again reinventing itself. Accenture's rapid expansion of its efforts to create value for clients through business process outsourcing, and its rebounding consulting business for both the private and public sectors, created a global, diversified services industry leader. At the same time, the company maintained its core values and continued to encourage people to reach their full potential in a world of increasing diversity.**

Chapter opening image: Despite challenges in the marketplace, Accenture was poised for a period of dramatic growth and success.

Joe Forehand knew how Leonard Spacek must have felt. Fifty years earlier, some of Spacek's own partners had criticized the legendary Arthur Andersen & Co. managing partner for investing in technology research during a period of tight budgets, with no clients footing the bill. Several partners dismissed the nascent effort as "Spacek's Folly." Some advised the young hires who had put their faith in Spacek's vision, including information technology pioneer Joe Glickauf, to seek their fortunes elsewhere. History proved Spacek right, of course. The initial, few-million-dollar investment he championed in the early 1950s was the seed money for what became Accenture, a multibillion-dollar global consulting and outsourcing giant.

As the Accenture CEO and his management team were leading the newly public company through the early months of 2002, Forehand was also feeling the heat. Wall Street analysts and institutional investors holding Accenture stock expected the newly public company to meet its quarterly earnings targets. They didn't want to hear that the global economy was still reeling from the shock of the September 11 terrorist attacks or that new business, particularly in the traditional consulting practices, was hard to come by. In fact, revenues from the company's consulting businesses would slip 7 percent for the fiscal year ending August 31, 2002, and another 10 percent in fiscal 2003. Several consulting firm rivals merged with stronger partners or went out of business during this period.

Chairman Joe Forehand (right) handed over the CEO reins to Bill Green (left) at the end of fiscal 2004.

To offset the consulting slump, Forehand and his team reduced spending across the board, including some cuts in personnel. Then they bet the company's future on a business that Forehand's high-profile predecessor George Shaheen hadn't fully embraced, and that in 2001 had accounted for a mere 17 percent of total revenues: outsourcing. Would this latest bet to transform Accenture pay off, or would subsequent commentators label it "Forehand's Folly"?

Accenture's performance in the intervening years strongly suggested that history proved Forehand right, just as it did Spacek. As it has at crucial junctures for more than a half century, Accenture embraced dramatic change to better serve the evolving needs of its clients and respond to shifting economic trends. Corporate as well as government clients sought Accenture's help to transform their businesses, cut costs and boost efficiencies via outsourcing. Outsourcing revenues soared 33 percent in 2002 and grew by another 37 percent in 2003. By the end of fiscal 2004, even as the traditional consulting business was rebounding, revenues from outsourcing amounted to nearly 40 percent of total revenues and were expected to hit 50 percent within a few years. Between 2001 and 2004, outsourcing helped fuel a 27 percent increase in Accenture's total number of employees to more than 105,000. Investors also liked what they saw. At the time of the 2001 IPO, Accenture's market value was roughly one-half that of outsourcing leader EDS. Three years later, thanks in large part to strong growth in outsourcing and the company's rivals' inability to keep pace, Accenture's market value roughly equaled that of EDS, CSC, BearingPoint and Perot Systems combined.

**On August 2, 2004, 861 people joined Accenture, putting the total employee headcount to more than 100,000 people. One of those 861 people was Juan Manuel De La Torre Álvarez, manager-Financial Services, Mexico City, Mexico.**



Accenture's ability to evolve was underscored in 2004 when the company led a successful bid by the Smart Border Alliance to win the bidding for the U.S. Visitor and Immigrant Status Indicator Technology (US-VISIT) contract to create a "virtual" border for the United States. What was at that time one of the largest contracts awarded by the U.S. Department of Homeland Security could total up to $10 billion over 10 years for Accenture and several contractors on its Smart Border Alliance team, including Raytheon, SRA and The Titan Corporation. With the US-VISIT project as the capstone to his 32-year career at the company, Forehand stepped down as CEO at the end of fiscal 2004, while retaining the title of chairman.

Bill Green, tapped by the Accenture board to succeed Joe Forehand as CEO, faced a new set of challenges. Working closely with Steve Rohleder, chief operating officer and former group chief executive of the Government operating group, Green took the helm of a dramatically different company than the one Forehand took over leadership of in 1999. Accenture comprised several distinct workforces—Consulting, Enterprise, Services and Solutions—with consultants representing less than half of total personnel. And it was a much more diverse workforce in every sense of the word. That fact drove company leadership to respond creatively to reemphasize the range of career development and advancement opportunities at Accenture, particularly following the retrenchment earlier in the decade. "You have to recognize there's an inclusiveness requirement that is really new to our leaders, to understand that in the past five years we have dramatically changed who we are, and our workforce has changed dramatically," Green said.

Green and his leadership team also took charge of a company that continued to build on its original guiding values. A focus on client service coupled with a commitment to do the right thing for employees has consistently guided decision making at Accenture. Combined with the willingness to take risks and the can-do mind-set that is the key ingredient in Accenture's "special sauce," these values placed Accenture at the forefront of the global consulting and outsourcing industry of the 21st Century.

Steve James served as chief operating officer under Joe Forehand and then as international chairman upon his retirement at the end of fiscal 2004.

### Hard Times

No one knew how the global business community would react in the months following the September 11, 2001, terrorist attacks. After the New York Stock Exchange took an initial plunge when it reopened for trading in mid-September 2001, most global stock markets actually rallied by year-end. But Accenture was getting clear indications that business conditions, already weak, weren't ready to improve significantly anytime soon.



Indeed, Accenture already was cutting back prior to the attacks of September 11. Less than a month after going public, Accenture announced on August 18, 2001, that it was eliminating 1,500 positions, 2 percent of its workforce, because of weak economic conditions in its top global markets and low employee turnover. The company also deferred the start dates for 1,000 recently hired employees. Smaller job cuts would follow in 2002 and 2003.

The information technology sector in particular was reeling from the global economic slowdown. The surge in global corporate IT spending that helped drive the company's financial results to record levels in the late 1990s left many companies with excess capacity and little need to invest further in IT services. Many of Accenture's largest clients in the technology arena were also coping with a drastic falloff in business. Green, who was running Communications & High Tech at the time, recalled, "We had 16 of our telecom clients go bankrupt in the same year. It wasn't a pretty sight. I put that down as a character-building experience."

The recession was off the radar of even the most experienced personnel. "As we saw the period where our business started to decline," Forehand said, "I don't think anyone thought the length and depth of the economic and technology spending recession would hit us like it did." Steve James, who served as COO under Joe Forehand and international chairman upon his retirement at the end of fiscal 2004, said

## Consulting Crisis.

The severe downturn took its toll on the entire consulting industry. In July 2001, McKinsey took the rare step of asking its partners to contribute up to $200,000 each in new capital to bolster the firm's finances. Headcount reductions came later at McKinsey and at Boston Consulting Group. In February 2002, Arthur D. Little, following the collapse of plans for an initial public offering of its high-tech operations, filed for Chapter 11 bankruptcy protection and offered itself for sale. And PriceWaterhouseCoopers Consulting, which had nearly been sold to Hewlett-Packard in the boom year 2000 for $18 billion, was sold to IBM in 2002 for a mere $3.5 billion. By November 2002, with no sign of an upturn in corporate spending on information technology in sight, *The Economist* magazine was describing a "crisis of confidence in consulting."



that he had weathered four recessions in 36 years with the company, but "this one we've just gone through [was] by far the hardest because it went on so long."

During the early 1990s slump, Shaheen and his management team were able to tell their partners to look beyond short-term results and help position the firm for the eventual recovery. Forehand and his team didn't have that luxury. Unlike their predecessors, they had to operate as the leaders of a publicly held corporation. And that meant sticking to the discipline of meeting quarterly earnings estimates, if Accenture wanted to build any credibility with Wall Street and institutional investors around the world. Forehand and his team may have been operating in uncharted territory when it came to the demands placed on public companies, but they were very much operating in the Accenture tradition of adapting to new challenges. Shaheen, after all, had been handed the reins of a newly formed consulting division with little operating infrastructure to speak of in 1989. Likewise, Spacek, Higgins and Glickauf rebuilt the postwar consulting business almost from scratch.

Forehand didn't have to look far to see what might happen if he failed. BearingPoint, formerly known as KPMG Consulting, had gone to the public markets several months before Accenture. But after it failed to meet quarterly earnings projections, its stock price had plunged nearly 50 percent in 2001's first quarter and remained stuck well below its offering price three years later.

## The Fall of Arthur Andersen.

Once the consultants and the audit and tax practice had fully separated their businesses following the 2000 arbitration decision, there was little contact between the two groups. Within a matter of months, even the most tradition-bound consultant had to concede that forfeiting the Andersen name was extremely fortuitous given the problems that were to challenge Arthur Andersen. Arthur Andersen's fall from accounting industry grace was swift. Enron, the rapidly growing energy trading firm based in Houston, was one of Andersen's largest audit clients. After a series of disclosures in late 2001 of charges and restated financial results that added $2.59 billion to Enron's books and reduced its previous five years' worth of earnings by 20 percent, Enron filed for bankruptcy in December 2001. The U.S. Securities and Exchange Commission was conducting a formal investigation of Enron by the end of October 2001.

**Joseph Berardino, CEO of the accounting firm Arthur Andersen, testifies in February 2002 before a Congressional subcommittee investigating the Enron Corporation bankruptcy.**



The U.S. Justice Department secured a guilty plea to obstruction of justice from David Duncan, the Arthur Andersen partner directly handling the Enron account who had overseen the shredding of Enron-related documents. The Justice Department indicted Arthur Andersen on obstructing justice in March 2002. Its reputation severely tarnished, Andersen began losing audit clients almost immediately. Joe Berardino resigned as the head of Arthur Andersen on March 26, 2002, and in June 2002, a federal jury found the firm guilty on one count of obstructing justice. As of August 31, 2002, Arthur Andersen in the United States no longer audited publicly traded companies. The non-U.S. member firms all went their own ways. This collapse marked the tragic end of a once-proud firm from which Accenture inherited some of its most enduring values. The U.S. Supreme Court voted unanimously to overturn the verdict in 2005, finding that the trial judge had improperly instructed the jury.

## External Oversight

One of the most important steps Accenture took in preparation for its IPO was to form a board of directors that included several independent members who weren't executives of Accenture. A series of business scandals in the early years of the decade—including the collapse of Enron—led to calls for greater corporate accountability and ultimately the 2002 passage of the Sarbanes-Oxley Act, which set new corporate governance rules for publicly traded companies. Accenture, as of August 2002, had complied with requirements that its CEO and CFO certify the accuracy of the company's financial statements. In October 2001, Accenture's initial board still contained a majority of corporate insiders, as defined by the New York Stock Exchange, but a number of external directors were added. By 2004, ahead of deadlines set by the New York Stock Exchange, Accenture's board comprised a majority of eight external directors of whom seven were considered independent of Accenture, and six directors who were employees of the company.

From 2001 through 2004, three new members joined the board: Dennis Hightower, former CEO of Europe Online Networks, S.A.; William Kimsey, former CEO of Ernst & Young Global, Ltd.; and Carlos Vidal, Accenture country managing director for Spain and managing partner-Financial Services in South Europe, Latin America, Central Europe, the Middle East and South Africa. Internal directors who left the board during that time were Karl-Heinz Floether, Joel Friedman, Steve James, Masakatsu Mori, Diego Visconti and Jack Wilson.

Pictured are the members of Accenture's first Board of Directors, 2001. Top row (left to right):

Jackson L. Wilson, Jr., Corporate Development Officer and Managing General Partner-Accenture Technology Ventures, Accenture

Steven A. Ballmer, Chief Executive Officer, Microsoft Corp.

Blythe J. McGarvie, Executive Vice President and Chief Financial Officer, BIC Group

William D. Green, Managing Partner-Communications & High Tech and Country Managing Director-United States, Accenture

Joe W. Forehand, Chairman & CEO, Accenture

Sir Mark Moody-Stuart, Former Chairman, Royal Dutch/Shell Group of Companies and Former Chairman, The Shell Transport and Trading Company

Wulf von Schimmelmann, Chief Executive Officer, Deutsche Postbank

Dina Dublon, Executive Vice President and Chief Financial Officer, J.P. Morgan Chase & Co.

Karl-Heinz Floether, Managing Partner-Financial Services, Accenture

Robert I. Lipp, Chairman and CEO, Travelers Property Casualty

Bottom row (left to right):

Joel P. Friedman, Managing General Partner-Accenture Technology Ventures, Americas, Accenture

Stephan A. James, Chief Operating Officer, Accenture

Masakatsu Mori, Country Managing Director-Japan and Managing Partner-Japan Operating Unit, Accenture

Diego Visconti, Country Managing Director-Italy and Managing Partner-Communications & High Tech, Europe and Latin America, Accenture

## Staring Change in the Face

By 2002 Forehand knew he had to do more than just cut costs and ride out the recession. To do so would leave an opening for a rival to take market share from Accenture or otherwise redefine the business. That wasn't the Accenture way. He knew it was time for the company to once again embrace change and reflect the new reality in the marketplace for its clients. Echoing one of Shaheen's favorite maxims, Forehand recalled, "We continue to stare change in the face every day and continue to challenge ourselves with, 'What do we have to do to remain relevant to our clients?' And I think that's what we've done over the last two to three years during the downturn."

The change staring Forehand in the face was increased client demand for outsourcing services, even during the depths of the recession. For instance, while Bill Green was in the process of coping with 16 of his telecom clients going belly up, in January 2002 AT&T signed a $2.6 billion, five-year contract for Accenture to manage its global call centers. That kind of demand led the Accenture management team to change the Accenture business model from their 50-plus-year history of being primarily a consulting business to more of a mix of consulting and outsourcing businesses.

"We transformed our business model to blend consulting and systems integration services—areas in which we have had broad experience for decades—with outsourcing services," Forehand noted in his 2002 letter to Accenture stakeholders. Accenture's existing outsourcing expertise focused on managing business processes, applications and technology infrastructure. The company also began adding outsourcing capabilities in customer information, billing systems, information technology services, supply chain management and human resources administration.

"The outsourcing business took off, both on the applications side and business process side," Green recalled. "We needed to have a delivery model that was cost effective and very efficient. We introduced our Global Delivery Network and we put all that in place. And we did all those things while we were in the middle of fighting the toughest economic environment ever. It wasn't just fighting the good fight in the marketplace, it was positioning the firm for the future."

Accenture Procurement Solutions employees at the Accenture Delivery Center in Chicago.

## Outsized Outsourcing Growth

The timing of the shift toward outsourcing couldn't have been better. In key ways it echoed the firm's ability to capitalize on large systems installations in the 1970s following the standardization of approach and implementation pushed through by Vic Millar and his team. Accenture once again was a leader in rapidly adapting to changing technologies and client needs. The number of client engagements mushroomed, with a 37 percent jump in outsourcing revenues in fiscal 2003 compared to just a 2 percent increase in net revenues. During that year alone, Accenture's Business Process

Outsourcing (BPO) solution units, with a network of more than 40 integrated delivery centers around the world, collected about $30 billion of customer debt for clients, handled more than 100 million incoming customer calls, processed more than 50 million customer bills, processed 100 million airline passenger reservations and were responsible for more than 29 million electricity and natural gas meter readings. The meter readings were among the services offered by Accenture Business Services for Utilities. Only 18 months old by the end of fiscal 2003, the unit was providing services to more than 6 million customers, more than any utility in North America.

Accenture created a limited partnership with Vancouver-based BC Hydro to provide customer service and other management services.

Among Accenture's more innovative outsourcing engagements during this period was the 10-year, nearly $1 billion agreement with Vancouver-based BC Hydro. The engagement involved the creation of a limited partnership between Accenture and BC Hydro that offered the electric utility and other North American utilities, customer service, procurement and office management services. The partnership estimated savings to BC Hydro at $187 million over 10 years.

And in July 2004, Accenture signed a seven-year outsourcing contract with electronics retailer Best Buy, under which Accenture agreed to manage and develop the full scope of the retailer's IT systems, infrastructure, and applications development and maintenance. Nearly 600



## Accenture-brand Outsourcing.

Many clients have thought that outsourcing is primarily about cutting costs. They may have given outsourcing a try, only to see initial savings diminish as their organization reverted to status quo behaviors. Accenture CEO Bill Green described outsourcing Accenture-style as "transformational." "When people come to Accenture for outsourcing services, it's not just about getting the costs lower," Green said. "It's about getting capability. Our differentiator in outsourcing is all about capability and flexibility.

"This isn't about what's core and what's non-core anymore," he added. "We've been asked to operate on behalf of clients some very mission-critical things that traditionally you would consider to be core to their business, like customer service. It's because what they're looking for is capability, not cost. And they see we're able to take that operation, evolve it, and continue to improve it over time and make it relevant to their customer base."

## Fore!

To enhance its global brand campaign, in 1994 Andersen Consulting took on sponsorship of the Andersen Consulting World Championship of Golf, which George Shaheen called "one of the most extensive marketing programs in our history." Under the direction of Jim Murphy, the initial three-year, $15-million-plus commitment created a nine-month-long golf tournament played on three continents. The first tournament began in Japan and ended in Arizona. The tournament provided what was then the richest purse in the history of golf, $3.65 million total, with $1 million to the winner among the top 32 golfers in world rankings (later expanded to 64 players).

**Golfing sensation Tiger Woods and Joe Forehand celebrate Woods' second consecutive Match Play tournament win in 2004.**



In 1999, the event evolved into the World Golf Championships and the company became a global umbrella sponsor of a series of events designed and sanctioned by the International Federation of PGA Tours. The first event in the World Golf Championships each year has been the Accenture Match Play Championship—a match-play tournament contested by the top 64 golfers in the world.

Tiger Woods won the Accenture Match Play Championship in both 2003 and 2004. And it was during this time period that Woods was retained by Accenture for marketing and advertising initiatives as a symbol of the company's new market positioning, High Performance Delivered.

The Accenture Match Play Championship became more than a golf event; it provided a forum for Accenture leaders and clients to explore new business opportunities in the midst of one of the world's most elite golf tournaments. Plus, the five days of television coverage to more than 140 countries—along with the television and print advertising—put the Accenture brand in front of current and potential client executives around the world.

Best Buy IT employees were identified to make the transition from Best Buy to Accenture. The contract was the latest in a decade-long, close working relationship between Accenture and the high-performance retailer. "It is rare for a business at the top of its game to undertake a transformation program to reshape its business model, but Best Buy is boldly doing so," said Joe Forehand.

The growth of outsourcing business processes was not confined to the U.S. market. Sainsbury's, the leading British supermarket chain, in February 2004 extended its existing seven-year transformational IT outsourcing engagement with Accenture by another three years in a deal valued at more than $1 billion. The Sainsbury's engagement represented one of Europe's largest IT transformation programs, with state-of-the-art capabilities spanning marketing, stores, e-commerce, trading, supply chain, finance, human resources, office and IT infrastructure. And in July 2004, Barclays Bank announced a major application outsourcing contract with Accenture. The six-year deal, worth more than £400 million (US$740 million), was among the largest applications-only outsourcing contracts ever signed.

In 2004, British supermarket chain Sainsbury's extended its outsourcing engagement with Accenture.

Accenture signed a landmark business processing outsourcing agreement with Deutsche Bank AG in 2004 that at the time was the largest, most comprehensive procurement outsourcing contract ever signed. In conjunction with that deal, Accenture also established Accenture Procurement Solutions as a formal solution unit within its BPO organization. Under the contract, the newly formed group assumed responsibility for many of the German financial services giant's procure-to-pay functions, including requisition, tactical sourcing, invoicing and payment processing.

Also in Germany, Fujitsu Siemens Computers signed an applications outsourcing deal with Accenture in mid-2004. The engagement was expected to cut Fujitsu Siemens's cost of supporting all Siebel applications by one-third. The $27 million, five-year engagement with Fujitsu Siemens, the leading European IT infrastructure supplier, grew out of an existing, three-year relationship during which Accenture designed and implemented one of the most advanced global Siebel customer relationship management solutions.

Outsourcing engagements also were likely to serve as vehicles for expanding client relationships to include other Accenture services. In early 2004, Accenture won a 10-year, $140 million applications outsourcing engagement with DSV Group, the leading supplier of transport and logistics services in the Nordic region. The partnership agreement placed the entire responsibility for DSV's information technology maintenance and future development with Accenture, using DSV's services center in Copenhagen and Accenture delivery centers in India.

## Risks and Rewards

As the size, duration and complexity of the largest of these engagements suggested, the push to become a leading player in the global outsourcing market led Accenture to make commitments that, taken together, would have severely strained the company several years earlier. Steve James drew a parallel with the construction industry. "I tell people that we used to be very good at building nice custom houses," James said. "Today, our clients are asking us to build stadiums, large skyscrapers and arenas that have much more complex uses."

Top: Fujitsu Siemens Computers, the leading European IT infrastructure supplier, signed a five-year, $27 million applications outsourcing engagement with Accenture in mid-2004.

Bottom: Bob Frerichs, chief quality and risk officer, discussed bottom-line benefits of quality improvements at an Accenture leadership meeting, 2004.

The enhanced financial stability and resources provided by the public share offering played a key role in Accenture's ability to operate at this level. And so did Accenture's passion and reputation for delivering on its commitments. "We've always been a company that focused on being exceptionally good at delivering what we committed to," James said. "Doing it in much more complex environments, with multiple sets of skills, is something that we have to make sure we are learning as we go and becoming much more effective at, given the complexity of these transformation projects we're doing today."

With greater size and complexity of engagements came greater rewards, as well as greater risks. "We were talking in the '80s about taking on mission-critical systems, but they were, for the most part, one system," noted David Hunter, senior partner-Strategic Programs and a member of the Executive Leadership Team. "Now we're taking on huge, corporate sets of systems, billion dollar-plus jobs. All of a sudden, you talk about risk increasing. It's way out there now in terms of the effect on shareholder value of our clients."

As Accenture's size and the size of its contracts increased, so did its risk management effort. Beginning in fiscal 2005, the company rolled out an enhanced quality and risk program aimed at improving execution and margins by applying best practices across disciplines to reduce the "cost of poor quality," including write-offs, changes to approved financials and legal costs. "The goal is to take the quality of our engagement work to the next level, and in doing so, take the savings from those improvements to the bottom line," said Bob Frerichs, the company's chief quality and risk officer and a member of the Executive Leadership Team. "It is vital to our marketplace performance and our reputation."

The latest emphasis on quality at Accenture was built on previous quality initiatives. From its earliest days installing mainframe computer systems, the company had senior partners travel to review systems work and ensure that the installations were meeting company standards. By the 1980s the emphasis had shifted to building quality assurance into the planning and execution process in the early stages, rather than as a follow-up exercise. Practice directors became responsible for reviewing every major proposal to ensure that personnel with the appropriate skills were assigned to the project, and that multiple partner reviews were built into the process. Each job also had quality assurance checkpoint reviews at specific points in the engagement.

No quality assurance process could be foolproof, of course. But the steps taken by the company to try and avoid or at least minimize mistakes often impressed clients, even when they were in disputes regarding the particulars of an engagement. One of the original Accenture board members, Wulf von Schimmelmann, got to know the company in the early 1990s while negotiating the resolution of disputes regarding an engagement for a consortium of German banks. As a managing director of one of the banks, von Schimmelmann "thought that we had dealt with this issue in a straightforward and honest and fair manner," said Vernon Ellis, who was directly involved in the negotiations. "We became good friends," Ellis added.

Accenture leadership emphasized that it didn't want to curb the risk-taking culture that has helped drive the company to new heights throughout its history. At the economy's lowest point in 2002, Green's Communications & High Tech group "took on three major jobs, worth over a billion dollars, that we had trouble executing," he recalled. "When I met with the board to talk about succession and becoming the CEO, they asked me about my choices. And I said if those opportunities were in front of us again today, I would pursue them like my life depended on them. I would execute them a little differently, because I've learned through this period, but when we ever lose the courage to be bold, to be innovative and to do new things, we ought to give it up."



## IPO Report Card.

Accenture management listed the need for a larger, permanent capital base, primarily to handle larger outsourcing engagements, as one of the main reasons for converting to public ownership. As it turned out, the company structured groundbreaking outsourcing deals, in terms of size and duration, without resorting to the type of capital commitments envisioned at the time of the IPO. "The recession taught us to be very stingy with capital," said then-CFO Harry You. In fact, many current and former partners agree that since the IPO, Accenture has been a much more disciplined company with much tighter management controls than in the past.

One of the biggest benefits of public ownership has been transparency. Forehand said that the legacy of a partnership, with little public disclosure of operating results and balance sheets, "led us to fear more transparency in our business. Ironically, that transparency actually has helped our brand enormously in the marketplace." Client management and boards of directors are able to look at Accenture's financial statements and see that it is a well-run company—with plenty of capital and virtually no debt—that is going be around for the duration of their contract.

## Virtual Visit

One of the boldest and most complex bids in Accenture's history was its proposal to design and implement a "virtual" border for the U.S. Department of Homeland Security as part of its US-VISIT program. Winning the project was considered such a long shot that it was code-named Seabiscuit, after the undersized U.S. racehorse that overcame great odds in the 1930s to beat the finest horses of its day. When a three-person Accenture team began actively working on the proposal in the spring of 2003 in the basement of the Reston, Virginia, office, the largest federal government contract the Accenture Government operating group had previously won was a five-year Defense Logistics Agency (DLA) contract awarded in 2000, noted Eric Stange. Stange served as US-VISIT program manager along with Steve Rohleder, who was running the Government operating group at the time. The scope of the DLA project was dwarfed by the scope of the US-VISIT contract, which would run for 10 years and could be worth up to $10 billion. Also weighing against Accenture was that its two leading rivals bidding on the US-VISIT contract, CSC and Lockheed Martin, already were working with the Department of Homeland Security on the initial phase of the US-VISIT program.

The Accenture team took the offensive, focusing on the outcomes of enhanced national security, improved integration of the immigration process and protecting privacy. They also needed to define the transformation necessary among the various government agencies involved in the program. Only then did the team focus on the technology necessary to effect such change. By November 2003, when the government issued its official request for proposal, the Accenture team numbered 100 strong. Stange didn't see the competing proposals, but later feedback from federal officials led him to conclude, "We had a stronger vision of the role technology would play in the process." As he suspected, the other two bidders focused on the technology in their proposals, rather than emphasizing the transformational process for which the technology was the means, not the end.

Top: One of the U.S. Department of Homeland Security kiosks at Chicago's O'Hare International Airport designed to check passenger visas.

Bottom: Prior to being named Accenture's chief operating officer in 2004, Steve Rohleder led the company's global Government operating group.

## Radio Tag

Not that the Accenture team downplayed the high-tech tools at its disposal. Using a nearby facility belonging to Raytheon, a subcontractor on its team, the Accenture-led team constructed a mock border-point kiosk at which the government team had their fingerprints scanned, a digital photo taken and a radio frequency identification, or RFID, tag attached to their passports containing relevant personal data. They also constructed a mock land-border crossing where a scanner read the RFID passport tags of the government officials inside a car. Even though Jim Williams, the federal official who directs the US-VISIT program, pushed the accelerator in his car to the floor while leaving the parking lot—and the car became momentarily airborne after hitting a speed bump—the scanner read the digital information contained on the RFID chips of all four government officials in the vehicle, Stange said, displaying the officials' pictures on an electronic billboard as they passed by.

Stange learned later that Accenture had outperformed its rivals both in terms of its technology and the transformational scope of its proposal. Accenture's business transformation vision carried the day, and the project Seabiscuit team, numbering 120 and growing, was told on June 1, 2004, that they had won the race.

"I think this is a milestone," said Forehand. "We really hit our stride with the US-VISIT program. To think of being able to win the largest IT contract ever awarded, to think of doing something that does, as we say in our vision statement, improve the way the world works and lives, makes this a real landmark."

### Consulting Rebounds

After several quarters of contraction, the consulting business began to rebound in 2003. In March 2003, New York City went "live" with 311, its single phone number service for New Yorkers needing access to non-emergency information. Accenture, working closely with the city's Department of Information Technology and Telecommunications, completed the project in just seven months. Fulfilling recently elected Mayor Michael Bloomberg's pledge to bring government closer to the people, the 311 service replaced 14 pages in the phone book that had listed municipal services, and was available in 171 different languages. The 24-hour service even functioned as designed during the city's August 2003 blackout—with the help of 35 Accenture volunteers. The

Above: Made to Order. Accenture helped Dell upgrade its supply chain management systems.

Left: New York City's 311 Call Center handles residents' non-emergency needs.

311 contract emphasized the importance Accenture had placed on public-sector consulting since the 1970s to help offset the dips in private-sector projects that were more closely linked to the business cycle. But by 2003, the private sector was picking up as well, and many clients turned to Accenture for help in taking costs out of their businesses so they could get more leverage out of rebounding revenues.

Dell is widely considered the computer industry gold standard when it comes to just-in-time manufacturing. But when Dell realized it could shave even more time off of its assembly process and cut its costs accordingly, it turned to Accenture for help in implementing a supply chain solution that allowed Dell to operate on no more than two hours of inventory—industry-leading performance at the time. In 1999, Dell finished the rollout to plants around the world. The program paid for itself five times over in the first 12 months of operation.

### One Global Firm

It was an extremely difficult period for many Accenture employees to live through, but the global downturn strengthened Accenture's competitive position. With many traditional rivals left in a weakened financial state, Accenture remained unmatched in terms of its global breadth and depth. Accenture was leveraging these strengths with scores of new and continuing engagements to drive growth in consulting revenues that was projected to exceed global growth in IT spending going forward. Once again, as it had many times in its history, Accenture showed its ability to quickly respond to changing conditions in the marketplace to best serve its customers' needs.

Top: Karl-Heinz Floether, group chief executive-Technology & Delivery.

Bottom: James Hall led the Technology & Systems Integration capability group before taking a new position in 2005 leading Accenture's client work at the National Health Service in England.

Case in point: a multiyear engagement undertaken for food, home and personal care products giant Unilever. The Netherlands-based company worked with Accenture to help Unilever create a more integrated regional organization in Latin America. The multimillion dollar effort, scheduled to conclude in 2005, created synergy across Latin America for Unilever by harmonizing processes and systems, integrating the separate countries' IT platforms. This undertaking enabled Unilever to launch shared services efforts in finance and human resources, and further create fuel for growth.

In Britain, Accenture achieved considerable penetration of the U.K. health care sector in late 2003 and early 2004. Under a 10-year agreement with the U.K. Department of Health totaling more than $3 billion, Accenture began work with the National Health Service to deliver its National Programme for IT in both the eastern and northeastern regions of England. Accenture professionals embarked on designing, building, deploying and operating key information systems to support the delivery of world-class patient care and services. At the heart of the National Programme for IT is the NHS Care Records Service, which is designed to provide a nationally accessible electronic care record for every patient in England. This service will support an estimated 350,000 NHS staff and improve health care benefits for 17 million citizens in these regions.

Accenture also leveraged its global industry groups to differentiate itself from rival consulting as well as outsourcing firms. That fact hasn't been lost on clients, said Karl-Heinz Floether, former group chief executive-Financial Services, named group chief executive-Technology & Delivery in 2005. "Whether we are taking an insurance system we developed in Spain and installing it for a client in Chicago, or we take a banking system developed in Spain and install it in the U.K., I think we get a lot of credit from our clients who say: 'You can see that there's "one firm"—and that's Accenture,'" Floether noted. A recent visit to Accenture delivery centers in India left clients with the same impression. "We had a couple of clients visiting our sites in India where they said, 'It's very clear, you go into an Accenture office in London or you go into an Accenture office in India, and you say, that's Accenture,'" Floether added.

Accenture tapped its multiple workforces to complete a supply chain transformation for Roche Pharmaceuticals, a $16 billion division of F. Hoffmann-La Roche, based in Switzerland. Accenture edged out the incumbent, IBM, as the integration partner to deliver an 18-month SAP-based program across 16 European sales affiliates and six plants. With the first release needing to be designed, built and implemented at five sales affiliates and one plant in just seven months, Accenture proposed using its Supply Chain Solution Center in Barcelona for delivering the application configuration and custom-built solution. About 70 percent of the overall project team consisted of consultants from Switzerland, while the remaining 30 percent from Barcelona included roughly a 60–40 mix of Consulting and Solutions workforces. "By drawing on our strengths as a global company, we brought the right expertise at the right time to deliver an ambitious plan on schedule," said Bruce Horton, partner-Supply Chain Management.

**Eye on Value. Mark Foster, group chief executive-Products.**

### Adding Value

Leveraging business groups and workforces was the key to setting the stage for future growth at Accenture, according to London-based Mark Foster, group chief executive-Products. "We have to start leveraging global and other assets more effectively in terms of the bundled value proposition we put on the table to both transform and run businesses for our clients," he noted. Focusing on adding value for clients has enabled Accenture over the past few years to raise its sights from clients with money earmarked for consulting, which dried up noticeably during the recent recession, to "the addressable market of how much of the value chain of a client can now turn into our value chain with a margin on it," Foster said. "That's actually a pretty much infinite marketplace," he maintained. "That shift of thinking has been absolutely fundamental to changing our mix of business in a very, very fundamental way."

Accenture's goal, which remains virtually unchanged from the firm's earliest forays into consulting, is to help solve clients' problems by bringing the best global resources we can focus on the problem, Foster noted. Accenture will continue to create capabilities and centers of excellence around the world that can do this, integrating the value chain for the client. "It's not about us being exporters of jobs from one place to another, or being a catalyst for that," as some critics of the global outsourcing trend allege, he added.

### High Performance

Green cautioned that bigger isn't always better. "The game we're playing isn't going to be about scale, it's going to be about differentiation and superior execution," Green stated. "And that plays right into the High Performance Business theme—our outcomes-oriented focus. Senior-level executives get it. If you're going to bet your job or your company on the advice and counsel and assistance of somebody, they better be aligned with delivering measurable results. That's what works for us."

Accenture had to hold itself out as a high-performance company if it was going to help clients become high-performance companies as well, he said. "It's not just about profits. It's about innovation, it's about being bold, it's about going to the next level," Green added. "It's important we represent to our clients that we have achieved that, and that we continue to relentlessly improve our overall business performance."

Top: Accenture enjoys an ever-increasing role in the Asia markets. Mylin Tan at the Accenture Delivery Center in Manila, 2002.

Bottom: Basilio Rueda led Accenture's Global Delivery Network, which in 2005 included 32,000 professionals focusing on systems integration, application outsourcing and business process outsourcing.

After being on a "stabilize and navigate agenda, we need to get back on a growth agenda," Green said. He saw "tremendous headroom" for expanding into adjacent markets that are "direct extensions of what we know how to do every day." He added, "The world has changed a lot in five years. Where the action is has changed a lot. Certainly we have opportunities in Asia that are astounding. Now for years we've been positioning ourselves to a footprint and a launch pad in Asia. I think we're entering the space where we need to execute on that."

While it didn't receive much publicity at the time, Accenture was an early pioneer in building business service centers in Asia in the mid-1980s when it opened a center in Manila under the direction of partner John Smith. The firm was responding to clients, mainly in the United States, who were on the cutting edge of searching for ways to reduce the costs of systems development. Manila was chosen as the site for the center primarily because of the large number of English-speaking residents and widespread familiarity with American idioms. The savings were significant in the 1980s, even with a relatively high telecommunications cost structure. Twenty years later, the sharp drop in global telecommunications costs would drive dramatic growth in outsourcing work to Asia.

In step with global economic trends, a significant portion of Accenture's growth over the next several years was expected to come from China. Accenture's global delivery center in Dalian, the north China coastal city an hour's flight from Beijing, had 300 employees as of mid-2004 and had nearly doubled within a year. In November 2004, Accenture opened its Guangzhou office, expanding its presence in southern China and adding to operations the company had maintained in

## Avanade.

One aspect of bringing the best global resources to clients means partnering with the right allies. For Accenture, that has meant creating more than 100 strategic relationships with market leaders. "Companies need the ability to act quickly—both to be competitive and to survive in a dynamic global economy," Steve Ballmer, CEO of Microsoft, noted. "Accenture has all of the elements to bring clients that level of agility: They offer a combination of deep industry experience, business acumen, technology leadership and global reach."

Ballmer would know. In addition to being an Accenture board member, he was instrumental in the creation of Avanade, one of Accenture's most significant joint ventures. Launched as a 50–50 venture by Accenture and Microsoft in March 2000, Avanade's goal was to deliver technology solutions based on the Microsoft enterprise platform.

One major hurdle to clear was the creation of a shared culture. "Microsoft people initially just couldn't understand why the Accenture people didn't love our technology," Ballmer said. "And the Accenture people couldn't understand why the Microsoft people couldn't manage to get their stuff reframed around the customer. Now the two sides get it."

As Joe Forehand noted, "One thing we did right was make it clear early on that we have primarily a governance relationship with the two parents, not an operational relationship. On the scale of helping to meddling, it's much more turned to helping." (By 2005, Accenture held an 80 percent stake in the venture, with Microsoft owning the remaining 20 percent.)

By 2005, Avanade had delivered projects to more than 1,700 government and business organizations around the world. Moreover, Gartner, Inc., a leading provider of research and analysis on the global IT industry, cited Avanade as a "Cool Vendor" for offering technologies or solutions that were innovative, impactful and intriguing.

Source: *Cool Vendors in IT Services and Outsourcing*, 2005. Gartner authors: Gartner RAS Core Research Note G00126362, B. Pring, M. Cantara, F. Karamouzis, M. Haines, R. Valdes. Publication date: March 21, 2005. For full report: http://www.avanade.com/_uploaded/pdf/pressrelease/avanade1385.pdf

**At a meeting in 2003, Avanade CEO Mitch Hill (left), Steve Ballmer and Joe Forehand discussed how best to leverage the alliance to drive greater growth.**

Above: Jane Hemstritch was named managing director of Accenture's Asia Pacific region in 2004.

Right: Thanks to rapid growth in international business process outsourcing and technology solutions businesses, Accenture had more than 10,000 employees in India by 2005. Asha Ahuja (right), manager at the Accenture Delivery Center in Mumbai, India, 2002.

mainland China for more than 10 years, with its offices in Beijing and Shanghai. The number of Accenture employees in the China practice was estimated to grow by 15,000 to 20,000 within the following years, drawing primarily upon demand for outsourcing services from Japan and Korea, as well as the Americas and Europe. "Our growth in this region reflects our deep commitment to China, an important market for Accenture," said Jane Hemstritch, managing partner-Asia Pacific and managing director-Accenture Australia.

Similarly, India remained a principal growth area for Accenture. From a relatively small, domestically focused but highly profitable consulting practice in the early 1990s, Accenture's operations in India grew dramatically, beginning with the liberalization of the Indian economy in the late 1990s. By the end of fiscal 2004, Accenture had more than 10,000 employees in India. The rapid buildup was driven by the company's global business process outsourcing and technology solutions businesses. "India represents a tremendous resource for Accenture," noted Hemstritch in mid-2005. "We expect to have 45,000 employees there within three years." By April 2005, India ranked second to the United States in terms of number of Accenture employees.

The ambitious Tiger Woods advertising blitz used the golf star's personality to highlight Accenture's High Performance Business message: *Go on. Be a Tiger.*



## Cultural Shifts

The dramatic growth of Accenture's outsourcing business involved internal cultural issues as much as financial or organizational ones. And some of the repercussions of this shift were felt throughout Accenture, particularly concerning issues of hiring and training a much more diversified workforce. Once again, Accenture retooled its business model to meet changing market conditions as it had done numerous times in previous decades. "We've done the right thing by creating separate workforces and trying to engineer each of them differently to recognize and be relevant to the men and women who chose to work here," Green said. "What's before us now is how we rationalize that and bring us all together on one common agenda."

Accenture's leadership focused on making up for ground lost during the recession. "On the one hand we did what we had to do to be good stewards of our business," Green said. "But we lost something in the area of skills, by reducing training budgets, and in personal connections and networking. In 2003 we established new budgets for training and fixed those issues. We have to be able to say to ourselves, if this adds value to our people and business, then we should do it."

The group's training budget may have been cut back sharply in 2002, but Gill Rider, chief leadership officer, hardly took the year off. She and her team spent much time that year working on new curricula for

Accenture's leadership and other training programs. In so doing they followed in the tradition of predecessors who had taken advantage of the slowdown in the early 1970s to write the Electronic Data Processing reference binders that played such a key role in the firm's direction. The stakes were just as high for Rider's effort, a fact that Accenture's leadership underscored when it decided to spend an additional $100 million on training and development in fiscal 2003 for a total of $391 million, and $411 million in fiscal 2004.

### First Class

Under the leadership of Rider and Jill Smart (who became managing partner-Human Resources in 2004), Accenture in 2003 for the first time began rolling out curricula fashioned to meet the distinct needs of Accenture's four workforces—Consulting, Services, Solutions and Enterprise. The courses drew upon the tradition established at the St. Charles facility in the early 1970s, and at Chicago's Knickerbocker Hotel before, of combining intense learning experiences with opportunities to network and socialize with co-workers after hours. On June 23, 2004, the training program reached a milestone of its own when the 10,000th person in fiscal 2004—Geraldine Bodescot, analyst-Resources, Paris—attended the workforce training course in St. Charles.

Top: Geraldine Bodescot (center), analyst-Resources, Paris, is congratulated by Bill Green (left) and Joe Forehand (right) on June 23, 2004. Bodescot became the 10,000th person in fiscal year 2004 to attend the workforce training course in St. Charles.

Bottom: Gill Rider became Accenture's chief leadership officer in 2002. "I like to think that Accenture has the characteristics of the best families; friendly and supportive with the highest integrity and respect for others," she said.



Forehand noted that tailoring the training courses to different workforces is merely catching up with reality. "Just a few years ago we were predominantly a consulting organization with a Consulting workforce and core concepts courses," Forehand said. "Today, compared to the Services workforce, Solutions (which is more of a technology skill path in our global delivery networks), plus our Enterprise workforce...the Consulting workforce is now [a] minority."

The new courses were part of a concerted effort at Accenture to ensure that "All our employees see themselves as being important citizens. There are no second-class people at Accenture," Forehand said. "Being able to provide a different value proposition for each workforce, but yet an integrated model as to how we look at progression and career opportunities, is what we've been working on." It wasn't the first time the company had made a dramatic shift in its hiring policy that would result in multiple workforces. In 1965, for example, the consulting practice made a dramatic break with tradition when, for the first time as a matter of policy, it recruited new hires without accounting training.

The company also introduced the Partner Career Management and Compensation program, a major change in the way partners managed their careers and how they were compensated. Led by Jorge Benitez, when he was managing partner-Partner Matters, the program was a recognition that different partners have different capabilities and that Accenture needed to strengthen and maximize those different capabilities to achieve greater success for the company. "We recognized that there's no one role that is the same for every partner," Benitez noted. "You may be in a selling role, and that may be very different than a delivery role. One isn't better than the other; they're both necessary. But the way that you would measure and evaluate the results of someone, or the way that you would build capabilities, is different."

As fiscal 2005 began, the company set the foundation for the Accenture Career Framework, a multiyear program designed to clarify the career paths and professional growth opportunities for all Accenture people, at all levels. The initiative was designed to clearly articulate and document what an employee in each of the workforces could expect in terms of career progression, type of work, rewards and training. The project also called for a transition to a single Senior Executive Career Model that would be consistent across all workforces, allowing Accenture to better recognize and reward the contributions of diverse senior professionals.

While renowned in the business world for the quality of its entry-level training, Accenture also began focusing on "leaders teaching leaders," in which experienced partners teach leadership skills to younger partners. Developed in part out of concern after the IPO that Accenture might risk losing some of its accumulated expertise as a number of partners retired, this leadership development program has been an enormous success, Rider said. It was expanded in 2004 to include other executive levels.



## Spanish Steps.

The first steps to reinvent Accenture's training program were taken at a January 2002 meeting of the company's management team in Madrid. The mood leading up to the meeting was bleak, both within the company and around the world. "This was not long after the economy really went into the tank and we were dealing with the 9/11 aftermath," recalled Chairman Joe Forehand. "The management team was pretty tested in terms of dealing with the abrupt demand falloff and pressing short-term issues."

Accenture leadership quickly focused, however, on the need to reinvest in training for the future, even if there would be no immediate payoff. "There was a rallying around our view that we must invest in our people in the tough times even if a total revamping of our training would not pay off in the near term," Forehand said. "Our leaders went back to our belief that training is a long-term differentiator and an important aspect of our 'Best People' core value," he noted. Several senior company leaders, already working almost non-stop to help steer Accenture through the severe economic downturn, volunteered to serve on the steering committee with Gill Rider, chief leadership officer, and design the new training program.

## Corporate Citizenship.

Employees participating in Accenture Development Partnerships initiatives are assigned to small project teams to provide consulting services. While helping conduct a strategic review for the Hope for African Children Initiative in 2004, James Anderson (right), an Accenture manager from the United Kingdom, visited a Cameroon community. He is pictured with brothers and sisters who had lost both their parents to HIV/AIDS and were receiving financial support for schooling.

Accenture has long sought to play a positive role, beyond day-to-day business affairs, in the various communities and societies in which it operates. In the United States, prior to converting the firm to public ownership, the partners had contributed to a non-profit foundation that distributed funds to various charitable organizations. Upon Accenture's initial public offering in 2001, the partners endowed a fund with shares to form the basis for an expanded global giving program. The company also created local charitable giving programs in most of the countries in which it operated.

The company refocused its charitable energies in 2003 with the creation of the Accenture Corporate Citizenship Council, headed by non-executive International Chairman Vernon Ellis. Community initiatives undertaken by Accenture have included helping fund an SOS Children's Village clinic to care for HIV-infected children in South Africa; helping stage the 2003 Special Olympics World Summer Games for 7,000 athletes with learning disabilities; and developing a website that enables teachers across Brazil to share best educational practices and other tips.

Through one of its major initiatives—Accenture Development Partnerships—the company has made consulting services available at reduced rates to non-governmental and donor organizations working in developing countries.



Rider said the company also is trying to pass along some of its shared heritage. "We're building into all of our training, in all of the curriculums, what we call community meetings, at which people come together in their geographies within their workforces," she noted. "We're trying to get back to the world in which we used to live of telling stories, because we sort of lost that storytelling mentality, which is crucial to getting the culture and values going."

During a succession planning exercise at St. Charles, Rider said she was impressed once again with the depth of talent within the company. Accenture's goal was to "get those people the right opportunities, the right cross-cultural experiences and the right options to become visible in the firm," she said. "I can't conceive that there is another company out there that can look one, two levels down and have so much talent ready to come on the way up."

Reflecting Accenture's growth in Asia to date, the company emphasized regional education in that part of the world. "We have to recognize that we have different [ethnicities], cultures and languages within this global company and we've got to recognize that more," explained David Hunter. While English remained the global language of business, and of Accenture, the company realized that it needed to offer basic core training courses in the languages of the local populations it was hiring in Asia. More senior personnel received training in English as required.

St. Charles staff helped set up an education center in the Asia Pacific region in Malaysia, which offered training courses taught in Japanese, Korean, Mandarin and English.

### Diversity

Kedrick Adkins, named Accenture's first chief diversity officer in 2003, noted that diversity of all kinds, including racial, gender and ethnic, needed to be promoted at every level within Accenture. The company, in order to continue to attract the best people and win the best clients, had to become as diverse as the global community in which it

Left: Kedrick Adkins became the company's first chief diversity officer in 2003.

Above: Accenture's diverse workforce enables the company to meet the challenges of the marketplace. Nellie Borrero has managed a number of Accenture's diversity initiatives.



operated, Adkins said. "We're going to have people from everywhere, not only in the U.S. but from around the world. And they have to feel as though this is a good place for them," he added. As for clients, "They have expectations for us relative to diversity and inclusion. It's getting harder and harder to sell work and to grow in an environment where we don't present the same kind of face to our clients that they have within their organization, be it gender or ethnicity."

Adkins has worked with Forehand, Green and the rest of the Accenture leadership team to help the company focus on making diversity a key element in recruiting, training and mentoring within Accenture. "I think we need to reground ourselves in what it takes to attract, retain and motivate the men and women who carry this place on their backs every day," Green said. "And to do that in a modern way, focusing on diversity and other issues, to recognize that we're not the same business that we've been historically."

This drive dovetailed with efforts to encourage and support the hiring and advancement of women at Accenture. "We put in place a number of things such as a part-time partner policy and flexible scheduling," Forehand said, to open more career paths to women. Accenture also created women's networks that could deal with the unique issues of women concerning advancement and retention.

## Talk the Talk; Walk the Walk.

Jorge Benitez was included in *Hispanic Business* magazine's 2004 list of the "100 most influential U.S. Hispanics." In 2005, he was named to lead the Consumer & Industrial Products operating unit in the Americas.

Jorge Benitez learned firsthand what it was like to experience the company's less-than-diverse culture of the early 1980s. Benitez and his family had emigrated from Cuba to Miami, Florida, in 1970, and he joined the consulting group in 1981. Benitez was keenly aware of not fitting in with the predominately white male, white-buttoned-down shirt culture of the Miami office. He became so self-conscious of having a first name that many co-workers found difficult to pronounce that he asked that people call him George. After a year or so as a consultant, however, he decided that subverting his cultural heritage in an effort to fit in was asking too much: "I said to myself, I don't really think I should change my name just because others have difficulty pronouncing it."

Benitez was made a partner in 1992 and became managing partner-Partner Matters in 2002, following Jesse Tutor's retirement. In accepting that position, one of the challenges he faced was ensuring Accenture's commitment to diversity. "I know that all the leaders I interact with, they're not questioning whether it's right to have respect for the individual or not, or whether it's right to have a stewardship or an integrity principle. They all believe it. It's inherent," he said. "We have to start living those values much more so in the context of what we do, not just what we believe."

Pam Craig, senior vice president-Finance, played a lead role in several initiatives seeking to advance and retain women at the company. Craig, on the left, participated in a panel discussion at the Womenfuture MainEvent 2002.

While noting that more work needed to be done in this and all aspects of supporting diversity, Forehand said he was honored to accept the 2003 Catalyst Award on behalf of Accenture in recognition of its innovative approaches to recruiting and advancing women.

Shortly after she was named a partner in 1984, Carla Paonessa recalled, all the women partners at the company could sit around one or two breakfast tables at a partners' meeting. Paonessa, who joined the educational training practice in 1978, said that in the mid-1980s, "bringing women into the leadership of the firm really needed a lot of attention, and we put a lot of focus on that as the years went by." The example set by Paonessa and other pioneering women partners not mentioned in earlier chapters, including Rosemary O'Mahony, Julie Nelson, Cristina Molinari, Jane Hemstritch, Pam Craig, Jill Smart, Philippa Reid, Lynn McMahon and Lori Lovelace, helped pave the way for a significant expansion in the number of women among the Accenture leadership. At the start of fiscal 2005 there were 244 women partners, equal to 11 percent of Accenture's 2,219 partners.

## Accent on the Future

Doing everything possible to continue to attract the best people to Accenture, and "recharging and reenergizing" those who have weathered the severe economic downturn of the past few years, were at the top of Green's agenda as he assumed the CEO role. "It's been a rough ride the last three years. We've got to get some of the heart and soul back in our business," he said. "We're working on making sure we

Accenture Technology Labs professionals explore how emerging technologies may impact business, part of the company's commitment to innovation. William Westerman and Tanya Leake in Palo Alto, California, discuss plans for an innovation workshop for client organizations, 2004.

are clear and relevant" on issues of career path and compensation for each of the company's workforces, Green added. "Yet being part of a winning team and a widely recognized, great enterprise is something special. That matters as well."

Some speculated at the time of the IPO in 2001 that Accenture's special culture and values wouldn't be able to survive the transition to public ownership. The severe economic downturn that followed didn't help the organization's odds. But the partnership values and culture have retained a special meaning at Accenture.

"We're probably at the beginning of an evolution of this thing that we call being a partner," Green said. "I think the principles of it will never change—that is the emotional attachment, the ownership, the feeling of authority and accountability are the things we have to continue to hone and get right. Maybe titles will change, maybe compensation will change, maybe career paths will change. But the principles—what have historically been the partnership principles, as we call them—are precious, and every day we have to work to make sure that those never change."

Green was leading a town hall meeting at the St. Charles campus in the summer of 2004. There were about 800 employees in the auditorium, and one employee in the back of the room said, "I've been here three weeks. I think I understand some of these values, but what is this thing called stewardship?"

"Stewardship is the first thing that partners talk about when they talk about what's special about this place," said Green. "It's their inheritance. It's what they feel their obligations are in turn to our enterprise and our men and women," those here today and those yet to come. Tenacious support for clients and employees, coupled with high standards and a willingness to embrace change, were the values that each generation of Accenture "stewards" has handed down to the next.

When Bill Green would meet with clients, the first thing the Accenture CEO heard was, "You have great people. We selected you, and we have a long-term relationship with you, because your people are the best." Green confirmed the importance of Accenture's people, noting, "The company with the best people wins."

Bill Green at the fiscal 2005 Kickoff. When asked to describe Green in three words, an Accenture colleague said, "He's funny, he's innovative and he knows how to take care of our people."

**Accenture has changed dramatically in response to changing client needs, evolving markets and competitive challenges over the past half century. And a culture is in place to ensure the company will continue to change in the future to meet these and similar needs. But some things about Accenture remain unchanged: Accenture has a passionate commitment to be the best, to do what it takes to satisfy client needs and to create opportunities for the next generation of Accenture people. And the values first articulated by the founding partners, that have guided generations of people to do the very best that they can in the interests of their clients, still thrive in the new Accenture.**

# Epilogue
# Horizon 2012



**By the fall of 2004, Accenture's senior leadership knew that it was time once again to "reinvent the enterprise," as Bill Green put it. In the space of a few years, the company had dramatically transformed itself at a speed that would have left more typical executives with a bad case of management whiplash—from the arbitration decision, renaming, conversion to public ownership and IPO to the naming of Green as CEO and appointment of new Executive Leadership Team members, not to mention greatly expanding its outsourcing business. The executives agreed that it was time to take stock of how far they had come in such a short time, and how the company should position itself for the future. "This is not just about sustaining, but extending our leadership," Green said.**

"Nobody had to blow the whistle," Green recalled in mid-2005. "Over the past 12 months, we all got to the space where we knew it was time once again to chart the destiny of the firm."

While many organizations would turn to their senior management to lead such an effort, Accenture drew upon its traditions of stewardship and training and tasked its next generation of leaders to, in effect, write the next chapter of the company's future. This practice had its roots in earlier planning efforts, notably Lincolnshire I and II, as well as Horizon 2000 in the early 1990s. Many of the current company leaders had played just such a role in planning the firm's future in the late 1990s under the auspices of the plan known as Horizon 2010. The leaders of tomorrow would assume a similar role in the latest planning process, dubbed Horizon 2012. "We needed to set the direction of the company, and get the next generation of leaders to own it," Green explained.

Between 40 and 50 of these next-generation leaders began meeting in earnest in early 2005. They represented the breadth of Accenture's businesses, including consulting, technology and systems integration, and outsourcing. The company's global reach also was represented among this group, including next-generation leaders from India, China and the Philippines, as well as Europe and the Americas.

It's no coincidence that rising stars from Asia had been involved in Horizon 2012 from day one. As Green noted in mid-2005, "We are involving more people from Asia in the planning process. They are a large part of the future growth for us—we need to embrace them in the evolving culture of Accenture." Indeed, in July 2005 Accenture announced its plan to add 30,000 to 50,000 positions over the next three years to its then-current payroll of 19,000 in Asia Pacific. Green added, "In outsourcing in particular, we need to defend against traditional and new entrants, mainly the Indian offshore firms, and extend the services we provide."

Left: Members of the Horizon 2012 team gathered in June 2005 to put the finishing touches on their recommendations. Among those participating in the session were (left to right) Sue Bresnahan, La Mae Allen Dejongh, Walt Shill, Lori Lovelace, Richard Clark, Armelle Carminati-Rabasse and Paul Nunes.

Right: Sander Van't Noordende addressed Accenture's go-to-market model during the June 2005 meeting of the Horizon 2012 team.



The overarching goal of Horizon 2012 is to "weave ourselves into our clients' businesses and operations," Green said. "We're changing the game from providing advice and services to providing outcomes and results. We are truly helping companies and organizations to become high-performance businesses. We are basing our successes on the successes of the clients we serve."

Could Joe Glickauf or the other Administrative Services pioneers of the post-World War II era have imagined more than half a century ago what today's Accenture would look like? It's not likely. The only thing Accenture employees can confidently predict about the future, said Green, is that "the needs of our clients will continue to change rapidly and we will have to be able to respond just as quickly and creatively." He added, "I look back five years, I never would have guessed that this is what we would be doing. What we will be in five years, we haven't even invented yet."

# Core Values

**Accenture people embrace six core values that shape the culture and define the character of the company. These core values guide behavior and decision making. Accenture people believe ongoing commitment to these values is necessary to ensure Accenture operates with the highest ethical standards and achieves its vision: To become one of the world's leading companies, bringing innovations to improve the way the world works and lives.**

### Stewardship
Building a heritage for future generations, acting with an owner mentality, developing people everywhere we are, and meeting our commitments to all internal and external stakeholders.

### Best People
Attracting and developing the best talent for our business, stretching our people and developing a "can do" attitude.

### Client Value Creation
Improving our clients' business performance, creating long-term, win-win relationships and focusing on execution excellence.

### One Global Network
Mobilizing the power of teaming to deliver consistently exceptional service to our clients anywhere in the world.

### Respect for the Individual
Valuing diversity, ensuring an interesting and inclusive environment and treating people as we would like to be treated ourselves.

### Integrity
Inspiring trust by taking responsibility, acting ethically, and encouraging honest and open debate.

# Timeline

## 1945

The United Nations is officially created on October 24, after China, France, the U.S.S.R., the United Kingdom, the United States and a majority of the 51 member states ratify its charter.

A moth flies into U.S. Navy computer and jams the machine. This marks the first official record of the use of the word "bug" in computing.

## 1946

The ENIAC electric computer, at a cost of $400,000, is completed.

Leonard Spacek (below) hires John Higgins and Joe Glickauf to bolster the firm's consulting practice.

## 1947

Dr. Edwin H. Land (below) introduces a new camera that can produce a developed photographic image in 60 seconds.

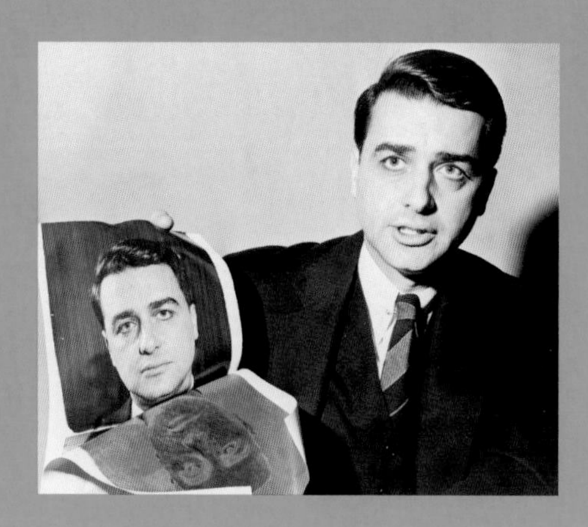

Arthur Andersen dies. Leonard Spacek assumes responsibility for operating the firm and strengthens the Administrative Accounting Division.

## 1948

IBM introduces the 402 accounting machine (tabulator).

Andersen begins a four-year engagement with Zenith Radio evaluating and overhauling manufacturing procedures.

## 1949

J. Presper Eckert and John W. Mauchly begin operating the BINAC magnetic tape computer for Northrop Aircraft.

The firm recommends that Southern California Edison Co. install an IBM punch card system (604). Upon review four years later, Andersen recommends continuing with the system.

# 1950s

## 1950

J. Presper Eckert and John W. Mauchly, inventors of the ENIAC electronic computer, sell their business to Remington Rand, which continues to develop the UNIVAC, the successor to the ENIAC.

First meeting of NATO Council Deputies in London.

After seeing a demonstration of the ENIAC computer, Joe Glickauf builds the Glickiac to demonstrate the applicability of computers for business.

## 1951

Glickauf demonstrates the Glickiac (above) at a special partners' meeting in Chicago and convinces the partners to invest in the firm's emerging computer practice.

## 1952

UNIVAC, used by the CBS television network, successfully predicts the election of Dwight D. Eisenhower (above) as U.S. president.

Jonas Salk tests a polio vaccine consisting of an injected dose of killed polio virus. In 1962, Albert Sabin produces an oral vaccine using a live, but weakened virus.

## 1953

James D. Watson and Francis Crick announce that they have determined the chemical structure of DNA.

Administrative Services begins the installation of a UNIVAC computer for a 15,000-employee payroll system at GE's Appliance Park facility.

The first Home Office Electronics School is conducted on the Chicago campus of Northwestern University.

## 1954

U.S. Senator Joseph McCarthy (below) conducts a series of hearings concerning communist infiltration of the U.S. government.

Higgins and Glickauf publish "Electronics Down to Earth" in *Harvard Business Review*. The article establishes the two partners as leading computer-for-business authorities.

Administrative Services tests computerization of payroll for GE, but finds completing it takes longer than the 40-hour work week. The system is reprogrammed and eventually works as planned.

The U.S.S.R. launches Sputnik (below), the first man-made Earth satellite.

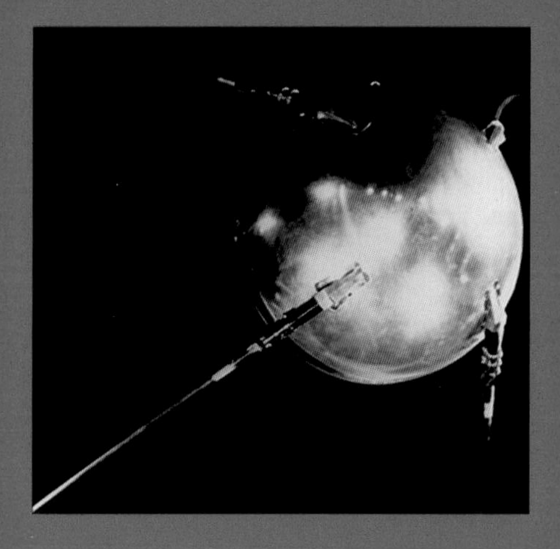

The Nautilus (above), the first nuclear submarine, revolutionizes naval warfare.

Egypt nationalizes the Suez Canal, prompting a war with Britain, France and Israel.

The first integrated circuits, or microchips, are manufactured independently by two scientists, Jack Kilby of Texas Instruments and Robert Noyce of Fairchild Semiconductor.



## 1955

Arthur Andersen opens its Mexico City office, its first outside of the United States.

## 1956

With Andersen's help, Commonwealth Edison becomes the first utility in the country to operate billing functions on a large-scale, general-purpose computer.

Andersen assigns Glickauf to develop Administrative Services outside of the United States.

## 1957

The firm opens offices in Brussels, London, Milan, Oslo, Rio de Janeiro, Santos, São Paulo and Paris. European Administrative Services activities initially are based in Milan.

Higgins (above) becomes director of U.S. operations for the firm as a whole. Glickauf takes over the Administrative Services Division.

## 1958

Administrative Services designs and installs a system for Bank of America that becomes the backbone for the BankAmericard (later renamed Visa).

## 1959

# 1960s

France grants independence to all its West African colonies, including Cameroon, Dahomey, Ivory Coast, Mali, Middle Congo, Niger, Senegal, Togo and Upper Volta.

The United States launches the Bay of Pigs invasion of Cuba.

Construction of the Berlin Wall (below) begins.

The Cuban Missile Crisis threatens the world with nuclear war.

Martin Luther King Jr. (above) delivers his "I have a dream" speech at a civil rights rally in Washington, D.C.

U.S. President John F. Kennedy is assassinated.

U.S. Congress passes the Civil Rights Act, prohibiting discrimination in employment on the basis of race, color, religion, nation of origin or gender.



## 1960

## 1961

## 1962

The firm expands into Asia with the opening of the Tokyo office.

## 1963

Wally Oliphant (above) becomes managing partner of the firm. Leonard Spacek becomes chairman.

## 1964

Art Welby initiates the Basic Systems Administrative Services School.

The firm installs responsibility reporting systems at several U.S. Air Force bases.

Martin Luther King Jr. and Robert F. Kennedy are assassinated.

Gordon Moore and Robert Noyce found Intel, and begin development of one of the first microprocessors for commercial production.

Japan's economy continues to grow; its gross national product (GNP) now ranks second only to the United States.

U.S. astronaut Neil Armstrong (above) is the first man to walk on the moon.

Digital Equipment introduces the PDP-8, the world's first computer to use integrated circuit technology.

The Cultural Revolution begins in China.

Israel captures East Jerusalem and the Golan Heights in the six-day Arab-Israeli War.

Dr. Christian Barnard performs the first heart transplant.



## 1965

Susan Butler (below) is the first professional woman hired by Administrative Services.

Administrative Services establishes the Basic Administrative Services Training School.

Administrative Services drops the requirement that new hires must work on an audit.

## 1966

## 1967

Administrative Services develops the Base V operating system, which is widely used by clients as the operating system for the popular System/360 Series of IBM computers (above).

## 1968

## 1969

Bill Ingersoll succeeds Joe Glickauf as head of Administrative Services.

# 1970s

GTE and AT&T begin experiments to transmit sound and image data using fiber optics.

The United States, North Vietnam and South Vietnam sign a peace agreement. Fighting continues until 1975, when the U.S. military fully withdraws; Vietnam is formally reunified in 1976 (below).

Arab oil embargo begins.

The Dow Jones Industrial Average drops to 570.01, approximately half of its peak in 1972.

U.S. President Richard Nixon (below) resigns.

## 1970

## 1971

The Center for Professional Development (above) at St. Charles, Illinois, opens.

Bill Mueller becomes head of the Administrative Services Division.

## 1972

The firm develops Lexicon, the first comprehensive computerized data dictionary for use in business computer systems.

Zenith Radio hires Andersen to develop software for a fixed-asset accounting system (detailed in the report below).

## 1973

International engagements include Fiat, La Société des Ciments Français and British Airways.

## 1974

The Chicago Board of Education hires Andersen to develop a full administrative system.

Andersen establishes the Technical Services Organization.

Francisco Franco, Spanish dictator, dies. His successor, the monarch Juan Carlos, makes vigorous efforts to restore democracy and a capitalist economy.

Bill Gates and Paul Allen found Microsoft.

Steve Jobs and Steve Wozniak, with Mike Markula, found Apple.

Chinese Chairman Mao Zedong dies. His death paves the way for economic reform and weakens the idea of the communist collective.

Students and fundamentalists in Iran begin to protest the government's excesses and demand removal of the Shah, leading to the Iranian revolution and Ayatollah Ruhollah Khomeini's fundamentalist regime.

Pro-communist insurgents in Afghanistan seize power in a coup, killing President Mohammad Daud Khan and overthrowing his government.

Margaret Thatcher (below) becomes prime minister of the United Kingdom, ushering in the transformation of the British economy.

After Iranian militants seize the U.S. embassy in Tehran, U.S. President Jimmy Carter places an embargo on importing Iranian oil.



## 1975

New York City engages Andersen to review the city's financial processes.

The firm develops its first real-time commercial software package, the Distribution Control System.

## 1976

Andersen forms Arthur Andersen & Co., S.C., an umbrella organization to facilitate international expansion.

## 1977

A major engagement at Yamaha Motor Company (above) leads to merging of American software with Japanese manufacturing methods.

## 1978

## 1979

Managing Partner Harvey Kapnick proposes spinning off consulting. After the failure of that proposal, Kapnick resigns and Richard Boland is selected as interim leader.

Susan Butler becomes the first female consulting partner.

# 1980s

Ronald Reagan is elected president of the United States.

IBM introduces the personal computer.

Reaganomics begins in full force, ushering in an era of deregulation, tax cuts and deficit spending in the United States.

Pope John Paul II is shot in an attempted assassination.

The compact disc, the digital alternative to the vinyl record, is introduced commercially.

*Time* magazine names the computer (below) "Man of the Year."

The U.S.S.R. boycotts the Los Angeles Olympic Games, in protest of the U.S.-led boycott of the 1980 Moscow Games.

Geraldine Ferraro becomes the first female vice presidential candidate in the United States.



## 1980

Duane Kullberg (below) elected managing partner.

Vic Millar succeeds Bill Mueller to become head of Administrative Services.

The Administrative Services Division is renamed Management Information Consulting Division (MICD).

## 1981

Andersen's Business Practice School is developed for Computer-Based Training.

## 1982

Management Information Consulting Division employs 5,100 people, with revenue totaling more than $250 million.

Harley-Davidson engages Andersen to implement just-in-time inventory techniques.

## 1983

Si Moughamian becomes managing partner of MICD.

London office begins a massive systems engagement to update the U.K. Department of Health and Social Security.

## 1984

## 1985

The first HIV tests are licensed for production.

## 1986

The Iran Contra hearings in the United States grab headlines.

The Chernobyl nuclear power plant (right) in Ukraine experiences the world's worst nuclear reactor accident, spreading radioactivity throughout northern and eastern Europe.

Andersen consultants work with the London Stock Exchange (above) in preparation for deregulated trading.

Millar leaves to form a consulting operation within Saatchi & Saatchi.

## 1987

Saatchi & Saatchi offers to buy the firm's consulting practice. The offer is rejected.

Consultants meet in London to discuss strategic planning and present their vision of the future.

Duane Kullberg implements major structural change, separating audit and tax from consulting.

## 1988

A dozen consulting group leaders meet at Manhattan's '21' Club. Kullberg dismisses Gresh Brebach, head of consulting in the United States, for organizing and leading the meeting.

George Shaheen takes over as the head of consulting in North America.

The Change Management Task Force studies the relationship between Arthur Andersen's audit and tax practice and the consulting practice.

The Andersen Consulting name is adopted.

Advertising campaign is launched.

## 1989

With the destruction of the Berlin Wall (above), East and West Germany are united.

Tim Berners-Lee invents the World Wide Web.

Partners vote to form Andersen Consulting as a separate strategic business unit.

Kullberg retires and is replaced by Larry Weinbach. Shaheen is ratified by oversight committee of the board to head the consulting practice. Dick Measelle is named head of Arthur Andersen audit and tax practice.

Arthur Andersen & Co., S.C. discloses merger discussions with Price Waterhouse. Talks break down in September.

Lincolnshire meeting leads Andersen Consulting toward business integration approach.

# 1990s

The space shuttle Discovery deploys the Hubble Space Telescope (above) 350 miles above the Earth.

Digital cell phone technology is first introduced in the United States. Mobile phone technology initially proliferated in the 1980s based on cellular networks.

Iraq is driven from Kuwait as a result of the Persian Gulf War (below).

The U.S.S.R. dissolves.

The Maastricht Treaty officially creates the European Union.

The North American Free Trade Agreement goes into effect.

With the first free multiracial elections in South Africa, Apartheid ends and Nelson Mandela is elected president.



## 1990

The U.S. Securities and Exchange Commission, in a "no-action letter," agrees that Andersen Consulting can enter into certain types of business relationships with Arthur Andersen audit clients.

## 1991

British Petroleum Exploration is among the firm's first major outsourcing engagements.

## 1992

Andersen Consulting's mission, core values and vision are developed and expressed in a series of initiatives known as Horizon 2000.

## 1993

The Asian Dynasty (above) initiative spearheads growth in the Asia Pacific region with the application of Horizon 2000 strategies.

Andersen Consulting assists in the privatization of YPF S.A., Argentina's giant oil and gas company.

Andersen Consulting launches Knowledge Xchange, a cutting-edge information sharing system.

## 1994

Andersen Consulting installs the most advanced customer relationship management system available at Barclays Bank.

The Arthur Andersen business unit forms Arthur Andersen Business Consulting.

Vernon Ellis, managing partner in charge of the Europe practice, reorganizes Europe into regions that cross country boundaries.

The World Trade Organization (below) is born.

Introduction of the Palm Pilot PDA (below).

IBM's Deep Blue computer plays chess with Gary Kasparov (Kasparov 1, Deep Blue 2, 3 draws).

Thailand's currency collapses, beginning the Asian economic crisis of the late 1990s.

Larry Page and Sergey Brin, Stanford University graduate students, put Ph.D. plans on hold to found Google.

Dow Jones Industrial Average hits 10,000 for the first time.

Despite crises in Asia, Russia and Brazil, downturns are less severe than expected. European economies revive after a slow period.

NATO forces (below) enter combat to protect Albanians in Kosovo.

## 1995

Andersen Consulting World Championship of Golf begins.

## 1996

Advertising campaign is launched on a global scale.

## 1997

Andersen Worldwide partners fail to elect a new CEO to succeed Larry Weinbach, as neither George Shaheen nor Jim Wadia receives the necessary two-thirds majority of the partner vote. The Andersen Worldwide board eventually appoints Bob Grafton as interim CEO.

Shaheen calls a controversial meeting of consulting partners to discuss resolution of differences with the audit and tax divisions through arbitration. The consulting partners vote unanimously to pursue arbitration, and the arbitration is filed in December.

## 1998

The Government industry group signs consulting agreement with the U.S. Department of Defense; part of a renewed focus on growing the government practice.

## 1999

George Shaheen (above) leaves the firm for Webvan, an e-commerce startup. Joe Forehand succeeds Shaheen as CEO.

# 2000s

The much-feared Y2K computer glitch fails to match the hype. In the United States alone, an estimated $100 billion was spent on upgrades, giving corporate productivity a boost.

The NASDAQ peaks at 5,049 points in March, only to fall repeatedly and bottom out, demonstrating market volatility fed by investor enthusiasm and anxiety.

Researchers with the Human Genome Project announce that they have mapped the human gene.

September 11 terrorist attacks on the United States kill 2,986 people.

Worldwide digital camera shipments top 40 million.

Global investment helps China upgrade its industrial structure, with high-tech industries contributing to more than 25 percent of Chinese industry growth.

The United States begins bombing Baghdad on March 19, marking the start of the 2003 Iraq War.

NASA successfully lands two rovers on Mars. During their exploration, the rovers (above) discover compelling evidence of water on Mars long ago, suggesting a possibility of life on Mars.

Around the world, cellular phone usage surpasses landline usage. The majority of U.S. households have one or more cell phones.



## 2000

An arbitrator's decision severs the contractual ties between Andersen Consulting and Andersen Worldwide.

Accenture is chosen as the new name of the firm, effective January 1, 2001.

At the October partners' meeting in Miami, Andersen Consulting leadership presents partners with the general framework for an Initial Public Offering (IPO).

## 2001

Partners approve IPO in April. Completed in July (above), it helps raise much-needed permanent capital.

Accenture immediately ranks among the 200 largest companies listed on the NYSE in terms of revenues.

In the immediate wake of the September 11 attacks, Accenture volunteers lead creation of Family Assistance Center in lower Manhattan.

## 2002

A federal jury finds Arthur Andersen guilty on one count of obstructing justice in the Enron case. (In 2005, the conviction is overturned by the U.S. Supreme Court.)

## 2003

Accenture secures Tiger Woods (above) as a symbol of high performance.

Accenture adopts High Performance Business strategy and marketplace positioning.

Accenture begins rolling out curricula fashioned to meet the distinct needs of Accenture's four workforces—Consulting, Enterprise, Services and Solutions.

## 2004

Accenture wins a major contract with the U.S. Department of Homeland Security to create a "virtual" border for the United States.

Bill Green (below left) is named CEO of Accenture. Joe Forehand (below right) retains the chairman role.

As laptop sales soar, the shift from desktop to laptop signifies a radical change in the way users perceive IT, just as the move from mainframe to desktop transformed business practices a generation earlier.

Many companies offer voice over Internet protocol (VOIP) calling as an alternative to copper-wire connections in use since Alexander Graham Bell's era.

Values. Driven. Leadership.

## 2005

Accenture's next-generation leaders begin the Horizon 2012 planning process to set the future direction of the company.

# Partners

In April 2001, Accenture partners voted overwhelmingly in support of a proposal to pursue an initial public offering, effectively charting the course for the end of exclusive partner ownership of the firm. This historic event was captured at the Annual Partners' Meeting in Dallas. The following list includes individuals who were admitted as partners of Accenture and its predecessor organizations.

July 1, 1951
John A. Higgins

July 1, 1952
Marvin Leonard Johnson

July 1, 1953
Joseph S. Glickauf

July 1, 1954
Frederick Cecil Lawrence
John E. Martin
Basil Anthony Regione

July 1, 1955
Henry George Trentin

September 1, 1955
Thomas Madison McDaniel

July 1, 1956
Charles E. Hemphill
Gale Hitchcock
William J. Mueller

July 1, 1957
David G. Morrison
John R. Spellman

July 1, 1958
John Herbert Bergstedt
Frank B. Gardner
John F. Umbs

July 1, 1959
David Bendel Hertz

July 1, 1960
Charles Griswold Abbott
Joseph E. Carrico
Lee S. Carter
Donald V. Kane
John D. Pardee
Irvin David Smith

July 1, 1961
Richard K. Gohr
Eric John Hibble
John Robert Kadow
Leighton F. Smith
Arthur Robert Voigt

July 1, 1962
Calvin G. Bauer
Eugene L. Delves
Gordon Lee Hamrick, Jr.
William C. Ingersoll
Charles R. Jewell
Kurt H. Schaffir
David Clyde Sullivan
Donald L. Thiry

July 1, 1963
Philip Eugene Barnes
Barrett M. Crawford
Robert Charles Hansel
David Lee Harvey
Leland Alfred Moody
Warren Francis Morgan

July 1, 1964
Guy Barbier
Donald B. Dixon
Frank M. Dwiggins
Richard Albert Nerad
Don L. Sneary
John Joseph Stephens

July 1, 1965
Stuart A. Clarke
Thomas F. Kelly
Alexander Edmund Simmons

July 1, 1966
Walter Searls Baker
Don G. Baker
John H. Curran
Ian Hay Davison
William Ellsworth Ellingson
John L. Fairfield
Richard J. Guiltinan
Billy O'Neill Hoskins
Reginald L. Jones
Donald Alfred Krueger
Vincent Anthony Melore
August L. Mollenkamp
Claude Onxley
Arthur Earle Welby

July 1, 1967
Donald D. Anguish
Arthur Ross Berger
Charles A. Bowsher
James A. Carty
Don Charles Eckert
Forest T. Fenton
Ronald N. Flores
Thomas M. Hallin
David R. Kaye
John E. Kindt
Robert Neil McDougall
Thomas J. Nessinger
Donald John Regele
Pierre Reveillion
Delton Roehm
Edward A. Schefer

July 1, 1968
Granville Rogers Gargiulo
H. Devon Graham
D. Clark Higgins
George William Marshall
Victor E. Millar
Donald C. Minard
Simon Moughamian
Patrick Daniel Murphy
James Frederick Shannon
Edward Jackson Smith
Martin H. Vandersteen

July 1, 1969
Charles Hansell Barineau
Walter Lee Bates
John R. Birkofer
Stanley L. Cornelison
Robert C. Engelstad
Walter Raymond Evans
Leon Fuller

Joseph R. Hausner
Richard C. LaVelle
Donald James McCubbrey
David O. Nellemann
Claude Pierre Remy
Billy Wayne Rhoades
David H. Woodham

July 1, 1970
Richard M. Boyle
Alfred E. Cambridge
Robert Eugene Evanson
Alvin Johnnie Hooker
Richard D. Johnson
Donald J. Kabat
Lamont La Robardier
Henry George Laun
Charles Paul McLarnon
Robert Jerome Parker
Emile Robert Poulin
Harford M. Robb
Alfred Ronneberger
F. Dean Taylor
Lucius P. Wheeler
Gwynn Rees Williams
Charles D. Winslow

July 1, 1971
Harold Sheldon Bott
John Laurie Buckworth
Edward John Case
Alexander David Ewing
Michel Falcotet
G. Frank Felder
George M. Hill
John W. Konvalinka
Robert L. Pedrazzini
J. Robert Prince
Paul L. Stock
Christiaan Van Aalst
John Beverely Warren
William Daniel Windham

April 1, 1972
Serge Audouin
Robert Martin Beals
George Robert Brian
Clifford Stanley Hicks
John T. Kelly
Edward T. Kennedy
John M. Kohlmeier
Paul William Landgren
Ronald L. Lowe
John A. Moga
Karl E. Newkirk
Gerald A. Taylor

September 1, 1972
Michael S. Noling

April 1, 1973
Luis I. Argumosa
Stephen L. Barnett
David M. Brunn
Charles H. Chapman
Allen R. Crossman
John R. Garrahy
Michael O. Hill
Edward A. Kennedy
Kevin B. Lavery
Charles M. Paulk
Leroy D. Peterson
Graham John Reddish
Jay N. Ross
Lloyd Joseph Russell
Michael E. Simon
Paul Lawrence Tom
Gerard Van Kemmel
Ray M. Whitworth
Jorge Zino Gutierrez

September 1, 1973
Robert F. Kelley

April 1, 1974
Charles A. Balch
Otto E. Becker
Gresham T. Brebach
Alan A. Burgess
Carlos Arturo Cervantes
John David Edwards
Louis P. Herremans
Hienz Horst Gunther Leist
Larry R. Levitan
W. Baker McAdams
Richard P. Moore
Paul T. Morey
Carlos Badger Quinn
Bruno Ricca
Thomas W. Sarowski
Roberto Silva
Clark David Stewart
Thomas H. Tebben
Robert L. Wilson

September 1, 1975
William S. Barnard
Challen O. Bonar
William L. Bramer
Jack L. Butts
Neil Doppelt
Stephen Renee DuMont
David Wilson Ehlers
Robert John Elliott
Robert L. Elmore
Michael Lynn Emmons
William A. Evenden
Robert J. Franz
Peter H. Fuchs

John J. Gullo
James S. Labick
Alain Legendre
Arthur S. Liss
Kazuo Miyazaki
Gerald L. Rydberg
Lloyd D. Seese
Arthur T. Stratman
Edward H. Wahtera
Dale H. Zempel

July 1, 1976
Joseph J. Carr

September 1, 1976
Robert Crandall Bruning
Herbert W. Desch
James C. Ellafrits
Francisco Javier Flores Ceja
Otis Andrew Gates
David L. Glavin
James Hartley Haas
Richard T. Howell
Thomas B. Kelly
John Kogan
Charles Lindas Lamme
Robert C. Manion
Donald E. Merz
Roger H. Nord
Padraic Declan O'Riordan
Stefanos Pantzopoulos
Barry Patmore
Frank Piccione
William F. Ramsaur
Thomas Karl Shaffert
John D. Smith
William G. Stoddard
Thomas G. Watrous
Vincent C. Watts
Donald P. Wingard
Stephen B. Zimmerman

September 1, 1977
Robert G. Baechle
Leslie F. Bergman
Melvyn Edward Bergstein
B. Michael Heath
Jerry L. Jana
Jack L. Mann
David J. Parks
Robert George Petrie
Alfred Schuler
George T. Shaheen
Luca Strambio de Castillia
Glen A. Terbeek
Randell C. Thomas
Peter C. Van Hull
James Randolph Yoakum

September 1, 1978
A. George Battle
Peter C. Bontinck
Graham R. Brough
Michel Carlier
William H. Choice
Emerson G. Dickey
Robert Meric Dymond
Peter Ehrensperger
David H. Fishburn
Friedhelm Goronzy
Guido T. Gysemans
William M. Hall
Frank P. Henderson
Richard Lee Linting
Edward F. Lukes
Thomas E. McCarty
Patrick F. McNally
Pedro Navarro
Drew Edmund Novak
Thad R. Perry
Jamie F. Picon
Luis Recio
Terry R. Schultz
W. Tunstall Searcy
Winton Starling
John Bartlett Strang
Kent L. Swanson
Donald Marvin Tomlin
Donald Ernest Warnecke
Victor T. Weber

September 1, 1979
Louis A. Amoroso
Alan D. Anderson
Willard N. Archie
John H. Blight
George L. Brown
John W. Bunnell
Susan B. Butler
Francois Charriere
Gary A. Close
Jon M. Conahan
Warner B. Croft
Ronald L. Cullum
Vernon J. Ellis
Timothy J. Forrest
Mamadou Gaye
Jean-Claude Guez
Lars L. Henriksen
Graham T. Henry
Carlos F. Ingouville
Stephan A. James
William G. Kelly
Carleton F. Kilmer
Robert A. Lauer
Ronald L. Luken

William H. McIntyre
Terence Victor Neill
Kazuaki Nishiwaki
William M. Noonan
Charles D. Petersen
Cesar Polanco
Mario A. Quiroga
Jorn K. Riewe
Donald Roberge
Herbert Sielhorst
Randy L. Stotler
Newell I. Troup
Jesse B. Tutor
William F. Underwood
William T. Van Lieshout
Dirk A. Vanderheyden
Harry L. Walter
Michael J. Winter
William John Yusko

September 1, 1980
Robert J. Ahern
Robert A. Anclien
David H. Armour
Jan M. Barents
Richard H. Beatty
Maurice Blackman
David J. Blume
George R. Bruha
Keith Burgess
Guy Chassang
Homer Lowery Dansby
Armand Victor de Rendinger
Alexander E. Dean
Abel R. Evelson
C. Robert Farwell
Persio De Luca Filho
Joel P. Friedman
James M. Fritz
Joel Garlot
Gary C. Garrett
Roy Wyatt Haley
Richard C. Haverly
Patrick J. Hogan
James W. McElwee
Federico Minelle
John William Murray
L. Dean Nelson
Dennis H. O'Brien
John R. Oltman
C. Anthony Ramsden
Anthony C. Rich
Ronald H. Rolland
Anthony J. Romanosky
Terrence Rosenberg
Roy E. Schoen

Lorenzo Secchi
Douglas W. Sewell
Cesare Sinicorni
Ronald James Sloan
Roger William Smith
Jorge Soldevila
Curtis G. Stangler
Richard W. Sullivan
Alan Richard Taylor
Jay E. Toole
Paul E. Vogelsang
John J. Warren
Brian J. Wilson
Derek B. Young

September 1, 1981

Timothy J. Admonius
Richard Andrew Babyak
Michael K. Bass
Peter Schumann Bauer
Bruce C. Baxter
Miguel A. Bermudez
Davis Hines Brannan
Richard T. Brant
Gabriel A. Bravo
Gerald R. Brundle
Donald Allen Bunch
James Klay Burns
John Allen Corsiglia
Ronald Kenneth Darling
William T. Darnton
H. William DeVitt
W. James Fischer
Barry Lionel Fradkin
Kuniaki Fujimoto
Michael F. Guheen
Donald B. Henry
Charles A. Horne
James V. Huson
John B. Kelley
Donald P. Lamers
M. Robert Leach
Jan A. Lourens
William Franklin McConnell
John A. Meier
Wayne E. Miers
Salomon Mizrahi
Masakatsu Mori
Jacque H. Passino
Roy F. Pearson
David Mark Rappaport
Jon D. Saunders
John Clive Skerritt
Douglas M. Smith
Barrett B. Smith
Robin Stainer
David J. Storm
Richard J. Stuckey
R. Hugh G. Thomson
Miguel Tobio
Marco Vigorelli
Gary Eugene Weatherly
Jack C. Wilkerson
Alastair Wood

September 1, 1982

Charlton Robbins Anderson
Ricardo J. Backer
James Stephen Barko
Kent F. Brooks
Henry S. Burgess
Bruce Gilbert Clark
James E. Collora
Paul J. Cosgrave
Yves Derville
Anthony J. Espina
James Brierton Flanagan
Joe W. Forehand
Jacques Habib
Jerry C. Hassebroek
Steven J. Johnson
Bruce B. Johnson
Philip A. Keirn
Neil F. Kidwell
Robert B. Lemon
Raymond A. Lenhardt
Richard A. Lobell
Thomas P. Maiero
Colin J. Markley
James S. Marpe
Luis Roberto Martins
Michael G. McGrath
Geoffrey Homer Nearing
Mark McRae Otway
Zandra Pedraza
Thomas D. Pincus
Aloysio C. L. Pontes
Henry J. Randazzo
Michael F. Rissi
Jan-Age Ronnestad
Keith Ruddle
Hugh W. Ryan
Melvin E. Schick
Joe L. Silman
Wilbur Lawrence Smither
Marc Howard Sternfeld
Michael L. Ward
Richard S. Wasch

September 1, 1983

Carlo Luigi Acabbi
Dow N. Bauknight
Robert I. Baxter
M. Kenneth Bien
Christian H. Billet
James C. Caldwell
Robert L. Christianson
M. John Craven
Richard S. Cuccioli
John E. Davis
Philip Z. Dolen
Thomas S. Edenton
Roger A. Gelfenbien
Thomas G. Grudnowski
Jeffrey T. Hamilton
William Jamieson
Byram T. Johnston
Thomas A. Kaminski
A. William Kapler
Steven A. Kruger
Ernesto J. Kuperman
Carl G. Longnecker
Patrick Lucas
Vincenzo Mancini
Lawrence H. Morrison
J. Patrick Mullaney
Dean A. Nichols
David A. Rey
John J. Rife
C. Thompson Ross
Ronald A. Tapp
Roger G. Willis
Jackson L. Wilson
Michael J. Young
Stephen R. Zimmer

September 1, 1984

David W. Andrews
Donald R. Asch
Nigel D. Backwith
James R. Barney
John B. Burke
J. Scott Cook
Ian R. Crouch
Douglas W. Cunningham
Donald L. Dall
Lucio Delgado
Kent A. Dolby
Roger E. Dunham
Stephen L. Farmer
Glover T. Ferguson
Eddy J. Fikse
Alan M. Fiorenza
Robert L. Grimm
Michael J. Gronemeyer
Stanley Joseph Gutkowski
Robert Halverson
Vance Edward Hitch
Keith F. Holden
James B. Hudak
Michael J. Huggins
Keith James Johnston
Hartmann Knorr
Carl A. Lilljeqvist
John A. McDorman
Robert H. Meixner
Jeffrey Miller
Brian M. Miller
Donald P. Monaco
Daniel M. Nycz
Carla J. Paonessa
Stephen G. Racioppo
E. Edwin Ramm
Gabriel Remolina
Ira M. Rosenmertz
Douglas A. Ryckman
Ronald B. Salvagio
Charles C. Searight
Stephen M. Smith
Donald L. Souter
John A. Steiner
Steven Wilson Stiling
Judith L. Teller
Luc J. Uzeel
Diego Visconti
Roy W. Walters
Francis H. Wildt
George D. Williams
Paul S. Wollam

September 1, 1985

Surjadi Adhiwidjaja
Alfonso A. Aliga Jr.
Renato B. Alto
Raul Eugenio Alvarado
Po Tim T. Ang
Rodolfo Q. Aquino
Antonio T. Aragon
Teofilo R. Asuncion
Jesus S. Ballesteros
Barbara J. Bashein
Kenneth P. Bergren
Donald W. Berkemeyer
Nigel Anthony Langhor Brooks
Leonard O. Brown
David L. Bushman
Marie T. Campagna
Guillermo N. Carague
Ignace Kokavi Clomegah
Rufo Colayco
John M. Crudele
Salvatore Michael Cutrona
Jaime G. del Rosario
Ferry Latuhihin Dharma
Orlando T. Diaz
James A. Dubsky
Adriano C. Dy
Budiman Elkana
Baltazar N. Endriga
Manuel E. Estrella
Milagros D. Fanega
Alfredo A. Figueras
Walter Fioramonti
Thomas K. Fox
James Victor Franch
Steven M. Freeman
Rene R. Fuentes
Akitomo Fujibayashi
Gerald R. Gallagher
Thomas C. Gaputis
Mario Gazanego
Qung W. Go
Manuel R. Guillermo
Antonio A. Henson
H. Curtis Herge
John Charles Hollis
Franklin Holz
James P. Honohan
Michael F. Hope
David R. Hunter
Willard A. Johnson
George Paul Jones
Mohammad Djoeana Koesoemahardja
Eugenio P. Ladrido
Antonio G. Lim
Wendy E. Lucas-Bull
Ferruccio Mangioni
Maximina Sindiong Martinez
Charles W. McDonough
Frances S. Monje
David Lewis Moore
Arden D. Moore
Ian S. Napier
Thongrut Ngarmcroh
Kiatisakdi Osothsinlp
Mario Pelosi
V. G. Perez
Waino Harold Pihl
Heru Prasetyo
Manuel S. Puno
Martin K. Ralston
Joseph W. Ratterman
Norman F. Rickeman
John Burton Robbins
Tulio Rodriguez
Jeffrey F. Roth
Steven P. Rothman
J. Steven Rushing
Elias R. San Pedro
Carmelito C. Salazar

Edward Jennings Sanderson
Carlos Osvaldo Schmidt
Edward M. Schreck
Wallace N. Sipos
Thomas J. Skelly
James P. Sweeney
Kenneth D. Theut
William A. Thurwachter
Glenn L. Timmerman
Philip M. Toomey
Byron A. Tsinikas
Cesar V. Tuazon
Thomas H. Tubergen
Emmanuel T. Velasco
Edwin B. Villanueva
Zainal Abidin Zahidin
Fortunato Juan S. Zalamea
Randy Zmrhal
Orlando S. Zorilla

September 1, 1986

Kedrick D. Adkins
Gerhard Aichberger
Ismael Alonso Ahijado
Arve Sogn Andersen
Richard Keith Anderson
Michael J. Arnold
Paul G. Backes
Robert Louis Baker
Catalino Y. Buktaw
Alfonso Capdepon
Daniel P. Carter
Christian Charvet
Scott M. Cleary
James Robert Corey
Benoit Coville
David A. Crow
Marc O. De Kegel
Robert W. Denner
James F. Drayer
Stephen A. Elliott
Guido Feller
Federico Feyles
Mario Fleck
Thomas D. Follett
Robert N. Frerichs
Silvio Jose Genesini
William T. Giblin
William D. Green
Oscar Humberto Guerra Van Rankin
Anthony C. Hancy
Gregg G. Hartemayer
Raad H. Hermes
Dennis Alan Hill
Michael R. Hudson
Frederick P. Huff
Andrew Hunter
Francois Jaquenoud
Muneo Katsumoto
Sudhindar K. Khanna
Richard A. LaBardi
Julio Lage Gonzalez
Peter C. Lamb
Jae-Hyung Lee
Alexa M. Lewandowski
Michele Liberato
Jeffrey P. Luker
Joseph S. Macies
Jose Luis Manzanares
Osvaldo Camilo Mendez
Harold C. Merrill
Richard D. Monroe
John C. Morris
Bruce B. Piper
Charles H. Porter
John D. Rollins
Kerry A. Schmitt
Douglas G. Scrivner
Kersi S. Shroff
Arthur Sinensky
John Stares
Marcelo Daniel Sternberg
David E. Stilerman
William E. Storts
Michael E. Surovik
Michael J. Thran
Robert L. Totterdale
Duilio Turrini
Keiichi Unno
Carlos Vidal
Herbert G. Vinnicombe
Brian W. Winne
Allen J. Wolpert
Naoji Yui

September 1, 1987

Thomas E. Arenberg
Robert L. M. Baldock
Stephen R. Baxter
James M. Bernstein
Denis Bourg
Stephen Lake Brant
Martin R. Brown
Alcides Brum
Michael L. Caine
James S. Carluccio
Joe K. Carter
Cherine Mohsen Chalaby
Joellin Comerford
Guenter Conrad
Jeffrey H. Cooper
Bjorn Ivar Danielsen
Irving Chase Decatur
Jean-Noel Deglaire
Toshio Fukuzumi
Marcello Gasco
Walter F. Geerts
Michael P. Gelhausen
Benoit Genuini
Mark E. Greenberg
Martino Grindatto
James D. E. Hall
F. Edwin Harbach
Jon Harrington
David E. Hoffman
Bradford L. Holcombe
William J. Hughes
Peter F. Kirn
Michael J. Klich
Mark D. Kuchel
William Martin Lattimer
Carol J. Lindstrom
Willem L. M. Lucassen
Eckardt Manske
Felipe Marcos
Andrew M. Marine
William J. Miller
Federico Montllonch
Diane Kohler Orndorff
Jack H. Redwine
Philip L. Schneider
Aram Edward Shishmanian
Carney R. Soderberg
Herbert D. Teel
Robert J. Turner
Klaus E. Wenger
John F. Wesselhoeft
Douglas Russell Willinger
David A. Yelich

September 1, 1988

Arnaud Andre
Daniel T. Beagley
Steven D. Blackledge
Dominique Brun
Peter S. Brzezicki
Michael A. Cabay
Gregory A. Carney
James C. Carolan
Willie J. H. Cheng
Jean-Paul Louis Eugene Choquel
Roderick Gong-Wah Chu
Christopher A. Coleman
Ian Conley
Carlos Consuegra
Carlos de Otto
Javier del Barrio
Claudio Della Penna
Kathryn A. Dessonville
Drew S. Dettling
Wayne Edward Donnelly
Peter A. Dunn
Harvey Richard Embree
Alessandro Falchero
Alan D. Flury
Hideo Furukawa
Michael B. Gaard
Larry Gan Nyap Liou
John Gibson
Richard J. Golden
Jose Luis Gonzalez H
David C. Griffiths
Stephen McLean Haggerty
Thomas P. Harig
Stephen D. Hawley
Jane S. Hemstritch
Joanne K. Holata
Peter Tiffany Hoversten
Robert H. Hunter
Early Blair Johnson
Vivienne Jupp
William D. Kalm
Dennis B. Karbach
Victor P. Kavals
Kohji Koyama
Kenneth Lee Lacey
Walter M. Laliberte
Dan Livio Lebas
Eric G. Leininger
Gert A. Lewies
Joseph A. Mantoan
Thomas R. Marshall
Beatriz Santos Martini
Robert P. McCarthy
Scott R. McKay
Massimo Merlino
Carol E. Meyer
James C. Mohr
Fabrizio Natali
Julieann F. Nelson
Keith G. Newton
Richard Roy Symes Niven
Jesus Olmedilla
Rosemary M. O'Mahony
Normand Paradis
Antonio M. Parente Ribeiro
Steven T. Patterson
Luis A. Paucar
Richard C. Peterson
Dale A. Raaen
Paul A. Racioppo
D. Michael Rappeport
Lewis B. Redd
James S. Reed
Michael William Reene
Jeffrey C. Reene
Klaus Reinhart
Jesus Rodriquez
Joseph A. Rohner
Roberto Romanin Jacur
R. Paul Russell
Luis Jose Sa Couto
Ulvi Sami
Alan M. Scheels
John G. Schoen
Grant R. Stephenson
Scott H. Strickland
Kevin H. Sullivan
Sheryl K. Sunderman
Javier Tapia
Raja Thuraisingham
J. Michael Urtso
Cory J. Van Wolvelaere
Guy Vandebrouck
William E. Warren
Warren H. Watkins
Robert O. Wetzel
Scott D. Williams
Vernon E. Williams
Peter R. Zirbel
Melvin C. Zwaig

September 1, 1989

Thomas R. Abraham
Terry Lee Adams
Samuel F. Altiero
Stephen J. Anderson
David G. Andrews
Ian H. Armstrong
Roderic Charles Mark Aston
Myron R. Badower
John M. Bean
Gregory D. Beltran
William R. Beshire
Piergiorgio Bianchetti
John Bladon
Robert E. Bloyd
Scott Brady
Christopher Brennan
Edward F. Burke
Susan L. Campbell
Enrico Castellano
Stefano Cavazza
Stefano Cianchi
J. Anthony Clancy
David R. Clinton
Larry L. Coates
Martin I. Cole

Thomas M. Compernolle
William C. Copacino
Alison J. Copley
Esteban Costa
William Thomas Cox
Alfonso de la Viuda
Didier Descamps
Paul S. Detlefs
Alistair A. Donald
Roger Mayer Dooley
Robert L. Edwards
Daniel J. Emmi
Marc Enjolras
David C. Escaravage
Fabrizio Fabbrini
Deon B. Fair
Thomas S. Fischer
Ricardo Flores
John G. Freeland
E. Kipp Friedli
J. Terence Gallagher
Lyle D. Ginsburg
Philippe Gire
James S. Greene
David M. Grubb
Michael R. Harris
Randy John Hendricks
Patrick A. Howard
R. Ann Jones
Karen J. Karbin
Gregg R. Karlberg
Kenton C. Keller
Thomas Kohler
Eugenio Kuri
Robert K. Laity
Thomas C. Lamming
Alex Wai-Leung Lau
David T. Lemme
Joy E. Lerner
Joo Boon Lim
Manuel de Carvalho
Lopes Alves
Ross N. MacDonald
Edward G. Mack
Ricardo Lobo Cruz
Martins
Gian Bruno Mazzi
Stephen Jay McCreadie
Mark A. McDowell
Antonio Mena
Ian David Milner-Brown
Cristina Molinari
Leonard A. Morris
Philip B. Moss
David John Mowat
Michael R. Naset
David T. Nass

Walter G. Nollmann
Michael J. Palmer
Claude Palmieri
Steven D. Phillips
V. Charles Pisciotta
Robert Charles Pitt
Hans Polbratt
Roderick C. Price
Dale H. Renner
Peter Albert Roberts
David J. Roessl
Jay H. Rosenfeld
Patrice Ruchon
Barry L. Rupert
Shunsaku Sakaki
Bruno Saracco
John V. C. Saylor
Stephen J. Schaus
Rodney G. Segraves
David E. Seibel
Joseph N. Shneider
Clifford M. Simms
Steven M. Singer
Marcus Karl Sipolt
Samuel B. Smart
Norman D. Smith
Scott Alan Smith
John J. Splavec
Guillermo Federico Stadler
Klas-Goran Stahl
Dan P. Steinman
Ronald Edwin Stewart
Einar Stokke
Kerry L. Stover
Adedotun Sulaiman
Martha R. Tuthill
Fernando Jorge Victorica
Georg Hans Virnich
Richard E. Von Hagen
Jeffrey S. Wilson
Garen L. Wisner

September 1, 1990

Roberto Alvarez
Peter Allan Andersen
Roy A. Andrews
G. Craig Apregan
Kenji Asai
Jacob P. Bosmann
Richard V. Boulger
Stephen T. Brown
Kevin M. Campbell
Marco Carrara
Charles W. H. Carter
John M. Catlett
Peter Ayrton Cheese
David W. Coyle

Cathy R. Culp
Robert Davidow
Michael C. Dickoff
Robert N. Duelks
Kenneth R. Ernst
Karl-Heinz Floether
James Duncan Flynn
Robert P. Gach
Uriel C. Galimidi
Susan K. Gampfer
Alberto Gandini
Jose Enrique Garcia
Paul F. Gelter
Gil Gidron
Jesus Gomez Esteban
Anthony Grant
Anna R. Harrington
Thomas J. Healy
Kent L. Holtgrewe
Isidro Huesa
Vance T. Hughes
Juan Alberto Illana
Elorduy
Raymond Hinley Jewitt
Steve A. Johnson
Jolinda G. Jones
Timothy G. Jury
Kaoru Kanazawa
Sharad K. Kapur
Kimberly A. Kelly
Richard R. Krahn
Patrick Lacombe
Adrian J. Lajtha
Orlando G. P. Lima
Howard C. Luks
Andrew J. Macpherson
Joseph A. Martha
Patrice Massat
Gary H. McClimans
William E. Mearse
Scott D. Myers
Jeffrey R. Pennington
Jose Manuel Perez de
Miguel
Joseph P. Phillips
Ossi Pohjola
Yvette D. Powell
Juan Carlos Prieto
Joseph J. Ragonese
Gill A. Rider
Giovanni Rizzotti
Eileen M. Rogers
Basilio Rueda Martin
Koetsu Sanga
Douglas W. Saugen
Joseph M. Schultz
Steven R. Shane

Gus E. Smith
Iain Somerville
Earl A. Stalter
Gregory J. Sterling
Walter R. C. Strickland
Michael P. Sullivan
Tsuneaki Takeuchi
Philip J. Tamminga
Dennis M. Terry
Donald E. Tucker
Luis Vassal'lo Reina
Ian Charles Watmore
Christopher K. Winans

January 1, 1991

Jacques Perrotto

January 21, 1991

Tauno J. Metsisto

February 1, 1991

Bruce A. Turkstra

April 1, 1991

C. Rudolph Puryear

September 1, 1991

Primo B. Aguas
Benjamin Aparicio
Carlo Alberto Baldissera
Pacchetti
Loren G. Beadle
J. Douglas Berto
Robert M. Berton
Giovanni Bolzan
Martin H. Borell
Harry H. Brakeley
Thomas E. Brydon
Douglas H. Calby
Barent W. Cater
Yew Chye Ching
Michael Ryan Collins
Pamela J. Craig
Kevin J. Dixon
Leonardus J. G. Etman
Stephen R. D. Fowler
D. Wayne Furphy
N. Martin Geddes
Philip G. Geiger
August W. Geise
Mark C. Goebel
Mark V. Goodyear
Frank R. Guillemyn
Charles L. Harris
James G. Harris
Martha M. Harris
Thomas J. Hartman
William R. Herman
Scott C. Hesaltine
Richard W. Hill

Mitchell C. Hill
Roger Ingold
Jose Ramon Jimenez
Christopher W. Kinder
Wendy B. Kingsbury
David A. Klemm
Fumio Koyama
Steven M. Kupres
Martin J. Leestma
Steven W. Louis
Constantinos
Louropoulos
Patrice Michelang
Hugh F. Morris
Hideshi Noda
James F. O'Byrne
Mark P. Pautsch
Steven B. Petchon
Jacobus G. Potgieter
David M. Pramer
Michael A. Rainey
Juan Pedro Raurell
David B. Rich
Donald J. Richards
David A. Richardson
Wayne J. Schachtel
Rolf Schulz
Jeffrey R. Smith
Doug Snedden
Stephen R. Sotzing
Thomas K. Spann
Manfred Stoll
Per Erik Stromso
James N. Wierzba
William E. Witnik
R. Curtis Worsey
Richard C. Wyman

October 28, 1991

Keith Stock

March 1, 1992

Julie Baddeley

September 1, 1992

James P. Adamczyk
David Langley Anderson
Christy G. Bass
Jorge L. Benitez
Hendrik Jan Blom
William Theodore Bourke
Thomas S. Brennan
Neil T. Brigham
Kevin Carnahan
Mary Kathryn Clubb
Colin K. Davies
Kenneth C. Dawson
Robert Howard Delves
Christopher S. DiGiorgio

Juan Domenech
Malcolm P. Dunn
Jose Antonio Fernandez
Bruce P. Froehlich
Jaime Gonzalez
David P. Hollander
Andrew J. Middleton
Tohru Murayama
John B. Nevins
Joyce A. Nitz
Fumio Ohue
Kevin A. O'Laughlin
Solly Patrontasch
John J. Patterson
Marco Peroni
Thomas D. Pollan
Jean-Francois Rambicur
Kevin P. Reedy
Donald A. Reynolds
Thomas Riggert
Stephen J. Rohleder
Bruno Ronchetti
Daniel L. Schriner
Rodney Drew Sellers
Yomtov Senegor
Steven J. Sullivan
Toshimasa Suzuki
David Charles Thomlinson
Mark A. Tillinger
Robert David Tyre
Ronald Arthur Veith
Josep Vicens
William G. Way
William P. Wheeler
Kim Zimmer

November 12, 1992

Saul Kaplan

September 1, 1993

Ryozo Akiyama
Michael W. Alber
Esteban Amengual
David Bruce Appel
Kenneth Wayne Baldwin
Randolph Cary Barba
Thomas Brendan Barry
Thomas Baubin
Thomas Rowe Bell
Leo Blennerhassett
James Richard Bolton
Terry L. Cardwell
Charles E. Crockett
Rita Francisca S. Cruz
Karen W. Dale
Renato Dedonatis
Alfredo Luis Della Savia
David Lewis Dinkin
William Christopher Draper
Mark Gregory Eyen
Pal K. Fevang
Gary J. Fitzgerald
Biagio Franco
Eduardo A. Gois
Trevor J. Gruzin
Blake Hanna
James F. Heddens
Thomas Herbst
Kohmei Higashi
Chyi-Yuan Hsieh
Sam Juul
Maher Hikmat Kaddoura
Tadashi Kashiwabuchi
Mardee Kasik
Scott Wilder Kerr
Joan C. King
Herve Le Guerer
Janet C. Lively
Joseph F. Lobbato
Robert T. Martin
Michael J. May
Jack O. McMillan
Yannis Methodios
Kenneth E. Mifflin
Kenneth Mitchell
Thomas Weld Moldauer
Keith H. Mueller
Pierre Nanterme
Gregory J. Owens
Gareth D. Paul
Mark F. Paulson
Susan R. Pearson
Roy K. Phelan
Thomas P. Prchal
L. Craig Ramsey
Sabine Reimers-Mortensen
Ralph Alan Riedel
Donald J. Rippert
Bradley A. Rosencrans
Francis J. Rovinski
Alan Salter
Scott Richard Sargent
Akihiko Sato
George P. Shaw
Glenn A. Sieber
David Charles Simpson
Jill B. Smart
Mark K. Snead
Mark Gerald Spelman
Miguel Susffalich
Richard John Taylor
Andre Telmosse
Bernardus Ter Braak
Steven A. Tesdahl
Mary A. Tolan
David G. Waller
John T. Warner
Michael Wetzer
Larry A. Winter
Yasunori Yoshimoto
Reinhard Ziegler

December 1, 1993

Thomas A. Nickles

January 1, 1994

Daniel R. Pfau

September 1, 1994

James F. Anderson
Ian G. Arthur
Andrew J. Blanchard
Timothy Michael Boudreau
W. Terence Breen
Robyn Hazel Brown
Steven Robert Burns
Paul Lonan Cantwell
Gianfranco Casati
Nancy H. Church
Christopher M. Cowan
Max L. Dannis
Marc P. Delesalle
Warren J. Dodge
Vitor Carlos N. Duarte
Javier Fernandez Luna
Fred M. Fosnacht
Mark Foster
Peter H. Franz
Stephen T. Freitas
Piercarlo Gera
Daniel G. Gillet
Barry A. Gleichenhaus
Paul V. Greenhalgh
Alan T. Harris
Thomas D. Hartwig
Alan J. Healey
David T. Heiser
David L. Hill
Thomas D. Hogan
Anthony N. Holman
James W. Johnson
Ikuo Karasawa
Steven P. Koppel
Albert M. Krall
Dana E. LaChapelle
Robert L. Laud
John W. Leffin
Jack R. Levy
Stephen M. Lorack
Constance L. Martin
Marcio Carvalho de Mattos
Ian S. May
Betty A. McCabe
Kurt H. Miller
Edgar Mokuvos
Gwendolyn B. Moore
Gregory P. Morgan
Randall F. Muck
Ettore Natale
Victor J. Orler
James Politoski
Michael A. Porges
Philippa Reid
Denise A. Rempe
Sverre Ruth
Jose Roberto Schettino Mattos
Helmut Schulte-Croonenberg
Steven Sho Ah Beng
Carmen Sierra San Miguel
Brian S. Sommer
Eric Siegfried Stange
Wendy M. Stops
Yasumasa Takeda
Christopher C. Teeter
Rainer W. Teschner
J. Dil Thomas
Michael S. Tilton
Penny L. Turner
Lennart Ulvskog
Hans van Doesburg
Stephen A. Wilcox
Rudiger H. Wolf
Brian L. York
Brian E. Younger

January 23, 1995

Patricia Y. Tsien

February 1, 1995

Leonard Sherman

September 1, 1995

R. John Aalbregtse
Sebastiao C. G. Albuquerque
Christopher A. Amirtharajah
Elisabeth A. Astall
Ellen M. Balaguer
Christopher E. Barbour
Stephen B. Barripp
Kenneth Beecham
Jose Bermudez Marcos
Justin Joel Brasuell
Richard Timothy Simmons Breene
Paul A. Burgess
Thomas M. Burke
Juan Manuel Castro
Stewart Robert Clements
Alison Lee Clew
Norman James Cook
Douglas Smith Coons
William Crothers
John Edward Cunningham
Thomas J. Dunne
Anne Teresa Dupont
Michael B. Elliott
Dan H. Elron
Robert L. Evans
Louis Fagalde
David J. Fitzgerald
Stephen M. Flynn
Paul A. J. Fockens
Charles Scott Forbes
Mikio Fujii
Wolfgang Gattermeyer
Andrew Mark Glassberg
Russell Herbert Gowland
Ann Katherine Haden
Elizabeth Ann Harding
Keith Frank Haviland
John Andrew Hay
John Wayne Henderson
John E. Highbarger
Thomas A. Hildebrandt
Chikatomo Hodo
Kah Soon Hoe
Edwin David Holt
Kenneth R. Jennings
Forest Daniel Jones
John T. Kunzweiler
Donald J. Laackman
David A. Langdon
Antonio C. Leocadio
Beng Choon Lim
Betty G. Lui
Richard Andrew Lumb
Paul G. Martinez
Raul Jose Fonseca Mascarenhas
John K. McCulla
William A. McErlane
Dermot James McMeekin
Dennis Ivars Melnbardis
Samuel W. Miller
John Robert Miller
Seiichi Mitsui
Vicente Moreno Garcia-Mansilla
Keisuke Morita
Matthew Mosetick
Christian Nibourel

David P. Nilsen
Glenn A. Noga
Petronio G. Nogueira
Brian Anthony O'Connell
John Patrick O'Halloran
Patrick G. O'Neill
Owen Vincent Perillo
Michael D. Petrushka
Thomas H. Pike
Victor Beech Riden
Beth Karin Roberts
Mark J. Ryan
Bryan Richard Saba
Paul Michael Schmucker
Robert Elliott Sell
Philip B. Sheibley
Rodolfo Guillermo Silberstein
Magnus Sjoeqvist
Daniel Thomas Smale
George Graham Smith
David Alan Stadler
Philip Walter Swallow
Jerry Robert Titus
Thomas G. Tynan
Mary Jo Veverka
Dorothy Vinson VonDette
Glenn G. Wattley
Christopher Antony Wearing
Simon John Whitehouse
David Edward Wilkins
Diane D. Wilson
Mark T. Wolfe

November 1, 1995

Cathy L. Greenberg

November 6, 1995

Mark Douglas Fleming

December 11, 1995

Staffan Canback

March 1, 1996

Peter Dubois

March 18, 1996

Peter Holmes

April 1, 1996

William A. Band
C. Scott Killips
Richard A. Moran
Donald E. Wallroth

April 16, 1996

Lawrence B. Leisure

May 13, 1996

Andrew Power

July 1, 1996

Robert B. Wiley

August 26, 1996

Richard C. Easton

August 30, 1996

Brian A. Johnson

September 1, 1996

Masud M. Arjmand
John D. Atkinson
Pradip K. Banerjee
John B. Baughn
Richard A. Bean
Royce Michael James Bell
Richard N. Berg
Richard F. Bergmann
David L. Bieber
Nicholas Billington
Pierre Bosche
Joerg Boysen
Michael D. Bozarth
Lucio Bozzoli-Parasacchi
Michael P. Brownell
Thomas Claussen
D. Gordon Cliff
William F. Cline
Stanley R. Craig
Johan G. Deblaere
Kathleen M. Duffy
John G. Edelblut
Bradley G. Englert
Carlos Escamez Abad
Mario Ezquerra-Plasencia
Rainer M. Famulla
Timothy M. Finnegan
W. Colin Fulton
Jose Galamba de Oliveira
Riccardo Gandus
Timothy Stephen Gbedemah
Alfonso Gonzalez Calvente
Pamela J. Gosda
William E. Gourgey
Bruno Grossi
Bhra Eka Gunapriya
Bong-Hoon Han
Timothy M. Hascall
Mark K. Hawn
James E. Hayes
James G. Hayes
Harry C. Hickling
John G. Hogan
Michael E. Hughes
Andrew Jackson
Nobuaki Katsuya
Kristian Kvam
Steven M. Lamont
Jorgen O. Lenz
Odell E. L'Heureux
Robert M. Linka
Hans-Dieter Lochmann
Eric F. Lonbois
Pierre Lumsden
Pascal Manhes
Lisa M. Mascolo
Leena Mayteedol
Michael A. McGinn
S. Kurt Menner
Jose Manuel Merino Aspiazu
Eric Monnoyer
William F. Morris
Just Erik Naess
Craig M. B. O'Flaherty
Nils Overaas
John Edward Percy
Edward F. Pool
Pierre Pouyfaucon
Sadeesh Raghavan
Jon C. Rands
Robert S. Rebitzer
Bruce S. Richmond
Charles J. Roussel
Michael J. Rusinko
William A. Schaffner
Takashi Shimodoi
Markku T. Silen
Andrew J. Simmonds
Janet A. Simons
Julian A. Sparkes
Gregory L. Storm
Willem Strauss
Toshiyuki Sugawara
Gregory J. Supron
Dean J. Teglia
Tomomichi Tomiie
Roy Aaron Underwood
Arnold R. Urson
Aziz Virani
Sergio F. Vulej
John T. Weisel
Randall L. Willis
Jon H. Wilson
Stephen Z. Zujkowski

September 11, 1996

Charles Kalmbach

September 16, 1996

Richard A. Genovese

September 30, 1996

Gregory E. Anderson

October 1, 1996

Noel A. Gordon

October 21, 1996

Michael Scott Galardi

November 1, 1996

Peter Weigert

February 14, 1997

Glenn H. Bryce

March 1, 1997

Richard H. Jones
Nat Sloane

April 1, 1997

James K. Mueller

September 1, 1997

Jonathon R.C. Allaway
James Burnes Anderson
James A. Astorian
Alan H. Barnes
Christian Baumgartner
Ingo M. Baussus Von Luetzow
Jeffrey A. Beech
Fabio Benasso
Giovanni Benedetto
Oliver J. Benzecry
Klaus Berentsen
Andrew Berger
Catriona M. Brash
James C. Bremhorst
Mark G. Bryant
Gregg L. Burt
Clive J. Butkow
Stuart G. Campbell
Paul Cartwright
Luca Casiraghi
Douglas M. Castek
Richard A. Chang
Brian A. Clark
Mitchell R. Cline
Shawn Collinson
Grieg W. Coppe
Anthony G. Coughlan
Andrew R. Curtis
William W. Dandridge
Charles H. Dean
Anthony J. deLeon
James M. Dickey
Nicholas Huw Edwards
James M. Ellis
Isao Endo
David J. English
Joseph R. Erickson
James O. Etheredge
Jean Faltz
Luiz C. Ferezin
Adrian Ruben Flint
Michael L. Gailey
Udo Glenewinkel
Hugues U. Gourbat
Steven E. Gratto
G. Victor Guyan
Henrik E. Hansen
Timothy A. Hanson
John Stewart Hawkins
Andrew M. Hay
H. Darryl Heath
Javier Hervas
Bradley J. Hitt
Martin H. Hodgett
Malcolm Howard
Andre P. Hughes
Edward W. Jensen
Rick D. Johnston
Neville K. Jones
Stefan A. Kampe
Apolonia Kersch
Peter-Paul M. J. Kissels
Robert S. Kloustin
Mats Koenig
Paul A. Kohlheim
Martin C. Leinweber
Dawna S. Levenson
Jonas Liljenberg
Leonid Lipchin
Roy S. Loomis
Iain D. Lopata
Yong Sun Mah
Keiji Matsuoka
Paul A. Matthews
John T. McHugh
Edward R. Meekins
Luca Mentuccia
Frank B. Modruson
Christer Mohlin
Kimio Momose
Ralf Naef
Hiroyuki Nishimura
Franklin C. Norman
Jean-Marc E. Ollagnier
Luis Sant'ana Pereira
Richard E. Phillips
Debra A. Polishook
Chris E. Politte
Verdele C. Polson
David M. Pugmire
Paul J. Purnell
Hans-Peter Remark
Alastair G. Robertson
Henry T. Rossi
Shane B. Ryan
Michael D. Scimo

Paul A. Shackelford
Yuji Shiga
Yaarit Annette Silverstone
Ole Skov
Peter J. Smart
Robin D. Smyth-Osbourne
Stephen C. Snyder
John H. Soles
David G. Sprows
Craig M. Stanley
David G. Steakley
Michael J. Steiger
Brian G. Strange
J. Guy Taylor
Stanton J. Taylor
Elizabeth A. Tinkham
Jan H. Toncar
Philippe Villaume
Patrice Vinet
Arnim E. Whisler
Andrew J. White
Richard John Wildman
Robert R. Zahm

September 22, 1997
Bret H. Bero

October 6, 1997
Dariusz K. Wiatr

November 3, 1997
Gavin Fraser

December 1, 1997
Bernward Niederwestberg
Jonathan R. Owen

January 1, 1998
Juergen Gerlach

January 15, 1998
Robert C. Moeller

February 1, 1998
Christer Bergquist
Robert Goodman

March 2, 1998
Allan V. Abelow

March 16, 1998
Robert A. Willett

June 5, 1998
Amy V. Snyder

July 6, 1998
Barry D. Jennings

August 3, 1998
Eileen H. Bedell

September 1, 1998
Juan E. Amador
Ronald L. Anderson
Yannis S. Arvanitis
Kenneth Auman
Samuel A. Awad
Sylvain Bacon
David A. Bebbington
Florentino Benito
Andrew David Bloch
Fernando Jimenez Boldrini
Rodney D. Bosma
Michael E. Boushka
Donald M. Bray
Charles Patrick Brown
William C. Brown
Antoine Brugidou
Mark J. Bruni
Serge E. Callet
Paul S. Cameron
Roberto Campagnola
Keith W. Carlson
Luis Ceniga
Daniel Hiok Khiang Chan
Lai Yong Chee
Tuck Oon Choong
Gianmarco Cividini
Ken G. Climie
Brian M. Cote
James D. Crowley
Alejandro Cuartero
Philippe H. Darneau
Paul R. Daugherty
Fritha A. Davidson
Jeffrey J. Davis
Andrew W. Davison
John L. Del Santo
Giorgio Di Paolo
Alexander P. Dickey
David R. Dietrich
Mark Wayne Dunaway
Matthew J. Edwards
Michael E. Egan
Robin D. Fall
Antonio L. Fernandez
Jaime Ferrer
Charles Boyd Findlay
Arnaldo Fornasiero
Albert H. Frazier
Robert Steven Frisch
Jerry Martin Garcia
Gustavo Gill
Jose Vicente Gimenez
Michael Goerner
Rafael Gomez Mallo
David Charles Graham
Douglas Arthur Green
Jeff Hamilton
Martha C. Hartman
Trevor M. Hatton
James O. Hernandez
Scott Andrew Elyard Herne
Luis Angel Herran
Kenneth C. Heubel
Paul Hewitt
Jennifer Hinshaw
James Terry Hintlian
Yves V. Humbert
Antonio Hurtado de Mendoza
Motoki Iidoi
Yutaka Iso
James M. Jackson
Sanjay Jain
Elbert S. Johnson
Kenneth A. Jones
Stephen Michael Jones
John Kenneth Kaltenmark
Paul L. Keane
Nicholas R. Kent
John P. Kinney
Larry L. Kirchner
Hiroaki Kodaira
Kenneth J. Kushnir
Toni C. Langlinais
Gong Li
Daniel T. London
Stefano Longhini
Philip A. Lopez
Trevor L. Lorge
Harald Luehrmann
Kenzo Maeda
Tore Magnussen
Silvio M. Mani
Juan B. Marin
Mark Mazzatta
Robert J. McCulloch
David Gordon McFarland
Charles Alexander McGrath
Timothy Medforth
Jeffrey G. Mehallick
Michael G. Mikurak
Quentin Morelle
Michael M. Morison
Eric R. Mouchous
Kevin O. Narcomey
Magnus Norrstroem
Alan C. Nowakowski
Frank J. O'Dea
Carlos Pedranzini
Howard Pennington
Annette N. Peterson
Audie T. Pili
Paul E. Primavera
Patrick Puechbroussou
Gregory S. Raynes
C. Ann Rettie
Leonardo Ricci
Frank Riemensperger
John M. Romanow
Ralf Runau
Ricardo Scheuer
Stephen T. Schwarzbach
D. Glenn Sedgwick
Grant S. Sheldon
Francis X. Shields
Sean Shine
Richard E. Simon
John J. Snopkowski
Stuart L. Solomon
Allan Paul Spence
Jeffrey V. St. Peters
Gary R. Stang
John T. Staton
Derek A. Steelberg
Michael B. Styve
Michael R. Sutcliff
Gerhard P. Thomas
Ushio Usami
Hendrik J. Velders
Olivier Vidal
Ouri Wachtel
John F. Walsh
John J. Walz
Barry J. Webster
Jeffrey Daniel Wiesner
Phillip M. A. Wiig
Susan Wollan Fan
Thomas E. Yager
Mark P. Younger
John Kenelm Zealley

September 28, 1998
Eileen Basho

November 1, 1998
Peter H. Weidermann

January 1, 1999
Gerold Hoerrmann
Richard Laub

February 1, 1999
Philippe Giry-Deloison
Rolf Graf

September 1, 1999
Brett B. Anderson
Duncan Armitage
Marylou Y. Bailey
Christopher M. Baker
Maurizio Barini
C. Keith Barringer
Bjorn Erik Bengtsson
Michael J. Bernaski
Uday Bhansali
David L. Blumberg
H. Keith Boone
Philippe Boueilh
Paul D. Calvin
Darrin J. Caramonta
Stuart Graham Carthy
Jaime Casanovas
Francisco Castellvi
Luca Fortunato Cesari
Richard A. Childs
Jon D. Craver
Frank D. Crocitto
Jorge Crudele
Gregory C. Cudahy
Michele Dagradi
Yvonne B. de Ridder
Etienne H. Deffarges
Philippe Delaide
Stephen J. Dempsey
Woodruff W. Driggs
John D. Dugan
Peter J. Effler
Jaime Falcao
James R. Farmer
Eberhard M. Fledel
Joseph D. Getto
Pierluigi Giannico
Richard E. Gillette
Graeme D. Gordon
Giuseppe Gorla
Siegfried Grohs
Timothy A. Hale
Norbert Hegner
Ivo Heukensfeldt Jansen
Marc J. Hillen
Mark A. Hodge
Montgomery Andrew Hong
Nobuhisa Horiguchi
Willy Huma
Stephen T. Hundley
Wayne T. Ingram
Mark William Joern
Patricia Jury Jones
John Daniel Karren
Ramez J. Katf
Steven I. Kauderer
Drew B. Keith
Stephen P. Kelly
Kazuhiko Kitamura
Benedikt J. Koch
Margaret A. Kostial
Nancy J. Laben
Dymphna Lehane

James R. Liebhart
Norbert Linn
Anthony G. Lombardo
Nicholas B. Lyon
Luis Maldonado
Juho Eruui Magnus Malmberg
Thomas O. Mann
Don McGill
Lachlan P. McNeill
Richard M. Melnicoff
Patrick M. Mills
Lorenzo Molina Morales
John Christopher Moran
Daniel J. Morris
Ronald Munk
Tim Murfet
David S. Muskat
Jorge Nicolau
Edward T. Novak
Jeremy Oates
John L. O'Connor
Fabrizio Perrone
Judith A. Phillips
Kevin A. Pollari
Friedrich J. Preiss
Barry Prince
Massimo Proverbio
Alberto Proverbio
David B. Quinones
Marco Rapaglia
Gavin Henry Rennie
David A. Ross
Earl P. Rousseau
Jeffrey B. Sakaguchi
Kathryn Ann Sanders
Stephan Scholtissek
Angela K. Selden
Ari T. Seppala
N. James Shachoy
Ameet A. Shah
Iain S. Smith
Michael J. Spencer
David Squire
Reinhold Stammeier
David J. Standridge
Charles E. Starr
Andrew Starrs
James N. Stephens
James R. Stolarski
Gregg M. Sweeney
Kazushi Taniguchi
Stephen D. Tibbs
Mark C. Trout
Thomas J. Van Dam
Luc Van der Biest
Alexander Van't Noordende
Jose Carlos Villela
Stan M. Vlasimsky
Bruce D. Voelker
Toennies-Hilmar Von Donop
Marc A. J. M. I. Vrouenraets
Henrique L Washington
Robert A. Weisstuch
Hugo Giles Were
Richard T. Wheeler
Duncan McCulloch White
Christian Wig
David A. Wilson
Masahiro Yoshida

September 6, 1999

William M. Gordon

September 7, 1999

Roger A. Pratesi

January 10, 2000

Cesar Muniz

January 31, 2000

Peter Kiehm

April 3, 2000

Patrick J. Leemputte

August 1, 2000

Albert James Viscio

September 1, 2000

David A. Abberton
Omar Abbosh
Oday Abbosh
Carmela A. Abiuso
David J. Abood
Anne Foss Abrahamsen
Michelle R. Adelman
Paul John Adler
Paula Adriao
Francisco Jos Aguado
Jorge Aguado
Scott K. Ahlstrom
Kennet W. Ake
Tamara D. Alairys
Ayad Al-Ani
Jerome J. Albright
Jose Jorge Alcobia
Alejandro C. Alcoverro
Michael A. Alfieri
W. Christopher Alger
Mark J. Allaby
Dawn J. Allan
Christopher J. Allen
Meryl A. Allison
Matias Alonso
Alexandra Altmann
Jane F. Ambrose
Javier Amezola
Eric A. Anderson
Grant Andes
Greg Andrews
David M. Andrews
John R. Andrews
Garth R. Andrus
Mario A. Angelastro
Theodore Ansusinha
David A. Antoniolli
Antonio Arce
Enrique Arias
Jose Luis Arias Gallo
William John Armstrong
Sandeep K. Arora
James W. Arrison
Les Brian Artman
Marcelo Astrachan
Eduardo Atihe
Christopher G. Atkins
Herve Auchere
Mary Ellen Austin
Katarina Axelsson
Alberto Ayuso
Ahmad Azhar
Soichi Azuma
Chris J. Bacic
Jae-Bong Bae
Paolo Bagnasco
James E. Bailey
Ann Frances Baker
W. Kent Baker
Anil R. Bakshi
Subramaniam Balasubramanian
Charles Ball
Muneatsu Ban
Jerome Barancourt
Michelangelo Barbera
Juan Barcena
Jose A. Barco
Thomas D. Barden
Nigel Barnes
Ian Barnetson
Rachael M. J. Bartels
Manfred E. Barth
David B. Baruch
Koos M. Basson
Martha J. Batista
Kathy L. Battistoni
Nathan E. Beadle
Sally Bean
Mark Beaton
Timothy Adil Becker
Arjun Bedi
Jeffrey I. Beg
John T. Bell
Phillip J. Bell
William M. Bell
Mick A. Bell
Nanci D. Bellante
Peter C. Bellas
David X. Bennett
Michael J. Benore
Karim A. Benrais
La Cinda S. Benson
Daniel Mark Benton
Michael M. Berens
Scott D. Berg
Ernst-Jan Bergman
Franz Bergmueller
Giancarlo N. Berry
Larry J. Berry
Bruno Berthon
Marc F. Bervoets
Jonathan F. Besse
Gianluigi Betti
Richard G. Bhanap
Holger Bill
Adrian Richard Bird
Gilles Biscay
Peter Nigel Blackadder
Alastair Murray Blair
Gregory Keith Blake
Robert V. Blakey
Tony Blakey
Arnaud Blandin
Dana Beth Blankenship
Jose Bleda
James Blomfield
Nigel Blower
David D. Boath
Pieter W. Boelens
Christophe Boitel
Jean Pierre Bokobza
Martin Fuhr Bolstad
Eugenio Bonomi
Marco Lauro Bonomi
Cody Boren
Lars Borjesson
Paul A. Boulanger
Michael L. Bowman
Karen M. Braeckmans
Paolo Branchi
Robert S. Brandt
Simon P. Bray
Nina L. Breen
Marco Bressa
Jerry H. Briggs
Edgar C. Britschgi
Marco P. Brocken
Chris Brocklesby
Randy A. Broda
David R. Brodwin
Rachel R. Brody
Mark C. Bronfman
Zachary R. Brooks
Maureen L. Brosnan
Richard L. Brower
Dave Brown
Thomas C. Brown
Fred W. Brown
Chris Broyden
Terry L. Bruehl
Wolfgang Brugger
Michael K. Buechling
Vincent E. Bugge
Jon Culver Bumstead
Christopher J. Burckhardt
Darren Burrows
Christopher T. Burton
Khan Busby
Thomas L. Butcher
Scott T. Butler
Kenneth Byrne
Brad P. Cable
John G. Callahan
Peter C. Callaway
Robert M. Calloway
Lisa L. Campbell
Nicholas Y. Campbell
Juan Camprubi
James Edward Canning
Jose Manuel Cantarero
Eugenio Capasso
Paolo Capone
Vito Caradonio
Ceri Carlill
Armelle Carminati-Rabasse
William John Carney
Chris Carrigan
Greg John Carroll
Visda M. Carson
Francisco M. Carton
David Cartwright
Francisco Carvajal
Victor Casas
Massimo Casiraghi
Gregory P. Caster
Carlos Castilla
Robert J. Castle
Ricardo M. Cerdan
Keith Joseph Cerny
Paolo Cerza
Martin Chalifoux
Min X. Chang

Lloyd W. Chapin
Eric Chapman
Philippe C. Chauffard
Jose Marcos Chaves
David M. Chen
Jodi M. Chen
Todd A. Chernik
Gregory P. Chestnut
Robert Chew
Youngcho Chi
Paul C. Chiu
Bum-Coo Cho
Chuan Neo Chong
Tong Ful Chow
Manoj Chowla
Serge E. Christin
Alex Christou
Michael H. Chung
Alberto Ciriello
Roberto Citton
Andrew Clarke
Robert C. Clauser
Robert C. Clement
Tim Clifford
Manuel Colao
Sergio Colella
James B. Coleman
Colleen K. Coleman
Mark T. Coleman
Michael F. Collins
Michael G. Condon
Daniel F. Conforti
Giovanni Contri
Steven G. Convey
David S. Cooper
Marcelo G. Cora
Silvano Corallo
Marian Corcoran
Kenneth Corless
Richard D. Cornelius
Craig Cornelius
Teutly Correia
Michael J. Costello
Nancy R. Costello
Paul T. Cottey
Richard J. Coughlin
Jean Louis Cougoul
Peter Roger Courtney
Thomas A. Cranley
Patricia Creedon
Karen Crennan
Pascal Cretot
Paul Crook
Phil J. Crosby
Alden Cuddihey
Scott G. Cumby
David T. Curran

John Michael Cusano
David R. Dahle
James J. Dailey
Pierre L. Dalton
Denise Damiani
Raffaella D'Angiolino
Margaret Harrison Darby
Daniel W. Darland
Ghazali Darman
Robert Lewis D'Avanzo
David A. Davidson
Christopher P. Davin
Jon Philip Davis
Mary Catherine Davis
Hans de Boer
Peter De Groot
Antony De Jong
Diego S. de Leon
Alessandro De Martini
Frikkie de Villiers
James De Watteville
Gert M. De Winter
Pieter W. de With
Paul J. Dean
Cheryl L. Deitcher
LaMae Allen deJongh
Vincent Delaporte
Catherine Delhaye
Vittorio Delmonte
Pascal A. Delorme
Stephen M. Demarest
Regis Demaria
Brian C. DeMay
Jean-Marc Deniau
Michael A. Dennis
Fabrice Dersy
Koen D. Deryckere
David Deschamps
Jan L. Dewitte
Carmen Diaz Madronal
Otto Diemer
Guido H. Dieperink
Roger W. Dik
Fraser M. Dillingham
Stanley DiLullo
Kenneth S. Dineen
Earle R. Dinsmore
Grant R. Dixon
Lucretia D. Doblado
Douglas R. Doerr
Michael T. Donohue
James C. Donohue
Arlene E. Donohue
Tony Doocey
Niall Peter Doran
Giuseppe Dosi
Alberto Dosset

Christopher J. Downey
John Martin Downie
Jonathan Doyle
Reid S. Drucker
Timothy D. Druzgala
Michael G. Duffy
Stephen Anthony Duffy
Stephen F. Dull
Jerome C. Dumaine
Todd A. Dunbar
Gary A. Duncan
David Boyd Durdan
Lloyd H. Dyer
Jack Dziak
Robert J. Easton
Philip Anthony Eaton
Terry R. Ecklund
W. Mark Edwards
Atsushi Egawa
Jens C. Egerland
Traci D. Egly
James M. Ehrhart
Don A. Eichmann
Scot K. Eisenfelder
Amr El Saadani
Mark N. Eleoff
J. Dean Elliott
Richard J. Emerson
Juan Enero
John F. Engel
Markus Enggist
Simon John England
Richard J. English
Michael H. Engoian
Robert Erickson
Mark D. Ernst
Peter P. Esparrago
Ennio Esposito
Mike Ethelston
Mark J. Euwe
Carrie Everhart
Pascal Eymery
Gilles Fabre
Anne-Cecilie Fagerlie
Victor Marcelino Farinas
Emanuele Farini
Quartara
George L. Farrington
Donavon J. Favre
W. Michael Fecko
Norman D. Fekrat
Alan R. Feldmann
Martin Ferguson
Jorge Fernandez
Casamayor
Jose Francisco
Fernandez Perdiz

Stephen David
Ferneyhough
Angel Ferreras
Vincenzo Ferro
Charles L. Filewych
Gary S. Fink
Kenneth A. Fishman
Erik Fjornes
Jose Maria Font
Jung Wei Foo
Michael S. Foong
Gill Ford
Kay N. Formanek
Marcelo C. Fortes
Drew W. Foster
Michael C. Fox
Luis Franquesa Castrillo
Mary Fratto Rowe
Jeffory Frayser
Todd N. Frech
James G. Fry
Ko Fukuzawa
Paolo Fumi
Hironobu Furusawa
Dieter G. Gable
Punita Gajree
Rafael Galan
Jeffery A. Galbraith
Andrea Galgoczi
Kelly P. Gallant
Jean-Yves Galley
Graham Mackenzie
Galloway
Thomas M. Gannon
Pedro Jose Garcia
Jose Luis Garcia Huerta
Miguel Angel Garcia-Diez
Alan M. Gardiner
Douglas F. Garfinkel
Randall Edward Gargas
David Gartside
Jean-Francois E. Gasc
Jennifer A. Gatewood
John L. Gattorna
Eric M. Gauthier
Xavier A. Gazay
Susie Gear
James W. Gearhart
Terrence M. Gee
Marc Gelle
Philip A. George
Anatole V. Gershman
Wim L. Geurden
Harold A. Ghering
Robert C. Gibbs
Ian S. Gibson
Dirk Gierlach

Glenn H. Gifford
Tim Gilchrist
Stuart K. Gilchrist
Olivier Jean Gillerot
John H. Gillespie
Brett Allen Ginter
Mark C. Giometti
D. Neil Gissler
Eric P. Gist
Thomas Gith
Bart H. Glass
Manuel M. Godinho
Aik Meng Goh
Lin Piao Goh
David Golding
Max S. Goldman
David S. Goldson
Jose Gomes
Raul Gonzalez Anton
John B. Goodman
Michael D. Goodson
C. Erickson Goodwin
David L. Gordon
Alexandre Gorine
Paul Gosling
Walter G. Gossage
James F. Gossage
Vincent Goutallier
Johnny Edward Gowdy
Geoffrey S. Graham
Raymond E. Grainger
Gina Graziosi Fine
Enrico Grazzini
Christopher M. Greer
Shawn T. Gregor
Thomas R. Greiner
Daniel G. Greteman
James C. Grimsley
Anja H. Groenewoud
Roy Gronli
Bradford S. Gruby
Tomas Guerrero
Philippe Guittat
A. J. Gupta
Gregory S. Guthridge
Gene A. Gutman
Jamie J. Gylden
Guido Haarmann
Jack B. Haberman
Greg L. Haertling
Richard B. Haggart
Jon E. Hagstrom
Scott M. Hahn
Daniel Joel Halabe
Geoffrey M. Halaburt
Bradley D. Hallin
Mark A. Halverson

Naoto Hanada
John E. Handley
Kevin Matthew Hanley
Arthur Hanna
Marc A. Hanna
Per Hannover
Jesper Hougaard Hansen
Nathan T. Hansen
Dana Hanson
Charles Waller Harkless
Michael Joseph Harrison
Jeffrey S. Hartigan
M. S. Hartley
Catherine A. Hartley
Teresa G. Hartmann
Lance P. Hartshorn
Andrew G. Hartvich
Carolyn F. Hassel
John Haswell
Toru Hatano
Peter Hawkins
Gary Howard Hay
Donagh Healy
Michael A. Healy
Bernhard A. Heck
Peter O. Heemskerk
Gary Heffernan
Jorg G. Heinemann
Craig H. Heiser
Kevin G. Heitz
Christer Hellstrom
Anders Helmrich
Iain Henderson
Michael Henry
Kimberly D. Hensley
Gregory R. Herman
Steven W. Hermann
Jose Luis Hernandez-Iriberri
Ellen J. Hertz
Dirk Heselmann
Robert W. Hetherington
Herman R. Heyns
Andrew T. Hickey
Cindy L. Hielscher
Bill Higbie
Michael K. Higgins
Katsushi Hioki
Stig Hjelmgaard
Thomas H. Hofbauer
Janet L. Hoffman
Kevin P. Hogan
Stephen L. Holland
Bradford Rickman Holmes
Sara Holmes-Woodhead
Rob W. Honts
Steve J. Hooper
Bruce John Horton
David J. Hosking
Andrew J. Hosking
Hans Hoss
Patrick R. Housen
Nicholas F. Howell
John J. Hrusovsky II
Friedrich Huber
Richard Thomas McDonald Huffer
Lon J. Huffman
John Bailey Hughes
Barton L. Hughes
John L. Humbert
Terry E. Hunley
Shelley L. Hurley
Steven Hurst
Jeffrey D. Hutcheson
Dwight N. Hutchins
Hans Hwang
Rizwan Ibrahim
Gary S. Ide
Antonio Iglesias del Rio
David Peter Ilett
Masahisa Inagaki
Mitsuo Isaji
Takashi Ishikawa
Angelo Italiano
Hiroshi Ito
Bjorn Ivroth
Kumar K. Iyer
Jaime Jackson
Hakon Jacobsen
Saleem Janmohamed
Giuseppe Jannelli
Goran Jansson
Glenn M. Javens
Scott Joseph Jecmen
Owen Jelf
Michael Jeltsch
Simon C. Jenkins
Parry Jenkins
Gregory J. Jenko
Wolfgang Jetter
James C. Johnson
Omobola Olubusola Johnson
Gregory Johnson
Robert J. Johnson
Shayne Johnson
Robert L. Johnson
Sue C. Johnson
Keith F. Johnson
Valerie L. Johnston
Tim J. Jones
Kevin R. Jones
Philip Edward Jones
Linda M. Jordan
Peter Edwin Jordan
Darryl W. Jue
Kevin K. Julian
Robert Jung
Pedro Jurado
Jonathan D. Kaehne
Henning Kaerner
Eliah M. Kahn
Brian Geoffrey Kalms
Raghu Kannan
Brian Andrew Kaplow
Atul K. Kapur
Altaf Kara
Ingemar Karlsson
Peter C.A. Karremans
Douglas L. Kasamis
Martin Kasper
Sergio G. Kaufman
Masahito Kazaoka
Joon-Neung Kee
William F. Kelly
Catharine J. Kelly
Stephen A. Kendrick
Rodney J. Kerger
Michael D. Kern
Sean M. Kerr
Martin Kerres
Rolf Ketelaar
Ingo Kett
Norbert Kettner
J. Patrick Keyes
Mitchell E. Kick
Hee Jip Kim
Chul Kim
Craig R. Kindleman
Lindsey King
Ina Kirchhof
John S. Kish
Koichi Kiyohara
Elizabeth C. Klee
Bernhard J. Klein Wassink
Susanne Kloess
Michael Knott
Yuhei Kobayashi
Michael K. Kobayashi
Martin Kochman
David J. Koehl
Kim M. Koeller
Pasi Koivunen
Yutaka Koizumi
Jussi Konkola
John D. Korry
Frank E.U. Korsstrom
Carsten Kracht
Tor Krattebol
Michelle L. Krause
Robert Kreuzer
Daniel P. Krueger
Xian Hong Ku
Ralf Kuhn
Ajit Kumar
Nalin Kumra
Matti Kurvinen
Eric Laffargue
Rod Keyes Laird
Mark P. LaLeike
Ted Clark Landis
Jonathan L. Lange
Gerhard Langst
Jean-Michel Lapisse
Brenda F. LaPorte
Tomas Larez
Kristian Larsen
Paul M. Larson
Daniel D. Lauderback
J. Scott Laughner
William John Laurie
Katherine D. LaVelle
Michael T. Lavelle
Richard Lawrence
Robert T. Lax
Bernard Le Masson
Bruno Le Moal
Nicolas Le Saux
Roberto Lecciso
Won-Joon Lee
John A. Lee
Sze-wing Lee
Sandra L. Leitch
Inaki Leiva
Xavier Lejeune
Mark Lelinski
Lori A. Lenehan
William F. Lenihan
Miriam Lenio
Bernard Lepere
Joel Leroux
Richard E. Lesher
Patrick W. Leung
Seth M. Levine
Mattias Lewren
Angel Li
Harald Lieder
Adriaan H. Lieftinck
Mark T. Lillie
Angelica Lim
Cherlyn C. Linden
Robert K. Lindsey
Ilkka Lipasti
Richard Kim Loane
Amy T. Loftus
Paul D. Loftus
Kevin P. Loftus
Ian Lomas
Bradley Hoffman Loose
Manuel Lopes da Costa
Ricardo Lopez Guinea
Lori L. Lovelace
George L. Lovett
Andrea Lucchesi
Lance A. Luther
Sami Juhani Luukkonen
Dirk Luyten
Mark John Lyons
Julian A. Mabe
Deborah MacArthur
Mauro Macchi
Douglas L. MacDonald
Bernardo Costa Macedo
Michele Maggiorotti
Josef Mago
Kevin L. Maher
Josep Maixenchs
Raju Makanjee
Jukka Makela
Asif F. Malik
Klaus Malle
Christopher P. Mammoser
Frank Thomas Mang
Steven Mankoff
David Mann
Joseph V. Marabito
Christian Marchetti
Mauro Marchiaro
Nitti L. Mardjan
Paolo Maresca
Olivier Jean Marie
Alessandro Marin
Toni L. Mark
E. Russell Martin
Rob Martin
Pietro Martinelli
Marty E. Martinson
Makoto Maruyama
Paolo Marzetti
Tony Masella
Xavier Massons
Thomas R. Mataconis
Michael A. Matella
Kenji Matsuda
Brian R. May
Trent A. Mayberry
Jon Mayne
James P. Mccleneghen
Bruce A. McCullough
David M. McCurley
Jim McDade
Mark P. McDonald
Nina T. McDonald

Paul E. McGowan
Jeff R. McGowan
Christopher J. McGrath
Neil M. McGregor
Meg T. McLaughlin
Mark G. McNulty
Robert B. McPherson
Curt W. Meeuwsen
Manish J. Mehta
Peter Meinhardt
Joakim Mellander
Eric J. Melulis
Andrew Mendoza
Laurent Mercier-James
Jair F. A. Merlo
Tor Mesoy
Thomas D. Meyer
Jacquelyn E. Middleton
Charles E. Mihaliak
Massimo Milanta
Myke L. Miller
George A. Miller
Richard E. Miller
Andrew Milligan
Stephen Anthony Mills
Agusti X. Miro
Domingo Miron
Lubos Miskuf
Koji Mitani
James E. Mitchell
James D. Mitchell
Kuniyuki Miyashita
Kohjiro Mizutani
Stein Erik Moe
Michael Mohnhaupt
Frederick Molineux
Rubens Moll
Steve Mollenkamp
Stephen John Molnar
Massimiliano Monaco
Paolo Monesi
Beat R. Monnerat
Alfredo Montalbano
Steven K. Moomau
Peter John Moore
R. Alan Moore
Jamie R. Moors
Brian J. Moran
Kurt E. Moreby
Juan Pedro Moreno
Guy V. Morgan
Gianluigi Morganti
Gael Comrie Morris
Alexandra Morris Robson
David I. Moskovitz
Chie Motoi
Karyn J. Mottershead
Jean-Francois F. Moufle
Jean Paul Moulin
Monty F. Mueller
Narendra P. Mulani
Dennis A. Mullahy
Donovan Herbert Muller
Laura D. Muller
Daniel S. Mullin
Hans-Joachim Muncheberg
Javier Mur
Katsuya Murashima
Stephen R. Murnen
Alistair Murray
Fabrizio Musmeci
Silvio Musso
Tatsuya Nagayama
Andy Naish
Yuji Nakamura
Yasuo Nakashima
Gerard Naouri
Tanya Nargolwalla
Thomas H. Neiger
Werner Neitzel
Tamas Nemeth
Mark R. Newall
Robert K. Newman
Mandla Bikwa Nhlapo
W. Anthony Nichols
John K. Nichols
Claudia Nieto
Hirokazu Nishikado
Yuji Nishimura
Thomas F. Nolan
Piero Nonino
A. Joe Norris
Paul North
Robert Lewis Northcutt
Ian Matthew Notley
Seiichiro Nukui
Fernando Nunez-Mendoza
Mark Oakes
Calvin A. O'Brien
Geoffrey O'Connell
Bruce L. O'Connor
Robert Brett Ogilvie
Norman Ogilvy
Robert F. O'Keefe
Dean W. Olmstead
Azad Ootam
Kathleen T. O'Reilly
Anne O'Riordan
Michael L. Orlowicz
Michael J. Orman
Stuart A. H. Orr
Neil A. Osborne
Bode Adesoga Ososami
Robert Ouellette
Sylvie Ouziel
Steven S. Ouzounian
Stanley M. Oyama
Stephen Michael Packard
Stephen Dowland Page
Massimo Pagella
Andrew R. Pahlman
Michael G. Pain
Mark Paling
Jorge Palmela
Michael E. Palmer
Jerry L. Palmer
Robert O. Palmer
George Papageorgiou
Pietro Papantuono
Thomas N. Parry
Craig W. Parsell
Gregory E. Pascuzzi
Aseet A. Patel
Rich Patrick
Eric W. Patton
Sam A. Paul
Timothy A. Peacher
David Malcolm Pearce
Mark H. Pearson
Miguel Peco
Alison Peden
David W. Pepping
Francis A. Perras
Mikael Persson
David T. Petersen
Zoe A. Peterson
Anastasia Petropulos
Darrell L. Petty
Antonio Pezzinga
Henning Pfaffhausen
Andreas Michael Pfeifer
Michelle B. Pfeifer
Kai Pfitzner
Gregory Thomas Phalin
Mark D. Phillips
Paul J. Pieper
Giorgio Pieragostini
William N. Pieroni
Jean-Marie Pierron
Willy Pillinger
Juergen Pinkl
Roberto Piraccini
Gregory J. Pitstick
Ali Piyarali
David E. Plesko
Matthew J. Podrebarac
Teresa L. Poggenpohl
John W. Poindexter
Jean-Laurent Poitou
Michael G. Pope
David L. Pope
Achille Poretta
Simon Ross Porter
James Porter
Parrish K. Potts
Anne M. Potvin
Blake A. Pounds
Grant D. Powell
Alex Anthony George Powell
Daniele Presutti
Piero Pronello
Andreas Przewloka
Scott A. Puopolo
Aidan Quilligan
Jose Ignacio Quintero
David E. Radvany
Barry Rafe
Thomas Raffeiner
Donald J. Ragas
Cheryl C. Railey
Anantha K. Raman
Balaji V. Ramarao
Antonio Carlos M. Ramos
Jack Ramsay
Steven S. Ramsey
Tor Jakob Ramsoy
Arne H. Ramstad
Giancarlo Ranaldi
Philip J. Rauen
Dhiren Rawal
Matthew V. Ray
Jazz Rayet
Manuela Re
Craig Rea
Juan Manuel Rebollo
Bernd Recker
Inigo Redondo
Jeronimo Reguera
Michael Rehm
Jan Rehnman
David Reid
Holger Reimers
Jeffrey Todd Relf
Rick H. Rene
Daniel W. Ressler
Scott S. Revare
Jose Antonio Revuelta
John J. Reynolds
Bernhard Rheinberger
Umar Riaz
Francisco Jose V. Ribeiro
John D. Rice
David T. Richards
Paul Richardson
Robert Mackellar Ritchie
Alfonso Rivero
Philippe Rixhon
Daniel W. Rizer
Eivind Roald
Stephen S. Roatch
Alain L. Robbe
Rick Robbins
Neville Roberts
Jon Robertson
Dean C. Robinson
Alan Robinson
Anthony Roby
Fausto Roda
John R. Roddy
Mark A. Rode
Michael J. Rogalski
John G. Rogers
Scott M. Rose
David A. Rossi
Jeremy Paul Rowe
David P. Rowland
Mark Graham Rowlands
Michael L. Rowley
Rafael Rubio
Michael D. Rudin
Fernando Rufilanchas
Michael Rundshagen
C. Holly Runyon
Christopher Rupp
Michael J. Russell
Carlos E. Rust
Kate Rutherford
Elizabeth L. Rutigliano
Christopher R. Rutledge
Richard A. Ryan
Rodolfo Sabater
Carsten Sachmann
Andres E. Sadler
Kenneth M. Saitow
Yasushi Saka
Ichiro Sakuda
Graciela Salgado Sarria
Marcus Salouk
Sushil Saluja
Heron A. Samara
Sudarshan Sampathkumar
Katherine J. Sample
Mark G. Samuelian
Antonio San Agustin
Jose Luis Sancho
Liv Guri Sandbaek
Richard J. Sands
Arak Sanprasert
Paulo Santos
Michael Sauter
Paul Ferris Saydah

Kenneth Scalet
Maria Scarcella
Eric Schaeffer
Guido Scherer
Daniel A. Schlegel
Hubertus Schleuter
John H. Schmidt
Hanno Kai Alexander Schmidt-Gothan
Stefan Schneider
Patrick O. Schneider
Jan L. Schotte
Denise M Schrimsher
Mark A. Schuler
Michael X. Schulz
Pablo D. Schuster
Thomas D. Schwenger
Michael Schworer
Anthony J. Scolini
Charlene A. Scott
Cheryl Anne Scott
Chin Siong Seah
Dana H. Sedgass
Pierre-Louis Seguin
M Andrew Seikel
Ryoji Sekido
Douglas W. Sellers
Christian Selmer
John F. Semmer
Takayasu Senba
Pollie Sengstake
John S. Sepple
Ralph Peter Seraphim
Jonas Serlachius
Jean-Michel Michel Servant
Jean-Marc E. Serve
David P. Shatto
Hiroshi Shinbo
Dean K. Shold
Christopher A. Shoup
Richard S. Siber
Julianto Sidarto
Gary Laurence Siegel
Riadh Sifaoui
James J. Sikora
Afonso Silva
Vasco Simoes
Rui Rio Simoes
Thomas M. Simoneau
Janet M. Simonitsch
Catherine M. Simons
Peter Simpson
Andrea P. Sinner
Witold Sitek
Michael J. Sivo
Joakim L. Sjoeman
Julian Skan
Thomas M. Skiba
Steven G. Skinner
Fraser Skirrow
Sigurd Skjaeveland
Richard L. Sklarin
Peter Skodny
Ian Daniel Slattery
Roland Smertnig
Jan-Coen Smit
Richard R. Smith
Nigel Smith
David A. Smith
T. Baker Smith
Edward D. Smith
William S. Smith
Wayne P. Sobon
Larry M. Socher
Lawrence F. Solomon
Pekka Somppi
Sham Soobiah
Claudio Sousa
Francesco Spinelli
Timothy John Staley
Gregory S. Stayin
Morten B. Steiner
Eyal Steinitz
Andrew B. Stengel
Joel A. Stern
Jonathan W. Stern
Harold A. Stern
Allen Emil Stiles
Jeffrey A. Stocker
Torbjoern Stockman
Peter C. Stockman
Mark P. Stoke
Ken B. Stoll
Jeffrey H. Stout
Terri E. Strauss
John A. Sundean
Karl Sussebach
Bente Svensson
Karin Svensson
Stephen J. Swartz
Michael S. Sweeney
Michael John Switek
Paul Joseph Sylvester
Nobuyoshi Takuma
Charles Tan
Judy S. Tan
Frank Jay Tappen
Kelly F. Tate
Gregory L. Tatum
Joao Pedro Tavares
Joao Antonio Tavares
Keith E. Tayloe
Roxanne Taylor
Stuart W. Taylor
Vincent Taylor
Michael R. Templin
Lay Lim Teo
Yoshimasa Terada
Thomas F. Terry
Atilla Terzioglu
Steven T. Thayer
Orapong Thien-Ngern
Marc Thiollier
Gregory A. Thorson
Nils Erik Thuden
Annika Thunberg
Matthew A. Tillman
Brendan Timmins
Barbara H. Titzrath
Henning Todte
Junya Tomatsuri
Takashi Tominaga
Masao Tomomune
Makoto Toyoda
Judy B. Trafas
Guido Traverso
Mark Treger
Pierluigi Troncatti
James K. Trowhill
Mike Steven True
Jack Tsai
George K. Tsantes
Yasuhiko Tsuchida
Stefano Tubino
Franco Turconi
Brett A. Turner
Harold C. Turner
Martin Derek Ullyatt
Fernando Usera
Sajid Usman
Maurizio Piero Vago
Francois Valerian
Rudy J. Valli
Risto Valtakari
Roswitha Adele Maria van der Markt
Edwin Van der Ouderaa
Julienne Van Der Ziel
James W. Van Pelt
Michel A. M. van Rosendaal
Peter Vanderslice
Jean M. Vandevelde
Jeffrey G. VanWie
Nam-Ung Vaque
Stephen A. Varley
C. Clark Varner
Andrew James Vautier
Mireya Velasco
Eric R. Veron
Rik M. Vervisch
Gregory L. Vestri
Paulo Vilares Vicente
Gary Vickers
Davide Vignotti
L. Thomas Vogel
Steve M. Voichick
Curt Volkmann
Druvaan B. von Drehnen
Hans Georg von Lewinski
Jos I. Vranken
Todd R. Wagner
Cathinka E. Wahlstrom
Salman Wakil
Patricia H. Walker
R. Brian Walker
John A. Wallace
Paula A. Walworth
Peter D. Warasila
Nicholas J. Ward
Richard Anthony Warner
Steven B. Warner
Frederic Watine
Karl C. Watkins
Sandra J. Wege
Olaf Wehrkamp
Joshua A. Weingast
David R. Weinstein
Sean Weir
Marie E. Weirich
James F. Weiss
Andrew Douglass West
Kevin Alistair Westcott
Adrian Westlake
Gregor Wick
Adrian Widmer
Friederike A. Wiertulla
Richard Duncan Wild
Angus Garvin Wildblood
Mark R. Willford
Andy M. Williams
Mark C. Williams
Simon C. Williams
Paul R. Wilson
Todd S. Wilson
David R. Wilson
Ole Winberg
Joseph D. Winslow
Richard B. Winston
Richard Boydell Wolff
Michael E. Wolk
Robert E. Wollan
David E. Wolski
James P. Wong
Carole L. Wong
Pauline Mary Elizabeth Wood
Gilbert D. Wootton
C. Cristian Wulf
Steve Wylie
Graham L. Wyllie
John A. Yacobi
Ahmet Yalcin
Peter H. Yen
Stanley John Stephen Young
Idar Ytterdal
Evelyn Zabo
Noor Azlin Zainal Abidin
Jeffrey C. Zaniker
Patrick T. Zelten
John A. Zerbe
Allan Ziirsen
G.L. Zunker
Stephen Ross Zutovsky
Marc Zwaaneveld
Debbie Masithole Zwane-Chikura

**October 1, 2000**

Bernd Venohr

**June 1, 2001**

Patricia Anslinger
William A. Bloom
Hans-Juergen Croissant
Jens Hanker
Robert A. Hohnen
Justin Jenk
Jens B. Junkermann
Alain Lancereau
Lance Harold Levy
Jeffrey Merrihue
Fumio Ohue
Tomoyasu Ozeki
Walter Pfeiffer
Thierry Pineau
Douwe Derk Tideman
Ruwan Upendra Weerasekera
Baerbel Wicha-Krause
Phil James Williams

**June 19, 2001**

Harry L. You

**July 1, 2001**

Paul-Michael Dahlheim
Axel Neidlein

**September 1, 2001**

Anders B. Abrahamsson
Kees C. Aerts
Thomas J. Agnew
Javed Ahmed
Darrin E. Ahrens
David J. Allen

Matthew J. Anderson
Jonathan S. Andrews
Yutaka Anma
Sheela P. Arkeri
Margaret Elizabeth Arky
George Attar
Olivier Aubert
John Audia
Akifumi Baba
Luigi Badaloni
Thomas P. Baecker
Andreas Baier
Jordi Ballesteros
Ana Baranda
Silvio L. Barboza
Roderick E. Barnard
Pedro Barsanti Vigo
Troy B. Barton
Michael P. Barton
Peter Baumann
Steven D. Beene
Richard O. Beggs
Philippe Bellamit
Jacob Benadiba Wahnich
Randall E. Berry
Pius Bienz
Manuel Alfredo Blanco Barrios
Lars A. Bohm
Valentijn Bonger
Saulo L. Bonizzato
Mark Boudreau
Michael A. Bova
James T. Bowler
David M. Boyle
Kim Ladota Bozzella
Brendan Walsh Bradley
Nigel P. Brady
Christophe Braun
Susann F. Bresnahan
Frank D. Brienzi
Thomas Buesch
Christian Bulletti
Raul Burgos Gonzalez
Ann V. Burns
Brian S. Burns
Vidya S. Byanna
Carlos Cadarso Marques
Lisa L. Caplan
Eduardo Carrizo
Johnny J. Cavaliero
Daniel L. Cavenaugh
Stefania Celsi
Foo Tuck Chan
Gavin John Chappell
Joseph D. Chenelle
Richard P. Clark

John L. Coffey
Michael J. Collins
Antonio Colmena
Jordi Colome
Ramon Colomina
Cory H. Courtney
Teresa S. Crabtree
Constance A. Cranos
Steven R. Culp
Ger M. Daly
Thomas H. Davenport
Michael R. David
Joseph E. Davis
David W. Day
Eric De Blauwe
Ian Ross De Snoo
Heinrich Degener
Allen J. Delattre
Gregory C. Dennis
R. Douglas Derrick
Jose Manuel Desco Agullo
Mark A. Detelich
Scott B. Deutschman
James R. Dicaprio
Francisco Javier Diez
Jose Luis Diez Ballesteros
Sara J. Dioguardi
Glenn J. Dispenziere
Marek Dobsa
Michael Andrew Donnellan
Christopher P. Donnelly
Kevin J. Dooley
Michael B. Doyle
John F. Drake
Michel Driessen
Marla J. Driscoll
Peter T. Duncan
John F. Durocher
Andrew James Dvorocsik
Barry C. Dyer
Ann G. Dyer
Giles A. Edmonds
Steven G. Edwards
John Erik Ellingsen
Richard P. Emery
Christian Engels
Wolf Henning Ettel
Nick Peter Evans
Phillip G. Everson
Craig R. Everson
John S. Fanguy
Marcos A. Fernandez
Daniele Ferrari
Guido Ferriani
Daniel V. Figueirido
Reiner Fischer

Jennifer V. Flake
James E. Flowers
Leonardo J. Framil
Per Ingvald Fredriksen
Michele K. Friedman
Sigurd Fristad
Maria Fullone
Anita Funken-Luce
Elena Gadol
Archie Galbraith
Adolfo J. Galue Amblar
Andrew Thorburn Garrick
Laurent Gatignol
Allen J. Gaudet
Michael A. Gavigan
Louanne Gemin
Roeland Gielen
Andrew Leonard Gillett
Mark J. Gilrain
Olivier Girard
Eivind Gjemdal
Irmgard Glasmacher
Roger Goncalves
Sanjay Gopal
Hiroshi Goto
Mary Beth Gracy
Eric Grison
Sean M. Hagarty
Fred G. Hajjar
Donald G. Hamilton
Simon James Wilfrid Hamilton
Thomas A. Hanley
Mikael Hansson
Simon J. Hargreaves
Gasser Haridy
Audrey R. Harrell
Scott F. Harrison
Steven B. Harrison
Scott A. Hathorne
Lissimahos Hatzidimoulas
Stephan Haupt
Marc Hauser
Gary John Haywood
Ulrich Heckenberger
James C. Hendrickson
Julio J. Hernandez
Dale R. Hersch
Thomas H. Hess
William Guy Hilbert
Greg J. Hodak
David M. Hodgson
Thomas Holtmann
Bernhard Holtschke
Ray Hopkins
Maureen S. Horgan

Timothy J. Hourigan
Karen Hoyndorf
F. Courtenay Huff
Mark Andrew Hughes
Shinji Igarashi
Koichi Ikegami
Michael A. Jackowski
Mark D. Jackson
Erik Jacob
Hendrik C.H. Jahn
Lindsay Katharine Johnston
Jorma Heikki Olavi Jokinen
Tom C. Kane
Michael John Leonard Kaye
Marty R. Kelliher
Carl S. Kiefer
Guy H. Kinley
Hugh Kirby
Peter Kirk
Geir T. Kjellevold
Michael Klein
Stefan Knipp
Eiichi Kokado
Shigeharu Komuro
Bernhard F. Kraft
Jakob Holmen Kraglund
Jeffrey A. Krause
Olaf Kreichgauer
Jaroslaw Kroc
Kazushi Kubokawa
Gabriele Kult
Julie E. Lamont
Russell K. Lath
Stephen M. Michael Lathrope
Kevin M. Laudano
Robert L. Laurens
Ed Lauwerens
Kenneth P. Lawhorn
Roberto Lazzari
Vincent Lebeault
Steven B. Lee
Suk-Geun Lee
Roger W. Lehman
Pino Leoni
Roberto Libonati
Paul A. Lichlyter
Alex Lin
Ben T. Little
Karen A. Lohss
Francisco Javier Lopez Espejo
Steven E. Lubowicz
Michael A. Lucarini

Anna Chiara Lucchini
Arnoud Maas
Alwin Kumar Magimay
Denise D. Malecki
Carl Christian Malm
Gianluca A. Marcopoli
Giovanni Mariani
Fabrice Mariaud
Eric E. Marin
Antonino Marino
Vitor Marques
Michele Marrone
Suzette L. Massie
Yuichiro Masuno
John B. Matchette
Guy Mather
Nishith Mathur
Lynn H. Mc Mahon
Debora B. McDonald
Stephen L. McMinn
Malcolm A. McNamara
Jonathan Patrick McQuoid
Sten Mejdahl-Hansen
Lourenco Mendonca
Thierry Mennesson
Tony Metcalfe
Valentin Andres de Miguel Luno
Natasha Elizabeth Jane Miller
James N. Miller
Kelly B. Miner
Raimon Miret
Clarence Mitchell
Giorgio Moise
Perry S. Moody
Noel C. Mooney
Lee Tony Moore
Terry L. Moore
Roberta Morandi
Marco Morchio
William H. Morris
Christophe Mouille
Josef C. Mueller
David G. Muir
Henrik R. Mulvad
Nobuhiko Muraoka
Joel Nadjar
Ramesh B. Nair
Russ Nash
Keith C. Nashawaty
Christina L. Naugle
Michael Paul Needleman
David L. Nichols
Kelly Nimmo-Guenther
Michael Nolte

Francisco Jose Nuez Campos
Matt Oakley
Thomas O. Oblak
Patrick T. O'Boyle
John M. O'Brien
Per Uno Oesterman
Pedro Olmos Lopez
Renato Osato
Marcus Osegowitsch
Oonagh O'Sullivan
Philip Otley
Cenk O. Ozdemir
Elizabeth J. Padmore
Duncan Brian Page
Jarkko Pallasaho
Purificacion Paniagua
Piyush M. Patel
John H. Patterson
William D. Perry
Kathleen B. Persian
Edwin M. Phanord
Elina Inkeri Piispanen
Guilherme J. Pinheiro
Adan Plaza
Troy R. Pliska
John P. Poisson
Andrew David Poppleton
Santiago Roberto Pordelanne
Sarah Gillian Pritchard
Robert Purks
Juha J. Pylkko
Kevin N. Quiring
Paolo Raimondo
Eric Carl Rasmussen
Tobias Rataj
Justin Rautenberg
John R. Ray
Michael J. Redding
Frank Rennekamp
Pedro M. Ribeiro
Seth W. D. Richman
Christopher S. Rigg
Michael M. Riley
Cato W. Rindal
Timothy A. Ringo
Antonio Rivas Perez
David T. Roberts
Gregory C. Roberts
Marcus D. Robinson
Buffie D. Rodri
William M. Rogers
Steven A. Rosati
Alessandro Rossi
Marco Rotondo
David M. Rouls
Carl Rubin
Jeffrey S. Russell
Kyriacos Sabatakakis
Joao C. Santos
Maria Jose Sanz Jimenez
Tsuyoshi Sato
Peter Scharf
Elisabeth S. Schmidt
Ingrid Schneider
Rikard Schroeder
Dirk Schuerbuescher
Andreas Hermann Schuler
Torsten Schumacher
Mike A. Scotten
Stephen M. Sell
Conrad M. Sheehan
Michael T. Shimota
Clive Lintorn Shore
Todd A. Sickles
Kenneth S. Silbert
Todd W. Singleton
Ravi Sirianukul
Russell Robert Smyth
Scott W. Softy
Julie A. Sokol
Jon David Solomon
David J. Sovell
Christine T. Sovereign
M. Scott Sparks
Marco Spaziani Testa
Thomas H. Spurr
Patrick J. St. James
John M. Stefanchik
Glenn A. Stolar
James P. Struntz
Andrew J. Sullivan
Alfredo Pablo Surroca Martin
Michelle R. Swanback
Paul A. Taffinder
Tomokazu Takeda
Marcello Tamietti
Eugene V. Tanski
Robin Tapp
Esther Tarres
Enrico Terenzoni
Philippe Terol
Nam Yew Thean
Glenn J. Thomas
Bryce B. Thompson
Steve J. Thomson
Carl-Peter Thorwid
William L. Trafton
Carlo A. Uchello
Olav Storli Ulvund
Fabio Pietro Vacirca
Maud M. van den Meiracker
Jerome Vercaemer
Marco Vernocchi
John Vickery
Philippe Vidal
Eduardo M. Vital
Gil J. Vogel
Anton von Bebenburg
Charles J. Waeltz
Gordon Walters
Bo Wang
Carl Ward
Nobuhiko Watanabe
Doug F. Watson
Shari K. Wenker
Stephan Werthschulte
James F. Whelan
Scott B. White
Clive Henry Hague Whitehouse
Steve D. Wick
Harry Wildeboer
Andrew Wilson
Kelly Wilson
Theresa Wise
Wai Yin Wong
Andrew W. Worley
Kennard L. Wottowa
Mark A. Wozniak
Rodney N. Wright
Garret R. Wu
Luis F. Zaninetti
Ignacio Zapater
Stephen Zatland
Daniel C. Zimmerman
Miguel D. Zweig

September 4, 2001
Gary A. Curtis

October 1, 2001
Ulrich Jakob Looser

November 12, 2001
Jouni Hakanen

December 3, 2001
Luigi Arrighini
Vincenzo Giovannitti

December 17, 2001
David A. Roberts

January 7, 2002
Adam Johnson

January 14, 2002
Gary Stephen Pusey

January 21, 2002
Douglas F. Hofmeister
John R. Hubbell

February 1, 2002
Eva Dewor

February 18, 2002
Thomas F. Van Horn

April 1, 2002
Robert C. Calvert

April 29, 2002
Donald A. Birchenough

May 1, 2002
John J. Ballow
Kazufumi Misawa

June 3, 2002
Mark Andrew Boyle

July 8, 2002
David O'Brien

August 7, 2002
Robert Suh

August 12, 2002
Allan Lord Tetley

August 20, 2002
Thomas Allen Kraack

August 27, 2002
George Abigail

August 29, 2002
Kris P. Denton

September 1, 2002
Toshihiko Aizawa
Stephen Martin Alessi
Claire Louise Allen
Steve Wayne Andre
Ansano Baccelli Jr.
George Clayton Baker
Alberto Bardaji Pascual
Stephen A. Barlock
Giuseppe Barzaghi
Joaquin F. Bas Monerris
Alex Bauer
Adrian Michael Bertschinger
Stephanie B. Bichet
Andreas L. Bienert
Jamie M. Bolton
Danilo Boretto
Scott R. Brennan
James Bentley Broms
Charles T. Brooks
Ad-Jan Brouwer
Edward Lambert Browne
Giovanni Paolo Bruno
Jean Cabanes
Philip Michael Calcutt
Filippo Caroselli
José Manuel Casado Gonzalez
Marco Cassinadri
John Celi
Philippe Chaniot
Manuel Chaure Bueno
Yoshio Chikayasu
Ricardo Chisman
Adrian Paul Clamp
Scot W. Clark
Serge Colle
John F. Coltsmann
Brian J. Condit
Michael A. Costonis
Christopher L. Crump
Owen Barrasford Davies
Bradley W. Davis
Patrizio Delicati
Andrew J. Desmond
Giovina Silvana D'Giacomo
Fernand Dimidschstein
David Joseph Dohnalik
Paul M. Duff
Segun Olakunle Egunjobi
Patricia Ann Endres
Paul Joseph Equale
Catherine Strother Farley
José Manuel Fernandes
Thomas M. Fischer
Simon Flack
Henry Clifton Fleming
Jason C. Freedman
Michael John Gallagher
Mark Gargiulo
Jean-Michel Gay
Ian David Geddes
Jordi Gibert Arce
Fiona E. Gibson
Vasathaven Govender
Rhonda F. Harrison
Mark R. Hennessy
Michael T. Hessler
Rodger Hill
Jochen Hollaender
Richard H. Holsman
Tetsuya Hotta
Khalid Husseini
Bridget Helen Jackson
Catherine Jestin
Kyle Kirkpatrick Jordan
Dhananjay M. Joshi
Paul A. Kline
Christopher John Kozina
Ittoop Johannes Kurian
Michel Lahyani

Alexander Landia
Jae-Han Lee
Stefan P. Lemke
John E. Lichtenstein
Eric Allen Livingston
John B. R. Long
Charlotta Elsa Desirée Lundell Berg
Luc Pierre Maes
Philippe Mallet
Carlos Mantas
Adrian Marcellus
Kathleen Mary Mcdivitt
Chris M. Merrill
Neil Miller
Julie E. Miller
Alexander William Milward
Peter Steen Mogensen
Michele Morelli
Remash Kumar Nair
Linh C. Nguyen
Luís Rafael Leite Nunes
Hiroaki Ohzono
Dawn Elizabeth Palmer
Shep Parke
Abelardo Pato Rodriguez
Gonzalo Perez Gasca
Massimiliano Pian
Kevin J. Pint
Gary A. Plotkin
Mark E. Potocki
Penelope G. Prett
Rajiv Rajput
María Ángeles Ramirez Fuentes
Prakash A. Rao
David M. Regan
Werner Reil
Daniel Francis Rice
Jeffrey Marden Riedel
James Alton Robbins
Timothy Robinson
David Zvi Ron
David Rowlands
Simon William Russell
Marco Salera
María Aránzazu Sanchez Hernandez
Tonje Sandberg
Dieter Helmut Schelzel
Andreas Schroeder
Marc Schuuring
Adriana Scozzafava
Theo Jan Simons
P. Dean Smith
Jesús Manuel Sualdea Martín
Steven Thomas
Andrea K. Thomson
Thomas Holman Thornton
Ross H. Tokmakian
Hubert Tresarrieu
Tomomi Ukaji
Geert van den Goor
Pallavi Verma
Jamie D. Walker
Christopher L. Ward
David John Whiteing
Andreas Wisser
Joseph Paul Wroblewski
Michael Joseph Yadgar
Naoyuki Yazawa
Michael E. Yeaman
Marco Ziegler

**November 1, 2002**
Petra Tielkes

**November 6, 2002**
Andrew Douglas Friars

**December 2, 2002**
Alastair Carmichael MacWillson

**January 1, 2003**
Michael Junker
Mark Roger Robertson

**January 6, 2003**
Jin K. Lee

**January 13, 2003**
Ronald D. Gillette
Patricia B. O'Brien

**January 15, 2003**
Stephen Sanders Simmerman

**February 12, 2003**
Robert H. Scheier

**February 17, 2003**
Michael Gerald Heideman

**March 3, 2003**
Cathy L. Bradley

**April 7, 2003**
Michael Farrell

**June 2, 2003**
Alton L. Adams

**June 24, 2003**
Jorman D. Granger

**August 1, 2003**
Walter Hennemann

**August 7, 2003**
Alexandre Manuel Oliveira

**August 19, 2003**
Gregg A. Clark

**August 28, 2003**
Andrew B. Zimmerman

**September 1, 2003**
Fernando Acevedo Frias
Greg S. Adler
Angelo Aliquo
Claudio Arcudi
James Herbert Arnott
Jack Elison Azagury
Lucy Bloem-Dunster
Franck Boubon
Santiago Jesus del Brio Gonzalez
Norbert Buening
Todd Stanley Cameron
Alessandro Cappelli
Jorge Carlos Castilla Ortuno
Ravi Chanmugam
France Leila Cyrenne
Libor David
Eric de Lavenne
Eloi Decottignies
Mauricio Deutsch Menache
Neil Deville
Gino B. DiGregorio
Oskar Ebbinghaus
Clare Filby
Stephen Michael Fraser
John Charles Gingrich
Lawrence Chear Wah Goh
Thomas K. Gosnell
Colin D. Grant
Richard E. Grassel
Ines Ramona Guzman Arrue
Ritchie Allen Hamm
Dean Francis Harford
Christina Marie Harper
Phillip E. Hazen
Jill R. Houck
Bernard Jaeck
Robert Scott Johnson
Lisa Marie Johnson
Sandra Auyer Jones
Emmanuel Jusserand
Chaitanya Madhukar Kamat
Saied R. Karamooz
Minh Nguyen Le
David Cruzen Link
Christopher Vernon Lucy
Maki Matsuzaki
Francois Matte
Kevin R. Meadows
Allen Merrill
Ross A. Meyercord
Paul E. Molnar
Carlos Morales Sanchez
Sergio A. Naylor
Drazen Nikolic
Yoshihiro Nomoto
Edmond C. O'Neill
Cary Satoshi Oshima
Harshad Parsot Parbhoo
Peter Kieron Pennifer
Giovanni Mario Pisanu
Eric A. Portman
Gregory Pryor
Soneel Raj
Gene Reznik
Jesus Rojas Seguido
Rafael Rovira Rius
Anoop Sagoo
Anneli Samuelsson
Stephanie K. Schnabel
Nakyang Seong
Ellyn Jo Shook
Thomas Sontheimer
Paul M. Squire
Seiichi Tamura
Andreas Thon
Stacey Titens
Sean David Toole
Yujiro Urakami
Mark Alan Vallaster
Joost van de Meent
Tom van der Spek
Marshall J. Wells
Greg Wilkinson
David C. Wilson
James Victor Wolak
C. David Wolf
Vincent Wah Kit Wong
Soichi Yonezawa
Alberto Zamora Reinoso
Jerome Douglass Zingg

**September 8, 2003**
Patrick Michael Byrne

**September 22, 2003**
Luis Emilio Taveras

**October 1, 2003**
Harald Deutsch

**October 17, 2003**
Arjang Zadeh

**November 1, 2003**
Darren Nippard

**November 13, 2003**
Jess I. Parks

**November 17, 2003**
Jonathan H. Kaplan
Robert Douglas VanWingerden

**December 1, 2003**
Andrew John Cleminson

**January 12, 2004**
Neil Canter
José T. Morales

**January 19, 2004**
Stephen Leslie Willis

**February 12, 2004**
Christopher F. Lange

**February 16, 2004**
William A. Phelps

**February 23, 2004**
Brian David Allatt

**March 1, 2004**
Scott William Hamilton
Timothy Roy Leger
Jian Ma

**April 5, 2004**
Norman Lindsay Wright

**April 26, 2004**
Gregory N. Bolino
Paul E. Rudolph

**May 1, 2004**
Augustin Manchon

**May 3, 2004**
Walter E. Shill
George Daniel Sullivan

**May 14, 2004**
Steven J. Grossmann

**July 1, 2004**
Warren John Harding

**August 1, 2004**
Jan Z. Kubat

**August 2, 2004**
Lloyd E. Johnson

**August 17, 2004**
Niul A. Burton

**August 23, 2004**
Shervin Talieh

**August 27, 2004**
Vincent K. Shepherd

August 30, 2004

Kevin F. Bandy
John Ho
Andrew James Hogenson
Brian J. Queenin
Rajan Srikanth

September 1, 2004

Shahid Ahmed
Vincenzo Aloisio
Christopher H. Atkinson
David Carl Auer
Vinod Bagal
Elizabeth Dodelin Bailey
Philippe Baratte
James George Bogues
Fabio Bonfanti
Erin M. Brannan
Michael Speros Brown
Michael Brueckner
Philip William Bulley
Adam Patten Burden
Werner Buttiens
Deborah Campbell
Giorgio Canocchi
Kevin Wade Carley
Jerel Lawrence Causey
Irving Chee Wei Chew
Bianca Moniz Chinelli
Timothy Eric Chron
Peter G. Colley
Avis Darzins
Pascal Denis
Sylvain Deslandes
Angelo D'imporzano
Kenneth Michael Dircks
Simon Roger Eaves
David M. Edmondson
Maged Fanous
Julien Faye
Hakan S. Franson
Elizabeth Fretwell
John Michael Gamberoni
Mohammed Ferhet Gause
Pascal Jean-Albert Gautheron
Carlo Gessi
Marcelo Gil Souza
John P. Grosvenor
Anish Gupta
Dominique Anne Hainebach
Claire Hall-Moore
Jeroen Haster
Brett Ivan Hayes
Roland Hess
Joerg Hoefer
Jan-Erik Hunn
Masayuki Ishizaki
Ralph Jahnke
Kelvin Paul Jauch
Albert Juanals
Uwe Jungmann
Keith Lane Ketcher
Max Alan Kleinman
Kevin Knarr
Louise Elizabeth Lackenby
Mark Dwayne Lambert
Damien Lasou
Matthew John Latham
Ji-Eun Lee
Keith Gregory Lippiatt
James Patrick Little
Michael A. Ljung
David J. Loffredo
Matthew Long
Stefano Lorenzi
Gregory P. Luethe
Piew Lum
Laurent C. Lutz
John P. Maguire
Jordi Majo
Scott P. Mall
Brad W. Martin
Daniel John Mathews
Gail E. Mc Giffin
William J. McDonald
Andrew James McGowan
Jennifer Susan McLaughlin
Sean E. McNamara
Mark T. McTiernan
Eric Mestre
Keith Middlemass
Troy G. Miller
Masaki Mochizuki
Nikolaus Mohr
Andrew Morlet
Filippo Moroni
Ciro Morra
Adam Munton
William Popayi Mzimba
Stuart D. Nicoll
Gayle S. Nix
Russell D. Norris
Koji Numahata
Stephen Alan Nunn
Charlie A. Nunn
Ma Pilar Olondo Serrano
Erik Andrew Olson
Stephen Philip O'Sullivan
Roberto Pagella
Mario Pascual-Heranz Caturla
Paul J. Peck
Pekka Pentti
Thomas Allen Pettit
Andrew Pitcher
Diego Alejandro Pleszowski Goldadler
Sergio Pollicino
John Proctor
Jeffrey P. Radack
Steven M. Randle
Martin William Rodgers
Shari A. Rogalski
Valerio Romano
Michael Russell
Pedro Luis Sanchez Gonzalez
Lorenzo Sanchez Hidalgo
Peter Andrew Sander
Alberto Sanz Acedos
Renato Scaff
Steve Alex Scemama
Kreg J. Schmidt
Daniel Schwartmann
Joan Sendra Font
Andrew Clement Shaw
Yutaka Shirai
Paolo Sidoti
Philip Smith
George D. Son Keng Po
Enrique Monteiro Soto
Amy Nicole Stern
Ken Sugiyama
Hettie Carl Tabor
Yoichi Tanaka
Yuen Ming Tang
Kris Peter Timmermans
Tokinao Tonomoto
Paul Tournier
David John Townshend
Pankaj Vaish
Jan Willem van den Bremen
Morten Vardal
Judy Kay Wade
Keki Wadia
Jose Oscar Wais
James Walker
Charles Eric Warden
Philip M. Watkins
Monica Weekes
Casey C. Wells
Karen Welsch
Ronald E. White
Gareth David James Wilson
Yushi Yanagawa
Carlos Yubero Arruga
Emile Zakhia
Inaki Zubasti Martinez

September 27, 2004

Paul Abel

October 25, 2004

Peter W. Buettgen
Patrick C. Cummings
Carlos Lopez-Abadia

November 1, 2004

Teresa Alvarez
Richard Thomas Blanc
Shelley Pittman

November 15, 2004

Michael C. Mueller

November 29, 2004

Gail L. Blauer
Steven L. DeHaven
Everett Dyer

December 1, 2004

Ismail Amla
Stephen J. Christie
Barbara J. Duganier
Hakan Hallen
Dana Jennings
Diane Shelgren
Andrew Wilson
Robert Wood

December 14, 2004

Steven J. Zucker

December 27, 2004

Richard D. Spitzer

January 1, 2005

Harry Meijer
Delia A. Newman

January 10, 2005

Andy Tinlin

January 24, 2005

Robert Edward Healy
Mark Knickrehm

February 1, 2005

Anthony Cliffe
Stephen A. Newton

February 7, 2005

Cindy L. Warner

March 1, 2005

Martin McPhee
Amy Valley

March 23, 2005

Gaylord N. Maines

March 28, 2005

Gregory K. Douglass

April 1, 2005

Henry Jack Lowe
Max Schaifers

April 4, 2005

W. Anthony Will

April 11, 2005

Gil J. Brodnitz

April 25, 2005

Michael J. Boyd

May 1, 2005

Christian Campagna
Gerhard Sundt

May 9, 2005

Arthur R. Bert

May 16, 2005

Christopher T. Goodman

May 31, 2005

Caroline Firstbrook

June 1, 2005

Ana C. Dutra
Tetsuya Shimonishi

June 20, 2005

N. Harlen Pyle

July 11, 2005

Christopher G. White

July 25, 2005

Craig S. Sands

August 22, 2005

Nancy Kaplan

Note: Given the evolution of the organization that became Accenture, identification of every individual admitted as a "consulting partner" was challenging. These pages represent our best attempt to provide an accurate and complete list. We apologize for any omissions or inaccuracies.

# Acknowledgments

The author wishes to acknowledge several people who contributed to the success of the Accenture corporate history. Peter Fuchs, retired Accenture partner and former head of its strategy practice, conceived of and brought the idea for this history to the Accenture leadership team. He has been its champion from start to finish, while also crisscrossing the United States for several months to conduct many of the videotaped interviews with current and retired Accenture partners. Peter has been motivated by his concern that the shared knowledge and values of a generation of Accenture leaders risked being lost if the company didn't act soon. The fact that Joe Glickauf's intellect and enthusiasm sparkles on the printed page and on videotape for current and future generations of Accenture employees to see is largely a tribute to Peter's perseverance. (It is also a tribute to Joe's *joie de vivre*: After two hours of videotaping in his Florida home in 2004, those of us working on the project were wilting in the heat and humidity—air conditioners and audio feeds don't mix—while Joe clearly could've given us two more hours. Later, the 92-year-old turned his attention to his two laptop computers—one for sending and receiving e-mail, and the other for tracking satellite positions.) Sadly, Joe—who served as a reviewer for the book—died in July 2005.

Bruce Weindruch, president and founder of The History Factory, has been involved in documenting and showcasing the history of Accenture, and its predecessor Andersen Consulting, for more than a decade. He was responsible for helping create the Andersen Consulting Heritage Center at the St. Charles Center for Professional Education. Bruce also conducted most of the videotaped interviews of the firm's leaders from the mid-1990s, acting as a one-man crew at one point as he lugged video and audio equipment across Europe. Bruce brought the author into the Accenture history project, and acted as a thoughtful and enthusiastic editor throughout the process of reporting and writing the history. He also wrote the narration for the accompanying DVD and selected and edited the video segments. Bruce works with a strong supporting cast, including Erin Purdy, who acted as project manager for the Accenture history project and was a source of boundless creative and technical support and enthusiasm, while also being a stickler for deadlines.

Brock Haldeman, Liz Haldeman, Drew Waiss and the team of designers at Pivot Design provided several creative options for the presentation of the Accenture history in book format, while meeting Accenture's detailed identity standards.

Michael Swenson, Accenture senior executive in charge of Internal Communications, acted as the history team's liaison with Accenture personnel around the world. In the process, Mike took multitasking to a new level without ever losing his cool, while also offering thoughtful editorial comments. Mike was supported by his team members, notably Phyllis Kennedy, Connie Dieter, Julie Carlson, Jayme

Silverstone and Kelly Rohrer. Mary Lou Brous also provided invaluable brand identity advice. Doris Hambacher, Accenture archivist, moved mountains of file boxes in several different locations to help find the material we needed to document the history. And Marilyn Taillon and Jan Hanczar, formerly lead members of the research library at the Center for Professional Education, worked as freelance researchers, sorting and filing thousands of documents in the Accenture archives, as well as those provided directly by retired partners in support of this project. They and the author shared work space in the "garden level" of Accenture's 180 N. LaSalle St. offices in Chicago, and they offered valuable insights into the culture of the company and some of its more colorful characters of the past two decades.

All of us involved in producing the Accenture history would like to thank Chairman Joe Forehand and Chief Executive Officer Bill Green for their support and foresight and for making company resources available to us as needed. We would also like to thank the overall project sponsor, Jorge Benitez, who leads the Consumer Industrial unit of the Products group in the Americas (and previously served as managing partner-Partner Matters), for his contributions and help in navigating the Accenture organization. General Counsel Doug Scrivner provided not only expert legal counsel, but his sharp eye and incredible recall helped refine the book's details. Lastly, we would like to thank the retired partner chapter reviewers who, often on short notice, provided us with crucial commentary and observations that helped us produce a more complete historical picture of Accenture, as well as the members of the Accenture Editorial Board, for their thoughtful comments.

**Chapter Reviewers**
Susan Butler, Jon Conahan, Gene Delves, Vernon Ellis, Joe Glickuaf, Charles Hemphill, Reginald Jones, John Kelly, Larry Levitan, Dick Nerad, Barry Patmore, Bob Prince, Jesse Tutor, Martin Vandersteen

**Editorial Board**
Jorge Benitez-Chairman, Joe Forehand, Bill Green, Steve Rohleder, Steve James, Masakatsu Mori, Jim Murphy, Gill Rider, Doug Scrivner, Carlos Vidal, Diego Visconti

Scott McMurray
August 2005

## About the Author

Scott McMurray brings more than 20 years' experience to business writing and research projects as founder and president of McMurray Group, Inc. A former senior writer with *The Wall Street Journal*, Scott specializes in finding creative ways to put clients' histories to work addressing present and future business challenges. Most recently, Scott worked closely with researchers and archivists at The History Factory as the author of a corporate history of Sacramento, California-based, Sutter Health, one of America's most innovative not-for-profit health care systems. Scott also is the author of a biography of a major Chicago law firm.

Scott is a graduate of Grinnell College with a Bachelor of Arts degree in American Studies and English Literature, and is a member of the Phi Beta Kappa academic honor society. He also attended the Harvard-Radcliffe Publishing Procedures Course, and is a member of the Authors Guild, an association of professional writers.

## Note on Sources

This history of Accenture draws upon numerous sources in order to tell the story of the company's dramatic growth. Principal source materials include more than 100 interviews with current and former Accenture partners conducted by The History Factory. The videotaped interviews were conducted primarily in 1995 and 1996 as part of the consulting practice's documenting of its history, and also in 2004 in anticipation of the creation of this history and accompanying DVD. In several cases, quotes from the videotapes were truncated or otherwise altered slightly to eliminate repetitive phrases, non sequiturs or related verbal slips that are common to interviews. In each instance the changes were carefully reviewed to ensure that the meaning of the quotation wasn't altered.

Among written source materials, *A Vision of Grandeur*, published by Arthur Andersen in 1988 to mark its 75th anniversary, as well as an unpublished history of the firm's consulting practice written in 1988 by former consulting partner Charles Hemphill, were valuable references. Another important reference work was an oral history of Leonard Spacek, *The Growth of Arthur Andersen & Co. 1928-1973: An Oral History*, published by Garland Publishing, Inc. in 1989. Accenture archival records including memos, subject files, company publications and images also were important sources of information on company events and clients.

Several former partners provided copies of company or personal memos and photos or other material that proved invaluable in adding a sense of depth and detail to the narrative. These former partners included Joe Glickauf, Gene Delves, Jack Garrahy, Martin Vandersteen, Vernon Ellis, Charles Balch, Duane Kullberg and George Shaheen.

## Image Credits

For pages with more than one image, credits read clockwise from top left unless noted.

**The 1950s: Sparking Innovation:** 4: (bottom right) SRI International 7: (top) Library of Congress, Prints & Photographs Division, HAER, ILL, 16-CHIG, 140-19 9: Library of Congress, Prints and Photographs Division, LC-USZ62-129751; Southern California Edison, Edison Historical Collection; El Paso Corporation 10: Courtesy of the Computer History Museum 11: (all) © Bettmann/CORBIS 13: The Drake Hotel 14: © Bettmann/CORBIS 16: (all) Schenectady Museum 20: Courtesy of the Computer History Museum 21: Courtesy of Hagley Museum and Library 23: Pennsylvania Railroad Technical & Historical Society Collection 24: Schenectady Museum 25: Reprinted with permission of the *Harvard Business Review.* Copyright © 1954 by the Harvard Business School Publishing Corporation: all rights reserved; University of Illinois Department of Computer Science 26: © Yousuf Karsh / Retna Ltd. 28: Courtesy of the Computer History Museum 30: (right) SRI International 31: SRI International **Late 1950s – Late 1960s: Coming of Age:** 34-35: © Accenture/Computer History Museum / Snape Photography 36: Courtesy of the Computer History Museum; Ford Motor Company Limited (U.K.); Jack Garrahy; Simmons-Boardman Publishing Corporation 44: (all) Ford Motor Company Limited (U.K.) 45: Cummins Inc. 46-47: (all) Chicago & North Western Historical Society 48: Simmons-Boardman Publishing Corporation 50: Courtesy of the Computer History Museum 51: © Marvin Koner/CORBIS 52: (top) © Bettmann/CORBIS 53: Library of Congress, Prints and Photographs Division, LC-USZ62-22789; Library of Congress, Prints and Photographs Division, LC-U9-17443 54: Reprinted by Permission of *Forbes* Magazine © 2005 Forbes, Inc. Image reprinted with permission of the estate of Leo Garel 55: Neil Beer/Photodisc Green/Getty Images 57: (all) Jack Garrahy 58: Courtesy of Zenith Electronics Corporation 62: (top) Chicago Historical Society **Late 1960s – Late 1970s: Setting Standards:** 82: Courtesy of California State Railroad Museum 83: Chicago Historical Society 84: (all) Tennessee Valley Authority 85: © New York *Daily News*, L.P. reprinted with permission 91: (right) © Bettmann/CORBIS 92: © David Lees/CORBIS **Late 1970s – Mid-1980s: Shifting Competition:** 100-101: PhotoLink/Photodisc Green/Getty Images 102: (bottom right) © Bettmann/CORBIS; (bottom middle) © Bettmann/CORBIS 108: © Bettmann/CORBIS 110: © Owen Franken/CORBIS 111: © Bettmann/CORBIS 113: Bay Area Regional Transportation 114: Copyright 1983 by Goldman, Sachs & Co. 119: Reprinted with the permission of the Free Press, a Division of Simon & Schuster Adult Publishing Group, *Reinventing the Factory* by Roy L. Harmon and Leroy D. Peterson. Copyright © 1989 All Rights Reserved 121: (top) Paul Schlismann Photography; (bottom left) Paul Schlismann Photography **1986 – 1989: Winds of Change:** 128-129: Courtesy of Leonardo Media/Le Meridien Piccadilly Hotel 130: (bottom middle) '21' Club 137: (bottom) Courtesy of Leonardo Media/Le Meridien Piccadilly Hotel 142: Michael Belenky 149: '21' Club 150: Reprinted with permission of *The Wall Street Journal*, Copyright © 1988 Dow Jones and Company, Inc. All Rights Reserved Worldwide 153: Reprinted with permission of *The Wall Street Journal*, Copyright © 1988 Dow Jones and Company, Inc. All Rights Reserved Worldwide 155: Copyright © 1989 by the New York Times Co. Reprinted with permission; Charlie Balch 156: Courtesy of Wyndham Anatole Hotel **1989 – 1997: The Consulting Firm of the Future:** 160: (bottom right) Copyright © 1989 by the New York Times Co. Reprinted with permission; (bottom left) Craig Cameron Olsen/Anderson Hopkins 165: Copyright © 1989 by the New York Times Co. Reprinted with permission 168: Craig Cameron Olsen/Anderson Hopkins 170: (top) Magdalena Caris Photography 191: Grzegorz Stanecki 192: Bob London 193: Photodisc / Getty Images **1997 – 2001: Becoming Accenture:** 203: Reprinted by Permission of *Forbes* Magazine © 2005 Forbes, Inc. 207: Jake Chessum/MS Logan 210: Bob London 211: Copyright © 2000 by The *Financial Times*. Reprinted with permission 212: Reprinted with permission of *The Wall Street Journal*, Copyright © 2000 Dow Jones and Company, Inc. All Rights Reserved Worldwide **2002 to Present: Building High Performance:** 228: (bottom left) Steve McCurry/Magnum Photos 234: © Reuters/CORBIS 237: Paul Fusco/Magnum Photos 239: Magdalena Caris Photography 240: (top) Copyright of Fujitsu Siemens Computers 242: (top) © Frank Polich/Reuters/CORBIS 243: Steve McCurry/Magnum Photos; Zubin Shroff **Epilogue: Horizon 2012:** 259: (all) Liz Townsend **Timeline:** 263: (top) Library of Congress, Prints and Photographs Division, LC-USZ62-118115; (bottom right) Southern California Edison, Edison Historical Collection 264: (top) Library of Congress, Prints and Photographs Division, LC-USZ62-117123; (middle right) Library of Congress, Prints and Photographs Division, LC-USZ62-111231 265: (top left) Library of Congress, Prints and Photographs Division, LC-USZ62-84982; (top right) NASA 266: (top left) © Bettmann/CORBIS; (top right) National Archives 267: (top right) NASA; (bottom right) Courtesy of the Computer History Museum 268: (top middle) Photo Courtesy of U.S. Army; (top right) Library of Congress, Prints and Photographs Division, LC-USZ62-13037; (bottom middle) Jack Garrahy 269: (top left) AP/Wide World Photos; (top right) © Peter Turnley/CORBIS 270: (top right) © Bettmann/CORBIS 271: AP/Wide World Photos; AP/Wide World Photos; © Bettmann/CORBIS 272: (top left) NASA; (top middle) AP/Wide World Photos; (bottom left) Craig Cameron Olsen/Anderson Hopkins 273: (top left) Courtesy of USRobotics; (middle left) AP/Wide World Photos; (top right) AP/Wide World Photos 274: (top right) NASA 275: Photo courtesy PDPhoto.org

# Index

The DVD on the inside back cover of this book—The People Behind the Accenture Story—is a companion piece to the business biography. In this compilation of more than 100 interviews, we hear in their own words how the actions and decisions of our people shaped Accenture and led to its growth and success, often despite great obstacles. Collectively, these stories serve as a source of inspiration and support for all current and future Accenture people.

# The People Behind the Accenture Story



The following individuals appear in the indicated DVD chapters.

Kedrick Adkins 4, 11, 14, 15
Skip Battle 3, 8, 10, 15
Eliseo Belmonte 16
Jorge Benitez 8, 10, 12, 13, 14, 15
Leslie Bergman 2, 3, 6, 9, 13, 15
Mel Bergstein 9
Alex Bhak 16
Pete Bott 15
Tim Breene 15
Keith Burgess 8, 9, 15
Susan Butler 1, 4, 15
Al Cambridge 3, 15
Aimie Chapple 16
Susan Christensen 16
Joellin Comerford 13, 15
Jon Conahan 11, 12, 15
Bill Copacino 11, 14, 15
Stan Cornelison 1
Pam Craig 4, 11, 15
Gene Delves 1, 15
James Ellafrits 1, 15
Vernon Ellis 2, 6, 8, 9, 15
Glover Ferguson 1
Jim Fischer 1, 9, 15
Karl-Heinz Floether 2, 6, 12
Joe Forehand Intro, 3, 4, 12, 14, 15
Mark Foster 13, 14, 15
Joel Friedman 9, 10, 11, 12, 13, 15
Peter Fuchs 3, 8, 9, 15
Benoit Genuini 2, 6, 9, 15
Joe Glickauf 1
Bill Green Intro, 1, 11, 12, 13, 14, 15
Jean-Claude Guez 2, 6, 9, 10, 15
Jacques Habib 2, 6, 9, 15
Dominique Hainebach 16
Chuck Hemphill 15
Jane Hemstritch 4, 7, 9, 12, 15
Lars Henriksen 2, 6
Mike Hill 15
David Hunter 1, 12, 15
Steve James 12, 14, 15
Reg Jones 4, 15
John Kelly 9, 12, 15
Ed Kennedy 15
Ji-Eun Lee 16
Larry Levitan 1, 13, 15
Lori Lovelace 4, 9, 14, 15
Tom McCarty 3, 5, 7, 8, 15
Mike McGrath 10, 15
Jennifer McLaughlin 16
Scott Mall 16
Ferrucio Mangioni 6
Bob Manion 3, 15
Carol Meyer 4, 9, 15
Vic Millar 3, 15
Masakatsu Mori 1, 5, 7, 15
Si Moughamian 3, 10
Bill Mueller 1, 2, 3, 4, 15
Jim Murphy 10, 12, 15
Pedro Navarro 6
Terry Neill 9, 15
Dick Nerad 15
Declan O'Riordan 3, 15
Carla Paonessa 3, 4, 8, 11, 15
Cris Parcelles 16
Barry Patmore 8
Charlie Paulk 1, 15
Pete Peterson 5, 11, 15
Bob Prince 3, 8, 9, 15
Gill Rider 4, 9, 12, 13, 15
Steve Rohleder 11, 15
Basilio Rueda 9, 13
George Shaheen 9, 10, 11, 13, 15
Martin Sherrill 16
John Skerrit 2, 13, 15
Ming Tang 16
John Tham 16
Don Thiry 2, 5, 15
David Thomlinson 14, 15
Jesse Tutor 11
Christiaan Van Aalst 2, 6
Martin Vandersteen 2, 6, 9
Carlos Vidal 15
Art Welby 15
Mike Whitney 16
Brian Wilson 5, 7, 9, 15
Jack Wilson 15
Steve Zimmerman 3, 15

The individuals included in the DVD chapters held many positions during their careers. The titles shown with the segments in the DVD are among the more significant titles held by these individuals.